Get the eBooks FREE!

(PDF, ePub, Kindle, and liveBook all included)

We believe that once you buy a book from us, you should be able to read it in any format we have available. To get electronic versions of this book at no additional cost to you, purchase and then register this book at the Manning website.

Go to https://www.manning.com/freebook and follow the instructions to complete your pBook registration.

That's it!
Thanks from Manning!

Linux in Action

DAVID CLINTON

MANNING

SHELTER ISLAND

Manning Publications Co.
20 Baldwin Road
PO Box 761
Shelter Island, NY 11964

Development editor: Frances Lefkowitz
Review editor: Ivan Martinović
Technical development editor: John Guthrie
Project manager: Deirdre Hiam
Copyeditor: Frances Buran
Proofreader: Tiffany Taylor
Technical proofreader: Reka Horvath
Typesetter: Gordan Salinovic
Cover designer: Marija Tudor

ISBN 9781617294938
Printed in the United States of America
1 2 3 4 5 6 7 8 9 10 – DP – 23 22 21 20 19 18

brief contents

contents

v

preface

No matter what you do or how long you've been doing it in the IT or programming world, if you're not learning new stuff, you're probably not doing it right. It's not that the platforms and paradigms are constantly changing. Nor is it that new business demands require fresh thinking. Or that the bad guys are constantly coming up with new ways to attack your servers. It's all of those things and more. You can't afford to stop learning. The trick is finding a way to learn the high-priority skills without turning the experience into a major detour.

It's my intention and desire that you should be able to read even a single chapter from this book, *Linux in Action*, and walk away feeling confident enough to take on something challenging and productive—something you wouldn't previously have even considered. If you hang around until the bitter end, you'll learn to work with critical and current technologies powering virtualization, disaster recovery, infrastructure security, data backups, web servers, DevOps, and system troubleshooting.

But why Linux? Because Linux powers most of the internet, most scientific research, and most commerce—in fact, most of the world's servers. Those servers need to be provisioned, launched, secured, and managed effectively by smart and well-trained people. Smart is what you bring to the table, and I think I can help with well trained.

Not sure you know enough about Linux to embark on such an ambitious project? Chapter 1 will quickly fill in the holes. After that, fasten your seat belt and prepare for a serious learning curve.

acknowledgments

It's impossible to reach the end of a book's long and sometimes tortured production cycle without reflecting on what it took to make it through. In the case of *Linux in Action*—as with my *Learn Amazon Web Services in a Month of Lunches*—survival required the talent and dedication of every part of the Manning team's deep bench.

Once again Frances Lefkowitz, as development editor, added significant clarity and purpose to each chapter, relentlessly keeping me focused and on track. Both Reka Horvath and John Guthrie patiently tested all the book's projects and added valuable operational insights along the way. The copy editor, Frances Buran, seems never to have met an adverb she approves—at least not when used by me. But the accuracy and grace of the text in its current form clearly indicate the quality of her judgment.

In her role as project manager, Deirdre Hiam effectively shepherded us through the last mile, successfully keeping all the many moving parts in sync. Each of the book's peer reviewers has left an important mark. They may not realize it, but all of their valuable observations were carefully noted, weighed, and, where possible, applied. Many thanks, therefore, to Angelo Costo, Christopher Phillips, Dario Victor Duran, Flayol Frederic, Foster Haines, George L. Gaines, Gustavo Patino, Javier Collado, Jens Christian B. Madsen, Jonas Medina de los Reyes, Maciej Jurkowski, Mayer Patil, Mohsen Mostafa Jokar, and Tim Kane.

This book is about more than just Linux administration skills. It also tries to impart the larger sense of responsibility successful administrators have for the servers and systems under their care. I was lucky to have benefited from a great mentor at the start of my career as a Linux system administrator. Peter Fedorow's attention to both fine operational details and the big global picture make him an especially effective admin. His dragging me kicking and screaming into the world of Linux virtualization hooked me on containers long before containers were cool. When everything's said and done, at least some of Peter's guidance is, no doubt, reflected here.

And finally, none of my professional (or private) projects would get off the blocks without the cheerful and helpful participation of my dear wife. We fully share the hard work, but the successes are mostly her doing.

about this book

Looking to learn to administer Linux computers? Excellent choice. While it can hold its own in the consumer desktop space, where Linux absolutely dominates is the world of servers, especially virtual and cloud servers. Because most serious server administration these days takes place remotely, working through a GUI interface of one sort or another just adds unnecessary overhead. If you want to manage the servers and network architectures that are currently attracting all the attention, you're going to have to learn your way around the Linux command line.

The good news is that the core Linux command set is going to work for you across geographic and corporate lines, just about anywhere computers and business intersect. The better news is that, relatively speaking, Linux skills have staying power. Because it's such a mature and stable operating system, most of the tools used a quarter century ago are still just as effective as ever, and most of the tools used today will probably still be actively used after another quarter century. Learning Linux, in other words, is a lifelong investment.

But you're busy and you've got deadlines. Well, I can't promise you that mastering Linux will be as simple as learning to tie your shoes. But I can help you focus like a laser so you can leave all the stuff you don't need lying on the highway, choking on your exhaust fumes (assuming you're not driving a Tesla, of course).

How am I going to pull that one off? *Linux in Action* turns technology training sideways. That is, while other books, courses, and online resources organize their content around categories ("Alright boys and girls, everyone take out your slide rules and charcoal pencils. Today we're going to learn about Linux file systems."), I'm going to use real-world projects to teach.

So, for example, I could have built an entire chapter (or two) on Linux file systems. But instead, you'll learn how to build enterprise file servers, system recovery drives, and scripts to replicate archives of critical data. In the process, you'll pick up the file system knowledge as a free bonus.

Don't think I'm going to cover every Linux administration tool. That's impossible: there are literally thousands of them out there. But don't worry. The core skills and functionality needed through the first years of a career in Linux administration will be covered, and covered well, but only when needed for a practical, mission-critical project. When you're done, you'll have learned no less than what you would have from a traditional source, but you'll also know how to complete more than a dozen major administrative projects, and be comfortable tackling dozens more.

Are you in? I thought so.

Who should read this book

This book is designed to help you acquire a solid range of Linux administration skills. Perhaps you're a developer who wants to work more directly with the server environment within which your applications will live. Or maybe you're ready to make your move in the server administration or DevOps worlds. Either way, you belong with us.

What should you already know? At the very least, you should be comfortable working with the files, networks, and basic resources of a modern operating system. Experience with system administration, network management, and programming languages definitely won't hurt, but are not required. Most of all, you should be unafraid of exploring new environments and enthusiastic about experimenting with new tools. One more thing: you're expected to know how to perform a simple and straightforward installation of a Linux operating system.

How this book is organized: A roadmap

Just a few words about the way the book is built. Each chapter of *Linux in Action* covers one or two practical projects—except chapter 1. Chapter 1, because it's designed to fill in any very basic gaps that might exist in your Linux knowledge, will be different from all the others. Don't need the basics? I'm absolutely sure you'll find lots of fun new toys to play with in chapter 2.

Along with the book's projects, I'll also introduce you to the individual skills and tools that you'll need. In addition, each chapter's projects usually build on the skills you've learned previously in the book. Just to show you that I mean business, here's a fairly complete list of the main projects (under the Chapter heading), skill domains, and tools you'll meet through the course of the book:

Chapter	Skill domains	Tools
1. Welcome to Linux	Shells, partitions, and file systems	Bash, man
2. Linux virtualization: Building a simple Linux working environment	Virtualization, file systems	VirtualBox, LXC, apt, yum/dnf
3. Remote connectivity: Safely access networked machines	Security, remote connectivity	ssh, scp, systemctl, ps, grep
4. Archive management: Backing up or copying entire file systems	Partitions and file systems, text streams	tar, dd, redirects, rsync, locate, split, chmod, chown
5. Automated administration: Configuring automated offsite backups	Scripts, system process management, security	scripts, cron, anacron, systemd timers
6. Emergency tools: Building a system recovery device	Partitions and file systems, device management	parted, GRUB, mount, chroot
7. Web servers: Building a MediaWiki server	Databases, networking, package management	PHP, MySQL (MariaDB), Apache web server, package dependencies
8. Networked file sharing: Building a Nextcloud file-sharing server	Package management, networking, security	snapd, file systems, encryption
9. Securing your web server	Networking, security, system monitoring	Apache, iptables, /etc/group, SELinux, apt, yum/dnf, chmod, chown, Let's Encrypt
10. Securing network connections: Creating a VPN or DMZ	Networking, security	firewalls, ssh, Apache, OpenVPN, sysctl, easy-rsa
11. System monitoring: Working with log files	System monitoring, text streams, security	grep, sed, journalctl, rsyslogd, /var/log/, Tripwire
12. Sharing data over a private network	Networking, partitions, file systems	nfs, smb, ln, /etc/fstab
13. Troubleshooting system performance issues	System monitoring, system process management, networking	top, free, nice, nmon, tc, iftop, df, kill, killall, uptime
14. Troubleshooting network issues	Networking	ip, dhclient, dmesg, ping, nmap, traceroute, netstat, netcat (nc)
15. Troubleshooting peripheral devices	Device management	lshw, lspci, lsusb, modprobe, CUPS
16. DevOps tools: Deploying a scripted server environment using Ansible	Scripts, virtualization	Ansible, YAML, apt

About the code

This book contains many examples of source code both in numbered listings and in line with normal text. In both cases, source code is formatted in a `fixed-width font like this` to separate it from ordinary text.

In many cases, the original source code has been reformatted; we've added line breaks and reworked indentation to accommodate the available page space in the book. In rare cases, even this was not enough, and listings include line-continuation markers (➥). Additionally, comments in the source code have often been removed from the listings when the code is described in the text. Code annotations accompany many of the listings, highlighting important concepts.

Linux distributions

There are currently dozens of actively maintained Linux distributions. Even though most of the Linux basics are common to all distros (distributions), there'll always be little things that'll work "here" but not "there." For practicality's sake, I'm going to concentrate mostly on two distributions: Ubuntu and CentOS. Why those two? Because each represents an entire family of distributions. Ubuntu shares its roots with Debian, Mint, Kali Linux, and others, while CentOS enjoys the company of Red Hat Enterprise Linux (RHEL) and Fedora.

That's not to say I don't value other distros like Arch Linux, SUSE, and Gentoo, or that what you'll learn in this book won't help you work with those environments. But fully covering the Ubuntu and CentOS families means grabbing the largest single slice of the Linux pie that I could reach using just two distributions.

Book forum

Purchase of *Linux in Action* includes free access to a private web forum run by Manning Publications where you can make comments about the book, ask technical questions, and receive help from the author and from other users. To access the forum, go to https://forums.manning.com/forums/linux-in-action. You can also learn more about Manning's forums and the rules of conduct at https://forums.manning.com/forums/about.

Manning's commitment to our readers is to provide a venue where a meaningful dialogue between individual readers and between readers and the author can take place. It is not a commitment to any specific amount of participation on the part of the author, whose contribution to the forum remains voluntary (and unpaid). We suggest you try asking the author some challenging questions lest his interest stray! The forum and the archives of previous discussions will be accessible from the publisher's website as long as the book is in print.

Other online resources

Stuck? Web search is your best friend, as it can quickly connect you with a wealth of existing Linux guides and troubleshooting expertise. But you shouldn't forget the StackExchange family of sites and, in particular, serverfault.com. If something's gone wrong with some system configuration or the network has disappeared, then the odds are high that someone else has experienced the same thing, asked about it on ServerFault, and received an answer already. Nothing yet? Then ask the question yourself. LinuxQuestions.org and ubuntuforums.org can also be helpful.

And those who enjoy video training will find a good range of Linux courses on Pluralsight.com, including more than a dozen of my own courses.

about the author

DAVID CLINTON is a system administrator, teacher, and writer. He has administered, written about, and created training material for many important technology subjects including Linux systems, cloud computing (AWS in particular), and container technologies like Docker. He's the author of *Learn Amazon Web Services in a Month of Lunches* (Manning, 2017). Many of his video training courses can be found on https://www.pluralsight .com/, and links to his other books (on Linux administration and server virtualization) can be found at https://bootstrap-it.com.

about the cover illustration

The figure on the cover of *Linux in Action* is captioned "Habit of an Armenian native of Persia in 1700." The illustration is taken from Thomas Jefferys' *A Collection of the Dresses of Different Nations, Ancient and Modern* (four volumes), London, published between 1757 and 1772. These are hand-colored copperplate engravings, heightened with gum arabic. Thomas Jefferys (1719–1771) was called "Geographer to King George III." He was an English cartographer who was the leading map supplier of his day. His work as a map maker sparked an interest in local dress customs of the lands he surveyed and mapped, which are brilliantly displayed in this collection.

Fascination with faraway lands and travel for pleasure were relatively new phenomena in the late 18th century, and collections such as this one were popular. The diversity of the drawings in Jefferys' volumes speaks vividly of the uniqueness and individuality of the world's nations some 200 years ago. Dress codes have changed since then, and the diversity by region and country, so rich at the time, has faded away. It is now often hard to tell the inhabitant of one continent from another. Perhaps, trying to view it optimistically, we have traded a cultural and visual diversity for a more varied personal life. Or a more varied and interesting intellectual and technical life.

At a time when it is hard to tell one computer book from another, Manning celebrates the inventiveness and initiative of the computer business with book covers based on the rich diversity of regional life of two centuries ago, brought back to life by Jeffreys' pictures.

Welcome to Linux 1

This chapter covers

- What makes Linux different
- Basic survival skills
- Getting help

This book turns technology training sideways. Although other books, courses, and online resources organize their content around *skills*, I'm going to use real-world *projects* as teaching tools. Each of the core skills and the functionality of Linux systems will be covered—and covered well—but only when needed for a project. When you're done, you'll have learned everything you would have from a traditional source, but you'll also know how to perform more than a dozen vital and sophisticated administration tasks and be comfortable tackling dozens more.

The first two or three chapters will quickly guide you through your initial introduction to the world of Linux servers. After that, you'll work through and adapt practical hands-on projects, and nothing but practical hands-on projects. Through those projects, you'll learn more than just commands and skills. Get ready to dive deeper and to eventually create solutions to your own business problems.

No single book can anticipate all the challenges that you'll face throughout your career. But, by demonstrating how to approach real-world problems using real-world tools, this book will make it a whole lot easier for you to use the vast resources available through both inline documentation and the internet. If your prior Linux experience is limited, this chapter introduces some basic command-line survival skills and points to places you can go for help when things don't work.

> **NOTE** As you'll see, a *command line* is an interface provided by an operating system (OS) that permits you to type text commands to control the OS or to query data it manages.

I should note that in this and every chapter, you're strongly encouraged to try everything out for yourself. There's no better way to really get to the core of an IT skill than actually doing it, realizing that it's not working the way you expected, and playing with it until it becomes yours forever. Good luck and have fun!

1.1   *What makes Linux different from other operating systems*

Linux is free, which means it's a lot easier than other OSs to install exactly where and when needed for any use you can imagine. Not having to worry about purchasing site licenses and jumping through Digital Rights Management hoops makes testing all kinds of hardware combinations and server configurations much more straightforward.

Linux makes it possible to do various really useful and creative things. For instance, you can load a Linux *live boot* image on a USB stick, boot a PC whose own hard disk has been corrupted, and then troubleshoot and fix the problem. (You'll learn how to do that in chapter 6.) Or, because Linux is a true multiuser OS, whole teams can concurrently log in to work locally or remotely, confident in the privacy and stability of the system.

Linux was built with some of the same technology and comes with most of the same tools as the deeply mature UNIX OS. This adds a great deal of stability and security. Linux distributions also provide sophisticated software package management systems that reliably install and maintain any of the thousands of free software applications available through online curated repositories.

But beyond free, Linux is *open source*, which means anyone can take the code base and reshape it into anything they want. Practically, this has spawned a vast ecosystem of specialty Linux distributions. A *distribution* (sometimes shortened to *distro*) is a customized stack of software that's packaged along with the Linux kernel and distributed with tools for installing a working version of Linux of user computers. Table 1.1 provides a very incomplete distro list to illustrate the kinds of things that are available.

Table 1.1   Some of the many available Linux distros

Purpose	Distribution
Security/anti-hacking	Kali Linux
	Parrot
Consumer desktop	Mint
	Elementary OS

Table 1.1 Some of the many available Linux distros

Purpose	Distribution
Lightweight (old hardware; diagnostics)	Puppy Linux
	LXLE
Internet of Things administration	Snappy Ubuntu Core
Enterprise server room	CentOS (community version of Red Hat Enterprise Linux)
	OpenSUSE (community version of SUSE)
Cloud computing	Amazon Linux (AWS AMI)
	Ubuntu Server (AWS AMI)
All-purpose (except lightweight)	Ubuntu

Can't find what you're after? Create your own. Need help? There's a large and active community online where, if someone hasn't already solved your problem, they'll know where to go to get it done. More than anything else, I'd say it's the community-based resources that really make Linux so powerful.

1.2 *Basic survival skills*

Before beginning with the enterprise-ready projects that make up the rest of the book, it's worthwhile to make sure we're starting on the same page. This chapter covers the Linux basics: the UNIX Filesystem Hierarchy Standard (including pseudo file systems), navigation (ls, pwd, and cd), file management tools (cat, less, touch, mkdir, rmdir, rm, cp, and mv), some tricks (like tab completion and file globbing), sudo, and where to turn for help (man, info, and journalctl).

It's possible you have enough experience already that you won't need any of that material. Feel free to skip this chapter altogether. Don't worry about the rest of us. We'll catch up.

Installing Linux

I'm not going to spend time talking about how to install Linux on your PC. It's not because installation is so ridiculously simple; it can sometimes get quite complicated. Rather, it's because the approach you choose depends on your specific circumstances. Describing one possibility or even half a dozen would do nothing more than annoy the 75% of you for whom those scenarios won't work.

Need some help getting started with installation? Check out *Learn Linux in a Month of Lunches* (Manning, 2016). Encountering a particular installation issue? Take a minute to write a brief but detailed description, and then use it to search the internet for help. Looking for a laptop or a desktop with Linux preinstalled? Search the internet for "pc with Linux preinstalled." Have some unused hardware and a USB stick? Search for "install Linux from usb." Prefer to install Linux as a virtual machine? Smart move. Stick around for chapter 2.

1.2.1 *The Linux file system*

It's often said that everything in Linux works through plain text files, so it probably makes the most sense to start by understanding the Linux file system. But before we can get to Linux, what's a *file system?* You can think of it as a data table (or an *index*) that creates apparent connections between individual files and groups of files with identifiable locations on a disk. Figure 1.1 can help you visualize how data spread across a disk partition can be exposed to system users within a directory structure.

Why would you need an index? A digital storage device like a hard drive or USB device isn't divided into physical divisions that can be used as organizing *folders* (or *directories,* as they're known in Linux circles). One particular file can reside in a location on the actual media that's a great distance away from another, nearly identical file created minutes or seconds apart, and all the parts of a single file might not be contiguous. Not only that, a file's geographic location on the disk won't necessarily remain static over time.

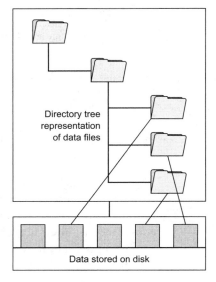

Directory tree representation of data files

Data stored on disk

Figure 1.1   Raw data on storage devices can be visually represented by the OS as organized directory hierarchies.

If you want your data to be reliably retrievable, you'll need some kind of index that can consistently point you to the resources you're after. A file system uses such an index to provide the appearance of an organized set of directories and files within a single disk division known as a *partition.*

> **NOTE**   In case you need to dig deeper on your own some time, it'll be useful to know that these days, the most commonly used Linux file system is ext4. But Linux can also work with storage drives that were formatted using file systems from other platforms like FAT32 and NTFS.

All the files in a disk partition are kept in directories beneath the root directory, which is represented by the / (forward slash) character. The way these directories are arranged is largely governed by the UNIX Filesystem Hierarchy Standard (FHS). You're going to see pretty much the same basic layout whether you're using a Linux distribution, UNIX, or even macOS. Figure 1.2 shows some of the most used, top-level directories.

Top-level directories—those directories located directly beneath the root—include /etc/, which contains configuration files that define the way individual programs and services function, and /var/, which contains *variable* files belonging to the system or individual applications whose content changes frequently through the course of normal system activities. You'll also want to know about the /home directory where individual users are given directories for their private files.

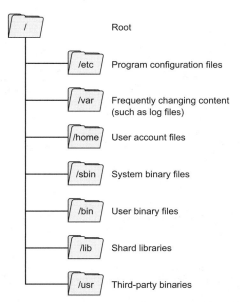

/   Root

/etc   Program configuration files

/var   Frequently changing content
(such as log files)

/home   User account files

/sbin   System binary files

/bin   User binary files

/lib   Shard libraries

/usr   Third-party binaries

**Figure 1.2   Common top-level
directories as defined by the UNIX FHS**

1.2.2   *Getting around: Linux navigation tools*

Here's where you'll learn the five most basic, must-have Linux navigation commands (ls, pwd, cd, cat, and less). Because the command line is not a particularly visual environment no matter what you're trying to do, you're going to rely a great deal on these five tools to orient yourself.

> **NOTE** I hope it's obvious that you should be trying each of these tools out for yourself on your own computer. That's the only way you'll learn.

The rest of the book requires a command-line terminal of one sort or another. Unfortunately, there's no single way to open a terminal window that'll work in all Linux distributions. For example, the terminal's location in the Ubuntu menu system won't necessarily match that of Fedora or Mint. And Ubuntu itself? Well, that depends on which version you're running.

The Ctrl-Alt-t keyboard combination should work in at least most environments, as will looking through the application menus searching for an item with *terminal* in the name. By default, once your terminal opens, your home directory (/home/yourname/) will be active.

ls (LIST)

No point hanging around the terminal if you can't see what's there. You can list the names of the files and subdirectories in your current directory using ls. The ls command with the l flag (*l* stands for *long*) lists not only the object names, but their file permissions, owner, group, file size, and time stamp. Adding a directory designation like /var/ displays the contents of that directory:

```
$ ls -l /var
total 40
drwxr-xr-x  2 root root    4096 May  3 06:25 backups
drwxr-xr-x 11 root root    4096 Jan 17 21:16 cache
drwxr-xr-x 39 root root    4096 Jan 17 21:16 lib
drwxrwsr-x  2 root staff   4096 Apr 12 2016 local
lrwxrwxrwx  1 root root       9 Aug 12 2016 lock -> /run/lock
drwxrwxr-x  7 root syslog  4096 May  3 06:25 log
drwxrwsr-x  2 root mail    4096 Aug 12 2016 mail
drwxr-xr-x  2 root root    4096 Aug 12 2016 opt
lrwxrwxrwx  1 root root       4 Aug 12 2016 run -> /run
drwxr-xr-x  5 root root    4096 Jan 17 21:16 spool
drwxrwxrwt  2 root root    4096 Nov  7 2016 tmp
drwxr-xr-x  3 root root    4096 Sep 11 2016 www
```

The h argument when added to ls -l displays file sizes in a human-readable format—kilobytes, megabytes, and gigabytes, rather than bytes, which tend to involve a great many hard-to-count digits:

```
$ ls -lh /var/log          ┌─ The total disk space (in MB)
total 18M               ◁──┘  consumed by files in this directory
-rw-r--r-- 1 root    root     0 May  3 06:25 alternatives.log
drwxr-xr-x 2 root    root  4.0K May  3 06:25 apt
-rw-r----- 1 syslog  adm   265K Jun  9 00:25 auth.log
-rw-r--r-- 1 root    root  312K Aug 12 2016 bootstrap.log
-rw------- 1 root    utmp     0 May  3 06:25 btmp
-rw-r----- 1 root    adm     31 Aug 12 2016 dmesg
-rw-r--r-- 1 root    root   836 May 21 14:15 dpkg.log
-rw-r--r-- 1 root    root   32K Nov  7 2016 faillog
drwxr-xr-x 2 root    root  4.0K Aug 12 2016 fsck
-rw-r----- 1 syslog  adm   128K Jun  8 20:49 kern.log
-rw-rw-r-- 1 root    utmp  287K Jun  9 00:25 lastlog
-rw-r----- 1 syslog  adm   1.7M Jun  9 00:17 syslog
-rw-rw-r-- 1 root    utmp  243K Jun  9 00:25 wtmp
```

> **NOTE** In general, you add arguments to Linux commands in one of two ways: a dash followed by a single letter (like the h that modifies ls), or two dashes introducing more verbose versions of the same argument. In the example, ls --human-readable generates exactly the same output as ls -h. Nearly all Linux commands come packaged with full documentation, which we'll explore later in the chapter.

Want to know what's going on beneath your current directory? Adding uppercase R as an argument to ls displays subdirectories and the files and subdirectories they contain, no matter how many nested layers of directories. Just to get an idea of how involved that can get, and therefore how useful it can be to properly visualize it, run ls -R against the /etc/ directory tree:

```
$ ls -R /etc
```

pwd (PRESENT WORK DIRECTORY)

In many cases, your current location within the file system will be displayed to the left of your command prompt. In this example, I'm in the network directory that lives just below /etc/:

```
ubuntu@base:/etc/network$
```

As you'll likely find yourself working on systems where that prompt isn't available, you might sometimes need a quick heads-up on your position. For that, typing pwd will print your present working directory:

```
$ pwd
/etc/network
```

cd (CHANGE DIRECTORY)

Once you've got a decent idea of where you are and what's immediately available to you in your current directory, you'll need to know how to change locations. Typing cd tells the command-line interpreter (which will usually be Bash) to move you to the directory you specify. When you first open a terminal session (often referred to as a *shell*), by default, you'll find yourself in your own account's home directory. If you run pwd, you'll probably see something like this:

```
$ pwd
/home/yourname
```

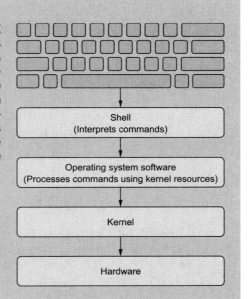

What's Bash?

Bash is probably the most popular UNIX shell. Great! But what's a shell? A *shell* is any user interface that interprets a user's commands, either through a command-line interface (CLI) or a graphical user interface (GUI). You can think of a shell (visualized in the figure) as a software layer meant to execute all appropriately formatted commands using the underlying kernel and hardware system resources. In other words, it's the way you talk to your computer.

The shell interprets the execution of user input commands.

Now, let's move back to the root directory by typing cd and a forward slash:

```
cd /
```

Run ls again to take a look at what's there. (You'll see the directories illustrated earlier in figure 1.2.) Notice the home directory from which you can access your *yourname* directory. To move to any of the subdirectories listed there, type cd and then the directory you'd like to visit. Because the path you're specifying here is *relative* to your current location, you don't need to preface the directory name with a forward slash character. The command cd . . will move you up one level in the directory hierarchy, from /home/*yourname*/ to /home/, for instance.

If, however, you've got more ambitious travel plans and you'd like to see parts of the world lying far beyond your current directory, you'll need to use an *absolute* path. That means you'll always use a path that begins with the root directory (represented by a forward slash). To move back to your home directory from somewhere else on the system, you'll type the forward slash, then home (which, you'll remember, exists within the root directory), and then your username. Try it:

```
$ cd /home/yourname
```

That said, typing cd without any arguments will take you back to the home directory of the current logged-in user.

cat (PRINT FILE CONTENTS TO OUTPUT)

Accessing the contents of text files within a terminal can sometimes be a bit tricky. The cat tool will print a file to the screen where it can be read, but not edited. This works pretty well for shorter documents like the fstab file in /etc/. The next example uses an absolute path so that the file can be found no matter where in the file system you happen to be at the moment:

```
$ cat /etc/fstab
```

> **NOTE** The name *cat* is actually short for *concatenate*, which reflects the tool's value in joining multiple strings or files into a single text stream.

Suppose the file you want to read contains more lines than will display in a single screen. Try viewing the /etc/group file:

```
cat /etc/group
```

The odds are that the first lines scrolled up and off your screen far too fast for you to have read them. What's the good of a plain text file if you can't read it? Of course, as you'll soon see, Linux has plenty of text editors for actively managing content, but it might be nice to be able to read a longer file, one screen at a time.

less (DISPLAY FILE CONTENTS)

Welcome to less—thus named, presumably, because it can quickly read and display *less* than the complete file contents (or perhaps to distinguish it from the older more command). You launch less by running it against an existing filename:

```
less /etc/services
```

Using less, you can scroll up and down through the file with the arrow, PgUp, PgDn, and spacebar keys. When you're done, press the q key to exit.

1.2.3 Getting things done: Linux file management tools

If you've got files and directories, you'll need to know how to create, destroy, move, and copy them. Files are often automatically created by some external process such as a software installation or an automated log generation or, say, by saving your work within an office productivity package like LibreOffice. There isn't much need to discuss all that here. I'll note, however, that you can quickly create an empty file using the touch command, followed by the name you'd like to give it:

```
$ touch myfile
```

You can then see the file listed within your current directory through the ls command. Displaying its contents with cat will, of course, display nothing at all because you've only just created the file:

```
$ ls
myfile
$ cat myfile
```

"Touching" an existing file with touch updates its time stamp without making any changes. This can be useful if, for some reason, you want to change how various commands like ls list or display a file. (It can also be helpful if you'd like your boss to think that you've been hard at work on a data file that, in fact, you haven't opened for weeks.)

Of course, you won't get too far in this fast-paced, dog-eat-dog world by just creating directories full of empty files. Eventually, you'll need to fill them with stuff and then edit the stuff that's already there. For that, you'll want to introduce yourself to a reliable text editor.

Before I throw myself headfirst into a very dangerous place, I should mention that lots of folks develop strong feelings for their text editors. Have you ever politely hinted to a Vim user that their venerable editor might not be as useful and important as it once was? Of course you haven't. You wouldn't be physically able to read this book if you'd done something like that.

I definitely won't be telling you which text editor you must use. I will, however, tell you that full-featured word processors like LibreOffice and MS Word should *never* be used for your Linux administration work. Those applications will add all kinds of hidden formatting to your documents that will break system-level files. What I can say is that, roughly speaking, there are three categories of editors that could work for you:

- If you prefer to work on documents from the GUI environment, then a simple *plain-text editor* like gedit (Ubuntu calls this *the Text Editor*) is great. Various syntax highlighting tools are also available to make coding and scripting more productive, and you can be confident that such a tool will save nothing but the text you see.

- For those times when you need to edit a file from inside a terminal session, then a *command-line editor* like nano (or Pico) with its intuitive interface can do the job.

- And, finally, there's *Vim* (or its original iteration: vi). Ah, Vim. If you're willing to invest a few months of your life into learning what is largely a nonintuitive interface, then you'll be rewarded with a lifetime of greatly enhanced productivity. It's that simple.

NOTE   All my books, articles, and course-related documents are written in gedit. Why? I like it.

Why not take a minute or two right now and make some edits to the myfile document you just created using each of the three text editors mentioned? For example:

```
$ nano myfile
$ vi myfile
```

For Vim, enter Insert Mode by pressing the i key and then typing your text. If you don't want to spend the rest of your life trapped inside Vim, you can save your work by pressing Esc, then type :w, and then exit by typing :q.

CREATING AND DELETING DIRECTORIES

Every object within a Linux file system is represented by a unique collection of metadata called an *inode*. I suppose you could say that the file system index discussed earlier is built from the metadata associated with all the many inodes on a drive. To display more information about the file you just created using touch, including inode information, you can use the stat command:

```
$ stat myfile
  File: 'myfile'
  Size: 0              Blocks: 0          IO Block: 4096   regular empty file
Device: 802h/2050d    Inode: 55185258    Links: 1                ⟵─┐  The file's inode ID
Access: (0664/-rw-rw-r--)  Uid: ( 1000/  ubuntu)  ⟵─────────────┘
                           Gid: ( 1000/  ubuntu)
Access: 2017-06-09 13:21:00.191819194 +0000
Modify: 2017-06-09 13:21:00.191819194 +0000        The file's permissions
Change: 2017-06-09 13:21:00.191819194 +0000        and ownership status
 Birth: -
```

As you can see, the output includes data describing the file's name, attributes, and time stamps. But it also tells you its inode ID number. It's important to be aware that when you move, copy, or delete a file or directory, all you're really doing is editing its inode attributes, not its ID. An *inode,* by the way, is an object used by UNIX systems to identify the disk location and attributes of files within a file system (as illustrated in figure 1.2). Usually there'll be exactly one inode for each file or directory.

Assuming that you're in your home directory, why not create a new directory that you can use for your experiments? For that, you'll use `mkdir`:

```
$ mkdir myplace
```

Now move to your new directory and create a file there:

```
$ cd myplace
$ touch newfile
$ ls
newfile
```

So you can see how deleting objects works, move back up to the parent directory (using `cd ..`) and delete the directory you just made. Oddly enough, the predefined command for deleting directories, `rmdir`, won't work in this case. Try it yourself:

```
$ cd ..
$ rmdir myplace
rmdir: failed to remove 'myplace': Directory not empty
```

"Directory not empty?" So what? This is a built-in check to prevent you from accidentally deleting directories filled with important files and subdirectories that you might have forgotten about. To get around this, there are a couple of things you can do.

One requires that you add the `--ignore-fail-on-non-empty` argument to the `rmdir` command, but that involves an awful lot of typing. Another approach would be to manually work through each subdirectory and individually delete every object you find. But that can sometimes be even worse. For those times when you are 100% sure that there's absolutely nothing you need beneath the directory, the quickest route is to add the `-r` flag (meaning *recursive*) to the `rm` command:

```
$ rm -r myplace
```

Now is probably a good time to tell you about one very important difference between working with a GUI desktop interface and the command line: the command line has no trash can. If you delete something using `rm` (or `rmdir`) and then regret it, by and large, you'll have no way of getting it back. But hey; think of all the disk space you'll have freed up.

COPYING AND MOVING FILES

For this next step, create a few more files and a new directory:

```
$ touch file1 file2 file3
$ mkdir newdir
```

You can make an identical copy of an object using cp. This example creates a copy of file1 within the directory newdir:

```
$ cp file1 newdir
```

By the way, the cp command knows what to do with this command line because it's smart enough to recognize *newdir* as a directory rather than a file. If there were no directory called newdir in the current location, cp would instead make a new copy of file1 named newdir. If you're anything like me, at some point you're probably going to accidentally misspell a command and end up with an odd new file rather than the directory you were after. In any case, check everything to confirm it all works out the way it was supposed to.

Unlike cp, the mv command will permanently move an object from one place to another. Therefore, if you were to move a file from your home directory to the newdir subdirectory, the original would no longer be available:

```
$ mv file2 newdir
```

Again, check the results for yourself. You can copy, move, or delete directories using the same commands as for files, adding the -r flag where necessary. Remember that you might be moving more than just the directory you see: any existing layers of unseen nested levels will also be dragged along for the ride.

FILE GLOBBING

Had I been there when they came up with the name *globbing*, I'd have definitely urged them to reconsider. Perhaps it's referring to a steaming swamp creature? Or an accidental discharge from the chemical plant up the highway? Actually, as it turns out, globbing (derived from the word *global*) describes applying wildcard characters to the filenames addressed by your commands.

If you need to move or copy multiple files and would like to avoid typing all the names individually, you can often apply the operation globally using the asterisk (*) wildcard. To move all the contents of the current directory to some other location, you might do something like this:

```
$ mv * /some/other/directory/
```

To move only files with names partially matching a particular sequence, try this:

```
$ mv file* /some/other/directory/
```

This command moves all files whose names begin with the letters *file*, but leaves everything else untouched. If you had files named file1, file2…file15 and wanted to move only those between file1 and file9, you'd use the question mark (?) instead of the asterisk:

```
$ mv file? /some/other/directory/
```

The question mark applies an operation to only those files whose names contain the letters *file* and *one* other character. It would leave file10 through file15 in the current directory.

DELETING FILES

As you learned earlier, objects can be deleted using rm. But keep in mind that these operations are effectively irreversible. If you wanted to delete file1 from the directory, you'd type:

```
$ rm file1
```

File globbing can be applied to rm the same way as to cp or mv, and with the same efficiency. So, for instance, this command

```
$ rm file*
```

deletes all files in the current directory whose names begin with the letters *file*. Adding the -r argument to a delete operation will make the action recursive and delete the contents of any subdirectories in the specified path:

```
$ rm -r *
```

In fact, that is a very dangerous combination, and even more so when you're working with root authority, giving you power over all system files as well. Think very carefully indeed before investing too much into an rm command.

1.2.4 *Keyboard tricks*

I doubt there's anyone who types just for the sheer joy of it. And I suspect that most people would really appreciate being told that they can get their typing done with, say, 40% fewer keystrokes. Well, I'm about to save you some fairly significant keyboard time.

CUTTING AND PASTING

First of all, despite anything you might have seen to the contrary, you can copy and paste text into and out of a terminal. It's true that the familiar Ctrl-c (copy) and Ctrl-v (paste) key combinations won't work for a Bash shell session, but Shift-Ctrl-c and Shift-Ctrl-v will. You can also cut and paste by right-clicking your mouse and selecting the appropriate operation from the menu. Believe me, that can make a very big difference. Just imagine you came across a really long command sequence from a reliable online source that looks something like this:

```
$ find ./ -name \*.html -printf '%CD\t%p\n' | grep "09/10/17"
➥ | awk '{print $2}' | xargs -t -i mv {} temp/
```

Do you want to type that whole thing in? Me neither. Here's where cutting and pasting comes to the rescue.

TAB COMPLETION

You'll really want to know about this one. Bash keeps track of your location and environment, and watches as you compose a new command. If the characters you've typed, based on the files and directories in your current environment, contain any hints about your ultimate goal, pressing the Tab key tells Bash to display its best guess on the command line. If you're happy with the suggestion, press Enter and you're on your way.

Here's an example. Suppose you've downloaded a software archive file thoughtfully named something like foo-matic-plus_0.9.1-3_amd64.deb. You'd like to copy it to a work directory where you can extract it. Normally, you'd have to type

```
$ sudo cp foo-matic-plus_0.9.1-3_amd64.deb /usr/bin/foo-matic/
```

But if the file is in your current directory then, assuming it's the only file in that directory that begins with *foo*, all you'll have to type is `cp foo` and press the Tab key. Bash fills in the rest of the filename for you. Because Bash can't read your mind, of course, you'll still have to type at least enough of the destination address to give tab completion something to work with.

Try it yourself. Use `touch` to create a file with some ridiculously long name, and then try deleting or copying it using tab completion. Here's what I came up with:

```
$ touch my-very-silly-filename_66-b.txt
$ rm my-<tab>
```

1.2.5   *Pseudo file systems*

A normal file is a collection of data that can be reliably accessed over and over again, even after a system reboot. By contrast, the contents of a Linux pseudo (or virtual) file, like those that might exist in the /sys/ and /proc/ directories, don't really exist in the normal sense. A pseudo file's contents are dynamically generated by the OS itself to represent specific values.

For instance, you might be curious to know how much total space you've got on one of your hard drives. Let me assure you that Linux will be only too happy to tell you. Let's use a command-line program called `cat` to read a file containing the number of bytes on the disk, designated by the system as sda:

```
$ cat /sys/block/sda/size
1937389568
```

> **NOTE** If the first storage device on a system is called /dev/sda, then, as you might guess, the second one would be called /dev/sdb and the third, /dev/sdc. Originally, *sda* probably stood for SCSI Device A, but I find that thinking of it as Storage Device A makes it more meaningful. You might also run into device designations like /dev/hda (hard drive), /dev/sr0 (DVD drive), /dev/cdrom (that's right, a CD-ROM drive), or even /dev/fd0 (floppy drive).

To get this kind of information, there are far simpler ways. You could right-click a drive's icon within your GUI file manager, for instance, but the pseudo files in /sys/ are the common source on which all system processes rely.

Don't happen to know your drive designation? No problem. Knowing that Linux organizes attached storage as *block devices*, you can move to the /sys/block/ directory and list its contents. Among the contents will be a directory called sda/. (Remember that sda stands for Storage Drive A.) That's the first drive used by your system on boot:

```
$ cd /sys/block
$ ls
loop0  loop1  loop2  sda  sr0
```

All the currently available block devices. A *loop device* is a pseudo device that allows a file to be used as though it's an actual physical device.

Change to the sda/ directory and run ls. Among its contents, you'll probably see files with names like sda1, sda2, and sda5. Each of these represents one of the partitions created by Linux to better organize the data on your drive:

```
$ cd sda
$ ls
alignment_offset  discard_alignment  holders    range      sda3       trace
bdi               events             inflight   removable  size       uevent
capability        events_async       integrity  ro         slaves
dev               events_poll_msecs  power      sda1       stat
device            ext_range          queue      sda2       subsystem
```

1.2.6 *Showing 'em who's boss: sudo*

For practical reasons, using an OS account that enjoys full administration powers for day-to-day computing activities is unnecessarily risky. On the other hand, fully restricting yourself to a non-administration account makes it pretty much impossible to get anything done.

Many flavors of Linux solve this problem by providing selected accounts with admin authority that under most circumstances are purely theoretical, but that can be invoked when necessary by prefacing a command with the word sudo. Once you confirm your identity by providing your password, your command will be treated as though it was issued by the root user:

```
$ cat /etc/shadow
cat: /etc/shadow: Permission denied
$ sudo cat /etc/shadow
[sudo] password for ubuntu:
```

The /etc/shadow file can't be displayed without sudo powers.

NOTE By default, the user created during the initial Linux installation will have sudo powers.

When illustrating command-line examples throughout this book, I use a command prompt of $ for commands that don't require administrator privileges and, instead of

$ sudo, I use # for those commands that do. Thus a non-admin command will look like this:

```
$ ls
```

And a sudo command will look like this:

```
# nano /etc/group
```

1.3   Getting help

One way or another, IT projects will always give you trouble. It can be complicated troubleshooting something you're trying for the first time, or maybe a task you haven't faced in so long that you've forgotten the exact syntax. You're going to need help. Here are some solid places to look.

1.3.1   Man files

By accepted convention, the people who create and maintain the software behind a Linux command also write a highly structured documentation manual known as a *man file*. When a Linux program is installed, its man file is nearly always installed with it and can be viewed from the command line by typing man followed by the command name. Believe it or not, the man system itself has a man file, so we'll start there:

```
$ man man
```

When you run this on your own computer, you'll see that NAME, the first section, includes a brief introduction, SYNOPSIS offers a detailed syntax overview, and DESCRIPTION provides a more in depth explanation of the program, which usually includes a list of command-line arguments and flags. If you're lucky, you'll also find some useful EXAMPLES.

Man files can sometimes be quite large, so skimming through the document looking for one particular detail is not always practical. For various historical reasons, the Ctrl-f combination that launches local search operations within more modern applications like web browsers and word processors isn't available. Instead, press the / key to get a text entry field at the bottom of the screen where you can type your search pattern. If the first highlighted result isn't what you want, press the n key (as many times as necessary) to search forward in the document for the same string until you find what you're looking for.

1.3.2   Info

The man system is great if you happen to know the name of the command or program you're after. But suppose the command name is the bit that you're missing. Type info at the command prompt, and you'll be transported to an environment that is, by Bash standards, downright interactive:

```
$ info
```

```
●  ubuntu@base: /usr/bin
File Edit View Search Terminal Help
File: dir,      Node: Top,      This is the top of the INFO tree.

This is the Info main menu (aka directory node).
A few useful Info commands:

  'q' quits;
  '?' lists all Info commands;
  'h' starts the Info tutorial;
  'mTexinfo RET' visits the Texinfo manual, etc.

* Menu:

Basics
* Common options: (coreutils)Common options.
* Coreutils: (coreutils).       Core GNU (file, text, shell) utilities.
* Date input formats: (coreutils)Date input formats.
* File permissions: (coreutils)File permissions.
                                Access modes.
* Finding files: (find).        Operating on files matching certain criteria.

Compression
* Gzip: (gzip).                 General (de)compression of files (lzw).
-----Info: (dir)Top, 179 lines --Top----------------------------------------
No 'Prev' or 'Up' for this node within this document.
```

Figure 1.3 The first screen of Info's main menu. Info links may appear different on your system depending on what software you've installed.

As you can see from figure 1.3, the content is arranged alphabetically by topic with headings like Basics and Compression. You can use the up and down arrow keys to scroll between lines; and, when you reach a topic of interest, you can press Enter to move to the topic's page.

Let's suppose that you want to learn more about file permissions. Scroll down through the Basics section until you get to File Permissions, and press Enter. The Menu section of this page indicates that the lines that follow are links to more pages another level down. The u key will take you back up one level, and pressing q will exit Info altogether.

I have the sense that Info isn't as heavily used in the community as it should be. In fact, I myself have a dark secret to share about Info—I worked with Linux for the better part of a decade before I even noticed it!

By default, the Info system might not be installed on some Linux server distributions. If typing `info` at the command prompt doesn't give you the satisfaction you're seeking, you can install it (on Ubuntu/Debian systems) using `sudo apt install info`.

1.3.3 *The internet*

No matter how dumb you may think you are, I can assure you that thousands of Linux administrators with all levels of experience have faced the same kinds of problems and solved them. Many of the solutions were the result of reaching out for help in an online community forum like link:serverfault.com or link:linuxquestions.org/questions.

Of course, you can always post your own questions on those sites, but why bother? Internet search engines do a great job indexing the questions that have already been asked and answered. A well-formed search query can usually get you to what you need much more quickly than starting the whole process over again from scratch.

The trick is knowing how to search intelligently. Typing my server crashed in the search field and hoping for the best probably won't be all that useful. You obviously need more detail. OK. What kind of server is it: an Apache web server? Did any error messages appear in your browser? Did the crash generate any log entries? It'd probably be a good idea to find out.

GETTING ERROR INFORMATION FROM SYSTEM LOGS

On nearly all modern Linux distributions (with the notable exception of Ubuntu 14.04), you can access all system logs through journalctl:

```
# journalctl
```

As you'll quickly see, running journalctl without any arguments will drown you in a torrent of data. You'll need to find some way to filter for the information you're after. Allow me to introduce you to grep:

The | (pipe) character uses the output of one command (journalctl, for example) as input for the next (grep).

```
# journalctl | grep filename.php
```

In this example, I use the vertical line (|) that's achieved on US keyboard layouts through the Shift-\ combination. This pipes the output of journalctl to the grep filter, which will print to the screen only those lines that include the string filename.php. I'm assuming, of course, that your web server is running PHP content and that there's a file named filename.php. Not that I'd ever do that. I usually give mine far more descriptive and useful names like stuff.php.

You can use grep in sequence to narrow your results further. Suppose there were too many journal entries for filename.php, and you realized you only needed the ones that also contain the word *error*. You could pipe the results of the first operation to a second grep command, filtering for *error*:

```
# journalctl | grep filename.php | grep error
```

In case you'd prefer to see only those lines that don't contain the word *error*, you'd add -v (for inverted results):

```
# journalctl | grep filename.php | grep -v error
```

SEARCHING THE INTERNET

Now imagine that the output you got from journalctl includes this text:

```
[Fri Oct 12 02:19:44 2017] [error] [client 54.208.59.72]
➥ Client sent malformed Host header
```

This might be useful. There's no point searching the internet for the date stamp or for that particular IP address, but I'll bet someone else has encountered `Client sent malformed Host header`.

To cut down on false positives, you might want to enclose the words in quotation marks so your search engine returns only results matching that exact phrase. Another way to minimize false positives is to tell the search engine to ignore pages containing a particular string.

In this rather silly example, you're searching the internet for a good introduction to writing Linux scripts. You find that, based on most of the results your search engine shows you for writing scripts, someone out there seems to think that you'd rather live in Hollywood. You can solve that problem by excluding pages that contain the word *movie*.

```
writing scripts -movie
```

Summary

- Just about any Linux command-line operation will make use of some or all of five basic tools: `ls`, `pwd`, `cd`, `cat`, and `less`.
- Linux uses pseudo file systems to expose data on the hardware environment to processes and users.
- Authorized users can invoke `sudo` to gain administration permissions for individual commands.
- There's a great deal of documentation and other help available through the man system, Info, and online.

Key terms

- A *file system* is made up of data files indexed in a way that allows the perception of a directory-based organization.
- A *process* is an active instance of a running software program.
- A *disk partition* is the logical division of a physical storage device that can be made to work exactly like a standalone device. Partitions are common organizational tools for all modern operating systems.
- *Bash* is a command-line user interface for executing system actions.
- *Plain text* that is usable for administration purposes is text made up of a limited set of characters and contains no extraneous formatting code.
- *File globbing* involves using wildcard characters to refer to multiple files with a single command.
- *Tab completion* employs the Tab key to suggest possible completions of a partially typed command.
- *Pseudo file systems* are directories containing files with dynamic data automatically generated at or after system boot.

Security best practices

Avoid working on your Linux machine as the root user. Use a regular user account instead, and, when you need to perform administration tasks, use `sudo`.

Command-line review

- `ls -lh /var/log` lists the contents and full, human-friendly details of the `/var/log/` directory.
- `cd`, by itself, returns you to your home directory.
- `cp file1 newdir` copies a file called file1 to the directory named newdir.
- `mv file?` `/some/other/directory/` moves all files containing the letters *file* and one more character to the target location.
- `rm -r *` deletes all files and directories beneath the current location. Use with great care.
- `man sudo` opens the man documentation file on using `sudo` with commands.

Test yourself

1   Which of the following Linux distributions is best suited for security operations?
   a   OpenSUSE
   b   CentOS
   c   Kali Linux
   d   LXLE
2   Which of the following tools allows you to edit text within a terminal session?
   a   nano
   b   gedit
   c   touch
   d   LibreOffice
3   What does adding the `-l` argument to the `ls` command do?
   a   Lists file details
   b   Lists information in a human readable format
   c   Displays only file names
   d   Displays subdirectories recursively
4   Which of the following commands will display your current location within the file system?
   a   touch
   b   pwd
   c   ls -c
   d   cd
5   What does the command `cat /etc/group` do?
   a   Displays the contents of the /etc/group file within a navigable interface
   b   Copies the /etc/group file to a new, specified location

    c Updates the last accessed value of the /etc/group file

    d Prints the contents of the /etc/group file to output (scrolling the contents to the screen)

6 Which of these commands will delete directories containing files and subdirectories?

    a `rmdir myfulldirectory`

    b `sudo rmdir myfulldirectory`

    c `rm -r myfulldirectory`

    d `rm myfulldirectory`

7 Assuming there's no directory named mynewfile, what will the `mv myfile mynewfile` command do?

    a Make a copy of the file myfile named mynewfile

    b Create an empty directory named mynewfile

    c Create an empty directory named mynewfile and move the myfile file into the new directory

    d Change the name of myfile to mynewfile

8 Which of the following will delete all files with the word *file* plus any number of characters in its name?

    a `rm file*`

    b `rm file?`

    c `rm file.`

    d `rm file??`

Answer key

1. c, 2. a, 3. a, 4. b, 5. d, 6. c, 7. d, 8. a

Linux virtualization: Building a Linux working environment

This chapter covers

- Finding the right virtualization technology
- Using Linux repository managers
- Building effective environments using VirtualBox
- Building containers with LXC
- How and when to closely manage VMs

Virtualization is the single most important technology behind almost all recent improvements in the way services and products are delivered. It's made entire industries from cloud computing to self-driving cars not only possible, but compelling. Curious? Here are two virtualization facts you'll need to know from the start:

- Linux absolutely dominates the virtual space.
- Virtualization makes it easier to learn any technology.

This chapter gives a good taste of the dominant enterprise virtualization technologies currently in use. But more to the point, it also enables you to use a virtualized environment where you can safely learn Linux administration skills. Why does this rather sophisticated technology show up so early in the book? Because it'll make it much easier for you to work through the rest of the chapters.

Need a fresh, clean operating system (OS) to try something new? Create one in a few seconds. Made a configuration error that's locked you out of your machine? No problem. Kill it and launch a new one. Along the way, you'll learn how to use Linux package managers to download, install, and manage all the software (like VirtualBox and LXC) that you'll need.

2.1 What is virtualization?

Once upon a time when you wanted a new server to provide some web server or document share for your company or its customers, you'd need to research, request budget approval, negotiate, order, safely house, provision, and then launch a brand-new machine. The process from start to finish could take months (trust me on that one— I've been there). And when increasing demand on that service threatened to overwhelm the server's capacity, you'd start the whole thing over again, hoping to eventually get the capacity/demand balance right.

A common scenario would see a company providing multiple but codependent services, each run on its own hardware. Picture a frontend web server deployed along with a database in the backend. When the dust settled, however, you'd often end up with one server deeply underused and one (usually right next to it on the rack) unable to keep up. But imagine you could securely share the compute, memory, storage, and networking resources of a single high-capacity server among multiple services. Imagine being able to carve virtual server instances out of that physical server by assigning them only the level of resources they need, and then instantly adjusting capacity to meet changing demands.

Now imagine being able to efficiently pack dozens of those virtual computers running multiple operating systems onto a single bare-metal server so that absolutely nothing is ever wasted. Imagine then being able to have those virtual machines (VMs) automatically spill over onto other physical servers as the first ones fill up. Imagine too the convenience of being able to kill a VM that's failed or in need of an update, and replace it so quickly that users might never realize anything has changed. Got that image in your head (hopefully, it's something like figure 2.1)? You're imagining *virtualization*.

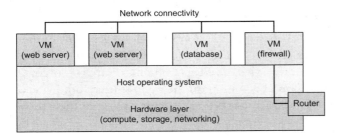

Figure 2.1 VM clients of a hardware host with connectivity to each other and to a larger network through an external router

That image is so attractive that it now dominates the enterprise computing world. At this point, I doubt there are many local or cloud-based server loads left that aren't running on some kind of virtualization technology. And the OS running the vast majority of those virtual workloads is Linux.

Amazon Web Services (AWS), by the way, lets customers rent capacity on (Linux) servers hosting millions of VMs that, in turn, run countless workloads, including many of the most popular online services. Figure 2.2 shows how an AWS Elastic Compute Cloud (EC2) VM instance serves as a hub for a full range of storage, database, and networking tools.

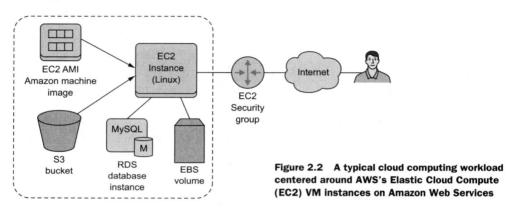

Figure 2.2   **A typical cloud computing workload centered around AWS's Elastic Cloud Compute (EC2) VM instances on Amazon Web Services**

Don't worry if some of those AWS details are a bit obscure—they're not the subject of this book in any case. But if you do find yourself wanting to learn more about Amazon Web Services, you could always read my book *Learn Amazon Web Services in a Month of Lunches* (Manning, 2017). And virtualization? There's my *Teach Yourself Linux Virtualization and High Availability* (LULU Press, 2017).

This next short section might feel a bit heavy, but it'll help provide some context for those of you interested in understanding how things are working under the hood. Successful virtualization uses some kind of isolated space on a physical computer where a guest OS can be installed and then fooled into thinking that it's all alone on its own computer. Guest operating systems can share network connections so that their administrators can log in remotely (something I'll discuss in chapter 3) and do their work exactly as they would on traditional machines. Those same shared network connections allow you to use the VMs to provide public services like websites. Broadly speaking, there are currently two approaches to virtualization:

- *Hypervisors*—Controls host system hardware to one degree or another, providing each guest OS the resources it needs (figure 2.3). Guest machines are run as system processes, but with virtualized access to hardware resources. AWS servers, for instance, have long been built on the open source Xen hypervisor technology (although they've recently begun switching some of their servers to the

equally open source KVM platform). Other important hypervisor platforms
include VMware ESXi, KVM, and Microsoft's Hyper-V.

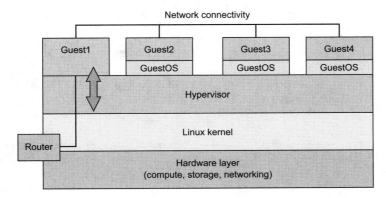

**Figure 2.3 A type 2 hypervisor architecture showing full operating systems installed
on each guest with some special administration duties delegated to Guest1**

- *Containers*—Extremely lightweight virtual servers that, rather than running as full
  operating systems, share the underlying kernel of their host OS (see figure 2.4).
  Containers can be built from plain-text scripts, created and launched in seconds,
  and easily and reliably shared across networks. The best-known container technology right now is probably Docker. The Linux Container (LXC) project that
  we'll be working with in this chapter was Docker's original inspiration.

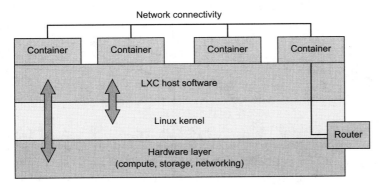

**Figure 2.4 LXC architecture showing access between the LXC environment
and both the Linux kernel and the hardware layer beneath it**

No one technology is right for every project. But if you decide to hang around for the
rest of this chapter, you're going to learn how and why to use two virtualization technologies: VirtualBox (a type 2 hypervisor) and, as I mentioned earlier, LXC (a container manager).

> **Design considerations**
>
> I wouldn't want you to walk away from this book without at least some basic guidelines for choosing virtualization technologies, so here are some thoughts:
>
> - Full-sized hypervisors like Xen and KVM (through a management frontend like Libvirt) are normally used for enterprise-sized deployments involving large fleets of Linux VMs.
> - VirtualBox (and VMware's Player) are perfect for testing and experimenting with live operating systems, one or two at a time, without the need to install them to actual PCs. Their relatively high overhead makes them unsuitable for most production environments.
> - Container technologies like LXC and Docker are lightweight and can be provisioned and launched in mere seconds. LXC containers are particularly well suited to playing with new technologies and safely building OS software stacks. Docker is currently the technology running countless dynamic, integrated fleets of containers as part of vast microservices architectures. (I'll talk a bit more about microservices in chapter 9.)

2.2   *Working with VirtualBox*

There's a lot you can do with Oracle's open source VirtualBox. You can install it on any OS (including Windows) running on any desktop or laptop computer, or use it to host VM instances of almost any major OS.

> **Installing VirtualBox on a Windows PC**
>
> Want to try all this out from a Windows PC? Head over to the VirtualBox website (https://www.virtualbox.org/wiki/Downloads) and download the executable archive. Click the file you've downloaded, and then work through a few setup steps (the default values should all work). Finally, you'll be asked whether you're OK with a possible reset of your network interfaces and then whether you want to install VirtualBox. You do.

VirtualBox provides an environment within which you can launch as many virtual computers as your physical system resources can handle. And it's a particularly useful tool for safely testing and learning new administration skills, which is our primary goal right now. But before that'll happen, you need to know how downloading and installing software on Linux works.

2.2.1   *Working with Linux package managers*

Getting VirtualBox happily installed on an Ubuntu machine is simple. It takes two commands:

```
# apt update
# apt install virtualbox
```

NOTE Remember that the # prompt means this command requires admin privileges, which are normally accessed by prefacing the command with sudo.

But what happened in our example? It all revolves around the software package manager called Advanced Package Tool (APT, more commonly known as *apt*). In the Linux world, package managers connect computers to vast online repositories of thousands of software applications, most of them free and open source. The manager, which comes installed with Linux by default, has a number of jobs:

- Maintains a local index to track repositories and their contents
- Tracks the status of all the software that's installed on your local machine
- Ensures that all available updates are applied to installed software
- Ensures that software dependencies (other software packages or configuration parameters required by the package you're installing) are met for new applications before they're installed
- Handles installing and removing software packages

Figure 2.5 illustrates some elements of the ongoing relationship between an online software repository and the package manager running on a Linux computer.

The system works incredibly well and, for historical and economic reasons, there's nothing quite like it outside of the Linux world. The thing is, though, that the manager you use will depend on your particular Linux distribution. By and large, if your distribution falls within the Debian/Ubuntu family, then you'll use APT. Members of the Red Hat family will use the RPM manager and Yum (or its new DNF replacement). Table 2.1 shows a partial list of distributions.

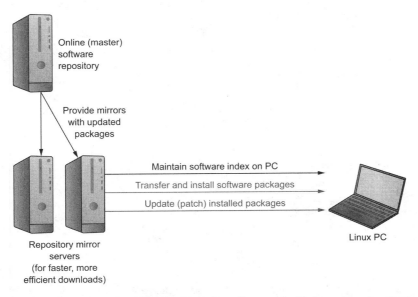

Figure 2.5 **The relationships among master software repositories, mirror download servers, and Linux running on an end user machine**

Table 2.1   **Package managers and distros**

Package manager	Distribution
APT	Debian
	Ubuntu
	Mint
	Kali Linux
RPM	Red Hat Enterprise Linux
	CentOS
	Fedora
YaST	SUSE Linux
	OpenSUSE

Besides using a package manager to install software from remote repositories, you may need to download software from a website. Often, you'll find packages that were formatted by their developers to work with APT or Yum once installed from the command line using a backend tool. Say, for instance, you want to use Skype. Heading over to its download page (figure 2.6) will let you download either a DEB or RPM file of the Skype for Linux package. You'd choose DEB if you're using a Debian-based distribution and APT, or RPM if you're in the Yum-loving Red Hat family.

WORKING WITH THE DEBIAN PACKAGE MANAGER

Once you download the file, you can install it from the command line using `dpkg`. Use the `-i` flag (for install). You'll need to make sure that you're running the `dpkg` command from the directory where the skypeforlinux-64 file is located. This example assumes that you saved the package to the Downloads directory in your user account:

```
$ cd /home/<username>/Downloads
# dpkg -i skypeforlinux-64.deb
```

The `dpkg` command should take care of dependencies for you. But if it doesn't, its output will usually give you enough information to know what's going on.

What's with that "-64"?

Linux, like other x86-based operating systems, comes in both 64-bit and 32-bit versions. The vast majority of computers manufactured and sold over the past decade use the faster 64-bit architecture. Because there's still older or development-oriented hardware out there, you'll sometimes need to run 32-bit, and you'll want the software you install to work with it.

You can check for yourself by running `arch` from the command line. Unless you know you're running on older hardware (something Linux does particularly well, by the way), you're safe assuming that you're a 64-bit kind of person.

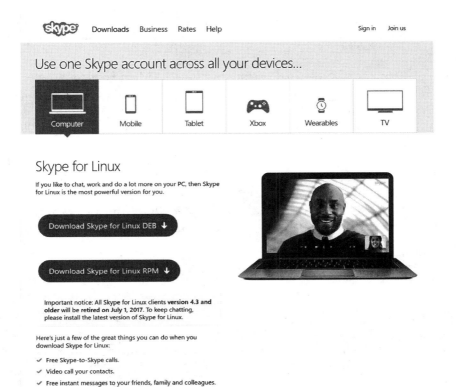

Figure 2.6   The download page for Skype for Linux. Note the separate links for the Debian (APT) and RPM (Yum) package managers.

INSTALLING VIRTUALBOX FOR THE RPM PACKAGE MANAGER

Earlier, I introduced `apt update` and `apt install virtualbox`. What did those brief commands do? To explain, I'll install the same VirtualBox software on a machine running the Fedora Linux distribution. Because I'll use Red Hat's DNF package manager, it'll require a few extra steps—which is a good thing, because running them will illustrate how the process works. The process is a bit involved, so table 2.2 lists the steps.

Table 2.2   Steps to install VirtualBox on Fedora

Task	Command
Add repo	`wget http://download.virtualbox.org/virtualbox/rpm/fedora/` ➥ `virtualbox.repo`
Update index	`dnf update`
Install dependencies	`dnf install patch kernel-devel dkms`
Install package	`dnf install VirtualBox-5.1`

NOTE These steps were designed for and tested on Fedora version 25 and do a great job illustrating the package management process. It all might work more smoothly on more recent Fedora releases, though.

Back on Ubuntu, APT knew what I meant by *virtualbox* when I added it to the `install` command. That's because a VirtualBox package is part of an online repository with which APT is already familiar. It turns out, however, that Red Hat and its children (like CentOS and Fedora) aren't quite as sociable, at least not out of the box, so I'll need to add the virtualbox repository to Yum.

From the previous chapter, you'll remember that third-party software configuration files are often kept within the /etc/ directory hierarchy, and, in that respect, yum/DNF is no different. Repository information is kept in /etc/yum.repos.d/, so you should change to that directory. From there, you'll use the wget program (usually installed by default) to download the .repo file. Here's how to do all that:

```
$ cd /etc/yum.repos.d/
# wget http://download.virtualbox.org/virtualbox/rpm/fedora/
        virtualbox.repo
```

> ### Installing software on Linux
> Specific directions for installing Linux software, including details like the precise URL I used earlier, are almost always available online. You can find those either on the software developers' own websites or through freely available guides. The internet is your friend.
>
> Make sure you specify the Linux distribution, release version, and architecture in your search engine phrases wherever necessary. I found details about the specific packages required for this project through my favorite search engine—so should you.

Having the .repo file in the right directory won't do much until you tell RPM what's changed. You do that by running `update`. The `update` command also checks the local repository index against its online counterparts to see whether there's anything new you'll want to know about. No matter what manager you're using, it's always a good idea to update the repo information before installing new software:

```
# dnf update                              All transactions with the repositories
Importing GPG key 0x98AB5139:    ◄──      are encrypted using GPG keys.
 Userid      : "Oracle Corporation (VirtualBox archive signing key)
       <info@virtualbox.org>"
 Fingerprint: 7B0F AB3A 13B9 0743 5925 D9C9 5442 2A4B 98AB 5139
 From        : https://www.virtualbox.org/download/
       oracle_vbox.asc                                        ◄──────────
Is this ok [y/N]: y
Fedora 25 - x86_64 - VirtualBox        120 kB/s |  33 kB      00:00
Dependencies resolved.
Nothing to do.              The VirtualBox references refer to the fact that I'm
Complete!                   running this Fedora host as a VM in VirtualBox.
```

The next step involves installing all the software dependencies that VirtualBox will need to run properly. A *dependency* is software that must already be installed on your computer for a new package to work. Back on Ubuntu, APT took care of these important details invisibly; Yum will also often take care of a lot of the backend details. But when it doesn't, forcing you to do it manually, the details are readily available from the same online sources discussed previously. Here's a truncated version of what that will look like:

```
# dnf install patch kernel-devel dkms
Last metadata expiration check: 0:43:23 ago on Tue Jun 13 12:56:16 2017.
[...]
Dependencies resolved.


================================================================================
 Package          Arch      Version                         Repository  Size
================================================================================
Installing:
dkms              noarch    2.3-5.20170523git8c3065c.fc25    updates     81 k
 kernel-devel     x86_64    4.11.3-202.fc25                  updates     11 M
 patch            x86_64    2.7.5-3.fc24                     fedora     125 k
Transaction Summary
================================================================================
Install  3 Packages
Total download size: 12 M
Installed size: 43 M
Is this ok [y/N]: y              Approve the operation by
Downloading Packages:            typing y before it will run.
(1/3): dkms-2.3-5.20170523git8c3065c.fc25.noarc 382 kB/s |  81 kB    00:00
(2/3): patch-2.7.5-3.fc24.x86_64.rpm            341 kB/s | 125 kB    00:00
(3/3): kernel-devel-4.11.3-202.fc25.x86_64.rpm  2.4 MB/s |  11 MB    00:04
--------------------------------------------------------------------------------
Total                                           1.8 MB/s |  12 MB    00:06
[...]
Running transaction
  Installing : kernel-devel-4.11.3-202.fc25.x86_64                    1/3
  Installing : dkms-2.3-5.20170523git8c3065c.fc25.noarch              2/3
  Installing : patch-2.7.5-3.fc24.x86_64                              3/3
  Verifying  : patch-2.7.5-3.fc24.x86_64                              1/3
  Verifying  : kernel-devel-4.11.3-202.fc25.x86_64                    2/3
  Verifying  : dkms-2.3-5.20170523git8c3065c.fc25.noarch              3/3
Installed:
  dkms.noarch 2.3-5.20170523git8c.fc25 kernel-devel.x86_64 4.11.3-202.fc25
  patch.x86_64 2.7.5-3.fc24
Complete!
```

A quick review of the successful operation

It's been a bit of a journey, but you're finally ready to install VirtualBox itself on your Red Hat, CentOS, or Fedora machine. The version number I used in this example came from the online guide used earlier. Naturally, by the time you get to try this out, it may no longer be 5.1.

DNF is obviously satisfied with the dependencies installed earlier.

```
# dnf install VirtualBox-5.1
Last metadata expiration check: 0:00:31 ago on Tue Jun 13 13:43:31 2017.
Dependencies resolved.
===============================================================================
 Package            Arch     Version                     Repository    Size
===============================================================================
Installing:
 SDL                x86_64   1.2.15-21.fc24              fedora        213 k
 VirtualBox-5.1     x86_64   5.1.22_115126_fedora25-1    virtualbox    68 M
 python-libs        x86_64   2.7.13-2.fc25               updates       6.2 M
 qt5-qtx11extras    x86_64   5.7.1-2.fc25                updates       30 k
Transaction Summary
===============================================================================
Install  4 Packages
[...]
Is this ok [y/N]: y
[...]
Creating group 'vboxusers'. VM users must be member
     of that group!
[...]
Installed:
  SDL.x86_64 1.2.15-21.fc24
  VirtualBox-5.1.x86_64 5.1.22_115126_fedora25-1
  python-libs.x86_64 2.7.13-2.fc25
  qt5-qtx11extras.x86_64 5.7.1-2.fc25
Complete!
```

Returns a list of all the packages that will be installed in this operation

Note that the process created a new system group. I'll talk about groups in chapter 9.

> ### VirtualBox add-ons
>
> You should be aware that Oracle provides an Extension Pack for VirtualBox that adds features like USB support, disk encryption, and some alternatives to the existing boot options. Take those tools into account should you ever hit a dead end running the standard package.
>
> You can also add extra file system and device integration between VirtualBox VMs and their host through the VBox Guest Additions CD-ROM image. This provides you with features like a shared clipboard and drag and drop. If the Vbox additions aren't already available through your host, install the Extension Pack on Ubuntu using this command:
>
> ```
> sudo apt install virtualbox-guest-additions-iso
> ```
>
> And then add it as a virtual optical drive to your running VM. Search online documentation concerning any extra packages that might be necessary for this to work on your host OS.

Before moving on to actually using virtualization tools like VirtualBox, I should leave you with at least a hint or two for tracking down other repository packages you might need. APT systems let you directly search for available packages using apt search.

This example searches for packages that might help you monitor your system health and then uses apt show to display full package information:

```
$ apt search sensors
$ apt show lm-sensors
```

The aptitude program, when installed, is a semi-graphic shell environment where you can explore and manage both available and already installed packages. If you can't live without your mouse, Synaptic is a full GUI package manager for desktop environments. And the Yum world is also fully searchable:

```
$ yum search sensors
$ yum info lm_sensors
```

2.2.2 Defining a virtual machine (VM)

I'm not sure whether you've ever put together a physical computer from components, but it can get involved. Defining a new VM within VirtualBox works pretty much the same way. The only significant difference is that, rather than having to get down on your hands and knees with a flashlight clenched between your teeth to manually add RAM and a storage drive to your box, VirtualBox lets you define your VM's "hardware" specs by clicking your mouse.

After clicking New in the VirtualBox interface, you'll give the VM you're about to build a descriptive name. As you can see in figure 2.7, the software should be able to correctly populate the Type and Version fields automatically. The Type and Version you select here won't install an actual OS, but are used to apply appropriate hardware emulation settings.

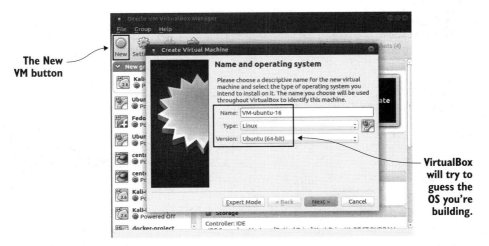

Figure 2.7   The Create Virtual Machine dialog: VirtualBox will try to approximate your OS and OS version to offer intelligent default choices later.

On the next screen, you'll allocate RAM to your VM. Unless you're planning something particularly demanding, like hosting a container swarm or running a busy web server, the default amount (768 MB) should be fine. You can certainly give it more RAM if necessary, but don't forget to leave enough for your host machine and any other VMs that might already live on it. If your host only has 4 GB of physical RAM, you probably won't want to give half of that to your VM.

Keep these limits in mind if you eventually decide to run multiple VMs at a time, something that will be useful for some of the projects you'll attempt later in the book. Even if each VM is only using the default amount of memory, two or three of them can start to eat away at the RAM needed for normal host operations.

The VirtualBox setup process now asks if you'd like to create a new virtual disk for your VM or use one that already exists (figure 2.8). What's a computer without a hard disk? There may be times when you want to share a single disk between two VMs, but for this exercise I'm guessing that you'll want to start from scratch. Select Create a Virtual Hard Disk Now.

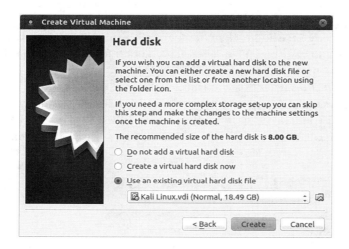

Figure 2.8   The Hard Disk screen. Note how, in this case, the non-default Use an Existing Virtual Hard Disk File radio button is selected.

The next screen (figure 2.9) lets you choose a hard disk file-type format for the disk you're about to create. Unless you're planning to eventually export the disk to use with some other virtualization environment, the default VirtualBox Disk Image (VDI) format will work fine.

I've also never regretted going with the default Dynamically Allocated option (figure 2.10) to determine how the virtual drive will consume space on the host. Here *dynamic* means space on the host storage disk will be allocated to the VM only as needed. Should the VM disk usage remain low, less host space will be allocated.

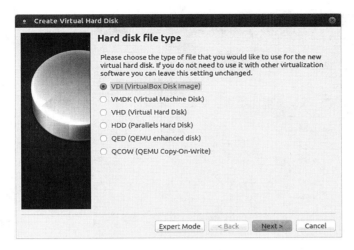

Figure 2.9 Virtual hard disks can be created using a number of formats. VDI is fine for VMs that will be used only within VirtualBox.

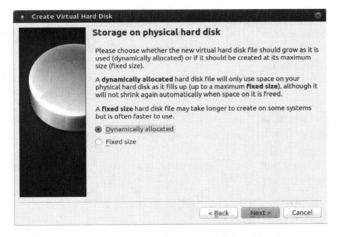

Figure 2.10 Dynamically allocated virtual disks will only consume as much space on their host's devices as they need.

A fixed-sized disk, on the other hand, will be given its maximum amount of space right away, regardless of how much it's actually using. The only advantage of Fixed Size is application performance. Because I generally only use VirtualBox VMs for testing and experiments, I'm fine avoiding the trade-off.

Because it knows it's Linux you're after, and because Linux makes such efficient use of storage space, VirtualBox will probably offer you only 8 GB of total disk size on the next screen (figure 2.11). Unless you've got unusually big plans for the VM (like, say, you're going to be working with some serious database operations), that will

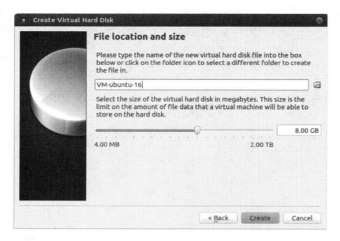

Figure 2.11   If necessary, your virtual disk can be as large as 2 TB or the maximum free space on the host device.

probably be fine. On the other hand, if you had chosen Windows as your OS, the default choice would have been 25 GB—and for good reason: Windows isn't shy about demanding lots of resources. That's a great illustration of one way Linux is so well suited to virtual environments.

> **NOTE**   You can, if you like, also edit the name and location VirtualBox will use for your disk on the File Location and Size screen.

When you're done, click Create, and the new VM will appear in the list of VMs on the left side of the VirtualBox manager. But you're not done: that was the machine. Now you'll need an OS to bring it to life.

2.2.3   Installing an operating system (OS)

Now that you've defined your new VM's virtual hardware profile, here's what you'll still need to do:

1   Download a file (in ISO format) containing the image of the Linux distribution you want to use.
2   Boot the new VM using a virtual DVD drive containing the ISO you downloaded.
3   Work through the standard OS installation process.
4   Boot the VM and launch the OS you installed previously.

Once you've settled on a distribution, you'll need to download an .ISO file containing the OS files and installation program. Finding the right file is usually a matter of searching the internet for the distribution name and the word *download*. In the case of Ubuntu, you could alternatively go to the https://ubuntu.com page and click the Downloads tab as you see in figure 2.12. Notice the various flavors of Ubuntu that are

Figure 2.12   The Downloads drop-down on the home page of Ubuntu.com. Note the range of versions Ubuntu offers.

available. If you're going to be using this VM for administration tasks, then the small and fast Server version is probably a better choice than Desktop.

Large files can sometimes become corrupted during the download process. If even a single byte within your .ISO has been changed, there's a chance the installation won't work. Because you don't want to invest time and energy only to discover that there was a problem with the download, it's always a good idea to immediately calculate the checksum (or *hash*) for the .ISO you've downloaded to confirm that everything is as it was. To do that, you'll need to get the appropriate SHA or MD5 checksum, which is a long string looking something like this:

```
4375b73e3a1aa305a36320ffd7484682922262b3
```

You should be able to get this string from the same place you got your .ISO. In the case of Ubuntu, that would mean going to the web page at http://releases.ubuntu.com/, clicking the directory matching the version you've downloaded, and then clicking one of the links to a checksum (like, for instance, SHA1SUMS). You should compare the appropriate string from that page with the results of a command run from the same directory as your downloaded .ISO, which might look like this:

```
$ shasum ubuntu-16.04.2-server-amd64.iso
```

If they match, you're in business. If they don't (and you've double-checked to make sure you're looking at the right version), then you might have to download the .ISO a second time.

NOTE You should be aware that there's more than one kind of hash. For many years, the MD5SUM algorithm was dominant, but SHA256 (with its longer 256-bit hashes) has been gaining in popularity. Practically, for large OS image files, one approach is probably no worse than the other.

Once your .ISO file is in place, head back to VirtualBox. With the VM you just created highlighted in the left panel, click the green Start button at the top of the app. You'll be prompted to select a .ISO file from your file system to use as a virtual DVD drive. Naturally, you'll choose the one you downloaded. The new VM will read this DVD and launch an OS installation.

Most of the time the installation process will go fine; however, including solutions to each of the many small things that could go wrong would require a couple of full chapters. If you do have trouble, you can consult the documentation and guides that are available for each Linux distro, or post your question on the *Linux in Action* forum on the Manning website and let the rest of us help.

When everything is nicely installed, there still might be a few more things to take care of before you can successfully boot into your VM. With your VM highlighted, click the yellow Settings icon. Here's where you can play with your VM's environment and hardware settings. Clicking Network, for example, allows you to define network connectivity. If you want your VM to have full internet access through the host machine's network interface, then, as shown in figure 2.13, you can select Bridged Adapter from the Attached To drop-down and then select the name of your host's adapter.

NOTE Using a bridged adapter might not always be your first choice, and it might sometimes present a security risk. In fact, choosing NAT Network is a more common way to provide a VM with internet access. Because many of the exercises in this book require network connectivity between multiple VMs (something that's complicated using NAT), I'll go with a bridge for now.

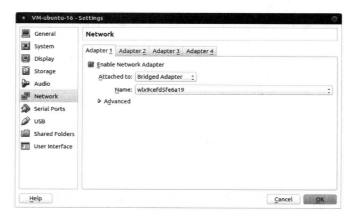

Figure 2.13 The Network tab of the Settings dialog where you can determine what type of network interface (or interfaces) to use for your VM

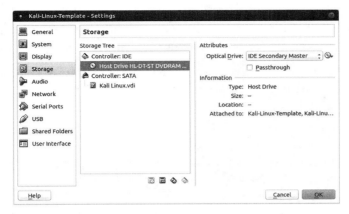

**Figure 2.14   Remove a virtual disk by right-clicking its link and selecting Remove.
You may need to do this to ensure that the VM boots to the right drive.**

You may never need this next piece of information, but you'll appreciate knowing about it if you do. In some cases, to get the VM to boot properly, you'll also need to remove the DVD from the drive, like you would for a "real" physical installation. You do that by clicking Storage. Click the first disk listed and then the Remove Disk icon at the bottom (figure 2.14). Make sure you don't accidentally remove your hard disk!

It's also possible that you might sometimes need to mount a DVD (or .ISO file) to get VirtualBox to recognize it. Clicking the + icon with the Controller:IDE line highlighted lets you select a file to serve as a virtual optical drive.

2.2.4   *Cloning and sharing a VirtualBox VM*

This section is a bit bonus-y, but who doesn't like free stuff? I'm going to tell you about two related tricks: how to organize your VirtualBox VMs to make spinning up new ones as quick as possible and how to use the command line to share VMs across a network.

CLONING VMS FOR QUICK STARTS

One of the most obvious advantages of working with VMs is the ability to quickly access a fresh, clean OS environment. But if accessing that environment requires going through the full install process, than I don't see a whole lot of *quickly*, until you throw cloning into the mix. Why not keep your original VM in its clean post-install state and create an identical clone whenever you want to do some real work?

That's easy. Take another look at the VirtualBox app. Select the (*stopped*) VM you want to use as a master copy, click the Machine menu link, and then click Clone. You'll confirm the name you'd like to give your clone and then, after clicking Next, whether you want to create a Full Clone (meaning entirely new file copies will be created for the new VM) or Linked Clone (meaning the new VM will share all the base files with its master while maintaining your new work separately).

NOTE   Selecting the Linked option will go much faster and take up much less room on your hard disk. The only downside is that you'll be unable to move this particular clone to a different computer later. It's your choice.

Now click Clone, and a new VM appears in the VM panel. Start it the way you normally would, and then log in using the same credentials you set on the master.

MANAGING VMs FROM THE COMMAND LINE

VirtualBox comes with its own command-line shell that's invoked using vboxmanage. Why bother with the command line? Because, among other benefits, it allows you to work on remote servers, which can greatly increase the scope of possible projects. To see how vboxmanage works, use list vms to list all the VMs currently available on your system:

```
$ vboxmanage list vms
"Ubuntu-16.04-template" {c00d3b2b-6c77-4919-85e2-6f6f28c63d56}
"centos-7-template" {e2613f6d-1d0d-489c-8d9f-21a36b2ed6e7}
"Kali-Linux-template" {b7a3aea2-0cfb-4763-9ca9-096f587b2b20}
"website-project" {2387a5ab-a65e-4a1d-8e2c-25ee81bc7203}
"Ubuntu-16-lxd" {62bb89f8-7b45-4df6-a8ea-3d4265dfcc2f}
```

vboxmanage clonevm will pull off the same kind of clone action I described previously using the GUI. Here, I'm making a clone of the Kali Linux template VM, naming the copy newkali:

```
$ vboxmanage clonevm --register Kali-Linux-template --name newkali
```

You can verify that worked by running vboxmanage list vms once again.

That will work nicely as long as I only need to use the new VM here on my local computer. But suppose I wanted other members of my team to be able to run an exact copy of that VM, perhaps so they could test something I've been working on. For that, I'll need to convert the VM to some standardized file format. Here's how I might export a local VM to a file using the Open Virtualization Format:

```
$ vboxmanage export website-project -o website.ova
0%...10%...20%...30%...40%...50%...60%...70%...80%...90%...100%
Successfully exported 1 machine(s).
```

> **The -o flag specifies the output filename: website.ova, in this case.**

Next, you'll need to copy the .OVA file to your colleague's computer. Bear in mind that the file won't, by any standard, be considered small and dainty. If you haven't got network bandwidth to spare for a multiple-GB transfer, then consider moving it via a USB device. But if you do take the network route, the best tool for the job is Secure Copy (scp). Here's how that might work:

```
$ scp website.ova username@192.168.0.34:/home/username
```

If that whole scp thing seems a bit out-of-the-blue, don't worry: help is on the way. The scp command will be fully covered in chapter 3 as part of the OpenSSH content. In the meantime, that scp command will only work if OpenSSH is installed on both computers, you've authorized access to the username account on the remote computer, and it's reachable from your local machine.

Once the transfer is complete, all that's left is, from the remote computer, to import the VM into that machine's VirtualBox. The command is simple:

```
$ vboxmanage import website.ova
```

Confirm that the import operation worked using list vms, and try launching the VM from the desktop:

```
$ vboxmanage list vms
"website" {30ec7f7d-912b-40a9-8cc1-f9283f4edc61}
```

If you don't need fancy remote access, you can also share a VM from the GUI. With the machine you want to share highlighted, click the File menu in VirtualBox and then Export Appliance.

2.3 *Working with Linux containers (LXC)*

VirtualBox is great for running operations requiring Linux kernel access (the way you would if you were using security features like SELinux, as you'll see in chapter 9), for when you need GUI desktop sessions, or for testing operating systems like Windows. But if you need fast access to a clean Linux environment and you're not looking for any special release version, then you'd be hard pressed to beat LXC.

> **NOTE** Like any complex system, LXC might not work well with all hardware architectures. If you have trouble launching a container, consider the possibility that there might be a compatibility issue. The internet, as always should be a helpful source of deeper information.

How fast are LXC containers? You'll see for yourself soon enough. But because they skillfully share many system resources with both the host and other containers, they work like full-bore, standalone servers, using only minimal storage space and memory.

2.3.1 *Getting started with LXC*

Install LXC on your Ubuntu workstation? Piece of cake:

```
# apt update
# apt install lxc
```

Now how about on CentOS? Well, the cake is still there, but eating it will take a bit more work. That's partly because Ubuntu was built for and on Ubuntu and Debian. By all means, give it a shot on CentOS, but I won't guarantee success. You'll first need to add a new repository, Extra Packages for Enterprise Linux (EPEL), and then install LXC along with some dependencies:

```
# yum install epel-release
# yum install lxc lxc-templates libcap-devel \
  libcgroup busybox wget bridge-utils lxc-extra libvirt
```

The backslash character (\) can be used to conveniently break a long command into multiple lines on the command line.

That's it. You're ready to get down to business. The basic LXC skill set is actually quite simple. I'm going to show you the three or four commands you'll need to make it all work, and then an insider tip that, once you understand how LXC organizes itself, will blow you away.

2.3.2   *Creating your first container*

Why not dive right in and create your first container? The value given to -n sets the name you'll use for the container, and -t tells LXC to build the container with the Ubuntu template:

```
# lxc-create -n myContainer -t ubuntu
```

The create process can take a few minutes to complete, but you'll see verbose output and, eventually, a success notification displayed to the terminal.

> **NOTE** You'll probably start seeing references to an alternate set of lxc commands associated with the relatively new LXD container manager. LXD still uses LXC tools under the hood but through a slightly different interface. As an example, using LXD the previous command would look like this: lxc launch ubuntu:16.04 myContainer. Both command sets will continue to be widely available.

There are actually quite a few templates available, as you can see from this listing of the /usr/share/lxc/templates/ directory:

```
$ ls /usr/share/lxc/templates/
lxc-alpine      lxc-centos     lxc-fedora       lxc-oracle      lxc-sshd
lxc-altlinux    lxc-cirros     lxc-gentoo       lxc-plamo       lxc-ubuntu
lxc-archlinux   lxc-debian     lxc-openmandriva lxc-slackware   lxc-ubuntu-cloud
lxc-busybox     lxc-download   lxc-opensuse     lxc-sparclinux
```

> **WARNING** Not all of these templates are guaranteed to work right out of the box. Some are provided as experiments or *works in progress*. Sticking with the Ubuntu template on an Ubuntu host is probably a safe choice. As I noted, historically, LXC has always worked best on Ubuntu hosts. Your mileage may vary when it comes to other distros.

If you decided to create, say, a CentOS container, then you should make a note of the final few lines of the output, as it contains information about the password you'd use to log in:

In this example, I called the container centos_lxc and used the centos template.

The root password is located in a directory named after the container.

```
# lxc-create -n centos_lxc -t centos
[...]
The temporary root password is stored in:
        '/var/lib/lxc/centos_lxc/tmp_root_pass'
```

You'll log in using the user name *root* and the password contained in the tmp_root_pass file. If, on the other hand, your container uses the Ubuntu template, then you'll use *ubuntu* for both your user name and password. Naturally, if you plan to use this container for anything serious, you'll want to change that password right away:

```
$ passwd
Changing password for ubuntu.
(current) UNIX password:
Enter new UNIX password:
Retype new UNIX password:
passwd: password updated successfully
```

By the way, that command is, in fact, passwd and not password. My guess is that the creator of the passwd program didn't like typing. Now use lxc-ls --fancy to check the status of your container:

```
# lxc-ls --fancy
NAME        STATE    AUTOSTART GROUPS IPV4      IPV6
myContainer STOPPED 0          -      -         -
```

Well, it exists, but apparently it needs starting. As before, the -n specifies by name the container you want to start. The -d stands for detach, meaning you don't want to be automatically dropped into an interactive session as the container starts. There's nothing wrong with interactive sessions: some of my best friends are interactive sessions, in fact. But in this case, running the lxc-start command without -d would mean that the only way to get out would involve shutting down the container, which might not be what you're after:

```
# lxc-start -d -n myContainer
```

Listing your containers should now display something like this:

```
# lxc-ls --fancy
NAME        STATE    AUTOSTART GROUPS IPV4        IPV6
myContainer RUNNING 0          -      10.0.3.142  -
```

The container state is now RUNNING.

This time, the container is running and has been given an IP address (10.0.3.142). You could use this address to log in using a secure shell session, but not before reading

chapter 3. For now, you can launch a root shell session within a running container using
`lxc-attach`:

```
# lxc-attach -n myContainer
root@myContainer:/#
```

> Note the information in the new command prompt.

You might want to spend a couple of minutes checking out the neighborhood. For
instance, `ip addr` will list the container's network interfaces. In this case, the `eth0`
interface has been given an IP address of 10.0.3.142, which matches the IPV4 value
received from `lxc-ls --fancy` earlier:

```
root@myContainer:/# ip addr
1: lo: <LOOPBACK,UP,LOWER_UP> mtu 65536 qdisc noqueue
        state UNKNOWN group default qlen 1
    link/loopback 00:00:00:00:00:00 brd 00:00:00:00:00:00
    inet 127.0.0.1/8 scope host lo
       valid_lft forever preferred_lft forever
    inet6 ::1/128 scope host
       valid_lft forever preferred_lft forever
10: eth0@if11: <BROADCAST,MULTICAST,UP,LOWER_UP> mtu 1500 qdisc noqueue
        state UP group default qlen 1000
    link/ether 00:16:3e:ab:11:a5 brd ff:ff:ff:ff:ff:ff link-netnsid 0
    inet 10.0.3.142/24 brd 10.0.3.255 scope global eth0
       valid_lft forever preferred_lft forever
    inet6 fe80::216:3eff:feab:11a5/64 scope link
       valid_lft forever preferred_lft forever
```

> eth0 is, in this case, the designation for the container's primary network interface.

> The container's IP address (10.0.3.142) and CIDR netmask (/24)

When you're done looking around your new container, you can either run `exit` to log
out leaving the container running

```
root@myContainer:/# exit
exit
```

or shut down the container using `shutdown -h now`. But before you do that, let's find
out how blazing fast LXC containers are. The `-h` flag I added to `shutdown` before
stands for *halt*. If I used `r` instead, rather than shutting down for good, the container
would reboot. Let's run `reboot` and then try to log in again right away to see how long
it takes for the container to get back up on its feet:

```
root@myContainer:/# shutdown -r now
# lxc-attach -n myContainer
```

How did that go? I'll bet that by the time you managed to retype the `lxc-attach` command, myContainer was awake and ready for action. Did you know that pressing the
up arrow key in Bash will populate the command line with the previous command?
Using that would make it even faster to request a log in. In my case, there was no
noticeable delay. The container shut down and fully rebooted in less than 2 seconds!

NOTE LXC containers are also easy on system resources. Unlike my experience with VirtualBox VMs, where running three concurrently already starts to seriously impact my 8 GB host workstation performance, I can launch all kinds of LXC containers without suffering a slowdown.

What's that you say? How about that insider tip I promised you? Excellent. I can see you're paying attention. Well, back in a terminal on the host machine (as opposed to the container), you'll need to open an administrator shell using sudo su. From here on, until you type exit, you'll be *sudo* full time:

```
$ sudo su
[sudo] password for username:
#
```

Now change directory to /var/lib/lxc/, and list the contents. You should see a directory with the name of your container. If you've got other containers on the system, they'll have their own directories as well:

```
# cd /var/lib/lxc
# ls
myContainer
```

Move to your container directory, and list its contents. There'll be a file called config and a directory called rootfs (the *fs* stands for file system):

```
# cd myContainer
# ls
config rootfs
```

Feel free to take a look through config: that's where the basic environment values for the container are set. Once you're a bit more comfortable with the way LXC works, you'll probably want to use this file to tweak the way your containers behave. But it's the rootfs directory that I really wanted to show you:

```
# cd rootfs
# ls
bin   dev  home  lib64  mnt    proc  run   srv   tmp  var
boot  etc  lib   media  opt    root  sbin  sys   usr
```

All those subdirectories that fill rootfs, do they look familiar to you? They're all part of the Linux Filesystem Hierarchy Standard (FHS). This is the container's root (/) directory but within the host's file system. As long as you have admin permissions on the host, you'll be able to browse through those directories and edit any files you want—even when the container isn't running.

You'll be able to do all kinds of things with this access, but here's one that can quite possibly save your (professional) life one day. Suppose you lock yourself out on a container. Now there's nothing stopping you from navigating through the file system, fixing the configuration file that you messed up, and getting back to work. Go ahead, tell me that's not cool. But it gets better.

It's true that the Docker ecosystem has gained many layers of features and sophistication since the technology moved out from under LXC's shadow some years ago. Under the hood, however, it's still built on top of a basic structural paradigm that will be instantly recognizable to anyone familiar with LXC. This means, should you be inclined to test the waters with the fastest-growing virtualization technology of the decade, you've already got skin in the game.

Summary

- Hypervisors like VirtualBox provide an environment where virtual operating systems can safely access hardware resources, whereas lightweight containers share their host's software kernel.
- Linux package managers like APT and RPM (Yum) oversee the installation and administration of software from curated online repositories using a regularly updated index that mirrors the state of the remote repository.
- Getting a VM going in VirtualBox requires defining its virtual hardware environment, downloading an OS image, and installing the OS on your VM.
- You can easily clone, share, and administer VirtualBox VMs from the command line.
- LXC containers are built on predefined, distribution-based templates.
- LXC data is stored within the host file system, making it easy to administer containers.

Key terms

- *Virtualization* is the logical sharing of compute, storage, and networking resources among multiple processes, allowing each to run as if it was a stand-alone physical computer.
- A *hypervisor* is software running on a host machine that exposes system resources to a guest layer, allowing the launching and administration of full-stack guest VMs.
- A *container* is a VM that, instead of full-stack, lives on top of (and shares) the host machine's core OS kernel. Containers are extremely easy to launch and kill, according to short-term need.
- A *dynamically allocated* virtual drive in VirtualBox takes up only as much space on your physical drives as the VM actually uses. A *fixed-size* disk, by contrast, takes up the maximum space no matter how much data is there.
- A *software repository* is a location where digital resources can be stored. Repositories are particularly useful for collaboration and distribution of software packages.

Security best practices

- Allowing an official package manager to install and maintain the software on your Linux system is preferred over doing it manually. Online repositories are much more secure, and downloading is properly encrypted.
- Always scan the checksum hashes of downloaded files against the correct hash strings, not only because packages can be corrupted during download, but because they can also sometimes be switched by man-in-the-middle attackers.

Command-line review

- `apt install virtualbox` uses APT to install a software package from a remote repository.
- `dpkg -i skypeforlinux-64.deb` directly installs a downloaded Debian package on a Ubuntu machine.
- `wget https://example.com/document-to-download` uses the wget command-line program to download a file.
- `dnf update`, `yum update`, or `apt update` syncs the local software index with what's available from online repositories.
- `shasum ubuntu-16.04.2-server-amd64.iso` calculates the checksum for a downloaded file to confirm that it matches the provided value. This means that the contents haven't been corrupted in transit.
- `vboxmanage clonevm Kali-Linux-template --name newkali` uses the vboxmanage tool to clone an existing VM.
- `lxc-start -d -n myContainer` starts an existing LXC container.
- `ip addr` displays information on each of a system's network interfaces (including their IP addresses).
- `exit` leaves a shell session without shutting down the machine.

Test yourself

1. Which of the following is a quality shared by both containers and hypervisors?
   a They both allow VMs to run independently of the host OS.
   b They both rely on the host's kernel for their basic operations.
   c They both permit extremely lightweight VMs.
   d They both permit extremely efficient use of hardware resources.
2. Which of the following is *not* the responsibility of a Linux package manager?
   a Sync the local index with remote repositories.
   b Scan installed software for malware.
   c Apply updates to installed software.
   d Ensure all package dependencies are installed.

3 Which of the following commands would you use to directly install a down-loaded software package on a Ubuntu system?

   a dpkg -i

   b dnf --install

   c apt install

   d yum -i

4 When creating a VM on VirtualBox, which of the following steps comes first?

   a Select a hard disk file type.

   b Choose between Dynamically Allocated and Fixed Size.

   c Remove the virtual DVD from the drive.

   d Configure the network interface.

5 Which of the following formats can be used for OS images?

   a VDI

   b VMI

   c ISO

   d VMDK

6 Which of the following commands would you use to save a VM to a .OVA for-matted file?

   a vboxmanage export

   b vboxmanage clonevm

   c vboxmanage import

   d vboxmanage clone-ova

7 Which of the following LXC command-line flags will start a container without automatically opening a new shell session?

   a lxc-start -t

   b lxc-start -a

   c lxc-start -d

   d lxc-start -n

8 By default, in which of the following directories will you find a container's file system?

   a /usr/share/lxc/

   b /etc/share/lxc/

   c /usr/lib/lxc/

   d /var/lib/lxc/

Answer key

1. d, 2. b, 3. a, 4. a, 5. c, 6. a, 7. c, 8. d

Remote connectivity: Safely accessing networked machines

3

This chapter covers

- Encryption and secure remote connections
- Linux system process management with systemd
- Extra secure and convenient password-free SSH access
- Safely copying files between remote locations with SCP
- Using remote graphic programs over SSH connections

They say that half the fun is getting there. Well, when it comes to working in a distributed computing world, not being able to get to your servers and remote resources is pretty much a show stopper. Because so much of the workload these days is being carried by the kind of virtual machine you saw in the last chapter, and because you can't just walk up to a virtual server, push the power button, and log in, you'll need some other access route. Welcome to the world of the Secure Shell (SSH).

3.1   *The importance of encryption*

In the beginning, there was Telnet for login connections over a network at any rate. The Telnet protocol was fast and reliable and, in an innocent world made up of smaller and simpler networks, perfectly serviceable. Back then, the fact that Telnet sessions sent their data packets without encryption wasn't a big deal.

I've been given to understand, however, that things have changed a bit over the past few decades. This internet thing where all the cool kids play these days is a bit bigger than it used to be, and network admins no longer all know each other by their first names. Apparently, security has now become the subject of some animated discussion. Or, in other words, if you're using Telnet to transmit private data that includes passwords and personal information in plain text over insecure networks, then you should assume it's no longer private. In fact, anyone on the network using freely available packet-sniffing software like Wireshark can easily read everything you send and receive.

Because everyone's regularly moving sensitive data across public networks, what's a poor admin to do? The solution is to encrypt the data being transferred. But just what is encryption?

To protect the privacy of data even if it falls into the wrong hands, security software can use what's known as an *encryption key*, which is a small file containing a random sequence of characters. As shown in figure 3.1, the key can be applied as part of an encryption algorithm to convert plain-text, readable data into what amounts to total gibberish. At least that's how it would appear before the key is applied through a reverse application of the same algorithm. Using the key on the encrypted version of the file converts the gibberish back to its original form. As long as you and your trusted friends are the only people in possession of the key, no one else should be able to make any sense of the data, even if it's intercepted.

When you log in to a remote server, you're doing nothing more than causing data packets containing session information to be sent back and forth between two

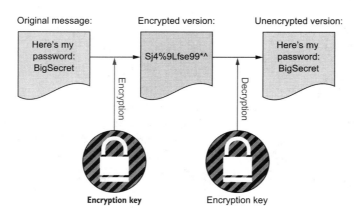

Figure 3.1 A private/public key pair to encrypt and decrypt the contents of a plain-text message. This figure illustrates a symmetric encryption design.

computers. The trick of *secure* communications is to quickly encrypt each of those packages before it's transmitted, and then, just as quickly, decrypt them at the other end. The SSH network protocol does this so quickly and so invisibly, in fact, that someone already used to connecting through Telnet sessions won't see any difference.

SSH was designed in the 1990s as a simple way for UNIX-like operating systems to safely encrypt the data transferred as part of remote logins. The OpenSSH implementation of the protocol is now so popular that Microsoft recently made it available natively for Windows.

3.2 Getting started with OpenSSH

In this section you're going to check to see if OpenSSH is installed and active on your machine. Then, if necessary, you'll install it. Because testing for a package's active status requires understanding how modern Linux distributions manage processes, you'll also take a detour into the world of systemd. When that's all done, you'll use OpenSSH to open a login session on a remote server.

If it's not already installed, running `apt install openssh-server` from an Ubuntu or Debian machine will give you all the software you'll need. But many versions of Linux distributions come with at least minimal SSH functionality right out of the box. To find what you've got under your hood (on Debian/Ubuntu-based machines, at least), you can use the package manager, dpkg.

The dpkg command-line tool manages and queries software packages that are part of the Advanced Package Tool (APT) system. Running `dpkg` with the `-s` flag and the name of a package returns the current installed and update status. If the package is already installed (as is true for this `gedit` example), the output will look something like this:

```
$ dpkg -s gedit                          Sample dpkg -s output
Package: gedit                           for the gedit package
Status: install ok installed      <---  The package status
Priority: optional
Section: gnome
Installed-Size: 1732
Maintainer: Ubuntu Desktop Team <ubuntu-desktop@
  lists.ubuntu.com>
Architecture: amd64
Version: 3.18.3-0ubuntu4
Replaces: gedit-common (<< 3.18.1-1ubuntu1)        Two of many
Depends: python3:any (>= 3.3.2-2~), libatk1.0-0    dependency packages
      (>= 1.12.4)
[...]
```

NOTE In chapter 2, you saw that you can search for available packages that aren't yet installed using `apt search packagename`.

As illustrated by figure 3.2, when you log in to a remote computer, your local PC is acting as a client of the remote server, so you'd use the openssh-client package. The

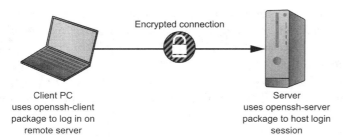

Encrypted connection

Client PC
uses openssh-client
package to log in on
remote server

Server
uses openssh-server
package to host login
session

Figure 3.2   Logging in to a remote server through an encrypted SSH connection

operating system (OS) on the remote server you're logging in to, however, is acting as a host for the shell session, so it must be running the openssh-server package.

You can run `dpkg -s openssh-client` or `dpkg -s openssh-server` to confirm that you've got the right package on your machine. Because they're built to host remote shell sessions, Linux containers will always have the full suite installed by default.

The server version also includes all the tools you'll find in the client package. This means that someone working on a machine with the openssh-server package installed will also be able to log in via SSH to other servers. Therefore, if the client package isn't already installed on your machine, installing the server package will cover you for anything you might need down the line.

On the other hand, security best practices teach us to limit access routes into our infrastructure to only what's absolutely necessary. If you don't think you'll need to log in to your desktop or laptop, then only install openssh-client:

```
# apt install openssh-client
```

Just because a package is properly installed doesn't mean that you'll be able to use it right away. Sometimes the configuration files are set to inactive by default. You'll see plenty of setup configuration examples as you work through this book, and you'll have a look at the OpenSSH configuration files a bit later in this chapter. But there's another common reason a Linux program might not work for you—it isn't running. You can use `systemctl status` to find out whether SSH is running on your machine:

```
$ systemctl status ssh
? ssh.service - OpenBSD Secure Shell server
   Loaded: loaded (/lib/systemd/system/ssh.service;
       enabled; vendor preset: enabled)
   Active: active (running) since Mon 2017-05-15 12:37:18
       UTC; 4h 47min ago          ◁─┐
 Main PID: 280 (sshd)          ◁──┐  │  SSH is currently active.
    Tasks: 8                      │
   Memory: 10.1M                  │   The process ID (PID) assigned
      CPU: 1.322s                 │   to SSH (280 in this example)
   CGroup: /system.slice/ssh.service
           ├── 280 /usr/sbin/sshd -D
           ├── 894 sshd: ubuntu [priv]
           ├── 903 sshd: ubuntu@pts/4
```

```
      ├── 904 -bash
      ├──1612 bash
      ├──1628 sudo systemctl status ssh
      └──1629 systemctl status ssh
[...]
```

As you can see from the Active line of the output, everything is fine. If you did have to crank it up yourself though, you'd use `systemctl` once again, but this time with `start` in place of `status`.

Bored with your new toy? `systemctl` `stop` will neatly put it away for you:

```
# systemctl stop ssh
```

You can force a process (like SSH) to automatically load on system startup using `systemctl enable ssh`, or to not load on startup with `systemctl disable ssh`. This code snippet enables SSH:

```
# systemctl enable ssh
```

That `systemctl` fellow seems nice enough, but you've barely had the chance to meet him. Right now OpenSSH awaits us, but I'll explain process management in greater depth at the end of this chapter.

3.3 *Logging in to a remote server with SSH*

Starting up remote sessions is a lot simpler than you might think. Make sure that you've got a second computer running somewhere with openssh-server loaded and to which you've network access. You could, for instance, fire up an LXC container the way you did in the previous chapter.

Now find that computer's IP address. If you're using an LXC container, it can give you everything you're after via the `lxc-ls --fancy` command. Here's an example showing one container called test that's not running, and a second called base that is running, using the IP address 10.0.3.144:

```
                              ┌─ Command to list LXC containers
# lxc-ls --fancy        ◁──┘  and their status details
[sudo] password for ubuntu:
NAME    STATE   AUTOSTART GROUPS IPV4         IPV6   ◁── Column headers
test    STOPPED 0         -      -            -
base    RUNNING 1         -      10.0.3.144   -
```

Alternatively, if you happen to be logged in to your server, you can get its public IP address using `ip addr`, which will spit out a rather nasty mess of characters listing all the local network interfaces. It looks something like this:

```
$ ip addr
1: lo: <LOOPBACK,UP,LOWER_UP> mtu 65536 qdisc noqueue
    state UNKNOWN group default qlen 1
```

```
link/loopback 00:00:00:00:00 brd 00:00:00:00:00
inet 127.0.0.1/8 scope host lo
   valid_lft forever preferred_lft forever
inet6 ::1/128 scope host
   valid_lft forever preferred_lft forever
8: eth0@if9: <BROADCAST,MULTICAST,UP,LOWER_UP>
      mtu 1500
qdisc noqueue state UP group default qlen 1000
link/ether 00:16:3e:ab:11:a5 brd
     ff:ff:ff:ff:ff:ff link-netnsid 0
inet 10.0.3.144/24 brd 10.0.3.255 scope
     global eth0
   valid_lft forever preferred_lft forever
inet6 fe80::216:3eff:feab:11a5/64 scope link
   valid_lft forever preferred_lft forever
```

The public network interface (in this example, eth0) ← points to `8: eth0@if9`

The inet line showing the interface's public IP address ← points to `inet 10.0.3.144/24`

In this case, the inet line numbered 8 in the interface is our primary interest. It shows an IP address of 10.0.3.144.

With that information in hand, to connect, you'll need to run ssh with the name of the account on the server you'll use to log in and the IP address. If this is the first time you've accessed the server from your PC, then you'll be asked to confirm the authenticity of the information your server's OpenSSH program sent back by typing yes. (That's *yes* by the way, not just the letter *y*.) Finally, you'll enter the password of the server account you specified (ubuntu, in my case), and you're in:

Request for confirmation

```
$ ssh ubuntu@10.0.3.144
The authenticity of host '10.0.3.144 (10.0.3.144)' can't be established.
ECDSA key fingerprint is SHA256:BPwiWLii7e+wPhFeLxJbYDjW53SgiBvZermGT9Hqck.
Are you sure you want to continue
➥    connecting (yes/no)? yes
Warning: Permanently added '10.0.3.144' (ECDSA) to the list of known hosts.
ubuntu@10.0.3.144's password:
```

Enter the password for your account on the remote server.

Didn't work out the way you expected? Looks like you're in for a terrific learning experience! The most common problem you're likely to encounter involves network connectivity, so why not sneak a peek at chapter 14? For now, though, use ping to test whether your two computers can see and speak to each other. Assuming you're running this from your local PC and testing its connectivity with a remote server using IP 10.0.3.144, a successful ping will look like this:

```
$ ping 10.0.3.144
PING 10.0.3.144 (10.0.3.144) 56(84) bytes of data.
64 bytes from 10.0.3.144: icmp_seq=1
➥    ttl=64 time=0.063 ms
64 bytes from 10.0.3.144: icmp_seq=2 ttl=64 time=0.068 ms
64 bytes from 10.0.3.144: icmp_seq=3 ttl=64 time=0.072 ms
64 bytes from 10.0.3.144: icmp_seq=4
➥    ttl=64 time=0.070 ms
```

Record of a successful response to a ping request

You can stop the ping requests and regain control of the command line by pressing Ctrl-c.

And failure will look like the following. To illustrate, I pinged an unused IP address:

```
$ ping 10.0.3.145
PING 10.0.3.145 (10.0.3.145) 56(84) bytes of data.        Record of an
From 10.0.3.1 icmp_seq=1                                   unsuccessful response
    Destination Host Unreachable          ◁─┘             to a ping request
From 10.0.3.1 icmp_seq=1 Destination Host Unreachable
```

3.4 *Password-free SSH access*

There's something a bit depressing about passwords. They're almost never used properly. They're either too short and/or easy to guess, or just overused for multiple accounts. And people seem to forget them with alarming frequency. If the only thing protecting your data is a password, then the odds are that it's not all that well protected.

That's why the industry players with the most credibility when it comes to security—like Amazon Web Services (AWS)—will, by default, disable password authentication altogether on their cloud instances. If you're concerned about the risk of unauthorized access to your servers, you might want to consider following their lead. Here's what that setting looks like in the /etc/ssh/sshd_config file on an Amazon Linux instance on the EC2 service:

```
# EC2 uses keys for remote access
PasswordAuthentication no
```

OpenSSH configuration files

Like anything else in Linux, the way OpenSSH behaves on a machine largely depends on settings in its plain-text configuration files. And, like most other programs, those configuration files can be found in the /etc/ directory hierarchy. In this case, they're in /etc/ssh/.

The configuration file whose settings control how *remote clients* will be able to log in to your machine is /etc/ssh/sshd_config. The /etc/ssh/ssh_config file, on the other hand, controls the way users on this machine will log in to *remote hosts* as a client. Besides limiting how people are allowed to log in to your systems through SSH, settings in these files can be used to control all kinds of behavior including, as you'll see a bit later in this chapter, whether you permit remote GUI access to local programs.

The alternative to SSH password authentication is to create a special key pair and then copy the public half of the pair to the remote host, which is the computer where you eventually want to log in. With encryption keys available at both ends of the connection, OpenSSH running on the host will now have a way to know who you are without having to demand a password. That's not to say passwords have no positive role to play in infrastructure security. In fact, you'll soon see how. Ideally, you should create what is called a *passphrase* and use it to authenticate yourself locally before using your key pair.

NOTE A *passphrase*, like a password, is a secret text string that you've chosen. But a passphrase will often also include spaces and consist of a sequence of real words. A password like 3Kjsi&*cn@PO is pretty good, but a passphrase like "fully tired cares mound" might be even better because of its length and the fact that it's relatively easy to remember.

3.4.1 Generating a new key pair

There's definitely more than one way to skin this cat. But since all good system administrators are, by training, lazy, I'll go with the approach that requires the fewest keystrokes. An unintended but happy consequence of this choice is that I'll get to introduce you to a much more sophisticated use of the pipe character (|).

You'll begin by creating a new public/private key pair on the client computer using the ssh-keygen program. You'll be asked for a key pair name, but, unless you've already got a pair called id_rsa, I'd just press Enter and stick with the default. As you saw previously, it's usually better to create a passphrase when prompted, especially if you share your computer with others. Remember, if you do opt to add a passphrase, you'll be prompted to enter it each time you use the key. Here's how all that will go:

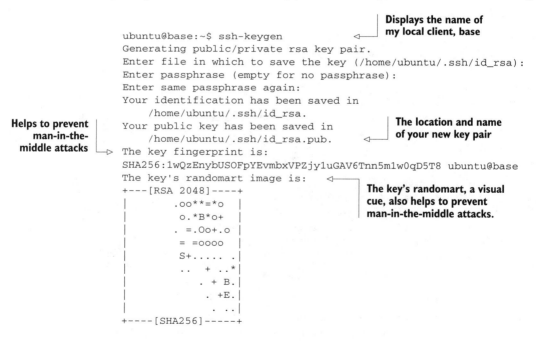

Well, now you're the proud owner of a shiny new RSA encryption-based key pair. Go ahead and use `ls -l` to display a long list of the contents of your .ssh/ directory. Notice how there are two files with the name id_rsa, but only one of them has the .pub filename extension. That file is the public half of the pair, and it's the file you'll eventually copy to the remote machine that will be your session host:

```
ubuntu@base:~$ ls -l .ssh
total 12
-rw------- 1 ubuntu ubuntu 1675 Jun  5 22:47 id_rsa
-rw-r--r-- 1 ubuntu ubuntu  393 Jun  5 22:47 id_rsa.pub
```

Which algorithm should you use?

Besides RSA (an acronym built from the last names of the three researchers who first described it: Ron Rivest, Adi Shamir, and Leonard Adleman), OpenSSH also supports the ECDSA and ED25519 signature algorithms. You'll find some rather obscure technical differences between the default RSA and both ECDSA and ED25519, which have the advantage of being based on elliptic curves. But all are considered reasonably secure. One thing to keep in mind with ECDSA and ED25519 is that they might not yet be fully supported with some older implementations.

You should no longer assume that DSA is supported by all implementations of OpenSSH. Due to suspicions surrounding its origins, DSA is widely avoided in any case.

3.4.2 Copying the public key over a network

Passwordless SSH access doesn't work until you copy the public key over to the host. As you can see in figure 3.3, the key pair is generally created on a client computer. That's because the private key should be just that: private. As much as possible, you want to avoid moving it around unnecessarily and exposing it to unfriendly eyes.

Once created, you can move the public key to the file .ssh/authorized_keys on the host computer. That way the OpenSSH software running on the host will be able to

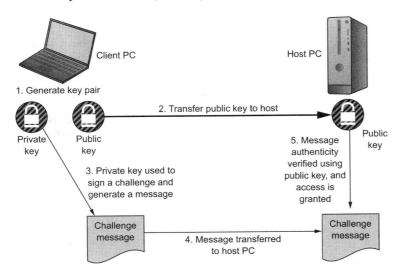

Figure 3.3 **The public key of a key pair must be moved to the host PC, while the private key remains on the client.**

verify the authenticity of a cryptographic message created by the private key on the client. Once the message is verified, the SSH session will be allowed to begin.

The first thing you'll need to do is figure out which user account on the host you'll be logging in to. In my case, it'll be the account called ubuntu. The key needs to be copied to a directory called .ssh/, which is beneath /home/ubuntu/. In case it's not there already, you should create it now using `mkdir`.

First, though, I'll introduce you to a cool shortcut: to run a single command, you don't need to actually open a full SSH session on a remote host. Instead, you can append your command to the regular `ssh` syntax like this:

```
ubuntu@base:~$ ssh ubuntu@10.0.3.142 mkdir -p .ssh
ubuntu@10.0.3.142's password:
```

You'll still need to provide the password to the remote host. But once that's done, you'll have a .ssh/ directory beneath /home/ubuntu/ on the host.

To make it easier for you to read, I split this next command into three lines using the backslash character (\), which tells Bash to read the next line as part of the current line. Make sure there are no characters (including a space) after the backslash. That's guaranteed to cause you grief:

The text is piped to the ssh command. →
```
ubuntu@base:~$ cat .ssh/id_rsa.pub \
 | ssh ubuntu@10.0.3.142 \
"cat >> .ssh/authorized_keys"
ubuntu@10.0.3.142's password:
```
← **The cat command reads the contents of the id_rsa.pub file.**

← **The text is appended to a file called authorized_keys.**

That single, multi line command will use `cat` to read all the text in the id_rsa.pub file and store it in memory. It will then pipe that text via an SSH logon on the remote host computer. Finally, it reads the text once again, this time on the host computer, and appends it to a file called authorized_keys. If the file doesn't yet exist, >> (the append tool) creates it. If a file with that name already exists, the text will be added to any content in the file.

That's it. You're ready to roll. This time, when you run the same old `ssh` command, there's no need to enter a password:

← **The login proceeds without a password request.**
```
ubuntu@base:~$ ssh ubuntu@10.0.3.142
Welcome to Ubuntu 16.04.1 LTS (GNU/Linux 4.4.0-78-generic x86_64)

 * Documentation:  https://help.ubuntu.com
 * Management:     https://landscape.canonical.com
 * Support:        https://ubuntu.com/advantage
Last login: Tue May 16 15:14:37 2017 from 10.0.3.1
ubuntu@tester:~$
```
← **The new command prompt indicates that you're on a different computer.**

3.4.3   *Working with multiple encryption keys*

There will be cases (like having to log in to a virtual machine instance running on Amazon's EC2 service) where you'll need to specify which key pair to use for a given session. This will definitely happen once you start building a collection of keys used for different hosts. To tell OpenSSH which key you're after, you add the -i flag, followed by the full name and location of the private key file:

```
ssh -i .ssh/mykey.pem ubuntu@10.0.3.142
```

Notice the .pem file extension in that example? That means the key is saved with a format that's commonly used to access all kinds of VMs, including Amazon EC2 instances.

3.5   *Safely copying files with SCP*

I'm sure you remember how the cp command copies files and directories from place to place within a file system. Well, in theory at least, there's no reason why that couldn't work just as well for copying files across a network. Except that it would be stark raving bonkers—the file contents would be exposed to anyone else who happened to be hanging around the network that day, or anyone who happened to be browsing through network log data some time later.

Forget that idea, unless you add an *s* for *secure* in front of that cp command. The SCP program copies files of any sort hither and yon using the SSH protocol for file transfer, relying on all the same keys, passwords, and passphrases. Assuming that you knew there was already a .ssh/ directory on the remote host you worked with earlier, here's how you could have transferred the public key (id_rsa.pub) to the remote host, renaming it authorized_keys:

```
ubuntu@base:~$ scp .ssh/id_rsa.pub \
   ubuntu@10.0.3.142:/home/ubuntu/.ssh/authorized_keys
```

> **WARNING** If there already was an authorized_keys file in that directory, this operation would overwrite it, destroying any existing contents. And, you can only copy or save files if the user accounts you're using have appropriate permissions. Therefore, don't try saving a file to, say, the /etc/ directory on a remote machine if your user doesn't have root privileges. Before you ask, logging in to an SSH session as the root user is generally a big security no-no.

You can, by the way, copy remote files to your local machine. This example copies a file from an AWS EC2 instance (represented by a fictitious IP address) to the specified local directory:

```
$ scp -i mykey.pem mylogin@54.7.61.201:/home/mylogin/backup-file.tar.gz \
   ./backups/january/
```
Saves the file to a directory
location relative to the
current work directory

The commands you've used up to this point have illustrated some important tools. But I should mention that there's a third (and official) way to safely copy your key over to a remote host—the purpose-built program called ssh-copy-id:

```
$ ssh-copy-id -i .ssh/id_rsa.pub ubuntu@10.0.3.142
```

> Automatically copies the
> public key to the appropriate
> location on the remote host

The nice thing about SSH sessions is that, unburdened by layers of GUI stuff, they're fast and efficient. But that can be a problem if the program you need to run on the remote host is of the graphic persuasion. The next section solves that problem for you.

3.6   *Using remote graphic programs over SSH connections*

Suppose you're trying to support a user in a remote location who's reporting trouble with a piece of desktop software like LibreOffice. If you feel that being able to launch and run the program could help diagnose and solve the problem, then it can be done using a graphic session (with the Linux X window manager) over SSH.

Having said that, don't expect miracles. Running ssh with the -X flag, using what's called *X11 forwarding*, will allow you to load a host machine-based program in the desktop of your client. Depending on a number of factors, including the quality of your network connection, your results may not meet your expectations. This is especially true of resource-heavy programs like LibreOffice. Nevertheless, it's always worth a try. Suffering through a little low bandwidth might still beat a two-hour drive to a client's office.

One more thing: don't try this on a server. In most cases, the OS version installed on a server or VM (like an LXC or a Docker container) comes with little or no graphic functionality. If you absolutely must, you can install the desktop packages to upgrade it. On an Ubuntu machine, it would look like this:

```
# apt update
# apt install ubuntu-desktop
```

With all of the disclaimers out of the way, I'd say it's time to see how this actually works. First off, open the sshd_config file on the host machine (the one whose program you want to run). You'll need to make sure that the X11Forwarding line has the value yes (although, for security considerations, it's probably not a good idea to leave it that way any longer than necessary):

```
# nano /etc/ssh/sshd_config
    X11Forwarding yes
```

> Edit the line to look
> exactly like this.

There's a similar line in the ssh_config file on the client machine that will also need to be set correctly:

```
# nano /etc/ssh/ssh_config
    ForwardX11 yes
```

> Edit the line to look
> exactly like this.

Because you've edited the configuration files, you'll need to restart SSH on both machines to make sure that your changes are live:

```
# systemctl restart ssh
```

And you're ready to go. To start a session that's graphic-enabled, add the -X flag to your ssh command:

```
$ ssh -X ubuntu@10.0.3.142
```

You'll see the regular command prompt, but you'll now be able to run a command that will launch a graphic program. Try something small. This should work on an Ubuntu system:

```
$ gnome-mines
```

Amazing! You're successfully running a remote program from a window on your local desktop.

OpenSSH brings a great deal more value to the table than the core features you've already seen. Once you've got a working SSH connection, there are all kinds of tricks you can pull off. Try mounting a local file system or directory on a remote machine, allowing remote users to seamlessly access your files. Or, through the magic of SSH tunneling, use port forwarding to permit the secure, private use of remote HTTP services.

3.7 *Linux process management*

As promised, now I'm going to revisit Linux process management so you can properly understand how programs like OpenSSH are handled. Knowing how these things work can make general administration and troubleshooting much more effective in the long run. But if you don't feel inspired to dive into such an involved topic right now, you can safely skip the rest of this chapter. You should have no problem following along with the rest of the book.

Just what is systemctl, and what's it actually doing? To properly answer those questions, you'll have to think for a bit about how Linux manages system processes in general. And because it's always nice to meet new friends, you'll also learn about some process-tracking tools to make understanding the way things work easier.

Software, as I'm sure you already know, is programming code containing instructions to control computer hardware on behalf of human users. A *process* is an instance of a running software program. An *operating system* is a tool for organizing and managing those instances/processes to effectively use a computer's hardware resources.

Organizing and managing processes for a complex multiprocess, multiuser operating environment is no simple task. To make it work, you'll need some kind of traffic cop to tightly control the many moving parts (figure 3.4). Let me introduce you to systemctl.

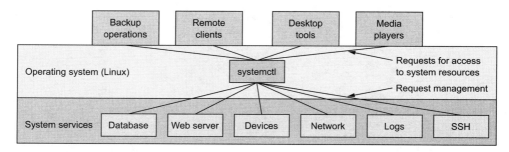

Figure 3.4   The availability and responsiveness of many system services are managed by systemd's systemctl process manager.

3.7.1   *Viewing processes with the ps command*

Let's pull out an electron microscope and see if we can't spot a process in its natural habitat. Type the following command into a terminal. It will do nothing (sleep) in the background (&) for 10 seconds and then stop. While it's running, though, type ps:

The PID of the command running in the background

```
$ for i in {1..10}; do sleep 1; done &
[1] 19829
$ ps
   PID TTY          TIME CMD
 19522 pts/17    00:00:00 bash
 19829 pts/17    00:00:00 bash
 19832 pts/17    00:00:00 sleep
 19833 pts/17    00:00:00 ps
```

The sleep process launched by the original command

The ps command to list running processes

What you'll see is a record of the two running processes spawned by that command, along with their PIDs: 19829 and 19832, in my case. If you run ps once again after waiting 10 seconds, you'll see those two processes are no longer running. You should also see a report of the successful completion of the sleep command:

```
$ ps
   PID TTY          TIME CMD
 19522 pts/17    00:00:00 bash
 20549 pts/17    00:00:00 ps
[1]+  Done                    for i in {1..10};
do
    sleep 1;
done
```

Normally, if you were to type just ps and run it, you'd probably get only two results. The first, a process called *bash* that represents the Bash command interpreter being used by your current shell session, and the most recent command (which, of course, was ps). But by looking at the PID assigned to bash (7447, in the following example), you know there are lots and lots of other processes already hard at work somewhere on your system. These will have been spawned by parent shells going all the way back to the init process itself:

```
$ ps
  PID TTY          TIME CMD
 7447 pts/3    00:00:00 bash
 8041 pts/3    00:00:00 ps
```

On an Ubuntu machine, the first process to wake up and get everything else going when a Linux computer boots is called *init*. As you'll soon discover, that name can be misleading, which is why the first process has a different name on CentOS. You can see for yourself that init is first by running the following ps command exactly the way it's printed here. I'll explain the details in just a minute:

The file responsible for process 1

```
$ ps -ef | grep init
root          1      0  0 12:36 ?        00:00:00 /sbin/init     ◄──────┘
ubuntu     1406    904  0 16:26 pts/4    00:00:00 grep --color=auto init
```

The rightmost column of the output (/sbin/init on the first line) represents the location and name of the file behind the process itself. In this case, it's a file called init that lives in the /sbin/ directory. The leftmost column on this first line contains the word root and tells you that the owner of this process is the root user. The only other piece of information that is of interest right now is the number 1, which is the PID of the init process. The only way you're going to get PID 1 is by getting there before anyone else.

Before moving on, it's worth spending a bit more time with ps. As you've seen, ps displays information about active processes. It's often important to have access to process-related information so you can properly plan and troubleshoot system behavior. You can expect to use ps early and often.

Adding the -e argument to ps as you did previously returns not only the processes running in your current child shell, but all the processes from all parent shells right back up to init.

> **NOTE** A *parent shell* is a shell environment from within which new (child) shells can subsequently be launched and through which programs run. You can think of your GUI desktop session as a shell, and the terminal you open to get a command line as its child. The top-level shell (the grandparent?) is the one that's run first when Linux boots.

If you want to visualize parent and child shells/processes, you can use the pstree command (adding the -p argument to display the PIDs for each process). Note how the first process (assigned PID 1) is systemd. On older versions of Linux (Ubuntu 14.04 and earlier, for instance), this would have been called init instead:

```
                                      CentOS users might need to install
                                      the psmisc package to run pstree.
$ pstree -p            ◄───────┘
systemd(1)─┬─agetty(264)        ◄──┐
           ├─agetty(266)           │  systemd, the top-level
           ├─agetty(267)           │  parent process
           ├─agetty(268)
           ├─agetty(269)
           ├─apache2(320)─┬─apache2(351)
           │              ├─apache2(352)
           │              ├─apache2(353)
           │              ├─apache2(354)
           │              └─apache2(355)
           ├─cron(118)
           ├─dbus-daemon(109)
           ├─dhclient(204)
           ├─dockerd(236)─┬─docker-containe(390)─┬─{docker-containe}(392)
           │              │                      └─{docker-containe}(404)
           │              ├─{dockerd}(306)
           │              └─{dockerd}(409)
           ├─mysqld(280)─┬─{mysqld}(325)
           │             ├─{mysqld}(326)
           │             └─{mysqld}(399)
           ├─nmbd(294)
           ├─rsyslogd(116)─┬─{in:imklog}(166)
           │               ├─{in:imuxsock}(165)
           │               └─{rs:main Q:Reg}(167)
           ├─smbd(174)─┬─smbd(203)
           │           └─smbd(313)
           ├─sshd(239)───sshd(840)───sshd(849)───bash(850)───pstree(15328)
           ├─systemd-journal(42)
           └─systemd-logind(108)
```

Go ahead and try all these commands on your machine. Even on a quiet system, you'll probably see dozens of processes; a busy desktop PC or server can easily have hundreds or even thousands.

3.7.2 *Working with systemd*

There's something interesting about that /sbin/init file you just saw: `file` is a venerable UNIX program that gives you insider information about a file. If you run `file` with /sbin/init as its argument, you'll see that the init file is not actually a program, but a *symbolic link* to a program called systemd. We'll talk more about symbolic links in chapter 12, but here's where you get to meet systemd:

```
$ file /sbin/init
/sbin/init: symbolic link to /lib/systemd/systemd
```

It took years of fragmentation and some vigorous political infighting, but nearly all Linux distributions now use the same process manager: systemd. It's a drop-in replacement for a process called *init*, which has long been the very first process started during the boot process of all UNIX-based operating systems. By *drop-in replacement*, I mean that, even if the way it gets things done can be quite different, to the casual observer, systemd functions like init always did. That's why the /sbin/init file is now nothing more than a link to the systemd program.

This is all a bit theoretical as you'll probably never actually invoke the systemd program itself by name, either directly or through its /sbin/init frontend. This is because, as you've already seen, the key administration tasks are handled by systemctl on behalf of systemd.

Technically, systemd's primary job is to control the ways individual processes are born, live their lives, and then die. The systemctl command you used previously is the tool of choice for those tasks. But, somewhat controversially, the systemd developers expanded the functionality far beyond the traditional role of process management to take control over various system services. Included under the new systemd umbrella are tools like a logging manager (journald), network manager (networkd), and device manager (you guessed it: udevd). Curious? The *d* stands for *daemon*, a background system process.

You'll cross paths with at least some of those systemd tools as you work through the book. Our next stop will be learning how to manage and, most importantly, back up file systems and archives.

Summary

- Encrypted connections are a critical part of all networked communications, and SSH is pretty much the industry standard.
- You can enable password-free SSH access by sharing the public key of a key pair.
- The OpenSSH package also allows for secure file copying and remote graphic sessions.
- On most modern Linux distributions, processes are managed by systemd through the systemctl tool.
- You can pipe data between commands using the | (pipe) character and filter streaming data with grep.

Key terms

- A *password* is a string of regular characters, while a *passphrase* can include spaces and punctuation.
- *RSA* is a popular encryption algorithm.
- *X11 forwarding* allows graphic programs to be run over a remote connection.
- A Linux *process* is all the ongoing activity that's associated with a single running program.
- A *shell* is a terminal environment that provides a command-line interpreter (like Bash) to allow a user to execute commands. When you're working from a Linux desktop PC or laptop, you'll generally access a shell by opening a terminal program (like GNOME Terminal).

- A *parent shell* is an initial environment, from within which new child shells can subsequently be launched and through which programs run. A shell is, for all intents and purposes, also a process.

Security best practices

- Always encrypt remote login sessions running over a public network.
- Avoid relying on passwords alone; like people, they're fallible.
- Key-based, passwordless SSH sessions are preferable to simple password logins.
- Never transfer files across public networks in plain text.

Command-line review

- `dpkg -s openssh-client` checks the status of an APT-based software package.
- `systemctl status ssh` checks the status of a system process (systemd).
- `systemctl start ssh` starts a service.
- `ip addr` lists all the network interfaces on a computer.
- `ssh-keygen` generates a new pair of SSH keys.
- `$ cat .ssh/id_rsa.pub | ssh ubuntu@10.0.3.142 "cat >> .ssh/authorized_keys"` copies a local key and pastes it on a remote machine.
- `ssh-copy-id -i .ssh/id_rsa.pub ubuntu@10.0.3.142` safely copies encryption keys (recommended and standard).
- `ssh -i .ssh/mykey.pem ubuntu@10.0.3.142` specifies a particular key pair.
- `scp myfile ubuntu@10.0.3.142:/home/ubuntu/myfile` safely copies a local file to a remote computer.
- `ssh -X ubuntu@10.0.3.142` allows you to log in to a remote host for a graphics-enabled session.
- `ps -ef | grep init` displays all currently running system processes and filters results using the string `init`.
- `pstree -p` displays all currently running system processes in a visual tree format.

Test yourself

1 The purpose of an encryption key is to:
   a Establish a secure network connection
   b Encrypt and decrypt data packets
   c Obscure sensitive data in transit
   d Ensure the reliability of data transmissions

2 You can check the status of a service using which of the following commands?
   a `dpkg -s <servicename>`
   b `systemd status <servicename>`
   c `systemctl status <servicename>`
   d `systemctl <servicename> status`

3 Which of these packages must be installed before a host server can accept remote SSH logins?

    a openssh-server

    b ssh-server

    c openssh-client

    d ssh-client

4 On a Linux distribution using systemd, the job of init is performed by which of these programs?

    a /lib/systemd/systemd

    b /bin/systemd

    c /sbin/init

    d /bin/init

5 Which of the following services is *not* a systemd service?

    a networkd

    b journald

    c processd

    d udevd

6 For passwordless SSH connections, where must the keys be placed?

    a Public and private keys on the host, private key on the client

    b Public and private keys on the host, public key on the client

    c Private key on the host, public key on the client

    d Public key on the host, private key on the client

7 What is the purpose of a passphrase in SSH sessions?

    a To authenticate your identity to the remote OpenSSH program

    b To authenticate your identity to the local OpenSSH program

    c To identify which key pair you want to use

    d To authenticate the status of the key pair

8 Which of the following will copy a remote file to the current directory on your local machine (assuming both the remote directory and file exist)?

    a `scp mylogin@10.0.3.142:/home/mylogin/filename .`

    b `scp mylogin@10.0.3.142/home/mylogin/filename .`

    c `scp mylogin@10.0.3.142:/home/mylogin/filename`

    d `scp mylogin@10.0.3.142:/home/mylogin/filename`
      ➥ `./home/myname/Documents`

Answer key

1. b, 2. c, 3. a, 4. a, 5. c, 6. d, 7. b, 8. a

Archive management: Backing up or copying entire file systems

Through the book's first chapters, you learned a lot about getting around both safely and efficiently in a Linux environment. You also learned to generate base working environments using the wonders of virtualization. From here on in, I'll focus on building and maintaining the infrastructure elements you'll need to get real stuff done.

Building IT infrastructures without a good backup protocol is like mortgaging your home to invest in your brother-in-law's, can't-go-wrong, cold fusion invention. You know the odds are that it won't end well. But before you can properly back up file systems and partitions, you'll need to understand exactly how file systems and partitions work. After that? What tools are available? When should each be used, and how will you put everything back together again if disaster strikes? Stay tuned.

4.1 Why archive?

Before we get to the why, just what is an *archive*? It's nothing more than a single file containing a collection of objects: files, directories, or a combination of both. Bundling objects within a single file (as illustrated in figure 4.1) sometimes makes it easier to move, share, or store multiple objects that might otherwise be unwieldy and disorganized.

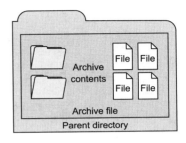

Figure 4.1 Files and directories can be bundled into an archive file and saved to the file system.

Imagine trying to copy a few thousand files spread across a dozen directories and subdirectories so your colleague across the network can see them too. Of course, using the proper command-line syntax arguments, anything can be done. (Remember `cp` from chapter 1? And `-r`?) But making sure you copy only the files you're after and not accidentally leaving anything out can be a challenge. Granted, you'll still need to account for all those files at least one time as you build the archive. But once you've got everything wrapped up in a single archive file, it's a whole lot easier to track. Archives it is, then.

But there are archives, and then there are archives. Which to choose? That depends on the kinds of files you're looking to organize and on what you plan to do with them. You might need to create copies of directories and their contents so you can easily share or back them up. For that, `tar` is probably going to be your champion of choice. If, however, you need an exact copy of a partition or even an entire hard disk, then you'll want to know about `dd`. And if you're looking for an ongoing solution for regular system backups, then try `rsync`.

Learning how to use those three tools and, more importantly, learning what real problems those three tools can solve for you will be the focus of the rest of this chapter. Along the way, we'll take a bit of a detour to see how to protect the permissions and ownership attributes for the files in the archive as they move through the archive life cycle. Finally, we'll take a peek at why Linux uses file permissions and file ownership in the first place.

4.1.1 Compression

One more note before we begin. Although the two are often used together, don't confuse archiving with compression. *Compression*, as figure 4.2 shows, is a software tool that applies a clever algorithm to a file or archive to reduce the amount of disk space

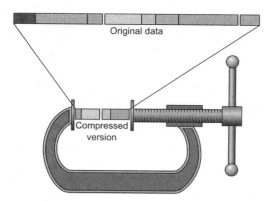

Original data

Compressed version

Figure 4.2 Object compression by eliminating statistical redundancy and/or removing less important parts of a file

it takes. Of course, when they're compressed, files are unreadable, which is why the algorithm can also be applied in reverse to decompress them.

As you'll see soon, applying compression to a tar archive is simple and doing so is a particularly good idea if you're planning to transfer large archives over a network. Compression can reduce transmission times significantly.

4.1.2 Archives: Some important considerations

Two primary reasons you'll want to create archives are to build reliable file system images and to create efficient data backups. This section describes those objectives.

IMAGES

What's an image? Remember those .ISO files you used to install Linux on a virtual machine back in chapter 2? Those files were images of complete operating systems, specially organized to make it easy to copy the included files to a target computer.

Images can also be created from all or parts of a live, working operating system (OS) so you can copy and paste the contents to a second computer. This effectively makes the second (copy) an exact clone of the first system in its current state. I've often done this to rescue a complex installation from a failing hard drive when I didn't feel like building up the whole thing again from scratch on its new drive. It's also great when you want to quickly provide identical system setups to multiple users, like student workstations in a classroom.

> **NOTE** Don't even think about trying any of this with Windows. For all intents and purposes, the Windows registry architecture makes it impossible to separate an installed OS from its original hardware.

Although we're going to spend the rest of this chapter talking about backups rather than images, don't worry. The tools we'd use for creating and restoring images are pretty much the same, so you'll be fine either way.

DATA BACKUPS

Backups should be a big part of your life. In fact, if you never worry about the health of your data, then either you're a Zen master or you're just not doing your job right. There's so much scary stuff that can happen:

- Hardware can—and will—fail. And it'll usually happen right before you were planning to get to that big backup. Really.
- Fat fingers (by which I mean clumsy people) and keyboards can conspire to mangle configuration files, leaving you completely locked out of your encrypted system. Having a fallback copy available can save your job and, quite possibly, your life.
- Data insecurely stored on cloud infrastructure providers like Amazon Web Services (AWS) can be suddenly and unpredictably lost. Back in 2014, this happened to a company called Code Spaces. The company's improperly configured AWS account console was breached, and the attackers deleted most of its data. How did Code Spaces recover? Well, when was the last time you heard anything about Code Spaces?
- Perhaps most terrifying of all, you could become the victim of a ransomware attack that encrypts or disables all your files unless you pay a large ransom. Got a reliable and recent backup? Feel free to tell the attackers just what you think.

Before moving on, I should mention that untested data backups may not actually work. In fact, there's evidence to suggest that nearly half of the time they don't. What's the problem? There's a lot that can go wrong: there could be flaws on your backup device, the archive file might become corrupted, or the initial backup itself might have been unable to properly process all of your files.

Generating and monitoring log messages can help you spot problems, but the only way to be reasonably confident about a backup is to run a trial restore onto matching hardware. That will take energy, time, and money. But it sure beats the alternative. The best system administrators I've known all seem to share the same sentiment: "Paranoid is only the beginning."

4.2 What to archive

If there aren't too many files you want to back up and they're not too large, you might as well transfer them to their storage destination as is. Use something like the SCP program you saw in chapter 3. This example uses SCP to copy the contents of my public encryption key into a file called authorized_keys on a remote machine:

```
ubuntu@base:~$ scp .ssh/id_rsa.pub \
   ubuntu@10.0.3.142:/home/ubuntu/.ssh/authorized_keys
```

◁── **Overwrites the current contents of the remote authorized_keys file**

But if you want to back up many files spread across multiple directories (a complicated project with source code, for instance) or even entire partitions (like the OS you're running right now), you're going to need something with more bite.

Although we discussed disk partitions and pseudo files in chapter 1, if you want to develop some kind of intelligent backup policy, you'll want to get a feel for what they look like. Suppose you're planning a backup of a partition containing your company's large accounting database; you probably won't get too far without knowing how much space that partition takes up and how to find it.

Let's begin with the df command, which displays each partition that's currently mounted on a Linux system, along with its disk usage and location on the file system. Adding the -h flag converts partition sizes to human readable formats like GB or MB, rather than bytes:

```
$ df -h
Filesystem      Size  Used  Avail Use% Mounted on
/dev/sda2       910G  178G  686G  21% /
none            492K     0  492K   0% /dev
tmpfs           3.6G     0  3.6G   0% /dev/shm
tmpfs           3.6G  8.4M  3.6G   1% /run
tmpfs           5.0M     0  5.0M   0% /run/lock
tmpfs           3.6G     0  3.6G   0% /sys/fs/cgroup
```

The root partition: the only normal partition on this system

Note the 0 bytes for disk usage. That (usually) indicates a pseudo file system.

The /run directory contains files with runtime data generated during boot.

The first partition listed is designated as /dev/sda2, which means that it's the second partition on Storage Device A and that it's represented as a system resource through the pseudo file system directory, /dev/. This happens to be the primary OS partition in this case. All devices associated with a system will be represented by a file in the /dev/ directory. (The partition used by your accounting software would appear somewhere on this list, perhaps designated using something like /dev/sdb1.)

NOTE Running df on an LXC container displays the partitions associated with the LXC host.

It's important to distinguish between real and *pseudo* file systems (file systems whose files aren't actually saved to disk but live in volatile memory and disappear when the machine shuts down). After all, there's no point backing up files that represent an ephemeral hardware profile and, in any case, will be automatically replaced by the OS whenever, and wherever, the real file system is booted next.

It's pretty simple to tell which partitions are used for pseudo files: if the file designation is tmpfs and the number of bytes reported in the Used column is 0, then the odds are you're looking at a temporary rather than a normal file system.

By the way, that df was run on an LXC container, which is why there's only one real partition, /. Let's see what it shows us when run on a physical computer:

```
df -h
Filesystem      Size   Used  Avail  Use%  Mounted on
udev            3.5G      0   3.5G    0%  /dev
tmpfs           724M   1.5M   722M    1%  /run
/dev/sda2       910G   178G   686G   21%  /
tmpfs           3.6G   549M   3.0G   16%  /dev/shm
tmpfs           5.0M   4.0K   5.0M    1%  /run/lock
tmpfs           3.6G      0   3.6G    0%  /sys/fs/cgroup
/dev/sda1       511M   3.4M   508M    1%  /boot/efi      ◁
tmpfs           724M    92K   724M    1%  /run/user/1000
/dev/sdb1       1.5G   1.5G      0  100%  /mnt/UB-16      ◁
```

This partition was created during installation to enable UEFI booting.

sdbl is a USB thumb drive containing an Ubuntu live boot image.

Notice the /dev/sda1 partition mounted at /boot/efi. This partition was created during the original Linux installation to permit system boots controlled by the UEFI firmware. UEFI has now largely replaced the old BIOS interface that was used for hardware initialization during system boot. Software installed on this partition allows UEFI integration with a Linux system. And /dev/sdb1 is a USB thumb drive that happened to be plugged into the back of my machine.

When you're dealing with production servers, you'll often see separate partitions for directories like /var/ and /usr/. This is often done to make it easier to maintain the integrity and security of sensitive data, or to protect the rest of the system from being overrun by file bloat from, say, the log files on /var/log/. Whatever the reason, for any particular disk design, you'll want to make informed decisions about what needs backing up and what doesn't.

You'll sometimes see the /boot/ directory given its own partition. I personally think this is a bad idea, and I've got scars to prove it. The problem is that new kernel images are written to /boot/ and, as your system is upgraded to new Linux kernel releases, the disk space required to store all those images increases. If, as is a standard practice, you assign only 500 MB to the boot partition, you'll have six months or so before it fills up—at which point updates will fail. You may be unable to fully boot into Linux before manually removing some of the older files and then updating the GRUB menu. If that doesn't sound like a lot of fun, then keep your /boot/ directory in the largest partition.

4.3 *Where to back up*

From an OS perspective, it doesn't make a difference where you send your archives. Feel free to choose between legacy tape drives, USB-mounted SATA storage drives, network-attached storage (NAS), storage area networks (SAN), or a cloud storage solution. For more on that, see my book *Learn Amazon Web Services in a Month of Lunches* (Manning, 2017).

Whichever way you go, be sure to carefully follow best practices. In no particular order, your backups should all be:

- *Reliable*—Use only storage media that are reasonably likely to retain their integrity for the length of time you intend to use them.

- *Tested*—Test restoring as many archive runs as possible in simulated production environments.
- *Rotated*—Maintain at least a few historical archives older than the current backup in case the latest one should somehow fail.
- *Distributed*—Make sure that at least some of your archives are stored in a physically remote location. In case of fire or other disaster, you don't want your data to disappear along with the office.
- *Secure*—Never expose your data to insecure networks or storage sites at any time during the process.
- *Compliant*—Honor all relevant regulatory and industry standards at all times.
- *Up to date*—What's the point keeping archives that are weeks or months behind the current live version?
- *Scripted*—Never rely on a human being to remember to perform an ongoing task. Automate it (read chapter 5).

4.4   Archiving files and file systems using tar

To successfully create your archive, there are three things that will have to happen:

1 Find and identify the files you want to include.
2 Identify the location on a storage drive that you want your archive to use.
3 Add your files to an archive, and save it to its storage location.

Want to knock off all three steps in one go? Use `tar`. Call me a hopeless romantic, but I see poetry in a well-crafted `tar` command: a single, carefully balanced line of code accomplishing so much can be a thing of beauty.

4.4.1   Simple archive and compression examples

This example copies all the files and directories within and below the current work directory and builds an archive file that I've cleverly named archivename.tar. Here I use three arguments after the `tar` command: the c tells tar to create a new archive, v sets the screen output to verbose so I'll get updates, and f points to the filename I'd like the archive to get:

```
$ tar cvf archivename.tar *
file1
file2
file3
```

The verbose argument (v) lists the names of all the files added to the archive.

NOTE   The `tar` command will never move or delete any of the original directories and files you feed it; it only makes archived copies. You should also note that using a dot (`.`) instead of an asterisk (`*`) in the previous command will include even hidden files (whose filenames begin with a dot) in the archive.

If you're following along on your own computer (as you definitely should), then you'll see a new file named archivename.tar. The .tar filename extension isn't necessary, but it's always a good idea to clearly communicate the purpose of a file in as many ways as possible.

You won't always want to include all the files within a directory tree in your archive. Suppose you've produced some videos, but the originals are currently kept in directories along with all kinds of graphic, audio, and text files (containing your notes). The only files you need to back up are the final video clips using the .mp4 filename extension. Here's how to do that:

```
$ tar cvf archivename.tar *.mp4
```

That's excellent. But those video files are enormous. Wouldn't it be nice to make that archive a bit smaller using compression? Say no more! Just run the previous command with the z (zip) argument. That will tell the gzip program to compress the archive. If you want to follow convention, you can also add a .gz extension in addition to the .tar that's already there. Remember: clarity. Here's how that would play out:

```
$ tar czvf archivename.tar.gz *.mp4
```

If you try this out on your own .mp4 files and then run ls -l on the directory containing the new archives, you may notice that the .tar.gz file isn't all that much smaller than the .tar file, perhaps 10% or so. What's with that? Well, the .mp4 file format is itself compressed, so there's a lot less room for gzip to do its stuff.

As tar is fully aware of its Linux environment, you can use it to select files and directories that live outside your current working directory. This example adds all the .mp4 files in the /home/myuser/Videos/ directory:

```
$ tar czvf archivename.tar.gz /home/myuser/Videos/*.mp4
```

Because archive files can get big, it might sometimes make sense to break them down into multiple smaller files, transfer them to their new home, and then re-create the original file at the other end. The split tool is made for this purpose.

In this example, -b tells Linux to split the archivename.tar.gz file into 1 GB-sized parts; *archivename* is any name you'd like to give the file. The operation then names each of the parts—archivename.tar.gz.partaa, archivename.tar.gz.partab, archivename .tar.gz.partac, and so on:

```
$ split -b 1G archivename.tar.gz "archivename.tar.gz.part"
```

On the other side, you re-create the archive by reading each of the parts in sequence (cat archivename.tar.gz.part*), then redirect the output to a new file called archivename.tar.gz:

```
$ cat archivename.tar.gz.part* > archivename.tar.gz
```

4.4.2   *Streaming file system archives*

Here's where the poetry starts. I'm going to show you how to create an archive image of a working Linux installation and stream it to a remote storage location—all within a single command (figure 4.3).

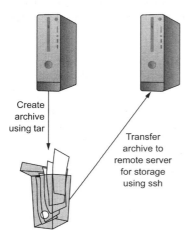

Create archive using tar

Transfer archive to remote server for storage using ssh

Figure 4.3   An archive is a file that can be copied or moved using normal Bash tools.

Here's the command:

```
# tar czvf - --one-file-system / /usr /var \
  --exclude=/home/andy/ | ssh username@10.0.3.141 \
  "cat > /home/username/workstation-backup-Apr-10.tar.gz"
```

Rather than trying to explain all that right away, I'll use smaller examples to explore it one piece at a time. Let's create an archive of the contents of a directory called importantstuff that's filled with, well, really important stuff:

```
$ tar czvf - importantstuff/ | ssh username@10.0.3.141 \
<linearrow />    "cat > /home/username/myfiles.tar.gz"
importantstuff/filename1
importantstuff/filename2
[...]
username@10.0.3.141's password:
```

You'll need to enter the password for your account on the remote host.

Let me explain that example. Rather than entering the archive name right after the command arguments (the way you've done until now), I used a dash (czvf -). The dash outputs data to standard output. It lets you push the archive filename details back to the end of the command and tells tar to expect the source content for the archive instead. I then piped (|) the unnamed, compressed archive to an ssh login on a remote server where I was asked for my password. The command enclosed in quotation marks then executed cat against the archive data stream, which wrote the stream contents to a file called myfiles.tar.gz in my home directory on the remote host.

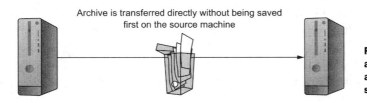

Archive is transferred directly without being saved
first on the source machine

**Figure 4.4   Streaming
an archive as it's created
avoids the need to first
save it to a local drive.**

As you can see in figure 4.4, one advantage of generating archives this way is that you avoid the overhead of a middle step. There's no need to even temporarily save a copy of the archive on the local machine. Imagine backing up an installation that fills 110 GB of its 128 GB of available space. Where would the archive go?

That was just a directory of files. Suppose you need to back up an active Linux OS to a USB drive so you can move it over to a separate machine and drop it into that machine's main drive. Assuming there's already a fresh installation of the same Linux version on the second machine, the next copy/paste operation will generate an exact replica of the first.

> **NOTE** This won't work on a target drive that doesn't already have a Linux file system installed. To handle that situation, as you'll see shortly, you'll need to use dd.

The next example creates a compressed archive on the USB drive known as /dev/sdc1. The `--one-file-system` argument excludes all data from any file system besides the current one. This means that pseudo partitions like /sys/ and /dev/ won't be added to the archive. If there are other partitions that you want to include (as you'll do for /usr/ and /var/ in this example), then they should be explicitly added. Finally, you can exclude data from the current file system using the `--exclude` argument:

**References
/usr and /var
partitions
explicitly**

**Excludes data from other partitions
when building the archive**

```
# tar czvf /dev/sdc1/workstation-backup-Apr-10.tar.gz \
  --one-file-system \
  / /usr /var \
  --exclude=/home/andy/
```

**Excludes directories or files within a selected
file system when necessary (poor old Andy)**

Now let's go back to that full-service command example. Using what you've already learned, archive all the important directories of a file system and copy the archive file to a USB drive. It should make sense to you now:

```
# tar czvf - --one-file-system / /usr /var \
  --exclude=/home/andy/ | ssh username@10.0.3.141 \
  "cat > /home/username/workstation-backup-Apr-10.tar.gz"
```

All that's fine if the files you need to archive (and only those files) are agreeably hanging out together in a single directory hierarchy. But what if there are other files mixed in that you don't want to include? Is there a way to aggregate only certain files without having to mess with the source files themselves? It's time you learn about `find`.

4.4.3   Aggregating files with find

The `find` command searches through a file system looking for objects that match rules you provide. The search outputs the names and locations of the files it discovers to what's called *standard output* (stdout), which normally prints to the screen. But that output can just as easily be redirected to another command like `tar`, which would then copy those files to an archive.

Here's the story. Your server is hosting a website that provides lots of .mp4 video files. The files are spread across many directories within the /var/www/html/ tree, so identifying them individually would be a pain. Here's a single command that will search the /var/www/html/ hierarchy for files with names that include the file extension .mp4. When a file is found, `tar` will be executed with the argument `-r` to append (as opposed to overwrite) the video file to a file called videos.tar:

The -iname flag returns both upper- and lowercase results;
-name, on the other hand, searches for case-sensitive matches.

```
# find /var/www/html/ -iname <1> "*.mp4" -exec tar \
 -rvf videos.tar {} \;
```

The { } characters tell the find command to
apply the tar command to each file it finds.

In this case, it's a good idea to run `find` as `sudo`. Because you're looking for files in system directories, it's possible that some of them have restrictive permissions that could prevent `find` from reading and, thus, reporting them.

And, because we're talking about `find`, I should also tell you about a similar tool called `locate` that will often be your first choice when you're in a big hurry. By default, `locate` searches the entire system for files matching the string that you specify. In this case, `locate` will look for files whose names end with the string *video.mp4* (even if they have any kind of prefix):

```
$ locate *video.mp4
```

If you run `locate` head-to-head against `find`, `locate` will almost always return results far faster. What's the secret? `locate` isn't actually searching the file system itself, but simply running your search string against entries in a preexisting index. The catch is that if the index is allowed to fall out of date, the searches become less and less accurate. Normally the index is updated every time the system boots, but you can also manually do the job by running `updatedb`:

```
# updatedb
```

4.4.4 *Preserving permissions and ownership...and extracting archives*

Did I miss anything? Actually, how to extract the files and directories from a tar archive so you can use them again. But before I get to that, there's another bit of business I promised I'd take care of—making sure that your archive operations don't corrupt file permissions and file-ownership attributes.

PERMISSIONS

As you've seen, running `ls -l` lists the contents of a directory in long form, showing you (from right to left) the file's name, age, and size. But it also repeats a name (root, in this example) and provides some rather cryptic strings made up of the letters *r*, *w*, and *x*:

```
$ ls -l /bin | grep zcat
-rwxr-xr-x 1 root root 1937 Oct 27 2014 zcat
```

Here's where I decipher those two leftmost sections (as annotated in figure 4.5). The 10 characters to the left are made up of four separate sections. The first dash (❶ in the figure) means that the object being listed is a file. It would be replaced with a *d* if it were a directory. The next three characters ❷ are a representation of the file's permissions as they apply to its owner, the next three ❸ are the permissions as they apply to its group, and the final three ❹ represent the permissions all other users have over this file.

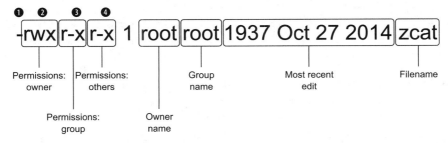

Figure 4.5   A breakdown of the data displayed by the `ls -l` command

In this example, the file owner has full authority—including read (r), write (w), and execute (x) rights. Members of the group and those in others can read and execute, but not write.

But what does all that really mean? Here, the file zcat is the script of a command-line program that reads compressed files. The permissions tell you that everyone has the right to read the script itself and to execute it (through something like `zcat myfile .zip`), but only the owner can edit (*w*) the file. If someone who's logged in to a different user account were to try to edit the file, they'd get a No Write Permission warning.

If you want to change a file's permissions, use the change mode (chmod) tool:

```
# chmod o-r /bin/zcat
# chmod g+w /bin/zcat
```

This example removes the ability of others (o) to read the file and adds write permissions for the group (g). A file's owner would be represented by the letter *u* (for user).

What's a group?

You can think of a group much the same way you might think of a regular user account: the things that both can and cannot do or access are defined by file permissions. The difference is that no one can log in to a Linux system as a group. Then why create groups, and what purpose do they serve? Here's the scoop.

Groups are a powerful and super-efficient way to organize resources. Here's a simple example. Consider a company with a few dozen employees who need some kind of server access, but not necessarily to the same resources. You can create a couple of groups called dev and IT, for example. When users are initially given their accounts, all the developers would be added to the dev group, and all the sysadmins would be added to IT group. Now, let's say that a system configuration file comes into use: rather than tediously adding file permissions for each of the 10 or 15 admins or so, you can give only the IT group access. All the IT group members will automatically be added, and all the developers will remain excluded.

Every system user along with many applications will automatically be given their own groups. That explains why files you create will normally be owned by *yourname* and be part of the *yourname* group. If you decide to stick around, you'll see more implementations of groups in chapter 9.

You'll find two other systems for describing permissions in Linux: numeric and mask. Talking about mask would be a bit distracting at this point, and, in any case, mask isn't used all that often. But you do need to understand the numeric system where each possible combination of permissions can be represented by a number between 0 and 7.

How-to guides and command documentation will often tell you to give a file 644 permissions (or something similar) in order for an operation to run successfully. For instance, invoking the private part of an encryption key pair will often not work unless it has permissions of either 400 or 600. You'll want to know how that works.

The read permission is always given the number 4; the write permission, number 2; and execute, number 1. A user with all three permissions is described by the number 7 (4+2+1=7). Read and write permissions, but not execute, is 6; read and execute but not write is 5, and no permissions at all is 0.

To change an object's permissions, you'd enter the final total scores for each category of user (that is, owner, group, and others). For example, updating the original status of the zcat file the way you did earlier using chmod g+w and o-r would require 755 (7 for the owner and then 5 for both group and others). Removing read permission from others would change that to 751, and adding write permissions to group would change that again to 771. Here's how you'd use `chmod` to apply that value:

```
# chmod 771 /bin/zcat
```

Here's a quick chart to help you remember all those details:

Permission	Character	Number
Read	r	4
Write	w	2
Execute	x	1

OWNERSHIP

What about those file ownership values? This one is straightforward: these are the values that define a file's owner (*u*) and group (*g*). Check it out yourself. From your home directory, create a new file and then list the directory contents in long form. You'll see that the values of both the owner and group match your user name. In this example, that's `username`:

```
$ cd
$ touch newfile
$ ls -l
-rw-rw-r-- 1 username username 0 Jun 20 20:14 newfile
```

I rarely go more than a couple of days without having to worry about file ownership. Suppose one of my users asks for a file. The file might be too large to email or might contain sensitive data that shouldn't be emailed. The obvious solution is to copy it if I'm on the same server. If I'm on a different server, I can always use `scp` to transfer the file and then copy the file to the user's home directory. But either way, I'll need to use `sudo` to copy a file to the user's directory, which means its owner will be root.

Don't believe me? Try creating a file using `sudo`:

```
$ sudo touch newerfile
[sudo] password for username:
$ ls -l
-rw-r--r-- 1 root root 0 Jun 20 20:37 newerfile
```
Note that the owner and group for this file is root.

Well now, that's going to be a real problem if my user ever needs to edit the file I was kind enough to send. Turns out that I wasn't being so helpful after all—unless I do the job properly and change the file's ownership using `chown`, which works much like the `chmod` command that you saw earlier. This example assumes that the account name of that other user is otheruser. Go ahead and create such an account using `sudo useradd otheruser`:

```
$ sudo chown otheruser:otheruser newerfile
$ ls -l
-rw-r--r-- 1 otheruser otheruser 0 Jun 20 20:37 newerfile   ◄─┐  Note the new file
                                                                 owner and group.
```

That's permissions and ownership. But what does it have to do with extracting your archives? Well, would you be upset if I told you that there was a good chance that all the files and directories restored after a catastrophic system crash would have the wrong permissions? I thought so. Think about it: you rebuild your system and invite all your users to log in once again, but they immediately start complaining that they can't edit their own files!

I think it will be helpful for you to see all this for yourself. So you can work through these examples on your own, create a new directory and populate it with a few empty files and then, if there aren't already any other user accounts on your system, create one:

```
$ mkdir tempdir && cd tempdir    ◄─┐  The && characters will execute a
$ touch file1                         second command only if the first
$ touch file2                         command was successful.
$ touch file3
# useradd newuser
```

Right now, all three files will be owned by you. Use chown to change the ownership of one of those files to your new user, and then use ls -l to confirm that one of the files now belongs to the new user:

```
# chown newuser:newuser file3
$ ls -l
-rw-rw-r-- 1 username username 0 Jun 20 11:31 file1
-rw-rw-r-- 1 username username 0 Jun 20 11:31 file2
-rw-rw-r-- 1 newuser  newuser  0 Jun 20 11:31 file3
```

Now create a tar archive including all the files in the current directory the way you did before:

```
$ tar cvf stuff.tar *
file1
file2
file3
```

To extract the archive, run the tar command against the name of the archive, but this time with the argument x (for extract) rather than c:

```
$ tar xvf stuff.tar
```

> **WARNING** Extracting an archive overwrites any files with the same names in the current directory *without* warning. Here, that's fine, but that won't normally be the case.

Running `ls -l` once again will show something you don't want to see. All three files are now owned by you...even file3:

```
$ ls -l
-rw-rw-r-- 1 username username 0 Jun 20 11:31 file1
-rw-rw-r-- 1 username username 0 Jun 20 11:31 file2
-rw-rw-r-- 1 username username 0 Jun 20 11:31 file3
```

That's not good, and I'm sure our friend newuser won't be happy about it either. What's the solution? Well, first of all, let's try to figure out exactly what the problem is.

Generally, only users with administrator powers can work with resources in other users' accounts. If I wanted to, say, transfer the ownership of one of my files to a colleague, because it requires a change to someone else's account, I can't do that. Generosity has its limits. Therefore, when I try to restore the files from the archive, saving them to the ownership of other users would be impossible. Restoring files with their original permissions presents a similar (although not identical) problem. The solution is to perform these operations as an administrator, using `sudo`. Now you know.

4.5   *Archiving partitions with dd*

There's all kinds of stuff you can do with `dd` if you research hard enough, but where it shines is in the ways it lets you play with partitions. Earlier, you used `tar` to replicate entire file systems by copying the files from one computer and then pasted them as is on top of a fresh Linux install of another computer. But because those file system archives weren't complete images, they required a running host OS to serve as a base.

Using `dd`, on the other hand, can make perfect byte-for-byte images of, well, just about anything digital. But before you start flinging partitions from one end of the earth to the other, I should mention that there's some truth to that old UNIX admin joke: *dd* stands for *Disk Destroyer*. If you type even one wrong character in a `dd` command, you can instantly and permanently wipe out an entire drive worth of valuable data. And yes, spelling counts.

> **NOTE** As always with `dd`, pause and think very carefully before pressing that Enter key!

4.5.1   *dd operations*

Now that you've been suitably warned, we'll start with something straightforward. Suppose you want to create an exact image of an entire disk of data that's been designated as /dev/sda. You've plugged in an empty drive (ideally having the same capacity as your /dev/sdb system). The syntax is simple: `if=` defines the source drive, and `of=` defines the file or location where you want your data saved:

```
# dd if=/dev/sda of=/dev/sdb
```

The next example will create a .img archive of the /dev/sda drive and save it to the home directory of your user account:

```
# dd if=/dev/sda of=/home/username/sdadisk.img
```

Those commands created images of entire drives. You could also focus on a single partition from a drive. The next example does that and also uses bs to set the number of bytes to copy at a single time (4,096, in this case). Playing with the bs value can have an impact on the overall speed of a dd operation, although the ideal setting will depend on hardware and other considerations:

```
# dd if=/dev/sda2 of=/home/username/partition2.img bs=4096
```

Restoring is simple: effectively, you reverse the values of if and of. In this case, if= takes the image that you want to restore, and of= takes the target drive to which you want to write the image:

```
# dd if=sdadisk.img of=/dev/sdb
```

You should always test your archives to confirm they're working. If it's a boot drive you've created, stick it into a computer and see if it launches as expected. If it's a normal data partition, mount it to make sure the files both exist and are appropriately accessible.

4.5.2 *Wiping disks with dd*

Years ago I had a friend who was responsible for security at his government's overseas embassies. He once told me that each embassy under his watch was provided with an official government-issue hammer. Why? In case the facility was ever at risk of being overrun by unfriendlies, the hammer was to be used to destroy all their hard drives.

What's that? Why not just delete the data? You're kidding, right? Everyone knows that deleting files containing sensitive data from storage devices doesn't actually remove them. Given enough time and motivation, nearly anything can be retrieved from virtually any digital media, with the possible exception of the ones that have been well and properly hammered.

You can, however, use dd to make it a whole lot more difficult for the bad guys to get at your old data. This command will spend some time writing millions and millions of zeros over every nook and cranny of the /dev/sda1 partition:

```
# dd if=/dev/zero of=/dev/sda1
```

But it gets better. Using the /dev/urandom file as your source, you can write over a disk with random characters:

```
# dd if=/dev/urandom of=/dev/sda1
```

4.6   *Synchronizing archives with rsync*

One thing you already know about proper backups is that, to be effective, they absolutely have to happen regularly. One problem with that is that daily transfers of huge archives can place a lot of strain on your network resources. Wouldn't it be nice if you only had to transfer the small handful of files that had been created or updated since the last time, rather than the whole file system? Done. Say hello to rsync.

I'm going to show you how to create a remote copy of a directory full of files and maintain the accuracy of the copy even after the local files change. (You'll first need to make sure that the rsync package is installed on both the client and host machines you'll be using.) To illustrate this happening between your own local machine and a remote server (perhaps an LXC container you've got running), create a directory and populate it with a handful of empty files:

```
$ mkdir mynewdir && cd mynewdir
$ touch file{1..10}
```
Creates 10 files named file1 to file10

Now use ssh to create a new directory on your remote server where the copied files will go, and then run rsync with the -av arguments. The v tells rsync to display a verbose list of everything it does. a is a bit more complicated, but also a whole lot more important. Specifying the -a super-argument will make rsync synchronize recursively (meaning that subdirectories and their contents will also be included) and preserve special files, modification times, and (critically) ownership and permissions attributes. I'll bet you're all-in for -a. Here's the example:

```
$ ssh username@10.0.3.141 "mkdir syncdirectory"
$ rsync -av * username@10.0.3.141:syncdirectory
username@10.0.3.141's password:
sending incremental file list
file1
file10
file2
file3
file4
file5
file6
file7
file8
file9

sent 567 bytes  received 206 bytes  1,546.00 bytes/sec
total size is 0  speedup is 0.00
```
Specify a remote target directory following the colon (:).

The verbose argument displays the files that were copied.

If everything went as it should, head over to your remove server and list the contents of /syncdirectory/. There should be 10 empty files.

To give rsync a proper test run, you could add a new file to the local mynewdir directory and use nano to, say, add a few words to one of the existing files. Then run the exact same `rsync` command as before. When it's done, see if the new file and updated version of the old one have made it to the remote server:

```
$ touch newfile
$ nano file3
$ rsync -av * username@10.0.3.141:syncdirectory
username@10.0.3.141's password:
sending incremental file list
file3
newfile
```

Only the new/updated files are listed in the output.

There's a whole lot more `rsync` backup goodness waiting for you to discover. But, as with all the other tools I discuss in this book, you now have the basics. Where you go from here is up to you. In the next chapter, however, you'll learn about automating backups using system schedulers. For now, there's one final thought I'd like to share about backups.

4.7   *Planning considerations*

Careful consideration will go a long way to determine how much money and effort you invest in your backups. The more valuable your data is to you, the more reliable it should be. The goal is to measure the value of your data against these questions:

- How often should you create new archives, and how long will you retain old copies?
- How many layers of validation will you build into your backup process?
- How many concurrent copies of your data will you maintain?
- How important is maintaining geographically remote archives?

Another equally important question: should you consider incremental or differential backups? Although you're probably going to want to use `rsync` either way, the way you sequence your backups can have an impact on both the resources they consume and the availability of the archives they produce.

Using a *differential* system, you might run a full backup once a week (Monday), and smaller and quicker differential backups on each of the next six days. The Tuesday backup will include only files changed since Monday's backup. The Wednesday, Thursday, and Friday backups will each include all files changed since Monday. Friday's backup will, obviously, take up more time and space than Tuesday's. On the plus side, restoring a differential archive requires only the last full backup and the most recent differential backup.

An *incremental* system might also perform full backups only on Mondays and can also run a backup covering only changed files on Tuesday. Wednesday's backup, unlike the differential approach, will include only files added or changed since Tuesday, and Thursday's will have only those changed since Wednesday. Incremental backups will be fast and efficient; but, as the updated data is spread across more files,

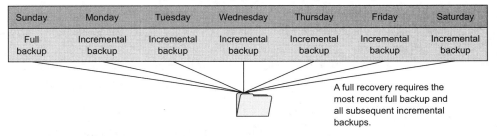

Incremental backup and recovery

A full recovery requires the most recent full backup and all subsequent incremental backups.

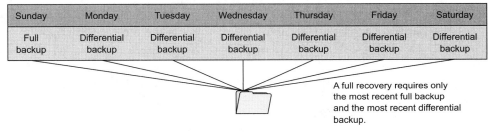

Differential backup and recovery

A full recovery requires only the most recent full backup and the most recent differential backup.

Figure 4.6   The differences between incremental and differential backup systems

restoring incremental archives can be time-consuming and complicated. This is illustrated in figure 4.6.

Summary

- Not having good backups can ruin your morning.
- The `tar` command is generally used for archiving full or partial file systems, whereas `dd` is more suited for imaging partitions.
- Adding compression to an archive not only saves space on storage drives, but also bandwidth during a network transfer.
- Directories containing pseudo file systems usually don't need backing up.
- You can incorporate the transfer of an archive into the command that generates it, optionally avoiding any need to save the archive locally.
- It's possible—and preferred—to preserve the ownership and permissions attributes of objects restored from an archive.
- You can use `dd` to (fairly) securely wipe old disks.
- You can incrementally synchronize archives using `rsync`, greatly reducing the time and network resources needed for ongoing backups.

Key terms

- An *archive* is a specially formatted file in which file system objects are bundled.
- *Compression* is a process for reducing the disk space used by a file through the application of a compression algorithm.

- An *image* is an archive containing the files and directory structure necessary to re-create a source file system in a new location.
- *Permissions* are the attributes assigned to an object that determine who may use it and how.
- *Ownership* is the owner and group that have authority over an object.
- A *group* is an account used to manage permissions for multiple users.

Security best practices

- Create an automated, reliable, tested, and secure recurring process for backing up all of your important data.
- Where appropriate, separate file systems with sensitive data by placing them on their own partitions and mounting them to the file system at boot time.
- Always ensure that file permissions are accurate, and allow only the least access necessary.
- Never assume the data on an old storage drive is truly deleted.

Command-line review

- `df -h` displays all currently active partitions with sizes shown in a human readable format.
- `tar czvf archivename.tar.gz /home/myuser/Videos/*.mp4` creates a compressed archive from video files in a specified directory tree.
- `split -b 1G archivename.tar.gz archivename.tar.gz.part` splits a large file into smaller files of a set maximum size.
- `find /var/www/ -iname "*.mp4" -exec tar -rvf videos.tar {} \;` finds files meeting a set criteria and streams their names to `tar` to include in an archive.
- `chmod o-r /bin/zcat` removes read permissions for others.
- `dd if=/dev/sda2 of=/home/username/partition2.img` creates an image of the sda2 partition and saves it to your home directory.
- `dd if=/dev/urandom of=/dev/sda1` overwrites a partition with random characters to obscure the old data.

Test yourself

1 Which of these arguments tells `tar` to compress an archive?

   a `-a`

   b `-v`

   c `-z`

   d `-c`

2 Which of these partitions are you *least* likely to want to include in a backup archive?

   a `/var`

   b `/run`

   c /

   d /home

3 The second partition on the first storage drive on a system will usually be designated by which of the following?

   a /dev/sdb2

   b /dev/srb0

   c /dev/sda2

   d /dev/sdb1

4 Which of the following will create a compressed archive of all the .mp4 files in a directory?

   a `tar cvf archivename.tar.gz *.mp4`

   b `tar cvf *.mp4 archivename.tar.gz`

   c `tar czvf archivename.tar.gz *.mp4`

   d `tar *.mp4 czvf archivename.tar`

5 Which of the following tools will help you put multiple file parts back together?

   a `cat`

   b `split`

   c `|`

   d `part`

6 What of the following will find all .mp4 files within the specified directories and add them to a tar archive?

   a `find /var/www/ -iname "*" -exec tar -rvf videos.tar {} \;`

   b `find /var/www/ -iname "*.mp4" -exec tar -vf videos.tar {} \;`

   c `find /var/www/ -iname "*.mp4" | tar -rvf videos.tar {} \;`

   d `find /var/www/ -iname "*.mp4" -exec tar -rvf videos.tar {} \;`

7 Which of the following will give a file's owner full rights, its group read and execute rights, and others only execute rights?

   a `chmod 752`

   b `chmod 751`

   c `chmod 651`

   d `chmod 744`

8 What will the command `dd if=sdadisk.img of=/dev/sdb` do?

   a Copy the contents of the /dev/sdb drive to a file called sdadisk.img

   b Destroy all data on the network

   c Copy an image called sdadisk.img to the /dev/sdb drive

   d Format the /dev/sdb drive and then move sdadisk.img to it

Answer key

1. c, 2. b, 3. c, 4. c, 5. a, 6. d, 7. b, 8. c

Automated administration: Configuring automated offsite backups

This chapter covers

- Automating administrative tasks with scripts
- Increasing security and system efficiency
- Backing up local data
- Scheduling automated tasks

If there's one thing that I'd hope I made sufficiently clear in the previous chapter, it's that regular and reliable system backups are absolutely *critical*. But, in many ways, the hard part is the *regular*. Keeping up with important tasks with immediate consequences is hard enough; remembering to run some dull daily or weekly backup is pretty much a nonstarter.

It's no secret: the single best solution to the problem is to configure an automated scheduler to perform the task for you and then forget about it. Until recently, the scheduler you'd use on Linux would almost certainly have been some variation of the software utility cron; and, in fact, that's still a great choice. But the systemd process manager you learned about back in chapter 3 has added systemd timers into the mix.

I'm going to cover both approaches in this chapter, but I'll also show you how to package backups and any other administration task into scripts, which can themselves be put on an automated schedule. To demonstrate how it all works in the real world, I'll craft a command to backup some data to an AWS Simple Storage Solution (S3) bucket and then use the command to create schedulers using both cron and systemd timers.

5.1 Scripting with Bash

A Linux *script* is a plain text file containing one or more commands compliant with Bash (or some other shell interpreter). Being able to string together multiple commands within a single file makes it possible to create executable routines that can rival programming languages in their complexity and versatility.

5.1.1 A sample script for backing up system files

To illustrate what a working script might look like, let me show you a short, nicely written example that's probably already active on your machine. Once we've worked through the script one line at a time, I'll tell you what it all has to do with this chapter. And don't forget the other important takeaway from this exercise: if you can read scripts, you can also write them. It's the exact same skill set.

This script uses a series of powerful tools to do something that's actually quite simple: create secure backups of four important system files to ensure a usable replacement in case the originals are somehow corrupted. Figure 5.1 illustrates the script's actions as a flow chart. Note that $FILE is a variable used to represent a set of filenames processed by the script.

Head over to the /etc/cron.daily/ directory and list the contents. You'll probably see a file called passwd. Display the file using less (or cat or nano or vim). It's your choice. If it doesn't happen to be there, this is what it looks like:

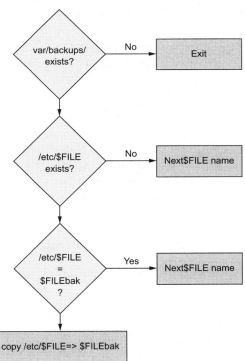

Figure 5.1 The decision flow traced by the passwd script

```
#!/bin/sh

cd /var/backups || exit 0

for FILE in passwd group shadow gshadow; do
        test -f /etc/$FILE              || continue
        cmp -s $FILE.bak /etc/$FILE     && continue
        cp -p /etc/$FILE $FILE.bak && chmod 600 $FILE.bak
done
```

Normally the # character introduces a comment that wouldn't be read by the interpreter. In this particular case, where both # and ! are used, Linux will read the comment and use its value (/bin/sh) as the active shell. The string is popularly known as the *shebang line*, though don't ask me why. Although sh is an alternative to bash, for our purposes right now, there aren't any practical differences between the two.

The next line in the script changes the directory to /var/backups/. If no such directory exists, it exits the script and issues an exit status code of 0, which signifies the command was successful:

```
cd /var/backups || exit 0
```

The || sequence (sometimes known as a double pipe) can be read as though it's the word *or*. So this line means: either change directory to /var/backups/ or exit the script. If everything goes according to plan, subsequent script operations will take place in the /var/backups/ directory.

> **NOTE** Exit codes are passed when a Linux command completes. A 0 will be passed to indicate success, whereas different numbers can be configured to specify some kind of error.

In the next part of the code, the line starting with for introduces a loop. Those of you with programming experience will have no trouble understanding what's going on here: the script will assign in turn each of the following four strings (passwd, group, and so forth) as the value of the variable FILE. It then executes the code block between the reserved words do and done:

```
for FILE in passwd group shadow gshadow; do
```

Here's a brief definition of some of those concepts:

- *Loop*—A sequence of actions delimited by reserved words to be repeated until a specified condition is met
- *String*—A contiguous sequence of characters
- *Variable*—A value that can change and can be dynamically incorporated into script actions
- *Reserved word*—A term interpreted according to a predefined meaning by the shell

Getting back to the script, the first of the following lines will test for the existence of a file in the /etc/ directory whose name matches the current value of the variable $FILE. If there isn't a file with that name in /etc/, then the script will continue by assigning the next string (the next filename) to the $FILE variable and testing for its existence:

```
test -f /etc/$FILE              || continue
```

If there is such a file in /etc/, then the script will compare (cmp) the contents of the file with the contents of a file of the exact same name plus the .bak filename extension in the current directory (/var/backups/). If the comparison operation (&&) is successful, the shell will continue the for loop and try the next string. If, on the other hand, the content of the two files isn't identical, then it will move to the next line:

```
cmp -s $FILE.bak /etc/$FILE      && continue
```

Then, at last, the script will deliver its payload: it copies the current version in the /etc/ directory to the /var/backups/ directory, adds .bak to its name, and tightens the file's permissions to prevent unauthorized users from reading it. The operation will overwrite any existing files with that same name. The -p flag in the example preserves the source file's original ownership attributes and timestamp:

```
cp -p /etc/$FILE $FILE.bak && chmod 600 $FILE.bak
```

What does that script do? It's designed to create copies of specified configuration files that have been updated since their last backup. Here's how it works: if files with the specified names exist in the active /etc/ directory and their contents are different from similarly named files in the /var/backups/ directory, then those in /etc/ will be copied to /var/backups/ and appropriately renamed and secured.

But what's the deal with those four files (passwd, group, shadow, and gshadow)? They're the files whose contents determine how individual users and groups will be able to access particular resources. For instance, if you were to look at the contents of /etc/passwd, you'd see a single line for every account that exists. In the following extract, you can see regular user accounts are assigned user and group IDs (1000, in the case of ubuntu), a home directory (/home/ubuntu/), and a default shell (bash). Some system users like syslog also have a default shell that is, curiously, set to /bin/false. This is a way of preventing a human user from logging in to the system using that account, which would be insecure:

ubuntu's user ID (1000), home directory (/home/ubuntu), and default shell (bash)

Non-user accounts shouldn't be used for login (/bin/false).

```
$ cat /etc/passwd
[...]
syslog:x:104:108::/home/syslog:/bin/false
_apt:x:105:65534::/nonexistent:/bin/false
sshd:x:106:65534::/var/run/sshd:/usr/sbin/nologin
ubuntu:x:1000:1000::/home/ubuntu:/bin/bash
mysql:x:107:111:MySQL Server,,,:/nonexistent:/
    bin/false
```

```
bind:x:108:112::/var/cache/bind:/bin/false
newuser:x:1002:1002:,,,:/home/newuser:/bin/bash
messagebus:x:109:114::/var/run/dbus:/bin/false
```

When you add a new user to your system using

```
# useradd -m alan
```

new lines will be added to each of the passwd, shadow, and group files. In fact, all related user administration operations can be performed from the command line (or through scripts) without the need to directly edit these files.

> **NOTE** Ubuntu prefers you use `adduser` `username` over `useradd` `username`, although both will work. One advantage of `adduser` is that a home directory will be automatically created, whereas `useradd` requires the -m argument. The command `adduser` will also prompt for a password for your new user. If you use `useradd`, you'll need to run `sudo` `passwd` `new-user-name` separately to set up a password.

Once upon a time, an encrypted version of each user's password would also have been included here. For practical reasons, because the passwd file must remain readable by anyone on the system, it was felt that including even encrypted passwords was unwise. Those passwords were moved to /etc/shadow. Using `sudo` permissions, you should take a look at that file with its encrypted passwords on your own system. Here's how:

```
$ sudo cat /etc/shadow
```

The /etc/group file contains basic information about all currently existing system and user groups. You can manually edit the group file to manage group membership. You could, for instance, give administrative rights to new users joining your team by adding their names to the sudo group. That line would look like this:

```
sudo:x:27:steve,newuser,neweruser
```

Don't add any spaces between names and commas. Doing so will result in immediate unhappiness.

   One last file: The /etc/gshadow file contains encrypted versions of group passwords for use if you sometimes want to allow group resource access to non-group users.

   As you might already have guessed, that script was a great example for this chapter because of where it lives: the /etc/cron.daily/ directory. Scripts saved to the /cron.daily/ directory will be executed each day. We'll get back to all that soon. For now, as another simple example, here's a script file called upgrade.sh to have apt automate updates to all my installed software:

```
#!/bin/bash
# Script to automate regular software upgrades

apt update
apt upgrade -y
```

As you no doubt recall, the `apt update` command will sync with indexes on the online repositories, ensuring that APT is aware of all the most recent packages and versions available. `apt upgrade` will download and install any relevant upgrades. `-y` will automatically answer Yes when asked to confirm the operation.

You're still not quite ready to run your script. Because you're going to be running the script as a program, you'll need to change the file attributes to make it executable. `chmod +x` followed by the filename will do that:

```
$ chmod +x upgrade.sh
```

That's it. You're now free to copy the file to the /etc/cron.daily/ directory where it can join passwd and others as they're run each day:

```
# cp upgrade.sh /etc/cron.daily/
```

Because it runs apt, the new script requires administrator permissions, but there's no need to include `sudo` in the command itself. Cron, by default, will always run as root. If you did want to run the script directly from the command line, you'd need to add `sudo` and preface the filename with a dot and forward slash to tell Linux that the command you're referencing is in the current directory:

```
$ sudo ./upgrade.sh
```

5.1.2 A sample script for changing filenames

Let me throw a couple more scripting tools at you. You've probably already come face to face with the fact that the Linux shell can sometimes misinterpret filenames that include spaces. Here's what it'd look like if you tried to `cat` the contents of a file called big name:

```
$ cat big name
cat: big: No such file or directory
cat: name: No such file or directory
```

The simple workaround is to enclose the complete filename in either single or double quotation marks like this:

```
$ cat 'big name'
Hello world
```

But that option won't always be available. In that case, you could automate a process to convert spaces within filenames to, say, underscore characters. Then, in the course of your journeys, when you came across a directory containing lots of offending filenames, you'd be able to execute a script to fix things fast. Well, here it is:

```
#!/bin/bash
echo "which directory would you like to check?"
read directory
    find $directory -type f | while read file; do
    if [[ "$file" = *[[:space:]]* ]]; then
    mv "$file" `echo $file | tr ' ' '_'`
    fi;
    done
```

The `echo` line prints its text to the screen and then waits for user input. The user will type in a valid directory like /home/ubuntu/files/, which will be assigned as the value of the variable `directory`. The `find` command will be invoked to return all file objects (`-type f`) in the specified directory. The set of filenames from `find` will be read, one at a time in a `while` loop, with each one tested for the presence of a space. If a space is found, `then` any spaces (' ') in the filename will be changed (`mv`) to underscores ('_'). And `fi;` stops the loop when there are no more filenames in the directory.

To try this out, create a directory with a few files containing spaces in their filenames, and then run the script for yourself. A directory that did look like this

```
$ ls
file name    file - name
```

should now look like this:

```
$ ls
file_name    file_-_name
```

> **NOTE** Think carefully about each of the steps that make up the script and be sure you understand exactly what's going on.

Let's spend a moment reminding ourselves of exactly where we are. It's always a good idea to make sure you're not staring at the trees and missing the forest. Here's what's happened so far:

- The chapter is about using scripts to create automated backups.
- You explored the script for backing up user admin files from /etc/ to /var/backup/.
- You learned about the care and feeding of those user admin files.
- You wrote your own simple script.

Here's what's still to come:

- You'll back up your own data to an AWS S3 bucket.
- You'll use cron and anacron to schedule regular backups.
- You'll learn how that's also done using systemd timers.

Scripts can be used for much more than backups and filenames. With the ever-increasing demands on servers and network environments, environments that sometimes require hundreds or even thousands of dynamically generated virtual microservices, manual administration is pretty much impossible. Through your career as a system administrator, you're probably going to need to create scripts to provision and launch individual and swarms of VMs, and to monitor massive and constantly changing environments.

5.2　*Backing up data to AWS S3*

Here are two reasons that I chose Amazon's AWS S3 as the target of the backup example I'm going to use:

- It's crucial to always keep copies of important data off-site.
- Archiving to S3 is something that's popular right now, and it's crazy easy.

That's it. The fact that this would be a great opportunity to shamelessly promote my book *Learn Amazon Web Services in a Month of Lunches* (Manning, 2017) that's chock full of everything you could possibly need to know about AWS had absolutely no impact on my choice. None. Well, maybe just a little.

At any rate, if you don't happen to have an AWS account of your own yet, you can still follow along with the next section and substitute a backup script of your own for the AWS one I'm going to show you. Alternatively, you could also visit https://aws.amazon.com and sign up for a new account. It won't cost you anything to open the account and, under the Free Tier, many services (including 5 GB of S3 storage) are available at no cost for the first year.

By the way, even after your Free Tier rights on AWS are over, storage still only costs around $0.025 per GB per month. That's probably cheap enough to make you change the way you think about off-site archives in general.

5.2.1　*Installing the AWS command-line interface (CLI)*

There's a lot of AWS administration you can do from your browser in the AWS's console, but that's not how real Linux admins get things done. If you're going to incorporate your backups to S3 into a script, it's going to have to be something that'll work on the command line. For that, look no further than Amazon's own AWS CLI. Because it runs on Python, you'll need to run at least Python 2 (version 2.6.5) or Python 3 (version 3.3). In addition, you'll need the pip Python package manager to handle the installation. As of this writing, Ubuntu is pushing to make Python 3 its default version, although other distributions might still favor Python 2.

If the following install command doesn't work, then you probably need to install pip. (Use either `apt install python-pip` or `apt install python3-pip`.) Here's the ultra-secret, insiders-only, I-can-reveal-it-to-you-but-then-I'll-have-to-kill-you hidden code that tells you which pip instalation you'll need. If it works, that's the right one. If it doesn't, try the other one:

```
$ pip3 install --upgrade --user awscli
Collecting awscli
  Downloading awscli-1.11.112-py2.py3-none-any.whl (1.2MB)
    100% |##############################| 1.2MB 946kB/s
Collecting PyYAML<=3.12,>=3.10 (from awscli)
  Downloading PyYAML-3.12.tar.gz (253kB)
    100% |##############################| 256kB 2.2MB/s
[...]
Collecting jmespath<1.0.0,>=0.7.1 (from botocore==1.5.75->awscli)
  Downloading jmespath-0.9.3-py2.py3-none-any.whl
Collecting six>=1.5 (from python-dateutil<3.0.0,>=2.1->
    botocore==1.5.75->awscli)
  Downloading six-1.10.0-py2.py3-none-any.whl
Building wheels for collected packages: PyYAML
  Running setup.py bdist_wheel for PyYAML ... done
  Stored in directory: /home/ubuntu/.cache/pip/wheels
    /2c/f7/79/13f3a12cd723892437c0cfbde1230ab4d82947ff7b3839a4fc
Successfully built PyYAML
Installing collected packages: PyYAML, pyasn1, rsa, colorama, six,
    python-dateutil, docutils, jmespath, botocore, s3transfer, awscli
Successfully installed PyYAML awscli botocore colorama docutils
    jmespath pyasn1 python-dateutil rsa s3transfer six
```

pip nicely displays real-time progress details.

A summary of all the packages installed by pip

5.2.2 Configuring your AWS account

You're now ready to link the local AWS CLI with your AWS account. To do that, you'll need to retrieve some access keys. From any page in the console, click the drop-down menu header with your account name on it (top right on the page), and then click the My Security Credentials link (figure 5.2).

Once you're on the Your Security Credentials page, click to expand the Access Keys (Access Key ID and Secret Access Key) section and note the warning that might appear: Existing Root Keys Cannot Be Retrieved. Then click the Create New Access Key button. You'll be shown your new access key ID and its accompanying secret access key. The former serves the same function as a login name, and the latter acts like its password. You can either download the access key and save it to a secure location on your computer or select, copy, and paste it somewhere.

To set things up, open a terminal on your local machine and run `aws configure` from the command line. You'll be asked for your access key ID, your secret access key, the AWS region you'd like to make default, and the format you'd like to use for output. You can leave those final two values blank if you like. The following example from the AWS documentation uses fake credentials (you should never publicly display a real key set):

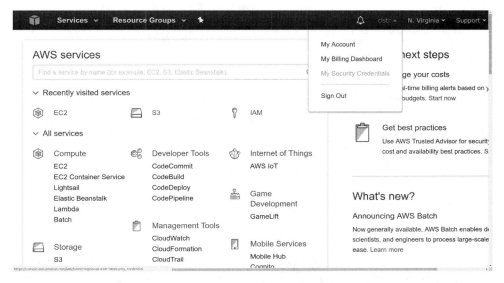

Figure 5.2   The AWS console with direct links to dozens of AWS services. Here the My Security Credentials link is visible.

```
$ aws configure
AWS Access Key ID [None]: AKIAIOSFODNN7EXAMPLE
AWS Secret Access Key [None]: wJalrXUtnFEMI/K7MDENG/bPxRfiCYEXAMPLEKEY
Default region name [None]: us-east-1
Default output format [None]:
```

Determines the AWS geographic center from which resources will be launched

Choose to have output displayed in text (default), JSON, or table format.

NOTE   When setting the default region name, bear in mind that local regulatory regimens can restrict the backup of some data to offshore servers.

You should now be all set to get to work. The following command line

```
$ aws s3 ls
```

will list all the S3 buckets in your account. *Bucket* is the term AWS uses for what we would call a directory.

5.2.3   Creating your first bucket

Assuming this is a brand-new account, nothing will be displayed. You should create a new bucket with the make bucket command: mb. One thing to keep in mind when choosing a bucket name is that it must be unique across the entire S3 system. As shown, something like mybucket probably won't be accepted:

```
$ aws s3 mb s3://mybucket
make_bucket failed: s3://mybucket/ An error occurred (BucketAlreadyExists)
 when calling the CreateBucket operation: The requested bucket name is not
 available. The bucket namespace is shared by all users of the system.
 Please select a different name and try again.
```

Instead, using less common words and adding a few numbers will probably work a lot better:

```
$ aws s3 mb s3://linux-bucket3040
```

One more step and we've got ourselves an off-site backup job. Assuming that the files you need to back up are in a directory called /dir2backup, located in your home directory, here's how it'll go:

```
aws s3 sync /home/username/dir2backup s3://linux-bucket3040
```

s3 sync works a lot like the rsync tool you met in chapter 4. The first time you run it, everything in the source directory will be uploaded to your S3 bucket; subsequently, only new or changed files will be transferred. Creating a script to run that sync command will be pretty much straightforward. Here's how it might look:

```
#!/bin/bash
/usr/local/bin/aws s3 sync \
 /home/username/dir2backup s3://linux-bucket3040
```

Note how I added the full path to the aws command (/usr/local/bin/aws). This is to make sure that Bash knows where on the system to find the command. You can confirm the location of aws using whereis:

```
$ whereis aws
aws: /usr/local/bin/aws
```

Having a great backup tool in place doesn't mean you'll use it. That requires some kind of task scheduler. You'll learn about a couple of those schedulers next.

5.3   *Scheduling regular backups with cron*

Cron comes in a number of flavors. Because that number is greater than one, you can expect that there's often more than one way to get a particular task done. To get a feel for what's there, list the objects in the /etc/ directory that include the letters *cron*:

```
$ ls /etc | grep cron
anacrontab
cron.d
cron.daily
cron.hourly
cron.monthly
crontab
cron.weekly
```

Of those, only anacrontab and crontab are files; the rest are directories. Let's begin by seeing how the directories work.

If you've got, say, a file system backup script in an executable file you want run at set intervals, you copy it to the appropriate directory: cron.hourly/ for execution each hour, cron.daily/ to be run daily, and so on. The cron.d/ directory is a bit different. It's meant for files whose contents precisely time the execution of commands.

Suppose you wanted to run that software upgrade job I scripted earlier once each Monday, but without the script. You could create a file in the /etc/cron.d directory with these contents:

```
21 5  * * 1  root apt update && apt upgrade
```

This example will run the upgrade at 5:21 each Monday morning. How does that work? Look at the first characters: 21 5. The first field (21) represents the number of minutes into the hour that you want the command run. In this case, it will run 21 minutes in. The next field is where you can specify which hour of the day (for example, 8 or 23). This one is 5, which means 5:00 a.m. The next two asterisks followed by a 1 indicate that you want the schedule followed on every day of the month, in every month of the year, on each Monday (1 represents Monday). To avoid confusion, either 0 or 7 can be used for Sunday. The root argument means that the command will be run as the root user.

Why so early? Because, presumably, competing demand for network bandwidth will be lower before everyone gets into the office. Why 5:21 rather than 5:00? Because you don't want to fall into the habit of scheduling all of your scripts for exactly the top of the hour (or any one time), as that might eventually cause a conflict. Better to stagger them.

You could add that line directly into the /etc/crontab file, and it would run the same way but without the need to create a separate file. But I wouldn't. Doing so might not unleash a zombie apocalypse on the world, but it's still a bad idea. You see, the crontab file is likely to be overwritten during system upgrades, and your custom commands will be lost.

Then what's the point of the crontab file? As you should be able to see from the file contents (figure 5.3), this is the scheduler that executes the scripts within the /cron.? directories. Take a minute or two to look through each command for yourself.

The test -x leading off the final three commands in figure 5.3 confirms that a binary program called anacron exists and is executable. If either of those is not true, then the scripts in the /cron.? directories will be run. The text -x command can be useful for scripting, in general, when you need to confirm to status of an object before launching a related operation.

You're definitely going to want to leave the /etc/crontab file for the professionals. But because Linux cares about both you and your feelings, they've given you your own crontab to play with. That one will run commands as your user rather than as root, with only the permissions available to you—and won't be overwritten during upgrades.

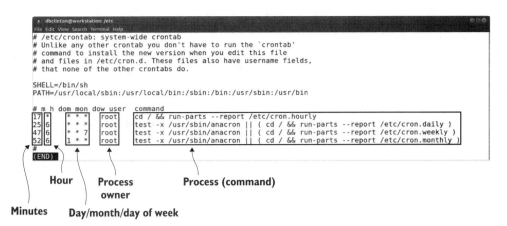

Figure 5.3   The well-documented /etc/crontab file showing four jobs, each designed to launch the contents of an /etc/cron.? directory

Care to see what you've already got scheduled? Run `crontab -l`. If you haven't added any commands yet, you'll probably get the No Crontab for *yourname* message shown in the following:

```
$ crontab -l
no crontab for ubuntu
```

You can edit your crontab using `crontab -e`. The first time you edit it, you'll be asked to choose a text editor. If you're already comfortable with Nano, go with that, as it's probably the easiest of the three listed:

```
$ crontab -e
no crontab for ubuntu - using an empty one     ⊲── Checks for existing jobs

Select an editor. To change, run 'select-editor'.     ⊲── Choose a text editor.
  1. /bin/nano              ⊲─┐
  2. /usr/bin/vim.basic        ├ The Nano editor selection
  3. /usr/bin/vim.tiny

Choose 1-3 [1]:
```

> **NOTE**   By default, on some systems a user won't be able to create crontab jobs unless a file called /etc/cron.allow containing their username is created. Debian/Ubuntu, however, allow individual crontab jobs right out of the box.

Those cron-based tools all work well for computers (like production servers) that are likely to be left running all the time. But what about executing important jobs on, say, your laptop, which is often turned off? It's all very nice telling cron (or cron.daily and so forth) to back up your files at 5:21 on a Monday morning, but how likely is it that you'll remember to get up to boot your laptop in time? Exactly—not likely at all. It's time to talk about anacron.

5.4   *Scheduling irregular backups with anacron*

The one cron file we haven't yet discussed is *anacrontab*, which is where you schedule operations to run at a set time after each system boot. If you wanted to back up those files on your laptop but couldn't guarantee that it would be powered on at any given time during the day, you could add a line to anacrontab.

What should catch your attention in the anacrontab file is that entries have only two columns to control timing, rather than the five used in `cron` commands. That's because anacron doesn't work on absolute time, but relative to the most recent system boot. Here's the file in all its glory:

```
# /etc/anacrontab: configuration file for anacron
# See anacron(8) and anacrontab(5) for details.
SHELL=/bin/sh
PATH=/usr/local/sbin:/usr/local/bin:/sbin:/bin:/
        usr/sbin:/usr/bin
HOME=/root
LOGNAME=root

# These replace cron's entries
1 5 cron.daily run-parts --report /etc/cron.daily
7 10 cron.weekly    run-parts --report /etc/cron.weekly
@monthly 15 cron.monthly run-parts --report
    /etc/cron.monthly
```

> **The directories within anacrontab's PATH. Files in these locations can be referenced without a full directory tree.**

> **This job executes any scripts in the /etc/cron.daily/ directory once a day.**

The `cron.daily` line in the anacrontab file, for instance, runs at one-day intervals, exactly 5 minutes after boot, whenever that happens to take place. The `cron.weekly` command, on the other hand, runs on seven-day intervals (meaning, when at least seven days have lapsed since the last run), 10 minutes after boot.

You might also be curious about those `cron.?` commands; weren't they already run through the /etc/crontab file? Yes, but only if anacron isn't active on the system. As you can see from the crontab file, anacron is given priority over cron. With all that in mind, here's how a backup script could be run for your laptop:

```
1    10    myBackupJob    /home/myname/backup.sh
```

This command runs the backup.sh script no more than once a day, 10 minutes after system boot. The job identifier is `myBackupJob`, and a log file of that name with job status information will be saved to the /var/spool/anacron/ directory.

5.4.1   *Running the S3 sync job*

Now, at last, with everything you've learned about scripting—AWS S3, cron, and anacron—you're finally ready to make a smart choice: what's the best way to schedule your backup? And, as always, the correct answer depends on context.

If you want to make sure the backup will get done even on a machine that's not always running, you can add a line like this to your anacrontab file (assuming that you've already got an executable script file of that name in /etc/):

```
1 10 myDailyBackup /etc/s3script.sh
```

This example runs the script each day (1), 10 minutes (10) after the system boots. For your 24/7 servers, syntax-specific directives could be added to your user's crontab or, within a file, to the /etc/cron.d/ directory (although you'd need to add a username like root to the cron.d version).

The next example runs the script at 5:47 each morning, every day of every month, every day of the week (* * *):

```
47 5 * * * /home/myusername/s3script.sh
```

◁─┐ **crontab syntax to run a script each day at 5:47 a.m.**

In this case, because we're talking about a simple script, you can also do that just as effectively by inserting the aws command itself into a cron file like anacrontab:

```
47 5 * * * username /usr/local/bin/aws s3 sync
    /home/username/dir2backup s3://linux-bucket3040
```

A specific command like this backup operation can be inserted directly into the crontab file. Note the username and the absolute location of aws. This clearly establishes both the ownership of the process you want to run and the file system location of the binary that will run it.

5.5   *Scheduling regular backups with systemd timers*

If there's a criticism of the new systemd timer alternative to cron, it'd probably be that it's noticeably more complicated and involves a few more steps to set up. Instead of simply creating your script and then copying the file into the right cron directory, you'll need to create and save two separate files to an obscure directory location (that's not yet standard across all Linux distros) and then run two systemctl commands.

Complicated, perhaps. But definitely not insurmountable. And systemd timers come with some significant advantages, including deeper integration with other system services (including logs) and the ability to execute commands based on changes to system state (for instance, someone connecting a USB device), rather than just set times.

I'll leave you to explore the specific, in-depth features that interest you on your own time. But I'll walk you through the steps it'll take to put together a simple backup. Your mission? Generate a dynamically named tar archive of the Apache-powered website running on your server. For the purposes of this demo, you can choose any directories to back up, and you don't have to configure and launch a website for this.

First off, take a look at the timers you might already have running. Mine are displayed in figure 5.4 through the systemctl list-timers --all command.

Those timers were all created automatically by the system. To create your own, start with a backup script. Digging deeply into my colorful and creative inner personality, I'll call my script file site-backup.sh. Here's how it looks:

```
#!/bin/bash
NOW=$(date +"%m_%d_%Y")
tar czvf /var/backups/site-backup-$NOW.tar.gz /var/www
```

◁─┐ **Assigns the system date to an environment variable $NOW**

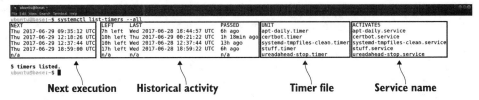

Figure 5.4 The command `systemctl list-timers --all` provides a rich range of historical data for all existing systemd timer jobs.

It would make identifying archives a lot easier if my archive filenames always included the date they were created. To do that, I assigned the current system date as the value of the $NOW variable and included it in the filename of the new archive. Here's how the resulting filename might look:

```
site-backup-11_28_2017.tar.gz
```

Don't forget to make your script file executable (`chmod +x site-backup-11_28_2017.tar.gz`). In fact, never forget to make your script file executable!

```
$ chmod +x site-backup.sh
```

Now you'll need to create your .service and .timer files. As I wrote previously, there's no single location where all service files are kept, but /lib/systemd/system/ and /etc/systemd/system/ will both work. Given a choice, I prefer /etc/systemd/system/ because, for me, it's an easy-to-remember and logical place. Your mileage may vary.

I'll begin with the .service file, which I'll call site-backup.service. *Service files* are common across systemd operations. They're meant to describe and define a system service in a uniform, predictable way. The `Description` value should contain whatever text you feel will accurately describe the service, and the `ExecStart` line points to the location of an executable resource: the script, in this case. This is all the information systemd needs to figure out what it is you want done:

```
[Unit]
Description=Backup Apache website

[Service]
Type=simple
ExecStart=/home/username/site-backup.sh

[Install]
WantedBy=multi-user.target
```

The executable resource to be run by the service

The .timer file, which is specific to systemd timers, tells systemd when you want the associated service to run. The association is set through the `Unit` line in the `[Timer]` section, which, in this case, points to my site-backup.service file. Note that, also in this case, the value of `OnCalendar` is set to execute every day (`*-*-*`) at 5:51 a.m., and the value of `Unit` is the site-backup.service file:

The schedule
settings to
control the
service
execution

```
[Unit]
Description=Backup Apache website - daily

[Timer]
OnCalendar=*-*-* 5:51:00
Unit=site-backup.service

[Install]
WantedBy=multi-user.target
```

The service unit with which
to associate this timer

With those files in place, you start the service using `systemctl start`. Additionally, you set it to load automatically every time the system boots with `systemctl enable`:

```
# systemctl start site-backup.timer
# systemctl enable site-backup.timer
```

Curious about the status of your service? `is-enabled` and `is-active` should be good for starters:

```
# systemctl is-enabled backup.timer
enabled
# systemctl is-active backup.timer
active
```

Finally, when you edit your .timer file, you'll need to update the system. In the process of practicing what you've learned in this chapter, you'll probably be doing a lot of editing. Naturally, you'll want to know how to do that. Well, here you go:

```
# systemctl daemon-reload
```

Summary

- Well-written Bash scripts can efficiently and reliably automate both complex and simple administrative tasks.
- Linux keeps user account and authentication information in plain text files (named passwd, group, shadow, and gshadow) in the /etc/ directory.
- You can back up local data to a S3 bucket and manage it through its life cycle directly from the command line.
- Copying an executable script to one of the /etc/cron.? directories causes it to be run at the appropriate interval.
- Adding a directive to the anacrontab file executes commands relative to system boots, rather than at absolute times.
- systemd timers can be set to run based on both absolute time and in reaction to system events, like changes to hardware states.

Key terms

- All Linux commands output *exit codes* upon completion: 0 represents a successful execution, but all positive integers can be set by a program to represent various failed states.
- Command-line access to AWS resources is secured by the use of *access keys* (Access Key ID and Secret Access Key).
- A *bucket* is an AWS object that works much the same way as a directory on an operating system.

Security best practices

- Lock down your system accounts (like syslog and, ideally, even root) to prevent their being used for remote logins.
- Include off-site backups in your security planning, which adds another layer of data reliability.
- Always protect your (AWS) access keys, not to mention passwords and encryption key pairs, from public exposure of any kind.

Command-line review

- `#!/bin/bash` (the so-called "shebang line") tells Linux which shell interpreter you're going to be using for a script.
- `||` inserts an *or* condition into a script. Think of this as either "the command to the left is successul" or "execute the command to the right."
- `&&` - inserts an *and* condition into a script. Think of this as "if the command to the left is successful" and "execute the command to the right."
- `test -f /etc/filename` tests for the existence of the specified file or directory name.
- `chmod +x upgrade.sh` makes a script file executable.
- `pip3 install --upgrade --user awscli` installs the AWS command-line interface using Python's pip package manager.
- `aws s3 sync /home/username/dir2backup s3://linux-bucket3040` synchronizes the contents of a local directory with the specified S3 bucket.
- `21 5 * * 1 root apt update && apt upgrade` (a cron directive) executes two apt commands at 5:21 each morning.
- `NOW=$(date +"%m_%d_%Y")` assigns the current date to a script variable.
- `systemctl start site-backup.timer` activates a systemd system timer.

Test yourself

1 What is the character used to introduce a comment in a Linux script?
   a `!`
   b `//`
   c `#`
   d `^`

2 What is the purpose of || in a Linux script?

   a Or

   b And

   c If

   d Comment

3 What is the data type kept in the /etc/shadow file?

   a Account group and shell data

   b Group membership data

   c Encrypted account passwords

   d Encrypted group passwords

4 Which of the following will create a new bucket on your AWS S3 account?

   a `s3 mb s3://mybucket`

   b `aws s3 mb s3://mybucket`

   c `aws s3 cb s3://mybucket`

   d `aws s3 sync mb s3://mybucket`

5 Which of the following commands will allow you to enter a cron directive that will be run as your own user?

   a `nano anacrontab`

   b `crontab -l`

   c `nano /etc/crontab`

   d `crontab -e`

6 Which of the following will run the command each Monday morning?

   a `21 * 1 * * root apt update && apt upgrade`

   b `21 5 * * 1 root apt update && apt upgrade`

   c `21 1 * * 0 root apt update && apt upgrade`

   d `21 5 * 4 * root apt update && apt upgrade`

7 Which of the following won't work well for computers that aren't always running?

   a crontab

   b anacron

   c systemd timer

   d anacrontab

8 What is the purpose of the `systemctl enable site-backup.timer` command?

   a Loads the site-backup timer manually

   b Configures the site-backup timer to load on system boot

   c Displays the current status of the site-backup timer

   d Forces the site-backup timer to run before the computer can close down

Answer key

1. c, 2. a, 3. c, 4. b, 5. d, 6. b, 7. a, 8. b

Emergency tools: Building a system recovery device

6

This chapter covers

- Recovering broken Linux systems
- Controlling resources with Linux live-boot drives
- Recovering data from damaged storage media
- Manipulating an inaccessible file system

Don't try to convince yourself otherwise: along with all the good stuff, you're going to have bad days with Linux. Sometimes you're going to forget the syntax for commands (which is why you should always keep a copy of this book within reach). You (or the users you support) are going to mistype commands and permanently destroy documents. Or, you're going to experience that sinking feeling when you realize that some important piece of hardware or software has failed. (That's gratitude after everything you did for it all those years.) Being properly backed up, as the last couple of chapters demonstrated, means that you can walk away from a nonfunctioning operating system (OS) or computer and rebuild it all somewhere else. But that's always going to be Plan B. Plan A is to recover.

This chapter is where I'll introduce you to key tools from the Linux recovery suite. You'll learn how you can use a live-boot device to load a fresh copy of Linux, mount the drive that's giving you trouble, and either update corrupted configuration files so you can boot normally again or rescue whatever data can be recovered before re-purposing or destroying the damaged drive. And you'll see how the files of a non-functional system can be *brought to life* and run within their own virtual environment, so you can do things like changing a user's forgotten password.

There's a lot that can go wrong when you try to throw hardware and software into a single box and expect them to play nicely together. I'm going to focus on cata-strophic events like these:

- Your computer boots, the hard drive is working, but Linux doesn't load.
- Your computer boots (as far as you can tell, anyway), but you're not quite sure whether the hard drive is fully functional.
- Everything works, but a software problem or lost password prevents you from logging in to Linux.

The specific problem you're facing will determine your plan of action to get yourself back in business. Figure 6.1 illustrates some diagnostic and recovery options, most of which I'll discuss later in this chapter.

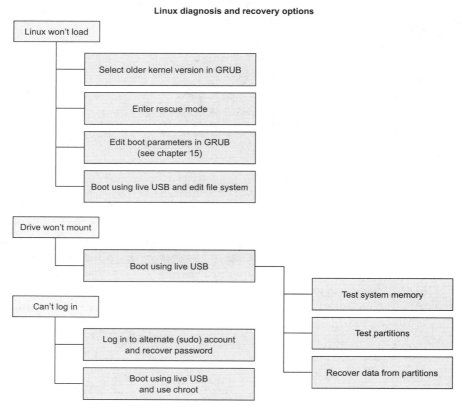

Figure 6.1   Common system problems along with diagnostic and solution considerations that we'll explore in this chapter

6.1   *Working in recovery/rescue mode*

Linux not letting you log in normally? Perhaps the boot process unexpectedly stops before displaying the login screen. You'll want some basic system administration tools.

But wait: if Linux won't load, how are you going to launch those tools? Well, even if Linux won't load all the way to a normal command prompt, often it'll get you to the GRUB menu. From there (as figure 6.2 shows), you can use the up and down arrow keys and then Enter to select a Linux kernel running in recovery mode. That, as you'll soon see, will open up a whole bag of tricks.

```
              GNU GRUB   version 2.02~beta2-36ubuntu3.9

 ┌───────────────────────────────────────────────────────────────────┐
 │*Ubuntu, with Linux 4.4.0-78-generic                               │
 │ Ubuntu, with Linux 4.4.0-78-generic (recovery mode)              │
 │ Ubuntu, with Linux 4.4.0-66-generic                               │
 │ Ubuntu, with Linux 4.4.0-66-generic (recovery mode)              │
 │ Ubuntu, with Linux 4.4.0-62-generic                               │
 │ Ubuntu, with Linux 4.4.0-62-generic (recovery mode)              │
 │ Ubuntu, with Linux 4.4.0-59-generic                               │
 │ Ubuntu, with Linux 4.4.0-59-generic (recovery mode)              │
 │ Ubuntu, with Linux 4.4.0-45-generic                               │
 │ Ubuntu, with Linux 4.4.0-45-generic (recovery mode)              │
 │ Ubuntu, with Linux 4.4.0-34-generic                               │
 │ Ubuntu, with Linux 4.4.0-34-generic (recovery mode)              │
 │ Ubuntu, with Linux 4.4.0-31-generic                               │
 │ Ubuntu, with Linux 4.4.0-31-generic (recovery mode)              │
 └───────────────────────────────────────────────────────────────────┘

      Use the ↑ and ↓ keys to select which entry is highlighted.
      Press enter to boot the selected OS, `e' to edit the commands
      before booting or `c' for a command-line. ESC to return previous
      menu.
```

Figure 6.2   The GRUB Advanced Options menu of an Ubuntu installation showing links to both current and older kernel versions, along with options for launching in recovery mode

Before you'll be able to take full advantage of those tools, however, you'll first need to understand what GRUB is and how it works. In the next several sections, I'm going to explain what GRUB does, how it can be used to access recovery tools, and how you can use those tools to get yourself out of some nasty jams.

6.1.1   *The GRUB bootloader*

What's *GRUB*? It's the GNU GRand Unified Bootloader. OK, what's a *bootloader*? It's the code an OS uses to bring itself to life when it's powered on. Figure 6.3 illustrates the process.

When a computer powers up, firmware instructions embedded in the basic system hardware identify the network, storage, and memory resources that are available. This was done through the BIOS system on older computers and, more recently, using UEFI (both of which you briefly met back in chapter 4).

Once the system finds a hard-drive partition containing a Master Boot Record (MBR), it loads the contents into active memory. On Linux systems, the MBR partition contains a number of files that, when run, present one or more loadable kernel image boot configurations. You can choose to load any of those configurations from the GRUB bootloader menu.

> **NOTE** Often, GRUB will load its default image automatically without asking for your opinion, unless a previous session fails to load. If you want to force the GRUB menu to appear, press the right Shift key as your computer boots.

6.1.2 Using recovery mode on Ubuntu

As you can see from figure 6.4, once Ubuntu is loaded in recovery mode, you'll be shown a menu of tools that address some common boot-time problems. It's worth trying each in turn, in case one of those ends up addressing your root problem. The clean option, for instance, removes unused files if you suspect the trouble stems from a full disk. And the dpkg option attempts to fix any broken APT-based software packages that might be gumming things up. (The dpkg tool might require that you first enable networking.)

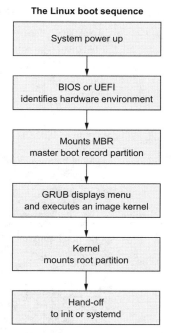

The Linux boot sequence

Figure 6.3   The key steps in the boot process of a Linux computer

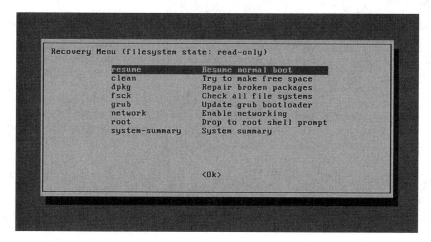

Figure 6.4   The Ubuntu Recovery menu with links to some basic diagnostic and repair tools, along with the option of opening a shell session as root

The root option opens a root command-line shell session for you where you'll have Bash at your disposal. In general, using a simple shell session for recovery rather than a full GUI desktop makes a lot of sense. That's because the fewer complicated services you've got running, the more likely it is that you'll be able to at least get your system going.

Once you do manage to get a working command prompt, you can start poking around to see if you can identify and fix the problem. At the very least, you'll look mighty cool doing that.

6.1.3 Using rescue mode on CentOS

The GRUB menu for CentOS offers a rescue kernel at boot time rather than a recovery mode. This kernel doesn't include a tool menu like Ubuntu's, but it will similarly drop you into a single-user shell session as root. Figure 6.5 shows the rescue boot option in CentOS GRUB.

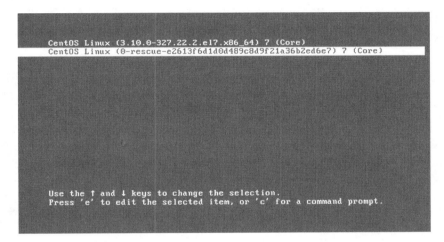

Figure 6.5 CentOS Linux offers a rescue kernel for booting directly to a single-user shell session for troubleshooting a damaged system.

Once you choose the rescue selection on your CentOS machine, what's next? You'll get to meet some useful tools through the rest of this chapter. But first, why not take a page from the Ubuntu playbook and manually apply some of the tools from the automated Recovery menu? "Easier said than done," I hear you say. "But just how do those tools work?" Over next page or so, I'm going to show you how to put some of your Bash and scripting skills to work figuring some of that out.

6.1.4 Finding command-line rescue tools

Got an Ubuntu machine running (this one won't work on Debian)? If there's code running the menu, it must already exist somewhere within the Ubuntu file system. Go take a look for yourself. Use locate to find it:

```
$ locate recovery-mode
/lib/recovery-mode
/lib/recovery-mode/l10n.sh
/lib/recovery-mode/options
/lib/recovery-mode/recovery-menu
/lib/recovery-mode/options/apt-snapshots
/lib/recovery-mode/options/clean
/lib/recovery-mode/options/dpkg
/lib/recovery-mode/options/failsafeX
/lib/recovery-mode/options/fsck
/lib/recovery-mode/options/grub
/lib/recovery-mode/options/network
/lib/recovery-mode/options/root
/lib/recovery-mode/options/system-summary
```

The 110n.sh script sets appropriate environment variables for the menu.

The recovery-menu script file

The script for reducing disk usage

If you navigate over to the /lib/recovery-mode/ directory, you'll see that the recovery-menu file is the script that displays the menu interface you saw back in figure 6.3. The options/ directory contains files for executing each of the menu items. For example, fsck will check and fix, if possible, any broken file systems.

Because you're now an accomplished Bash scripting expert, why not take a look at each of the scripts in the options/ directory to see if you can figure out how they work? Here are the contents of the fsck script to get you going. Note the way the script is nicely documented (using the # character) to help you understand what's going on:

```
$ cat /lib/recovery-mode/options/fsck
#!/bin/sh

. /lib/recovery-mode/l10n.sh

if [ "$1" = "test" ]; then
  echo $(eval_gettext "Check all file systems")
  exit 0
fi

# Actual code is in recovery-menu itself
exit 0
```

The 110n.sh script is called to set the environment.

This comment tells you where the real action takes place.

Here are a couple of things you can try on your own. Manually run the clean script on a Ubuntu machine. What happened? Then try carefully editing the /lib/recovery-mode/recovery-menu script (make a backup copy first). Change something simple, like the menu title or one of the script descriptions. Then reboot your machine and, from the GRUB menu, go into Recovery Mode to see what the recovery environment looks like. With some variations and exceptions, you should be able to put those scripts to good use elsewhere, including on CentOS.

6.2   *Building a live-boot recovery drive*

As you probably already know, those .ISO OS images you employed for your VirtualBox VMs back in chapter 2 can also be written to a CD or USB drive and used to boot a *live* session of the OS. Such live-boot devices let you load fully functioning Linux sessions without having to install anything to a hard drive. Many people use such drives to confirm that a particular Linux distribution will run happily on their hardware before trying to install it. Others will run live sessions as a secure way to maintain their privacy while engaged in sensitive activities like online banking.

It turns out that those live boot drives are also a fantastic tool for system rescue and recovery. Remember our second disaster scenario from earlier in this chapter?

> *Your computer boots (as far as you can tell, anyway), but you're not quite sure whether the hard drive is fully functional.*

Plugging a live-boot drive into a troubled computer and launching Linux with all of its administration tools can help you figure out what's really going on—and give you the tools to fix it. I'm going to show you how to create a live-boot USB drive and then how to use it. But first, a quick look at some of the most useful distro images currently available.

6.2.1　*System rescue images*

If you happen to already have a DVD or USB drive with a full Linux system (like Ubuntu) lying around anyway, then that'll be your simplest solution because most of the software you'll need will come preinstalled. Assuming you've got a network connection, you can always install other packages during a live session. Otherwise, the following sections describe some specialty images.

BOOT-REPAIR

If it's an Ubuntu system you're trying to rescue, then you'll want to try out Boot-Repair. A small and fast Boot-Repair live-boot checks your GRUB settings and, if necessary, rebuilds them. It can, as shown in figure 6.6, also perform other useful administration tasks. This one has saved the day for me more times than I can remember.

Boot-Repair can also be installed on an already-launched live session. The website (https://help.ubuntu.com/community/Boot-Repair) has great instructions.

Figure 6.6　The Boot-Repair desktop with the System Tools menu visible

GPARTED LIVE

If your problem relates to corrupted partitions that can damage your data or prevent you from successfully booting, the GParted Live image brings the full-featured and powerful GParted partition editor to a live CD or USB. Like Boot-Repair, GParted can also be installed and used from any normal Linux session. If you know your problem is partition-related, however, the full live-boot version can be the quickest and most direct way to fix it. Unlike Boot-Repair, GParted is built to be used on about any Linux distribution, rather than just Ubuntu.

SYSTEMRESCUECD

Another alternative, SystemRescueCd, is a lightweight image built on the Gentoo Linux distribution. As it comes with loads of useful system recovery tools, SystemRescueCd makes a great USB to carry around with you. (The CD is also great, although it doesn't fit so easily into back pockets, and sitting down safely can be a challenge.)

6.2.2   *Writing live-boot images to USB drives*

Before you can write any .ISO image, you'll need to download it. I think I'm safe assuming that you're OK finding the right page on the website of the distro you're after to get that done. But you might not know that large downloads can sometimes be corrupted during their journeys across the internet. Worse, they can be switched with malware by intrusion or man-in-the-middle attackers. That happened to some people downloading Mint Linux a while back.[1]

Besides checking to make sure the website you're on is properly encrypted (your browser should show some kind of lock icon in the URL bar), your best defense is to generate a hash on the downloaded file and compare it to the hash provided by the website. (Hashes were discussed back in chapter 2.)

The hashes will sometimes be displayed right on the image download page, but some distros make them a bit harder to find. Canonical (the fine people who give us Ubuntu) has not exactly bathed itself in glory on this one. There is a single page (https://help.ubuntu.com/community/UbuntuHashes) with links to all its hashes. Finding that page from the download site isn't simple. You're usually better off using a reliable internet search engine. Figure 6.7 shows you what the hashes for Ubuntu 17.04 will look like.

Once you find the published hashes for your image, you'll compute the hash for the file you've downloaded and compare the two values. This example generates the SHA256 hash for the SystemRescueCd image from the same directory to which it was downloaded:

```
$ cd Downloads
$ ls | grep systemrescue
systemrescuecd-x86-5.0.2.iso
$ sha256sum systemrescuecd-x86-5.0.2.iso
a2abdaf5750b09886cedcc5233d91ad3d1083e10380e555c7ca508
   49befbf487  systemrescuecd-x86-5.0.2.iso
```

---

[1] See Kelly Fiveash, "Linux Mint Hit by Malware Infection on Its Website, Forum After Hack Attack," *Ars Technica*, February 22, 2016, http://mng.bz/irPi.

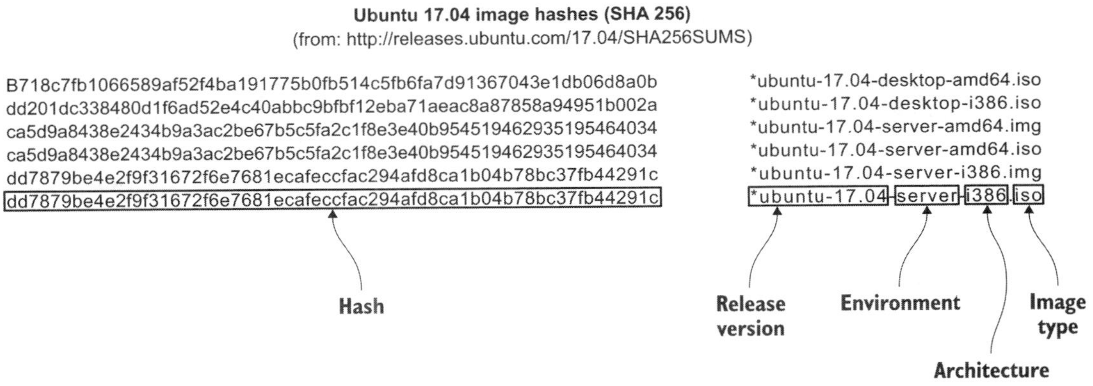
Ubuntu 17.04 image hashes (SHA 256)
(from: http://releases.ubuntu.com/17.04/SHA256SUMS)
B718c7fb1066589af52f4ba191775b0fb514c5fb6fa7d91367043e1db06d8a0b *ubuntu-17.04-desktop-amd64.iso
dd201dc338480d1f6ad52e4c40abbc9bfbf12eba71aeac8a87858a94951b002a *ubuntu-17.04-desktop-i386.iso
ca5d9a8438e2434b9a3ac2be67b5c5fa2c1f8e3e40b954519462935195464034 *ubuntu-17.04-server-amd64.img
ca5d9a8438e2434b9a3ac2be67b5c5fa2c1f8e3e40b954519462935195464034 *ubuntu-17.04-server-amd64.iso
dd7879be4e2f9f31672f6e7681ecafeccfac294afd8ca1b04b78bc37fb44291c *ubuntu-17.04-server-i386.img
dd7879be4e2f9f31672f6e7681ecafeccfac294afd8ca1b04b78bc37fb44291c *ubuntu-17.04-server-i386.iso
Hash
Release version
Environment
Architecture
Image type

Figure 6.7 SHA256 hashes for the various images of Ubuntu 17.04, currently available for download

With a reliable image of one kind or another safely downloaded, it's time to create that recovery tools live-boot drive. If both your current computer and the live-boot USB you're creating will run Debian, Ubuntu, or a derivative, the simplest approach is to use the Ubuntu Startup Disk Creator.

The Creator tool is available from the regular GUI menus and, as you can see from figure 6.8, is straightforward. Select an .ISO from somewhere on your hard drive and a target USB (or CD) where you'd like the image written. The Creator will take care of the rest.

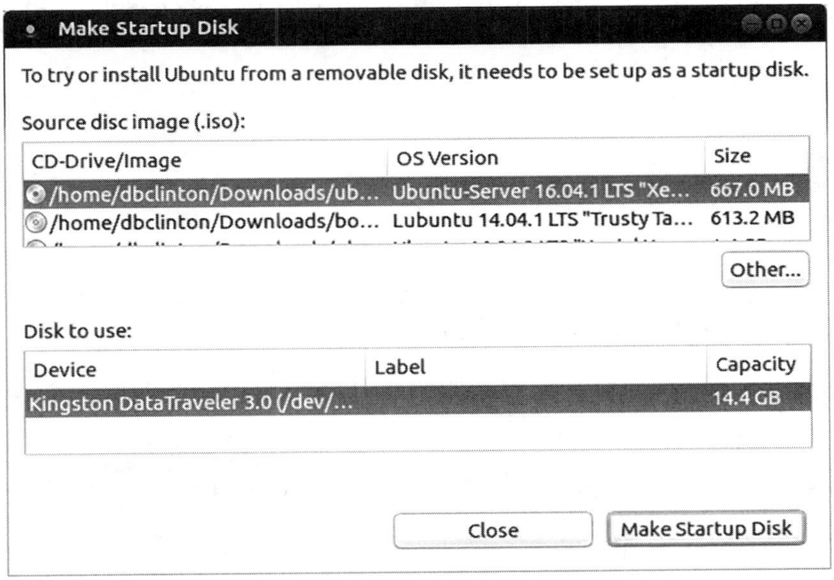
Make Startup Disk
To try or install Ubuntu from a removable disk, it needs to be set up as a startup disk.
Source disc image (.iso):
CD-Drive/Image
OS Version
Size
/home/dbclinton/Downloads/ub... Ubuntu-Server 16.04.1 LTS "Xe... 667.0 MB
/home/dbclinton/Downloads/bo... Lubuntu 14.04.1 LTS "Trusty Ta... 613.2 MB
Other...
Disk to use:
Device
Label
Capacity
Kingston DataTraveler 3.0 (/dev/... 14.4 GB
Close
Make Startup Disk

Figure 6.8 Ubuntu's Startup Disk Creator with an Ubuntu Server 16.04 image and target USB drive selected

If, on the other hand, you need a live-boot device built from a different distro (you're trying to rescue a CentOS machine and want to use CentOS tools to do it), then you'll need to dust off your old friend dd. If you want a CD or DVD-based live bootable, dd running on any Linux host is up to the job. But if the image will be written to a USB drive and if you happen to be working on an Ubuntu host, you'll first need to modify the image by adding an MBR to the .ISO archive so that BIOS and UEFI firmware will know what to do with it. Figure 6.9 represents how the process looks.

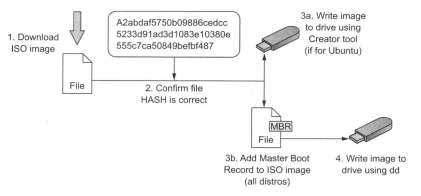

Figure 6.9   The steps necessary for writing a working live-boot USB image

On Ubuntu hosts, you use isohybrid for that image modification. The apt package containing isohybrid is called syslinux-utils. Once that's installed, move to the directory containing the downloaded image and run isohybrid using the image filename as the sole argument:

```
# apt update
# apt install syslinux-utils
$ cd ~/Downloads
$ isohybrid systemrescuecd-x86-5.0.2.iso
```

The next steps should work no matter what distribution you're on. Carefully identify the system designation for your target device. As you'll remember, df lists all the currently recognized file systems along with their designations:

```
$ df -h
Filesystem Size Used Avail Use% Mounted on
udev       3.5G    0 3.5G   0% /dev
tmpfs      724M 1.5M 722M   1% /run
/dev/sda2  910G 183G 681G  22% /
tmpfs      3.6G 214M 3.4G   6% /dev/shm
tmpfs      5.0M 4.0K 5.0M   1% /run/lock
tmpfs      3.6G    0 3.6G   0% /sys/fs/cgroup
/dev/sda1  511M 3.4M 508M   1% /boot/efi
tmpfs      724M  92K 724M   1% /run/user/1000
/dev/sdb1   15G  16K  15G   1% /media/myname/KINGSTON
```

This is my root file system. I definitely don't want to overwrite that!

The file system on my removable USB drive

In this example, there's a file system mounted on my Kingston USB device called /dev/sdb1. This tells me that the device itself is known as /dev/sdb.

If you plan to write the image to an optical drive like a CD or DVD, then you get its designation through lsblk, which stands for *list block devices*. The drive itself must be writable. Here my DVD drive is known as sr0:

```
$ lsblk
NAME    MAJ:MIN RM    SIZE RO TYPE MOUNTPOINT
sda       8:0    0  931.5G  0 disk
├─sda1    8:1    0    512M  0 part /boot/efi
├─sda2    8:2    0  923.8G  0 part /
└─sda3    8:3    0    7.2G  0 part [SWAP]
sdb      8:16    1   14.4G  0 disk
└─sdb1   8:17    1   14.4G  0 part /media/clinton/KINGSTON
sr0      11:0    1   1024M  0 rom
```

The writable DVD drive

The moment of truth. No more putting it off. It's time to unleash dd on your poor, defenseless file system and write your image to your USB.

First unmount the drive itself so dd can get full access. Then write the archive. In this example, I used the systemrescuecd-x86-5.0.2.iso image and wrote it to the drive at /dev/sdb.

Careful! Typing sda instead of sdb (in this particular case) will irretrievably overwrite your host file system and ruin your day, not to mention your life. Naturally, you should also make sure there's nothing important on the USB drive, as that will definitely disappear:

```
# umount /dev/sdb
# dd bs=4M if=systemrescuecd-x86-5.0.2.iso \
    of=/dev/sdb && sync
```

The added sync command ensures that all cached data is immediately written to the target disk.

It might take some time for dd to finish writing the image to your USB device, but, when it's done, you should be able to plug the drive into a computer, power it up, and enter a live session. This is assuming that your computer is configured to boot from a USB drive. If it isn't, you can force it to boot to a selected device this one time by entering the Boot menu during the boot process. Each PC manufacturer designates its own keys for such things (often displaying a list of keystroke options during the startup process). But pressing one of F1, F9, or F12 early in the boot sequence will often work.

You could also enter the setup utility (either BIOS or UEFI) to permanently set the order used to boot devices. Accessing the setup utility might also happen through a range of keys: I've seen F2, F10, Del, and Enter.

6.3　*Putting your live-boot drive to work*

You can do a lot of things with this Linux-in-a-pocket drive that you've created. The following sections describe a few common scenarios and the ways you might address them.

6.3.1　*Testing system memory*

If you've experienced sudden and unexpected system crashes, a likely culprit is your physical memory (RAM). Like all hardware, RAM will eventually fail. The problem is that you can't properly test your RAM for errors while it's being used by a running OS. Instead, you've got to catch it before the OS loads. Fortunately, as the proud owner of a Linux live-boot drive, you've already got everything you'll need for this job. As figure 6.10 shows, one of the menu items that will be displayed after booting to an Ubuntu drive is Test Memory.

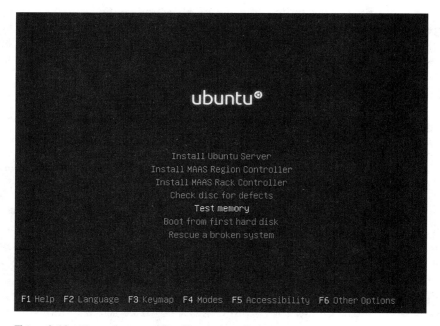

Figure 6.10　The main menu of an Ubuntu installation process showing Test Memory

Selecting Test Memory (using the up and down arrow keys and pressing Enter) takes you to the Memtest86+ program (figure 6.11). That program runs multiple scans of your RAM, displaying any errors it finds. Honestly, I'm not sure that the tool will ever stop on its own; I've certainly never reached that point. But if it returns no errors after running for at least a few full passes, you're memory is probably not the cause of your trouble. Which can be either good news or bad news...after all, you still don't know what's causing your crashes.

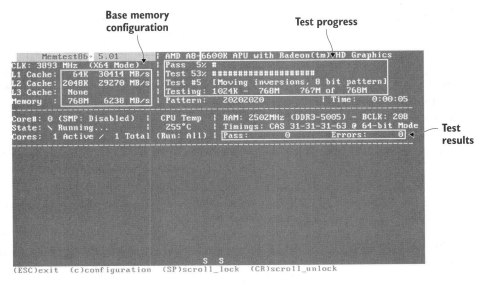

Figure 6.11   The Memtest86+ tool shows the location and kind of any errors in your RAM memory.
This system is clean (so far).

NOTE   Besides Test Memory, the Rescue a Broken System option in the main
menu of an Ubuntu installation process will give you a working Bash shell.

CentOS installation disks include their own link to Memtest86+ in the Troubleshooting menu (figure 6.12).

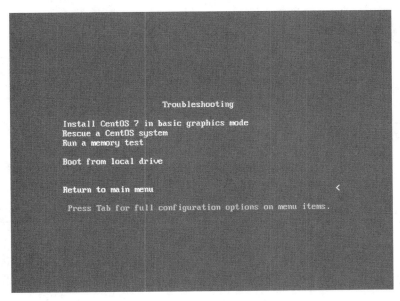

Figure 6.12   The Troubleshooting menu linked to from the main menu on a CentOS installation disk

6.3.2   *Damaged partitions*

A *partition* is really metadata pointing to the location on a physical disk occupied by a file system. They're fragile things, those partitions, and it doesn't seem to take much to upset them. If disk data is somehow corrupted and the exact addresses of a partition's start and end points are changed or lost, then the file system on the partition will become unreachable. And if a file system is unreachable, then the data on the file system is as good as gone.

Can't access your partition? It's time to boot up your new SystemRescue drive. SystemRescue is a lightweight package, so don't expect all the GUI miracles of a full-featured distro. Things like laptop touch pads and automatic WiFi connectivity might not work the way you expect. But it's a quick way to get some powerful rescue tools into play. As you can see in figure 6.13, the default boot option will open a special command-line shell.

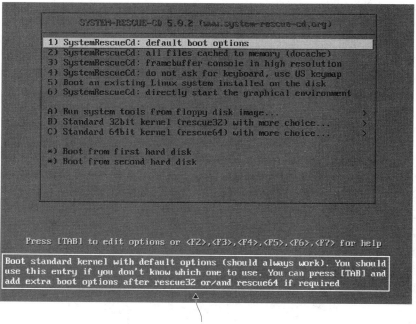

When a menu item is highlighted
above, the description appears.

Figure 6.13   The Boot Options menu displayed during SystemRescue startup. Note the detailed explanations for each option at the bottom of the page.

As you gear up toward rescuing your stricken partition (or its data), SystemRescue provides some useful orientation information along with the command line, including networking and text-editing basics (figure 6.14). Worry not: both Vim and Nano are available from the command line. And typing `startx` will load a fast and light GUI desktop.

Network setup information

```
         SystemRescue-Cd          5.0.2              tty1/6
                  http://www.system-rescue-cd.org/
  Type net-setup eth0 to specify ethernet configuration.
  If your PC is on an ethernet local network, you can configure by hand:
    ifconfig eth0 192.168.x.a (your static IP address)
    route add default gw 192.168.x.b (IP address of the gateway)
  To be sure there is an ssh server running, type /etc/init.d/sshd start.
   You will need to create an user or to change the root password with passwd.
  Available console text editors : nano, vim, qemacs, zile, joe.
  Web browser in the console: elinks www.web-site.org.
  Ntfs-3g : If you need a full Read-Write NTFS access, use Ntfs-3g.
  Mount the disk: ntfs-3g /dev/sda1 /mnt/windows
  Graphical environment :
   Type startx to run the graphical environment
   X.Org comes with the XFCE environment and several graphical tools:
    - Partition manager:..gparted
    - Web browsers:.......firefox
    - Text editors:.......gvim and geany

root@sysresccd      %  _
```

Figure 6.14 The SystemRescue shell. Note the text editors available by default (including Nano) and also that typing `startx` launches a graphical desktop.

If you're going to need network access to download or install more tools, perhaps, or to transfer data, you'll type `net-setup` at the command prompt, select the correct interface, and indicate whether your network is wired or wireless. If it's wireless, you'll enter your WiFi router's SSID and its encryption key (which will probably use ASCII rather than hex characters). In most cases, you'll want to let DHCP auto-detect your network.

With a damaged partition to worry about, your primary concern right now will be recovery. If there's any chance that the physical disk itself might be failing, then your first task must be to secure its data. For that, I'd use dd at the SystemRescue command prompt to create a perfect copy of the partition in its current state and save it to a healthy disk of equal or greater capacity. After running lsblk to confirm the designations of both partitions, the copy operation might look something like this, where the failing disk is /dev/sda and the empty partition on your target drive is /dev/sdc1:

```
# dd if=/dev/sda of=/dev/sdc1
```

With that done, you're free to see whether you can save the original copy. Type `test-disk`. You'll be asked how you'd like session events logged, which disk you want to recover, and which partition type to expect to find. More often than not, TestDisk will guess the right one and highlight it as the default.

You'll then find yourself facing a screen that looks like the one in figure 6.15, where you can ask TestDisk to analyze your disk, looking for existing partitions. When you've discovered and appropriately marked your damaged partitions, you can write the changes to disk, and you should be able to successfully boot once again.

```
TestDisk 7.0, Data Recovery Utility, April 2015
Christophe GRENIER <grenier@cgsecurity.org>
http://www.cgsecurity.org

Disk /dev/sda - 8589 MB / 8192 MiB - VBOX HARDDISK
      CHS 1044 255 63 - sector size=512

>[ Analyse  ] Analyse current partition structure and search for lost partitions
 [ Advanced ] Filesystem Utils
 [ Geometry ] Change disk geometry
 [ Options  ] Modify options
 [ MBR Code ] Write TestDisk MBR code to first sector
 [ Delete   ] Delete all data in the partition table
 [ Quit     ] Return to disk selection




Note: Correct disk geometry is required for a successful recovery. 'Analyse'
process may give some warnings if it thinks the logical geometry is mismatched.
```

Figure 6.15   The TestDisk Partition Repair page, where partitions discovered through Analyze can then be edited and recovered using the other tools

Wait…that's it? What about all the fine print? Does "discovered and appropriately marked your damaged partitions" cover the complex process in a way that's at all useful? Nope. But, then, why are you reading this chapter? I'd say it's either because you're trying to prepare for some future catastrophe or because the future is now and you're looking at your broken partition.

If it's the future that worries you, then following along with me as I work through the narrowly focused details of one or two hypothetical solutions won't help all that much. Besides, I'm not going to advise you to purposely corrupt a real partition so you can try out TestDisk for real. And if you've got your own real-world problem to deal with, then it's highly unlikely that any example I happen to choose will be useful to you. Practically, the best I can do is let you know that such software exists and teach you how to get it running. Oh, and there's some pretty good documentation available at https://cgsecurity.org/testdisk.pdf.

6.3.3   Recovering files from a damaged file system

If it turns out that you can't fully rescue your disk, perhaps you managed to revive your partitions just enough to allow access to the files but not enough to reliably boot from the disk. Then your new priority is to save as many important files as you can.

The simplest approach is to use the regular Linux file system management tools from any kind of live-boot session. If you're not sure about the partition's designation, running lsblk will, as always, get you up to speed.

It's possible that your partition won't yet be accessible as a file system because it hasn't been mounted. If, in fact, it doesn't show up among the results of a df command, then you'll have to *mount* it, meaning assign it to a location within a file system where it can be accessed. You can fix that one quickly enough by creating a new directory where your partition will be mounted and then using the mount command. I chose to create my temporary mount point directory in /run/, but any unused location you happen to find (like /media/ or /mnt/) will do as well. Let's assume, as before, that the partition is called /dev/sdc1:

```
# mkdir /run/temp-directory
# mount /dev/sdc1 /run/temp-directory
```

From here on in, any healthy files from the stricken file system will be available to copy or edit from within temp-directory. They'll probably also automatically show up in any GUI desktop file management tool you might want to use.

RECOVERY USING DDRESCUE

Didn't work? Time to pull out the heavy guns. The data-recovery tool, ddrescue, copies files between file systems. But there's something else it does at the same time that should put a smile on your face: it analyzes your files and attempts to repair any that are broken. No tool is guaranteed to fix everything that's gone sour, but by reputation, ddrescue is as good as you're going to get.

If it's not already installed on the live boot you're using, ddrescue comes as part of SystemRescue by default. Grab it from your repository. Then identify the troubled partition (/dev/sdc1 in this example), the partition where you want the image saved, and the name and location of a log file where a record of operation events can be written. Having a log file allows ddrescue to continue a stopped operation rather than starting again from scratch. My example uses an external drive (of greater capacity than the source drive) mounted to a directory called /run/usb-mount:

Note: for CentOS, the command would be yum install ddrescue.

```
# apt install gddrescue
# ddrescue -d /dev/sdc1 /run/usb-mount/sdc1-backup.img \
 /run/usb-mount/sdc1-backup.logfile
```

Tells ddrescue to ignore the kernel cache and access the disk directly

You can test the rescue by using dd to write the backup image to a new, empty drive (called /dev/sdd/ in my example) and then booting the system to the new drive:

```
# dd if=backup.img of=/dev/sdd
```

Even if you find that you still can't boot the partition, it may now be possible to use it to reliably access important individual files. Either way, you're ahead of where you would have been.

FILE RECOVERY USING PHOTOREC

Another tool that can help you grab files off a damaged drive is PhotoRec. One look at the interface tells you that it must have come from the same place as TestDisk. And, in fact, both were created and are maintained by Christophe Grenier of CGSecurity. To load the program, type

```
# photorec
```

Once you identify the file system that needs rescuing, which file types you want to include, and the location to which you'd like the files saved, the files are saved to numbered directories using the `recup_dir.?` prefix:

```
$ ls recup_dir.12
f1092680.elf
f0668624.png
f0853304.xml
f0859464.xml
f0867192.txt
f0977016.gz
f0982184.xml
[...]
```

Something to keep in mind about PhotoRec is that the files are all given new numbered filenames while retaining their original file extensions. This can sometimes make finding individual files difficult, but it sure beats losing them altogether.

6.4   *Password recovery: Mounting a file system using chroot*

You know that the passwords chosen by the people you support are probably not strong enough to protect your infrastructure against a serious attack. And even the few exceptions to the rule are probably being reused on multiple servers and accounts. You beg and nag and beg and nag, but it seems like a losing battle. All is not entirely lost.

The problem of keeping track of sufficiently complex passwords can be largely solved by using a good password vault like KeePass2 or LastPass. And the problem of overusing passwords can be at least blunted by implementing a single sign-on solution such as Kerberos. Still, uh-ohs are always going to happen.

What happens to the one or two users who care enough to dream up good, strong passwords for each server they access? Every now and then they forget a password. That won't be a problem if there's another admin with `sudo` power who can log in to the server and run `passwd` to create a new password for the user:

```
# passwd username
[sudo] password for yourname:
Enter new UNIX password:
Retype new UNIX password:
passwd: password updated successfully
```

But if your unlucky and forgetful user was the only admin with an account on that machine, you've got trouble. Except that you don't. The grandfather of all Linux virtualization, `chroot`, is going to save your day. Here's one way that it might work.

Use a live-boot drive to power up the server that's got you locked out, run `lsblk` to determine the designation of your root partition on the server's hard disk, and mount the root partition to a temporary directory:

```
# mkdir /run/mountdir/
# mount /dev/sdb1 /run/mountdir/
```

Then whisper the magic words, and you're in:

```
# chroot /run/mountdir/
root@ubuntu:/#
```

That's all it takes. At this point, you're free to run commands as though you were working on a running version of the physical hard drive. Use `passwd` to give your admin a new password to replace the lost one. And, after typing `exit` to shut down your `chroot` session, reboot the machine (without the live-boot USB). Everything should now be fine.

> **To encrypt or not to encrypt?**
> Encrypting the data on your storage drives using a tool like ecryptfs or dm-crypt makes it a great deal less likely that your data will be compromised. But on the other hand, many of the rescue and recovery operations discussed in this chapter won't work on an encrypted volume.

Striking a balance between security and accessibility isn't an exact science. Many admins leave local servers and desktop workstations unencrypted because those are at least protected by locked office doors, but they insist that mobile devices be encrypted.

Summary

- Linux recovery modes provide access to administration tools useful for repairing systems that won't boot normally.
- Live-boot drives allow you to boot your choice of Linux distros independently of the file systems on a computer's physical drives.
- Purpose-build distros like SystemRescueCd are lightweight versions of Linux that come preinstalled with a full range of rescue tools.
- Damaged partitions can sometimes be restored using tools like TestDisk.
- Data from damaged partitions can sometimes be recovered using tools like ddrescue and PhotoRec.
- File systems can be mounted and administered using a virtual process called `chroot`.

Key terms

- *GRUB* is a bootloader that manages the images to be used in the Linux boot process.
- A *hash* (checksum) is a cryptographically generated value that can be checked against a master copy to confirm an image's authenticity.
- A partition's *Master Boot Record* (MBR) for a CD/DVD will be different than for a USB, requiring special attention for creating live-boot USBs.
- The tool `chroot` opens virtual root shells within mounted file systems.

Security best practices

- Always confirm that downloaded images are authentic by checking their hashes. And avoid downloading from unencrypted (HTTP rather than HTTPS) websites.
- Carefully consider whether or not to encrypt the data at rest on your system drives, balancing accessibility against security.
- Enforce the use of password vaults and single sign-on services for users of your infrastructure.

Command-line review

- `sha256sum systemrescuecd-x86-5.0.2.iso` calculates the SHA256 checksum of a .ISO file.
- `isohybrid systemrescuecd-x86-5.0.2.iso` adds a USB-friendly MBR to a live-boot image.
- `dd bs=4M if=systemrescuecd-x86-5.0.2.iso of=/dev/sdb && sync` writes a live-boot image to an empty drive.
- `mount /dev/sdc1 /run/temp-directory` mounts a partition to a directory on the live file system.
- `ddrescue -d /dev/sdc1 /run/usb-mount/sdc1-backup.img /run/usb-mount/sdc1-backup.logfile` saves files on a damaged partition to an image named sdc1-backup.img and writes events to a log file.
- `chroot /run/mountdir/` opens a root shell on a file system.

Test yourself

1 Which of the following will allow you to access a damaged Linux machine's own recovery mode?
   a SystemRecovery
   b GRUB
   c Hitting CRTL+Right Shift during boot
   d chkdsk
2 Which user account is used by default for a Linux recovery mode shell session?
   a root
   b The initial account created during installation

    c admin

    d guest

3 What is the goal of the Clean option in the Ubuntu Recovery Mode menu?

    a Find and remove viruses

    b Remove unused program files

    c Remove unused user accounts

    d Clean up a session and shut down

4 Booting a Linux live-boot device will do which of the following?

    a Launch a system recovery environment

    b Launch a file recovery environment

    c Launch a Linux session using host machine partitions

    d Launch a Linux session using only live-boot partitions

5 What tool do you need in order to create a live-boot image that can be used to boot from a USB device?

    a ddrescue

    b GRUB

    c isohybrid

    d ecryptfs

6 The sha256sum program is used for what purpose?

    a Opening a virtual shell session on a mounted file system

    b Managing Linux images at system startup

    c Generating hashes to authenticate file integrity

    d Managing file recovery from damaged drives

7 Which of the following will write a SystemRescue image to the second block device on your system?

    a `dd if=systemrescuecd-x86-5.0.2.iso of=/dev/sdb`

    b `dd if=/dev/sdb of=systemrescuecd-x86-5.0.2.iso`

    c `dd if=/dev/sdc of=systemrescuecd-x86-5.0.2.iso`

    d `dd if=systemrescuecd-x86-5.0.2.iso of=/dev/sdb2`

8 What does the `chroot` command do?

    a Creates a live-boot image that can be used to boot from a USB device

    b Opens a virtual shell session on a mounted file system

    c Generates hashes to authenticate file integrity

    d Removes unused program files

Answer key

1. b, 2. a, 3. b, 4. d, 5. c, 6. c, 7. a, 8. b

Web servers: Building
a MediaWiki server

This chapter covers

- Building dynamic web servers using Apache
- Managing backend application data with SQL databases
- Identifying and resolving application package dependencies
- Installing and configuring a MediaWiki CMS

Got a small company blog to publish, or 30 years of technical and corporate data spanning 100,000 pages? You'll need some kind of content management system (CMS). In case you're wondering, a *CMS* is an application designed as a framework for the creation and administration of digital content. Popular CMS applications you might have encountered include WordPress and Joomla.

A *wiki* can be a particularly effective way to manage large communities of contributors. It's a kind of CMS whose architecture is intentionally decentralized, allowing users to freely collaborate not only on the content itself, but on the larger structure of the entire data collection. A *wiki engine* is a platform on which wikis are

130

built, usually using some kind of simple and intuitive markup language. MediaWiki is a popular example of an open source wiki engine, but Atlassian Confluence is a mature commercial alternative.

MediaWiki itself may not be all that important to us right now. I only chose to focus on installing MediaWiki because it's a great way to illustrate the process of building a web server (often known as a *LAMP server*) on Linux. Considering that more than two of every three web servers on the internet today are running on Linux, that's a big deal.

Don't get me wrong: MediaWiki doesn't lack for charm. It is, after all, the CMS originally created to power the tens of millions of articles that make up Wikipedia and the other Wikimedia Foundation projects. If you're looking for a robust and reliable way to manage a great deal of media content, whether private collections documenting your company's processes or public-facing help pages, you could do a lot worse than MediaWiki. But those specific use cases aren't common enough to justify inclusion in a core-skills kind of book like this one.

Working through a MediaWiki deployment can, however, teach you about the software packages that make up a Linux web server and how they fit together to make those two out of three websites possible. As a Linux admin, there's a good chance that you'll be asked to build web servers to support all kinds of applications, so you've got an interest in learning how to do this stuff, right?

7.1 Building a LAMP server

If you or your business has information, applications, or services, the odds are that you'll want to make them available for consumption by web browsers. A *web server* is software running on a computer that allows locally hosted resources to be viewed and consumed by visitors to a website. To be clear, the term *web server* is also often used to describe the computer hosting the web server software.

> ### Static or dynamic websites?
> This section will guide you through the process of building a *dynamic* website. That's a website whose pages are generated with the help of server-side operations. It's also possible to create *static* websites that, for the most part, provide only plain HTML files that delegate all the work to the client web browser.
>
> For simpler sites, static can be a fast and affordable option. But because there's nothing Linux-y about that, I'll say no more about the subject here. Chapter 6 of my *Learn Amazon Web Services in a Month of Lunches* (Manning, 2017), on the other hand, includes a nice demonstration of using AWS's S3 to host a static site.

As illustrated in figure 7.1, most Linux web servers are built on the four pillars of what's known as a LAMP server. The letters *LAMP* stand for Linux, the Apache web server administration software, either the MySQL or MariaDB database engine, and the PHP server-side scripting language (or, alternatively, Perl or Python). Those, in addition to Linux, with which I'd hope you're already familiar, will be the focus of this chapter.

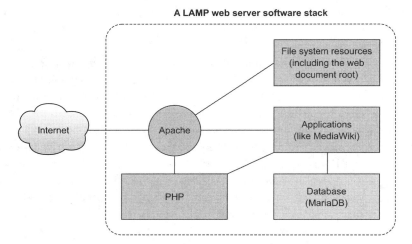

Figure 7.1   The Apache web server software exposes HTTP-based resources to external clients and coordinates internal services.

The LAMP server is such a common Linux configuration that Ubuntu, at least, has its own installation meta package. The caret (^) at the end of this example identifies the target as a special package bundled together to make installing common software stacks simpler:

```
# apt install lamp-server^
```

That one command will, after asking you to create a database password, automatically drop a working web server on top of your system, leaving you with nothing to do besides create some website content. Directing your web browser to the server's IP address should display a welcome page created when Apache was installed.

But automation isn't always the best solution. Sometimes you'll want to customize your software stack by specifying particular release versions to ensure application compatibility, or by substituting one package for another (MariaDB over MySQL, for instance, as you'll soon see). Setting things up manually will be particularly helpful in this case, as it'll force you to better understand how each bit works. That's the approach I'll take in this chapter. Here's a list of what needs doing to get you to your goal:

1 Install Apache
2 Add a web page or two to the web document root
3 Install an SQL engine (MariaDB in this case)
4 Install the PHP server-side scripting language
5 Install and configure MediaWiki

7.2   *Manually setting up an Apache web server*

Web server software has one primary job—to guide site visitors to the right directories and files on the server host—so appropriate website resources should be made available. Practically speaking, entering a uniform resource locator (URL) address in your browser address bar is really a request for the web server software running on a remote website host to retrieve a web page, video, or other resource from the host file system and load it in your browser. Web server software will usually integrate closely with other systems on the host server like networking, security, and file system tools so that access to local resources is well managed.

Although it's a volatile market, the open source Apache HTTP server tends to dominate the web server market across all platforms. Because it's so popular, and despite the fact that Apache has serious competitors including Nginx (also cross-platform) and Microsoft's IIS (which runs exclusively on Windows servers), I'm going to stick with Apache. (C'mon. Did you *really* think I'd devote an entire chapter to IIS?)

7.2.1   *Installing the Apache web server on Ubuntu*

Installing Apache itself is easy. On Debian/Ubuntu, it's `apt install apache2`. If you're following along on an Ubuntu machine, once Apache is installed, there's nothing stopping you from opening a browser and visiting your live website right away. You'll be greeted by the introduction page seen in figure 7.2.

> **NOTE**   The URL you'll use to reach an Apache site running on your workstation is *localhost*. If, instead, you chose to work on an LXC container or VirtualBox VM, then you'll use the machine's IP address for the URL. To make sure you'll have network access to sites running on your VirtualBox VM, ensure it's configured to use a bridged adapter (the way you did it in chapter 2).

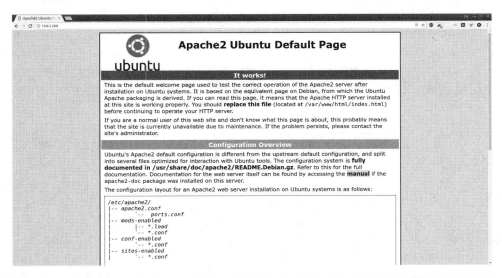

Figure 7.2   The Apache default page displayed in browsers directed to your server's URL or IP address includes some important basic configuration and navigation information.

Ubuntu makes things easy. But where's the fun in that? Once again, learning how it works on CentOS will help you understand what's happening under the hood. Even if you don't happen to have a VM or container running CentOS, Fedora, or Red Hat right now, I'd recommend you at least familiarize yourself with the CentOS way of doing things.

The CentOS processes you'll see in this chapter are different than Ubuntu's. For clarity, I decided to separate the two, placing all CentOS directions in their own section: 7.6. If you're aiming to install Apache on CentOS, head there for details.

7.2.2   *Populating your website document root*

Fantastic! You've got yourself a working website. Considering that there's nothing on the site besides the Apache welcome page, don't expect to win any awards (or generate much revenue). You're going to need to add some content. And to do that, you'll need to know where the content goes.

The content's location is controlled by the DocumentRoot setting in an Apache configuration file. On CentOS systems, the configuration is set in the httpd.conf file in the /etc/httpd/conf/ directory. Ubuntu users will find it in a file called 000-default.conf in the /etc/apache2/sites-available/ directory. Either way, searching the configuration file for DocumentRoot will probably show you a value like this:

```
DocumentRoot "/var/www/html"
```

This means that Apache will direct all incoming browser requests to files in the /var/www/html/ directory. You can change this value to point to any location on your file system you'd like. In fact, although it's not a topic for this book, if you plan to host multiple websites on your server, you're able to point to multiple file system locations.

If you've never done it before, why not take a couple of minutes right now and build a simple website of your own? Create a text file called index.html in your document root. (This file will overwrite Apache's welcome page using the same name.) You can type some welcome text of your own in the file along with a link to a second HTML file and a graphic image. Make sure to create that second file along with an image. The index.html file might look like this:

```
<h2>Welcome!</h2>
Take a look at our <a href="info.html">company history</a>.
<br>
And how about a look at our new company logo: <img src="logo.png">
```

7.3   *Installing an SQL database*

Take a quick look at the US government's Bureau of Labor Statistics (BLS) Occupational Outlook Handbook page for Network and Computer Systems Administrators (http://mng.bz/kHN3) as shown in figure 7.3. Given all the content displayed on each of the page's nine tabs, there's quite a lot of text. But I suspect that very little of it was manually added to this page by a human being.

What's more likely is that the database on the BLS server contains terabytes of raw data, within which can be found structured information related to each of the many thousands of included occupations. That data is probably then organized by information categories (Summary, Work Environment, and so forth). When I requested this page from the BLS menu (or through an internet search engine), the BLS web server might have requested the relevant raw data from the database and dynamically organized it on the page the way you see it in figure 7.3.

Figure 7.3   A page from the Bureau of Labor Statistics. The What Network and Computer Systems Administrators Do header was probably expanded from something like this: What $selected_occupation Do.

There are many more ways that a website can make use of dynamic access to a database engine installed in the backend, but that was a good illustration. The kind of database engine most likely used for a BLS-like project (or for our MediaWiki site) is called a *relational database*, which is a tool for organizing data into tables made up of columns and rows. The data contained within an individual row is known as a *record*. A record is identified by an ID value known as a *key*, which can be used to reference records between tables.

The *Structured Query Language* (SQL) is a standardized syntax for managing data on relational databases. A *database engine* is software for managing relational database data and exposing it to administrators and automated processes using SQL syntax.

I'll show you how to create and display a simple database table in a moment. But first, you'll have to install your own database engine so you can follow along yourself. Because our long-term goal is a full LAMP server, it would make sense to install this on the same computer/VM/container where you built your Apache web server. (The CentOS way can be found at the end of the chapter.)

```
# apt update
# apt install mariadb-server
```

Install MariaDB on your server.

Why did I choose MariaDB over MySQL? They both work with the exact same MySQL standards. In fact, they were both initially created by the same people. Both are great, but, right now at least, MariaDB seems to be the beneficiary of more active development and support. In addition to those two, there are other important SQL database engines in heavy use around the IT world, including Oracle, PostgreSQL, and Amazon's Aurora, which was built specifically for AWS workloads.

Why not check the status of the database (DB) you've just installed? You can confirm the DB is running using `systemctl`:

Whether you've got MySQL or MariaDB installed, Linux refers to the DB using the mysql command.

```
# systemctl status mysql
? mysql.service - MySQL Community Server
   Loaded: loaded (/lib/systemd/system/mysql.service;
       enabled; vendor preset: enabled)
   Active: active (running) since Wed 2018-05-02 12:26:47 UTC; 6h ago
  Process: 396 ExecStartPost=/usr/share/mysql/mysql-systemd-start post
       (code=exited, status=0/SUCCESS)
  Process: 318 ExecStartPre=/usr/share/mysql/mysql-systemd-start pre
       (code=exited, status=0/SUCCESS)
 Main PID: 395 (mysqld)
    Tasks: 28
   Memory: 126.3M
      CPU: 20.413s
   CGroup: /system.slice/mysql.service
           ??395 /usr/sbin/mysqld

May 02 12:26:29 base systemd[1]: Starting MySQL Community Server...
May 02 12:26:47 base systemd[1]: Started MySQL Community Server.
```

7.3.1   Hardening SQL

Once MariaDB's installed, it's always a good idea to harden your database security, so you'll want to run the mysql_secure_installation tool. If you weren't prompted to create a root MariaDB password during the installation process (something that's quite common), then you'll need to run mysql_secure_installation, as that's also how you'll set up your authentication. Running this tool presents the following interactive dialog:

```
# mysql_secure_installation
```

Note that this command may require sudo privileges, which will cause trouble later. Stay tuned.

```
NOTE: RUNNING ALL PARTS OF THIS SCRIPT IS RECOMMENDED FOR ALL MariaDB
      SERVERS IN PRODUCTION USE!  PLEASE READ EACH STEP CAREFULLY!
```

```
In order to log into MariaDB to secure it, we'll need the current
password for the root user.  If you've just installed MariaDB, and
you haven't set the root password yet, the password will be blank,
so you should just press enter here.
```

```
Enter current password for root (enter for none):    ⟵
OK, successfully used password, moving on...
```
Enter the password of the database root user, not the Linux root user.

```
Setting the root password ensures that nobody can log into the MariaDB
root user without the proper authorisation.
```

```
Set root password? [Y/n]
```

The values recommended by mysql_secure_installation are aimed at preventing anonymous and remote users from accessing your data. Unless you're planning to use this database only for testing, and it won't contain important or sensitive data, you'll want to accept the defaults.

> **NOTE** If the mysql_secure_installation only works when run using sudo, then create your password that way. But keep in mind that this will create a problem that will need fixing later. You'll see how to address that in the next section.

7.3.2 SQL administration

Now, as promised, I'm going to show you some simple database administration commands. The fact is you might never have to run any of these commands directly because most databases are accessed from within application code, rather than from the command line. Considering how inconvenient it would be to manually manage the thousands or even millions of data records commonly included in SQL databases, this makes a lot of sense. You'll see a perfect example of this automated application/database relationship a bit later in this chapter when we finally get to installing and configuring MediaWiki.

Still, you may sometimes need to handcraft your own database. Perhaps you need some test data to work with while you're putting a new application together. Or maybe your new business is starting off slowly and, rather than investing in a new application, for now it makes sense to manage your customers manually. You should at least know how it's done.

Feel free to skip to section 7.4 if you feel you're not up to a database dive right now. But before you go, there's one more important thing I should talk about.

By default, you'll access and administer the databases in your MariaDB or MySQL installations using the root user. That's a bad idea. For security reasons, individual databases should be owned and managed by regular database users who have been given only the authority they need to do their specific jobs. Nevertheless, for this demo, I'm going to throw caution to the wind and, for the sake of simplicity, use the root user. Later, when I show you how to set up your MediaWiki database, I'll do it properly by creating a non-root user.

ACCESSING THE DATABASE

Whether you've installed MariaDB or MySQL, you log in to your shell using mysql, followed by -u root. This tells the database that you want to authenticate as the root user. The -p means you'll be prompted for your MariaDB password:

```
$ mysql -u root -p          ◁──┐  Log in by specifying a user, and
Enter password:                  prompt for the user's password.
Welcome to the MariaDB monitor.  Commands end with ; or \g.
Your MariaDB connection id is 10
Server version: 5.5.52-MariaDB MariaDB Server

Copyright (c) 2000, 2016, Oracle, MariaDB Corporation Ab and others.

Type 'help;' or '\h' for help. Type \c to clear the current input statement

MariaDB [(none)]>   ◁──┐  The [(none)] value will change to
                          the name of an active database.
```

Here's where the trouble I hinted to earlier might rear its ugly head. MariaDB might not let you log in unless you run the mysql command as sudo. If this happens, log in using sudo and provide the MariaDB password you created. Then run these three commands at the MySQL prompts (substituting your password for your-password):

```
> SET PASSWORD = PASSWORD('your-password');
> update mysql.user set plugin = 'mysql_native_password' where User='root';
> FLUSH PRIVILEGES;
```

The next time you log in, you should no longer require sudo and, more importantly, MediaWiki should be able to do its job properly. With that little trouble out of the way, take a look around your SQL environment. Here's how to create a new database:

```
MariaDB> CREATE DATABASE companydb;  ◁──┐  Most MySQL commands must end with a
                                          semicolon (;). Forgetting this will prevent
                                          the execution of the command.
```

Suppose your company needs to store customer contact information. You might create a new table for contacts within your database like this:

```
MariaDB> use companydb
MariaDB> CREATE TABLE Contacts (
    ID int,
    LastName varchar(255),
    FirstName varchar(255),
    Address varchar(255),        ┌─ This is the last part of a
    City varchar(255)            │  single command, stretched
);                          ◁──┘  over seven lines for clarity.
```

Just got your first customer? Congrats! Here's how you'd enter the new information:

> **This line establishes which columns in the table will have new values added.**

```
MariaDB> INSERT INTO Contacts (ID, LastName, FirstName, Address, City)   ◁
VALUES ('001', 'Torvalds', 'Linus', '123 Any St.', 'Newtown');
```

Want to see what you've done? To display all the data in your new `Contacts` table, type `select *`:

```
MariaDB> select * from Contacts;
+------+----------+-----------+-------------+---------+
| ID   | LastName | FirstName | Address     | City    |
+------+----------+-----------+-------------+---------+
|    1 | Torvalds | Linus     | 123 Any St. | Newtown |
+------+----------+-----------+-------------+---------+
1 row in set (0.00 sec)
```

Note the ID value in your table, which can be used as the key value for your records. When you're all done, you can close the MariaDB shell by typing `exit`.

If, as I noted earlier, you might never need to perform any of those tasks manually, why bother reading about it here? Because, to integrate automated operations with your databases, you'll almost certainly need to include variations of MySQL syntax within scripts and application code someday. Even the simplest of web shopping portals lives on external data. You may not be the one doing the coding, but the odds are that someone you know or love will, and they may need your help making the database connection. All in a day's work for a tireless Linux sysadmin.

CREATING A MEDIAWIKI DATABASE USER

There's one more bit of database administration. As you've seen, MariaDB comes with an active root user out of the box. But because that user has full admin rights over all the tables in the system, it isn't a good idea to use root for day-to-day operations. Instead, from a security perspective, you're better off creating unique users for each database consumer and giving them only the access rights they need.

Let's log in to MariaDB one more time and create a new database called `wikidb` for MediaWiki to use later. Then you'll create a user that you'll call mw-admin. The `FLUSH PRIVILEGES` command enables the new settings and grants the mw-admin user full control over the `wikidb` database:

```
mysql> CREATE DATABASE wikidb;
Query OK, 1 row affected (0.01 sec)
mysql> CREATE USER 'mw-admin'@'localhost' IDENTIFIED BY 'mypassword';
Query OK, 0 rows affected (0.00 sec)
mysql> GRANT ALL PRIVILEGES ON wikidb.* TO 'mw-admin'@'localhost'
    IDENTIFIED BY 'mypassword';
mysql> FLUSH PRIVILEGES;
Query OK, 0 rows affected (0.00 sec)
mysql> exit
```

7.4   Installing PHP

The final LAMP ingredient is the PHP scripting language. *PHP* is a tool that can be used to write your own web applications. Prebuilt PHP applications are often used by third-party applications like MediaWiki to access and process system resources. It's safe to assume, therefore, that you'll be needing the *P* in your LAMP server.

7.4.1   Installing PHP on Ubuntu

Despite what the examples you've seen so far might suggest, Ubuntu installations aren't always simpler than CentOS. But here's one more task that goes down quicker the Ubuntu way. Want the latest PHP? apt install php is all it takes for Ubuntu to grant your desire. Because you'll want it to play nicely with Apache, you'll also need an extension:

```
# apt install php
# apt install libapache2-mod-php
```

You should get into the habit of restarting Apache whenever making changes to a web server's system configuration. Here's how:

```
# systemctl restart apache2
```

That's it. PHP should now be live.

7.4.2   Testing your PHP installation

To make sure your PHP installation is live (and to learn about PHP's local environment and resource integration), create a new file using the .php filename extension in the Apache web document root directory. Then fill the file with the remaining lines of text as shown here:

```
# nano /var/www/html/testmyphp.php
<?php
phpinfo();
?>
```

Now head over to a browser, enter the IP address of the machine that's running PHP (or localhost, if it's the desktop you're working on) and the name of the file you created:

```
10.0.3.184/testmyphp.php
```

You'll be treated to a long web page (like the one you see in figure 7.4), broken down into many sections, that describes your computer and the ways PHP talks to it.

> **NOTE** When you're done, make sure to either delete or restrict access to the testmyphp.php file. Exposing this kind of information about your system to the public is a serious security breach.

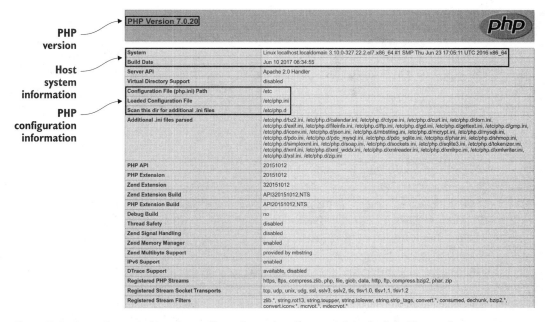

PHP version

Host system information

PHP configuration information

Figure 7.4　A small sample from the configuration and environment data displayed by `phpinfo`

As before, getting all this done on CentOS will come later. For now, let's give MediaWiki its very own database.

7.5　*Installing and configuring MediaWiki*

Got documents and media to share (as we discussed at the start of this chapter all those pages ago)? You've come to the right place. Here's how that process will break down:

1. Download and unpack the MediaWiki archive package
2. Identify and install necessary software extensions
3. Connect MediaWiki to your MariaDB database
4. Run and test the installation.

Head over to the MediaWiki download page (www.mediawiki.org/wiki/Download), and click Download MediaWiki to get the latest package. If you'd rather pull the file directly into your server via the command line, you can right-click the Download link, select Copy Link Address, and paste the address into a terminal window along with the wget program:

```
$ wget https://releases.wikimedia.org/mediawiki/1.30/\
    mediawiki-1.30.0.tar.gz
```
◁ The exact address (and version) will probably have changed by the time you read this.

NOTE If you get a `-bash: wget: Command Not Found` error when running the previous command, then you'll need to install wget.

Running `tar` against the downloaded archive creates a new directory containing all the extracted files and directories. You'll want to copy that entire directory hierarchy to the location on the file system where it'll do its work. If MediaWiki is going to be the only web application hosted on your server, that will probably mean your web root directory:

```
$ tar xzvf mediawiki-1.30.0.tar.gz
$ ls
mediawiki-1.30.0  mediawiki-1.30.0.tar.gz
# cp -r mediawiki-1.30.0/* /var/www/html/
```

If MediaWiki is going to be just one of a number of applications, then you might want to create a subdirectory within the document root that will expose the service in a practical and predictable way. Putting the files into a directory called /var/www/html/mediawiki/, for instance, would mean that your users would find MediaWiki at www.example.com/mediawiki, assuming that you're using example.com as your public domain.

From this point, the MediaWiki browser interface takes over. Point your browser to the index.php file in the MediaWiki directory on your server's IP address (or localhost if you're running all this on your desktop). If you copied the files to the /var/www/html/ root, then it would look something like this:

```
10.0.3.184/index.php
```

If, instead, you created a subdirectory for MediaWiki, it might look like this:

```
10.0.3.184/mediawiki/index.php
```

Normally, when I install an application for the first time, I'll follow the instructions of a good online guide, preferably one created and maintained by the project developers themselves. More often then not, such a guide will provide me with a long list of package dependencies that I'll quickly read (often too quickly) and then copy and paste into an `apt install` command.

This time, however, I've turned the process upside down and installed just the bare bones of the Apache, MariaDB, and PHP packages. I know that this won't give MediaWiki enough to work with, and that's exactly what I want. What better way to learn about how all the complex bits are supposed to fit together?

7.5.1   *Troubleshooting missing extensions*

The people who designed the MediaWiki setup process intelligently understood that things wouldn't always go smoothly. If it turns out that there's something missing from your configuration, rather than failing silently, you'll get an error page containing helpful information. In this case, as illustrated by figure 7.5, I seem to be missing a couple of PHP extensions: mbstring and xml.

MediaWiki 1.29 internal error

Installing some PHP extensions is required.

Required components

You are missing a required extension to PHP that MediaWiki requires to run. Please install:

- **mbstring** (more information)
- **xml** (more information)

Figure 7.5   A helpful error page telling me that my system is missing two extensions and providing links to appropriate PHP documentation pages

I'll use apt search to see what packages relate to mbstring. Since I'm running PHP 7, the php7.0-mbstring package seems like the one most likely to put a smile back on MediaWiki's flowery face:

```
$ apt search mbstring
Sorting... Done
Full Text Search... Done
php-mbstring/xenial 1:7.0+35ubuntu6 all
  MBSTRING module for PHP [default]

php-patchwork-utf8/xenial 1.3.0-1build1 all
  UTF-8 strings handling for PHP

php7.0-mbstring/xenial-updates 7.0.18-0ubuntu0.16.04.1 amd64
  MBSTRING module for PHP
```

> **Provides multibyte string encoding for PHP 7**

A similar search for both xml and php (apt search xml | grep php) told me about a package called php7.0-xml that seemed likely to satisfy MediaWiki's XML requirements. I'll install both packages and then use systemctl to restart Apache:

```
# apt install php7.0-mbstring php7.0-xml
# systemctl restart apache2
```

The beautiful thing about the way all this works is that you (and I) don't need to understand what multibyte string encoding or even XML is and why it is that Media-Wiki feels so completely lost without them. As long as we can trust an application's developers, there's nothing wrong with following their instructions. That assumes we can trust the application's developers, something that's often hard to assess. The philosophy underlying the entire Linux package management system is built on the premise that the managers of official repositories have already done the vetting job for us. It's up to us to hope they're right.

Getting back to our example, if everything goes according to plan, refreshing the browser page should take you back to the initial MediaWiki intro page. When the page loads, you'll see a warning about a missing LocalSettings.php file and a link to set up the wiki. When you click the link, you'll get to select a language preference and then, the MediaWiki Environmental Checks page and…more trouble!

The biggest issue is the absence of a *database driver*. That would be the software used to negotiate between PHP and, in our case, MariaDB. Not having that installed is, indeed, a killer. Although the suggested package shown in figure 7.6 is php5-mysql, `apt search` tells us that we're more likely to see success with the php-mysql package.

Also throw in the suggested PHP extensions for APCu (part of a framework for caching and optimizing PHP intermediate code) and ImageMagick (an image-processing tool). Another restart for Apache and another refresh of the browser window, and you should be all set:

```
# apt install php-mysql php-apcu php-imagick
# systemctl restart apache2
```

You'll see a Continue button at the bottom of the page. Use it.

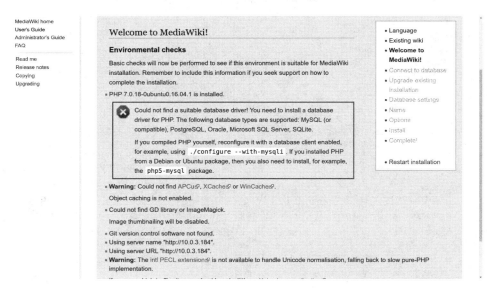

Figure 7.6 The bright *x* indicates a show-stopping hole in our configuration; other notes present less severe warnings.

7.5.2   *Connecting MediaWiki to the database*

The information you provide through the Connect to Database page tells MediaWiki:

- What kind of database you've got installed on your system (MySQL or compatible, in this case)
- Where the database lives (it can be remote or even cloud-based, but this is on the local server, so `localhost` is the correct value)
- The name you'd like to give the database that MediaWiki will use (I'll use the wikidb database I created earlier)
- The name of the existing database user account (mw-admin in this case)
- The password of the current database account (this allows MediaWiki to access MariaDB and create and administrate its database; see figure 7.7)

NOTE   That didn't work? If MediaWiki can't connect to your database, confirm that you're using the right password, but also make sure that you're able to log in to a MariaDB shell from the command line.

If all goes well, you'll be taken through a series of screens from which you'll enter configuration details like database settings, a name for your wiki (something like Company Documentation for this example) and a username, password, and contact email address for a wiki administrator account. This account is not connected to the accounts you already have on the Linux host or MariaDB.

Some optional setup questions let you set preferences for user rights, copyrights for the wiki content, a mail server to send notification emails, and add-on software extensions for things like an in-browser WikiEditor or anti-spam software. With the possible exception of the return email address, the defaults should work.

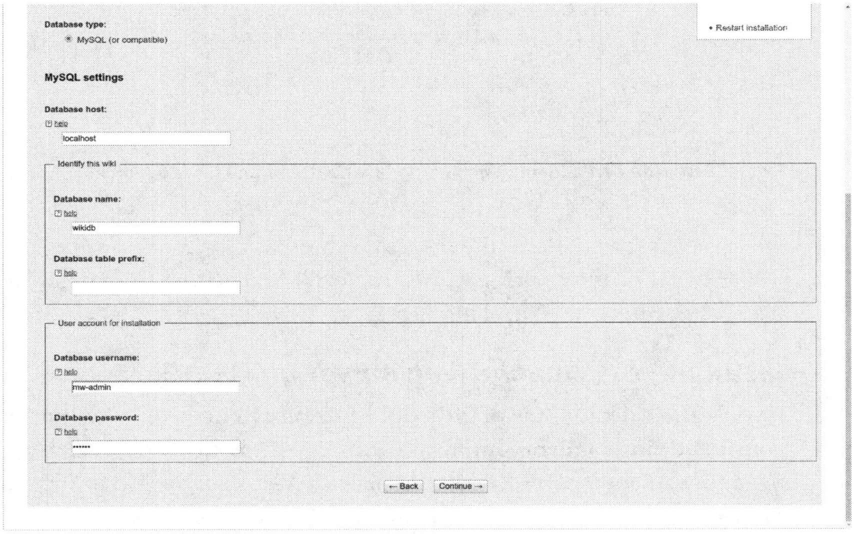

Figure 7.7   Part of the MySQL settings page where you tell MediaWiki how to connect to the database

When you're done, MediaWiki starts its installation process. When that's complete, it prompts you to download a file called LocalSettings.php and then save it to the Media-Wiki root directory (/var/www/html/ in this example). You can use scp to copy the file you've saved to your user's home directory:

```
$ scp LocalSettings.php ubuntu@10.0.3.184:/home/ubuntu/
```

And then, from a command line on your server, move it to the document root:

```
# cp /home/ubuntu/LocalSettings.php /var/www/html/
```

With everything in place, head back to the browser page at the same address you used earlier (something like 10.0.3.184/index.php). This time, as you can see in figure 7.8, you'll find yourself on the main page of your brand-new wiki. From here on in, it'll be your job to start packing your wiki with the many fruits of your wisdom and experience.

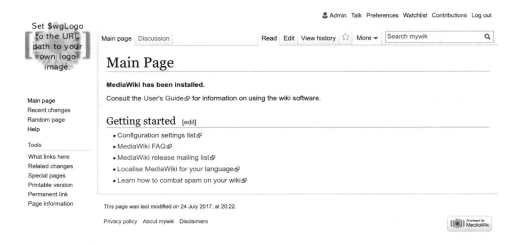

Figure 7.8   You can add and edit the page's contents and links by clicking the Edit tab at the top.

Feel free to spend some time with the MediaWiki User's Guide (www.mediawiki.org/wiki/Help:Contents). Here's where you'll learn how to work with files and to write using the simple markup language.

7.6   *Installing the Apache web server on CentOS*

If you want to avoid some of the trouble we experienced in our Ubuntu installation efforts, consider doing some preemptive research to find out exactly which release versions you'll need for each part of the LAMP puzzle. A quick trip to the MediaWiki Installation Requirements page (http://mng.bz/4Bp1) should give you all the information you'll need to install the Apache web server (or httpd, as it's known on CentOS). Once that's done, getting the software is simple:

```
# yum install httpd
```

By default, Apache won't be running. Remember how to fix that on systemd? No peeking! I hoped you guessed this:

```
# systemctl start httpd
# systemctl enable httpd
```

The command `systemctl start` launches the service, and `enable` causes it to start every time the computer boots. To confirm that Apache is running, you can use `curl` to print a web page to the terminal, specifying `localhost` to tell `curl` that you're after the default page being served locally. You may need to install `curl`...I'm sure you're OK with that by now. If `curl` spits out something that starts this way, then Apache is obviously doing its job:

```
$ curl localhost
<!DOCTYPE html PUBLIC "-//W3C//DTD XHTML 1.1//EN"
  "http://www.w3.org/TR/xhtml11/DTD/xhtml11.dtd"><html><head>
<meta http-equiv="content-type" content="text/html; charset=UTF-8">
    <title>Apache HTTP Server Test Page
         powered by CentOS</title>
    <meta http-equiv="Content-Type" content="text/html; charset=UTF-8">
[...]
```

The title attribute for this Apache test index.html page

But here's something strange: that successful `curl` command means that Apache is running and, hopefully, you know that you've got network connectivity between your computer and your CentOS VM through the bridged adapter. (Chapter 14 will be helpful if you're having trouble with that.) But you probably still won't be able to load the page from a GUI browser. The odds are you'll get a This Site Can't Be Reached error, instead. What's the problem?

This error illustrates another interesting way that the Ubuntu philosophy differs from CentOS's. By default, Ubuntu ships without a firewall of any sort. (Because there are no open network services beyond basic infrastructure, that's not nearly as crazy as it sounds.) Apache is ready to accept incoming external traffic as soon as it's installed. Naturally, there are plenty of ways to shut down network access to fit your needs, but out of the box, you're open to the world. CentOS, on the other hand, comes with all ports securely shut tight. If you want your web server to receive inbound HTTP requests, you'll first need to open the HTTP port (which, by convention, is port 80).

7.6.1 Understanding network ports

What, by the way, is a *network port?* It's nothing more than a way to identify a particular server resource to network users. Imagine that your server is hosting two separate applications. Visitors can reach your server using either its public IP address or a corresponding DNS domain name (like 172.217.1.174 for google.com). But how will a browser know which of the two applications you want to load?

Applications can be told to listen for traffic coming to the server when a predetermined port is specified. Thus, one application could use port 50501 and another, port 50502. As you can see in figure 7.9, the first application would, therefore, respond to incoming requests using 192.168.2.10:50501 (assuming that 192.168.2.10 is your server's IP address), and the second application would expect traffic using 192.168.2.10:50502.

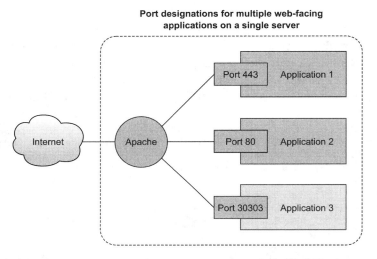

Figure 7.9   Applications configured to listen on separate network ports (80 = insecure HTTP; 443 = secure HTTPS; 30303 = a custom application)

We'll come back to ports later in the book in chapters 9 and 14. But it's your web server software (like Apache) that will do most of the heavy lifting for servers hosting multiple websites, automatically translating ports into local file system locations. If you're considering opening up your web server to more than one site, software configuration guides (like those at http://mng.bz/w6h4) are the place to start.

7.6.2   *Controlling network traffic*

How do you control access to your network? One way is through *firewall rules*. On CentOS, that's handled through the firewalld service and its firewall-cmd tool. In this case, you'll want to add the http service and, through the --permanent flag, ensure that the rule will be active each time you restart the service or boot the computer. (I'll have much more to say about firewalls in chapter 9.) To apply the changes, restart the service:

```
# firewall-cmd --add-service=http --permanent
success
# systemctl restart firewalld
```

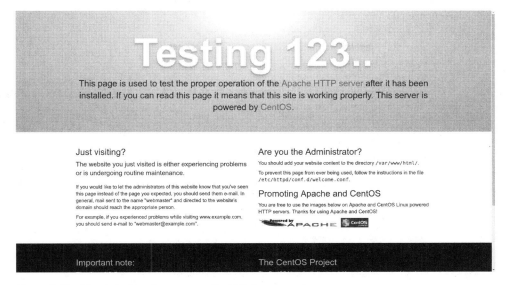

Figure 7.10 The default web page on a CentOS Apache web server

With that done, you should be able to successfully load the CentOS version of the Apache test page (figure 7.10).

7.6.3 *Installing MariaDB on CentOS*

Again, the installation itself is simple. You'll need to manually start MariaDB, however, and then use `enable` to configure it to load on system boot:

```
# yum install mariadb-server
# systemctl start mariadb
# systemctl enable mariadb
```

From here, you can follow the MariaDB setup steps outlined earlier as part of the Ubuntu installation process.

7.6.4 *Installing PHP on CentOS*

At the time of writing, the default version of PHP available though the CentOS repository was still 5.4, which is well behind the latest version available from the Ubuntu repository. The problem is that the current MediaWiki version (1.30) will not work with anything older than PHP 5.5.9. By the time you read this, the issue might have resolved itself. If it hasn't, you'll need to use web searches to find repositories containing more up-to-date versions of PHP to install.

I'm not mentioning this because CentOS happens to be a version or two behind at the moment, but because things like that happen all the time; there are important lessons to learn. The first lesson is to always check the package version before installing it. All Linux package managers make all kinds of information available for you before you jump in. Get in the habit of reading. Following is the software summary information for the PHP installation package:

**dnf displays an installation summary
before launching the action.**

**Note the PHP version dnf
will, by default, install.**

```
# dnf install php
Using metadata from Sun Jul 23 10:37:40 2017
Dependencies resolved.
======================================================================
 Package          Arch         Version              Repository    Size
======================================================================
Installing:
 libzip           x86_64       0.10.1-8.el7         base          48 k
 php              x86_64       5.4.16-42.el7        base         1.4 M
 php-cli          x86_64       5.4.16-42.el7        base         2.7 M
 php-common       x86_64       5.4.16-42.el7        base         564 k

Transaction Summary
======================================================================
Install  4 Packages

Total download size: 4.7 M
Installed size: 17 M
Is this ok [y/N]:
```

**The installation will not
begin until you explicitly
authorize it.**

It's also important to keep in mind that both newer and older versions of software packages can coexist within the repository system at the same time. Remember that you've got choices. And remember, too, that the most recent one is not always the one you want. This can be because another application you're working with might break with the latest version of this package or because a newer version might not be stable or secure enough for your project.

> **NOTE** There's a good chance that you might one day need to install a package that's not part of an official Linux repository. This is neither a crime nor an immoral act, so there's no reason to feel guilty. But you should be aware that you will be fully responsible for making sure that compatibility with other services and applications is maintained, and that your non-repo package and configuration survive system updates. And, of course, you must be extra careful to ensure that the package itself doesn't contain malware.

Whether or not you use the official CentOS PHP repository version, you'll probably need to manually add individual modules to support your intended operations. Following online guides to setting things up will prove useful. But you can run `yum search php-` to check for available modules, and then `yum info` and the name of an interesting choice to learn more about a specific package:

**The php-mysql package
for 64-bit architectures**

**Because a MySQL-like database
is installed, it makes sense to
look for related modules.**

```
# yum search php- | grep mysql
php-mysql.x86_64 : A module for PHP applications that use
   MySQL databases
php-mysqlnd.x86_64 : A module for PHP applications that use
   MySQL databases
php-pear-MDB2-Driver-mysql.noarch : MySQL MDB2 driver
php-pear-MDB2-Driver-mysqli.noarch : MySQL Improved MDB2 driver
[...]
# yum info php-mysql.x86_64
Available Packages
Name        : php-mysql
Arch        : x86_64
Version     : 5.4.16
Release     : 42.el7
Size        : 101 k
Repo        : base/7/x86_64
Summary     : A module for PHP applications that use MySQL databases
URL         : http://www.php.net/
License     : PHP
Description : The php-mysql package contains a dynamic shared object
            : that will add MySQL database support to PHP. MySQL is
            : an object-relational databasemanagement system. PHP is
            : an HTML-embeddable scripting language. Ifyou need MySQL
            : support for PHP applications, you will need to install
            : this package and the php package.
```

**Use yum info to
learn more about an
interesting package.**

**This is the package name you'll use
with yum to install the module.**

After installing PHP and any additional PHP modules, restart Apache to ensure that Apache can incorporate the new modules into its service:

```
# systemctl restart httpd.service
```

As was described during the Ubuntu setup process earlier in the chapter, use `phpinfo` to confirm PHP is properly installed.

Summary

- Web server packages like Apache coordinate connectivity between system resources such as databases and files, and expose website resources to clients.
- Available software package versions can vary between Linux distributions, and the release version you need can depend on your specific project.
- Package dependencies can be met with the help of search tools and metadata provided by package management systems (like APT and Yum).
- Applications will often need access to a database engine and will, therefore, need to be given valid authentication information.

Key terms

- A *wiki* is a tool for creating and managing distributed, collaborative projects.
- A *content management system* (CMS) is an application designed to make creating, sharing, and editing digital content easy.
- A *web server* is software designed to safely and reliably expose server resources to remote clients.
- *DocumentRoot* is the Apache setting determining where on the file system the web server will look for website files.
- *Structured Query Language* (SQL) is a syntax for managing data in relational databases.
- *Package dependencies* are programs or extensions required for the proper function of installed applications.

Security best practices

- Ensure your system firewall settings permit appropriate client access to system resources but block all other requests.
- In most cases, it's not a good idea to allow remote root access to your database.
- Never leave a file running `phpinfo` exposed on a public-facing website.

Command-line review

- `apt install lamp-server^` (a single Ubuntu command) installs all the elements of a LAMP server.
- `systemctl enable httpd` launches Apache on a CentOS machine at every system boot.
- `firewall-cmd --add-service=http --permanent` permits HTTP browser traffic into a CentOS system.
- `mysql_secure_installation` resets your root password and tightens database security.
- `mysql -u root -p` logs in to MySQL (or MariaDB) as the root user.
- `CREATE DATABASE newdbname;` creates a new database in MySQL (or MariaDB).
- `yum search php- | grep mysql` searches for available packages related to PHP on a CentOS machine.
- `apt search mbstring` searches for available packages related to multibyte string encoding.

Test yourself

1 Which of the following packages would you need to install to provide a database for a LAMP web server?
   a mariadb
   b httpd

    c mariadb-client

    d mariadb-server

2 Which of these platforms enables networking between browser clients and data resources on a server?

    a Apache

    b Perl

    c PHP

    d systemctl

3 `localhost` is a designation used to invoke

    a The DocumentRoot of a remote client

    b The DocumentRoot of the server from which the command is run

    c The .conf file on a web server

    d The default HTTP port on a host server

4 Where, by default, is the DocumentRoot of an Apache web server?

    a /var/www/html/

    b /var/html/www/

    c /etc/apache2/

    d /home/username/www/html/

5 Which of the following commands will allow web browser traffic into a CentOS web server using port 80?

    a `firewalld --add-service=http`

    b `firewall-cmd --add-service=https`

    c `firewall --add-service=https`

    d `firewall-cmd --add-service=http`

6 Which of the following commands will let you successfully log in to your MariaDB shell?

    a `mariadb -u root`

    b `mysql root -p`

    c `mariadb -r -p`

    d `mysql -u root -p`

7 Which of the following `yum` commands will display contextual data about the specified package?

    a `yum search php-mysql.x86_64`

    b `yum describe php-mysql.x86_64`

    c `yum info php-mysql.x86_64`

    d `yum data php-mysql.x86_64`

8 Which of the following tools is optional for running MediaWiki on a LAMP server?

a php-mysql

b mbstring

c php-imagick

d php7.0-xml

Answer key

1. d, 2. a, 3. b, 4. a, 5. d, 6. d, 7. c, 8. c

Networked file sharing: Building a Nextcloud file-sharing server

After your introduction to the LAMP web server and text-based content management collaboration in the previous chapter, I'm sure you started thinking about other ways you could use the technology stack. Perhaps your mind didn't immediately turn to the problem of enterprise file sharing, but that's not a bad place to go to learn more about the ways Linux provides web services.

The kind of file sharing I'm talking about has nothing to do with people illegally exchanging copyrighted movies and books. Nor am I referring to peer-to-peer sharing protocols like BitTorrent, even though they can be used for perfectly legitimate purposes. Rather, I'm talking about companies with large collections of documents and other media files that must be accessible, but also safely and securely maintained.

Imagine a project involving dozens of developers divided into a handful of teams and spread over three or four physical locations. In addition to their code, which might live in private repositories, each team produces lots of design documents, video demos, project funding proposals, and recordings of video chats, not to mention contracts and Statements of Work in PDF format. For this kind of system to work, you'll need to make it all securely available across an insecure network, but in a way that carefully controls access so only the right people see the right resources.

We're going to set up a Nextcloud server to illustrate how that can be done using some important Linux administrative skills. You'll see Ubuntu's new snapd package manager, learn about expanding the limits of an Apache configuration, understand how applications manage their configuration, and see how data storage can span multiple devices.

8.1 Enterprise file sharing and Nextcloud

Nextcloud is an open source software suite that can use storage capacity for saving, editing, and consuming a wide range of document types, including services like audio/video call hosting. Nextcloud also provides client applications that allow users on Linux, Windows, MacOS, and smartphone platforms to engage with media resources.

Using Nextcloud, you can create your own private version of Dropbox or Google Drive, but on your terms and without having to worry about unexpected changes to availability or service/privacy agreements.

> **NOTE** Nextcloud is a fork of the older ownCloud project. While both are still alive, Nextcloud seems to have a more robust team of active developers and a richer feature set.

Great. Nextcloud has some real benefits. But going it alone means you're on the hook for the costs and complexity of data hosting, replication, and backups. Is Nextcloud worth all the trouble and expense when you can get lots of storage at little or no cost from the Dropboxes and Google Drives of the world?

Good news—you can have it both ways. For particularly sensitive data, you can keep the whole thing in-house. But, as you'll soon see, you can also build a Nextcloud server as your frontend to finely control how users interface with your media, and have the data itself automatically and securely saved to cheaper, reliable third-party services, including Dropbox, Google Drive, and Amazon's S3. If, down the line, you find you need to migrate your data away from say, Dropbox, you can do it without your users ever noticing the change.

But is all that Linux-y enough to justify giving it a full chapter in this book? I think it is. Sure, Nextcloud is a third-party technology that only sits on top of the Linux stack, but it's nevertheless closely interwoven with the Linux OS. More to the point: moving through the deployment process will introduce you to those Linux administration skills listed earlier.

8.2 *Installing Nextcloud using snaps*

At this point in the book, I'll bet you're already a bit frustrated with the conflicts between the package managers used by Linux distributions. As I've mentioned, it's not APT versus Yum; there are also managers used by individual distros like Arch Linux and SUSE.

Wouldn't it be nice if a single set of Linux applications could be uniformly installed and managed across the whole range of distributions using a single tool? While we're at it, why can't people all just get along without having to engage in such costly wars? And how about all those rainy days we've been having: you call that summer?

I have the solution to at least one of those problems: Ubuntu's snaps. I should mention that none of the projects in this book rely on snaps, so if the topic doesn't interest you, there's nothing preventing you from skipping this section and joining up with us once again at section 8.3 in a couple of pages. No hard feelings.

Now where was I? Oh, yes. *Snaps* are software packages that are, by design, entirely self-contained. All you need is a Linux distro that's snap-compliant and the name of a package. (As of this writing, most distros including CentOS and OpenSUSE are either already there or getting close.) If you run this command from a Linux terminal

```
# snap install blender
```

it automatically installs the full Blender 3D creation suite, along with all the environment dependencies and extensions it'll need. Updates and patches will also be handled for you behind the scenes.

Blender is only an example. Being a heavily graphic program, it'll only make sense to install that snap on a Linux desktop version; you won't get good mileage on a server.

Snap is still a work in progress. Because there are plenty of applications that don't have a snap version yet, APT and its friends won't be going anywhere in the immediate future. But the technology has significant advantages, and there's a growing crowd of major industry players joining. You can only gain by introducing yourself.

> **NOTE** Ubuntu *Core* is a special lightweight distribution primarily built to work with Internet of Things (IoT) devices like smart appliances and connected cars, and with swarms of Docker-powered containers. By design, Core uses only snaps for its package management.

The snap system is more than a package manager. As you can see in figure 8.1, snaps are themselves isolated sandboxes with limited access to other system resources.

As this figure shows, communication with other snaps is achieved through a system of interfaces that connect only where appropriate. Snaps are given access to special

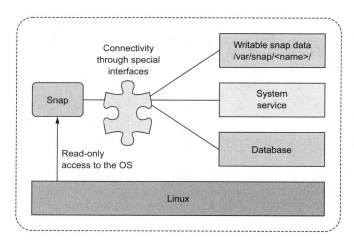

Figure 8.1   Snap architecture: notice how exchanging data between snaps and system resources is carefully controlled to maintain security isolation.

locations in the file system (within /var/snap/<snapname>/) where they can write their data. In case snap isn't yet installed on your machine, you'll want the snapd package:

```
# apt install snapd
```

> The snapd package may not yet be available for CentOS 7, but the dnf install snapd command will work on Fedora 25.

Application developers have already built hundreds of snaps, which are managed through a number of sources including the Ubuntu Store (https://snapcraft.io). You can search for available snaps from the command line using snap find and a keyword describing what you're looking for. Here are some of the results from a search of snaps containing the keyword server:

```
$ snap find server
Name                       Version    Developer    Summary
minecraft-server-jdstrand  16.04.10 jdstrand       Minecraft server packaging
                           for Ubuntu Core
thinger-maker-server       1.3.0      thinger       Thinger.io Internet Of
                           Things Server
rocketchat-server          0.57.2     rocketchat    Group chat server for 100s,
                           installed in seconds.
tika-server                1.16       magicaltrout Tika Server for metadata
                           discovery and extraction
kurento-media-server       6.6.1      surjohn       kurento-media-server on
                           snappy
nats-server                0.9.4      nats-io       High-Performance server
                           for NATS
kms-serverproxy-demo       6.6.0      surjohn       kurento service server
                           side proxy demo
lxd-demo-server            git        stgraber      Online software demo
                           sessions using LXD
[...]
```

It turns out that Nextcloud was among the first major application projects to add its package as a snap. Running `snap install nextcloud` on a brand-new, clean Ubuntu 17.04 VirtualBox VM will give you a fully functioning Nextcloud server without having to manually install all the LAMP elements first:

```
# snap install nextcloud
2017-07-25T21:07:41-04:00 INFO cannot auto connect core:core-support-plug
    to core:core-support: (slot auto-connection), existing connection state
    "core:core-support-plug core:core-support" in the
    way
  nextcloud 11.0.3snap7 from 'nextcloud' installed
```

This error message won't affect the installation; logging out and in again before installation will avoid it altogether.

When the snap is installed, use a browser to navigate to your VM's web root (using the VM's IP address that, as you recall, can be retrieved using `ip addr`). Once the page is loaded, you'll be asked to create an admin account, and you're off to the races.

Why Ubuntu 17.04, and why VirtualBox?

It seems that integrating snaps into the LXC environment went a bit more slowly than hoped, and it wasn't yet available for LXC containers previous to Ubuntu 16.10. Since I'm currently running Ubuntu 16.04 on my workstation, launching a VirtualBox VM built on an Ubuntu 17.04 ISO image is the quickest and simplest solution.

This is another illustration of the value of learning to use multiple virtualization technologies: when one fails you, another will probably work.

8.3 Installing Nextcloud manually

If installing the Nextcloud snap is so straightforward, why would you ever want to do it the old-fashioned, manual way? Here are a couple of reasons. One is that snaps can be a bit too simple and don't allow for a lot of flexibility in design and configuration. Another is that, as I write this, at least, you won't be able to add and fully administer applications using the snap version. You'll soon see how valuable that can be. And hand-crafting your application installations means learning more about the inner workings of your Linux system and about identifying and overcoming problems. What's not to love about that?

8.3.1 Hardware prerequisites

It's always a good idea to check an application's documentation to make sure that you've got enough hardware and software muscle to handle the load. Figure 8.2 shows Nextcloud's System Requirements web page. If you're planning to host a simple, lightly used server providing for a few dozen users, then you'll find Nextcloud is fairly easy to get along with, demanding nothing that can't be handled by an off-the-shelf container.

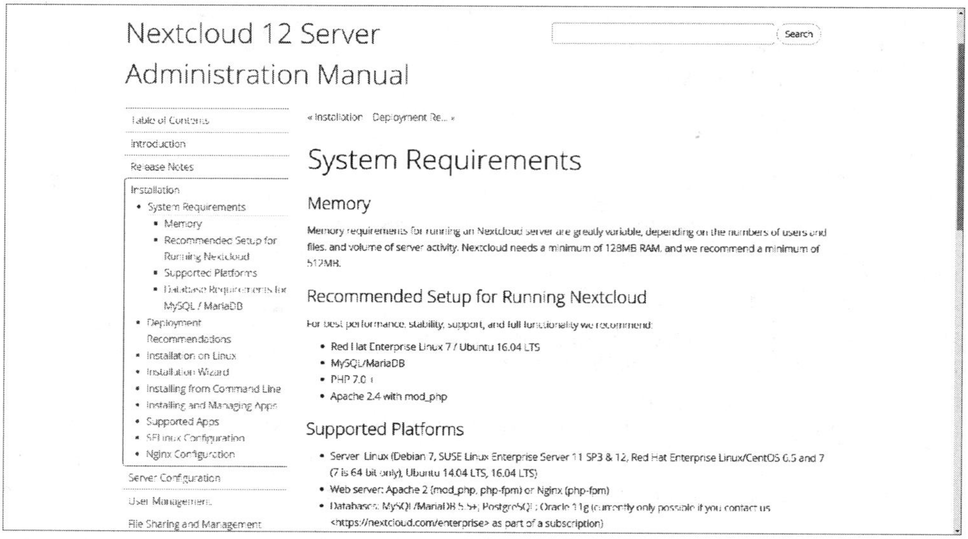

Figure 8.2   Hardware and software requirements for both recommended and minimal Nextcloud installations

Any old minimal hardware configuration will work fine for our technology testing, but I wouldn't want to rely on a single LXC container running an old PC to serve tens of thousands of users and terabytes of data.

Planning an enterprise-scale deployment? Nextcloud provides a useful, multilevel Deployment Recommendations guide to provisioning full-strength platforms (http://mng.bz/8ZAO). Here, for instance, is what Nextcloud recommends for a smaller workgroup with up to 150 users accessing up to 10 TB of data:

- One server with two CPU cores
- 16 GB of RAM
- Authentication through Lightweight Directory Access Protocol (LDAP, a widely used distributed information protocol)
- Red Hat Enterprise Linux or Ubuntu 16.04 with vendor support
- Apache with a TLS/SSL encryption certificate
- The MySQL or MariaDB database
- The Btrfs file system mounted with `nodatacow` for Nextcloud data partitions to permit *zero* downtime backups
- Caching with memcache to speed up access performance

NOTE   *Btrfs* is a file-system type that, although less widespread than ext4 (mentioned briefly in chapter 1), was designed to provide exceptional performance and data reliability at large scale. But, as of release 7.4 (August 2017), Red Hat Enterprise Linux has deprecated its support for Btrfs.

8.3.2   *Building a LAMP server*

The next step should be simple enough by this point. I'd recommend firing up a brand-new container or VM rather than using the one left over from your MediaWiki project, if for no other reason than that it'll be good practice. Here are all the packages you'll need for your server in a single command. I threw in wget and nano in case they're not already installed:

```
# apt install apache2 mariadb-server libapache2-mod-php7.0 \
  php7.0-gd php7.0-json php7.0-mysql php7.0-curl php7.0-mbstring \
  php7.0-intl php7.0-mcrypt php-imagick php7.0-xml php7.0-zip \
  wget nano
```

To keep the base image as small as possible, packages like nano often aren't installed by default on new LXC containers.

If you're not picky about using MySQL rather than MariaDB, and you're on an Ubuntu server, then you could just as easily spare yourself a lot of typing and go with the LAMP server metapackage I mentioned in the previous chapter. Again, don't forget the caret (^) at the end of the package name:

```
# apt install lamp-server^
```

Once installed, remember to run the MySQL secure installation tool:

```
# mysql_secure_installation
```

If you chose the MariaDB route and found yourself having to use sudo with that command, here's the quick fix I showed you in chapter 7:

```
MariaDB [(none)]> SET PASSWORD = PASSWORD('your-password');
MariaDB [(none)]> update mysql.user set plugin = 'mysql_native_password'
   where User='root';
MariaDB [(none)]> FLUSH PRIVILEGES;
```

With your LAMP software installed and a database up and running, you're now ready to tell Apache how you want it to work with your application.

8.3.3   *Configuring Apache*

To ensure that Apache will be able to communicate with Nextcloud, there are a few relatively simple adjustments you're going to have to make. First, you should enable a couple of Apache modules through the a2enmod tool. The *rewrite* module is used to rewrite URLs in real time as they're moved between a client and the server. The *headers* module performs a similar function for HTTP headers.

```
# a2enmod rewrite
# a2enmod headers
```

If you're not planning to use this server for any other purpose, putting the Nextcloud application files in the Apache document root would work. Because the value of the DocumentRoot entry in the 000-default.conf file in your /etc/apache2/sites-available/ directory already points to /var/www/html/, there's nothing left to do. But placing Nextcloud's data files in the default document root presents a potential security risk. You'll probably want Nextcloud in some other part of your file system.

There are two ways to tell Apache how to find site files that aren't in the document root. The Ubuntu method involves adding a new section to your existing 000-default.conf file that contains all the necessary information. Most people seem to prefer creating a new .conf file in the /etc/apache2/sites-available/ directory for each new service. Both work fine, but here's what the separate file should look like, assuming you placed the application in /var/www/ rather than the document root.

> **Listing 8.1   Contents of a /etc/apache2/sites-available/nextcloud.conf file**

```
Alias /nextcloud "/var/www/nextcloud/"        ◁──┐  Associates the contents of the
                                                  │  /var/www/nextcloud/ directory
<Directory /var/www/nextcloud/>                   │  with the Nextcloud host (or site)
  Options +FollowSymlinks
  AllowOverride All

 <IfModule mod_dav.c>
  Dav off
 </IfModule>

 SetEnv HOME /var/www/nextcloud           ◁──┐  Assigns environment variables
 SetEnv HTTP_HOME /var/www/nextcloud          │  that define how the Nextcloud
                                              │  application works
</Directory>
```

A similar directive using the Ubuntu method would involve adding a section in your 000-default.conf file. It might look something like this.

> **Listing 8.2   Sample Nextcloud directive in the 000-default.conf Apache setup file**

```
<VirtualHost *:443>                           ◁──┐  Note how this example uses
    ServerName bootstrap-it.com                   │  the 443 HTTP secure port.
    DocumentRoot /var/www/nextcloud
    ServerAlias bootstrap-it.com/nextcloud    ◁──┐  Directs traffic targeted at the
</VirtualHost>                                    │  bootstrap-it.com/nextcloud address
                                                  │  to the custom document root
```

As you can see in figure 8.3, when Apache reads this config file, it redirects all incoming traffic addressed to example.com/nextcloud to the application files in /var/www/, assuming that your domain is example.com. As before, an IP address will work just as well.

Finally, you'll need to create a symbolic link in the /etc/apache2/sites-enabled/ directory pointing to the nextcloud.conf file you created in /etc/apache2/sites-available/:

```
# ln -s /etc/apache2/sites-available/nextcloud.conf \
 /etc/apache2/sites-enabled/nextcloud.conf
```

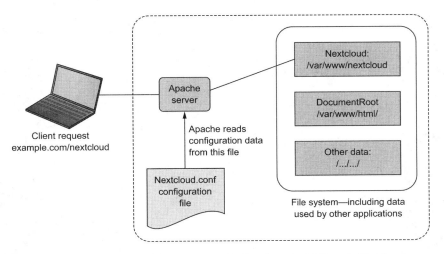

Figure 8.3   Apache reads configuration files in /etc/apache2/sites-enabled/ and uses their settings to redirect requests.

But why? And what's a symbolic link? When Apache starts, it reads the contents of /etc/apache2/sites-enabled/ looking for site configurations to load. Those configurations won't actually exist in /etc/apache2/sites-enabled/, but there'll be symbolic links to the real files in /etc/apache2/sites-available/.

Why not tell Apache to read /etc/apache2/sites-available/ in the first place and cut out the middleman? Because hanging it all on symbolic links makes it easy and convenient to quickly disable a site and then, when you've finished a round of edits, re-enable it once again. Rather than having to delete and rewrite the real file, you'll only need to play with an easy-to-manage link to it.

Symbolic links? They're objects that represent files or directories living elsewhere on a file system. They allow a user to execute or view a resource in one place, even though the resource itself is elsewhere. You'll learn more about symbolic links when you get to chapter 12.

8.3.4   *Downloading and unpacking Nextcloud*

You can download the most recent Nextcloud package from the Nextcloud Install page (https://nextcloud.com/install). If you're installing to a container or VM, or from a server without a desktop GUI installed, then the most convenient approach is to get the package's download URL and grab the package from the command line.

One quick way to get that URL from the Nextcloud site using a regular session on your own PC is to click the Download tab beneath Get Nextcloud Server and then, as you can see in figure 8.4, the Details and Download options button. Right-click the .tar.bz2 link, and select Copy Link Address from the menu.

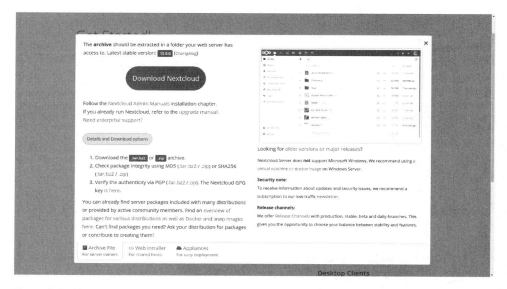

Figure 8.4   Links to Nextcloud download archives: either .tar.bz2 or the .zip format will work.

You can copy the .tar.bz2 URL into a `wget` command either by right-clicking in the terminal and selecting Paste, or by pressing Shift-Ctrl-v. Here's how the command will look:

```
$ wget https://download.nextcloud.com/server/releases/nextcloud-12.0.0.tar.bz2
```

Don't forget to click the MD5 or SHA256 hash links displayed when the Details and Download Options button is clicked. Then confirm that those values are identical to the hashes you generate from the downloaded archive.

You'll notice that the file you downloaded has a .tar.bz2 extension rather than the .tar.gz you saw back in chapter 4. A .gz archive is created using a different compression algorithm than a .bz2 archive. Which one's better? It seems that gzip archives take less time (and resources) to compress, but produce larger archives than BZ2. Therefore, your choice will depend on whether your operation values speed or storage space.

Unpacking a .tar.bz2 archive requires the `xjf` arguments, rather than the `xzf` you'd use for a .gz:

```
$ tar xjf nextcloud-12.0.0.tar.bz2
```
⊲ **The j argument is invoked to decompress a BZ2-compressed archive.**

The next step involves copying the unpacked files and directories to their new home, which, following the best practices I mentioned earlier, will be in /var/www/. That's a location outside the document root.

Adding -r to the copy command will copy the files recursively to include subdirectories and their contents:

```
# cp -r nextcloud /var/www/
```

Two more small steps and you're good to go. Apache will need full access to all the files in the Nextcloud directories in order to do its job. You could have the root user own them, but that means you'd have to give visiting users root powers to access those files. As you might imagine, giving everyone on the internet that kind of access to your files poses a wee bit of a problem.

Many web servers use a special system user called *www-data*. The next command uses chown (that you already met back in chapter 4) to turn the user and group ownership of all those files over to the web server user www-data. Using the uppercase -R will (like the lowercase -r you used with cp) apply the command recursively to all files and directories in the directory hierarchy:

```
# chown -R www-data:www-data /var/www/nextcloud/
```

Apache has no idea of the kinds of stuff we've been up to while it wasn't looking. You'd better let it in on the fun by restarting the service:

```
# systemctl restart apache2
```

If that restart wasn't successful, then make a note of any error messages and see if there's anything you can fix. You can also dig a bit deeper into the logs by displaying the last 10 entries in the Journal using the tail command. There might, for instance, be a reference to a specific line in the nextcloud.conf file:

```
# journalctl | tail
```

But if everything went well, then direct your browser to your container's IP address followed by nextcloud. You'll be taken to a page where you're asked to create a new admin account and provide valid login credentials for your MariaDB database. Unless you've created a different database user account for this purpose, you'll use root and the password you gave it earlier:

```
10.0.3.36/nextcloud
```

NOTE There are both security and logistical advantages to associating database resources with non-root database users. When you have more than one application using the resources of a single database, keeping the applications separate by creating multiple isolated accounts is recommended.

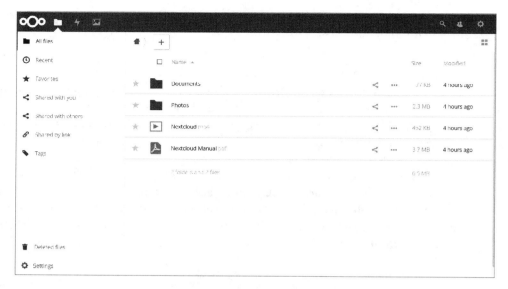

Figure 8.5   The main Nextcloud console, complete with sample folders and files. You can work with objects here as you would using an OS file manager.

Once your information is digested, you'll be shown links to Nextcloud's client apps and then dropped into the administration console you see in figure 8.5. That's where you can upload, view, and share documents and media files.

As the site administrator, you can also create groups and users, assign permissions and quotas, and manage how the site functions. Now, let's look at how to manage Nextcloud.

8.4   *Nextcloud administration*

As a Nextcloud site grows in complexity and as your needs change (for example, perhaps it'll be more efficient to manage growing resources with scripts), you'll sometimes need to work with administration resources at the command-line level. It'll be good to know where things are and what they look like.

Rather than using /etc/ the way many Linux applications do, Nextcloud keeps its main configuration file (named config.php) in the /var/www/nextcloud/config/ directory. The file contains authentication and environment information, along with key database connection details. Here's a quick peek at that file:

```
<?php
$CONFIG = array (
  'instanceid' => 'ociu535bqczx',
  'passwordsalt' => '',
  'secret' => '',
  'trusted_domains' =>
  array (
    0 => '10.0.3.36',
  ),
```

The server's public domain or, in this case, IP address

All encrypted authentication codes have been redacted for security reasons.

```
            'datadirectory' => '/var/www/nextcloud/data',
            'overwrite.cli.url' => 'http://10.0.3.36/nextcloud',
            'dbtype' => 'mysql',
            'version' => '12.0.0.29',
            'dbname' => 'nextcloud',
            'dbhost' => 'localhost',
            'dbport' => '',
            'dbtableprefix' => 'oc_',
            'dbuser' => 'oc_admin',
            'dbpassword' => '',
            'installed' => true,
    );
```

The location of the account and document data on the file system

Like any good Linux application, Nextcloud has a full-featured command-line shell called *occ command*. To use it, you'll need to prepend a surprisingly detailed string to run commands as the www-data user using PHP. Typing sudo -u www-data php occ -h displays basic syntax help, whereas list prints a full list of available commands:

```
$ cd /var/www/nextcloud
$ sudo -u www-data php occ -h
$ sudo -u www-data php occ list
```

For now though, let's ignore those command-line tools and head back to the browser console. As you can see in figure 8.6, clicking the gear icon at upper right presents links to the Users page (where you manage users and groups), the Apps page (with a menu of available apps that can be enabled), and the Admin page (where you manage security settings, services, and applications).

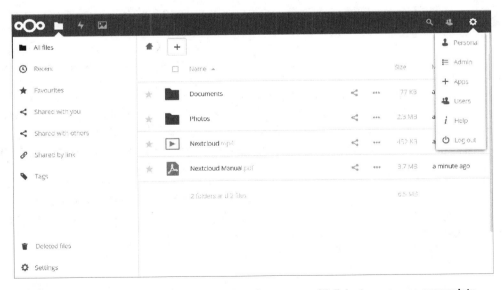

Figure 8.6 Clicking the gear icon displays a drop-down menu with links to resources appropriate to your account privileges.

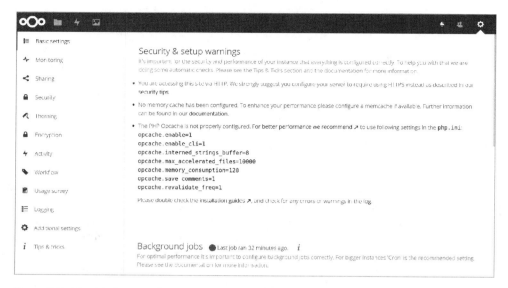

Figure 8.7   The Admin page with links to various admin apps in the left panel, and warnings and status information in the middle

If you click through to the Admin page, you'll probably see some security and setup warnings. As you can see in figure 8.7, the fact that my site isn't configured to use the encrypted HTTPS protocol for data transfers is a matter of concern. Nextcloud definitely has a point on this one, and it's something I plan to address in chapter 9.

HTTPS is all about encrypting data as it moves between a server (like the one running Nextcloud for you right now) and the browser on your visitors' PCs. This is critically important, as you don't want to expose your data in transit to anyone on any network between you and your users. But you should also be concerned about your data when it's at rest.

Encrypting the files on your server will prevent anyone who somehow gains access to your storage drives from mounting them and reading their content. Who might that be? Imagine someone hacking into your network. Or someone walking off with your physical server. If the files are encrypted, they'll provide the thieves with little or no value.

To enable encryption, click the Encryption link on the left panel and then select the Enable Server-side Encryption check box. As figure 8.8 illustrates, you'll be shown a list of some consequences you should consider. When you've read through that, click the Enable Encryption button.

No going back now. Only going forward…

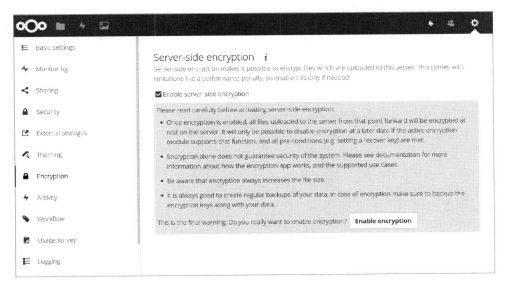

Figure 8.8 Enabling server-side encryption in Nextcloud is a simple, one-click process, but you should be conscious of the consequences.

8.5 *Using AWS S3 as the primary Nextcloud storage*

The thing about storage is that you have to find space to put it all. And, because all storage devices will eventually fail without warning, you'll need multiple copies of each device. Figuring out how to provision, connect, and maintain such storage arrays is time-consuming, and keeping it going is relatively expensive. But there's hope.

Cloud storage is comparatively cheap and, as you can read in my *Learn Amazon Web Services in a Month of Lunches* book (Manning, 2017), simple to set up. Because the big cloud providers invest vast funds in data security and resilience, their services are pretty much guaranteed to be more reliable than anything you could put together. Therefore, using cloud-based data as a backend to your locally hosted Nextcloud site is a serious option to explore. Here's how it works.

You'll first need to enable the External Storage Support app bundle. From the gear icon at top right, click the Apps item, and then the Disabled Apps link in the left panel. As figure 8.9 shows, the External Storage Support option appears in the list. Click Enable.

From the command line on any computer with the AWS CLI installed and configured for your AWS account (the way you did it back in chapter 5), create a new bucket with a globally unique name:

```
$ aws s3 mb s3://nextcloud32327
```

Again, as you did back in chapter 5, retrieve a set of account access keys from the Your Security Credentials page in the AWS console. You can also use an existing set of keys if you've got one available.

Figure 8.9   The list of currently available apps, including External Storage Support

Now head back to your Nextcloud console, click Admin from the gear drop-down, and then click the External Storage link, which should be visible in the left panel. This opens the External Storage page, where you can click the Add Storage drop-down and select Amazon S3 from the list. (The list also includes Dropbox and Google Drive.)

You'll be prompted to enter the S3 bucket you want to use along with your access and secret keys. All other fields, which allow you to customize your configuration using things like nonstandard ports or SSL encryption, are optional. When you're done, clicking the check mark to the right saves your settings and sets Nextcloud off trying to authenticate with AWS.

If you're successful, you'll see a happy green circle to the left, as is visible in figure 8.10. If it doesn't work, the most likely cause is that you somehow used invalid authentication keys. It can't hurt to confirm network connectivity to the internet and, in particular, AWS.

You can test your new storage configuration by copying and pasting a file from your computer into the folder in your Nextcloud console. Then, from your AWS CLI, list the contents of your bucket:

```
$ aws s3 ls s3://nextcloud32327
testfile.pdf
```

Of course, you'll need to test it the other way too. Copy a local file to the bucket from your command line:

```
$ aws s3 cp test.txt s3://nextcloud32327
```

The test.txt file should appear in your console. Glorious multi-platform storage integration.

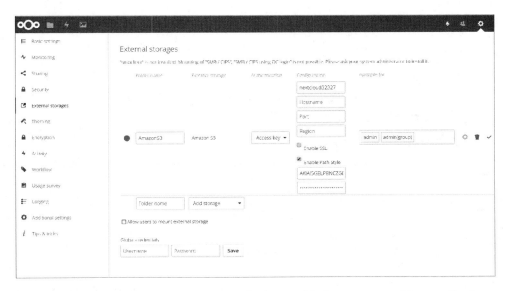

Figure 8.10 **The External Storages setup page for Amazon S3 shows a successful connection to my S3 bucket.**

Summary

- Planning your data storage strategy requires balancing between cost and ease of use on one side versus security and control on the other.
- Ubuntu's snaps are a distribution-neutral package management system that also provide secure, read-only isolation run environments.
- In order to know how to route incoming HTTP traffic, Apache reads either multiple host definitions in a single .conf file or multiple host-definition files.
- Web servers generally provide resources to visitors using a special web server user account to balance access against system security.
- Nextcloud keeps its configuration files in the /<DocumentRoot>/nextcloud/config directory and, in particular, in the config.php file.
- Authenticating Nextcloud to an AWS S3 bucket is a matter of providing the bucket name and the access keys.

Key terms

- A *snap* is a packaged application that can, using snapd, be autonomously installed on most modern Linux distributions.
- A *symbolic link* is a file system object representing a file or directory in a different location. Symbolic links in the /etc/apache2/sites-enabled/ directory point to files in /etc/apache2/sites-available/ that are read by Apache when it starts.
- *Archives* can be compressed using the BZ2 algorithm as an alternative to gzip or zip.

Security best practices

- Avoid keeping Nextcloud data files in the document root.
- Make sure that all public-facing files from your website are owned by the www-data user rather than the root user.
- Keep database resources used by separate applications isolated by creating separate user accounts.

Command-line review

- `a2enmod rewrite` enables the rewrite module so Apache can edit URLs as they move between a client and server.
- `nano /etc/apache2/sites-available/nextcloud.conf` creates or edits an Apache host-configuration file for Nextcloud.
- `chown -R www-data:www-data /var/www/nextcloud/` changes the user and group ownership of all website files to the www-data user.
- `sudo -u www-data php occ list` uses the Nextcloud CLI to list available commands.
- `aws s3 ls s3://nextcloud32327` lists the contents of an S3 bucket.

Test yourself

1 A snap is which of the following?
   a An Internet of Things driver for managing devices
   b An isolated environment for securely running applications
   c An Ubuntu-centric package manager
   d An application packaged for use as a self-contained resource
2 Which of the following commands will list all packages currently installed on the system?
   a `snap list`
   b `snap find`
   c `snap ls`
   d `snapd ls`
3 Which of the following is a rationale for not installing the Nextcloud files to the document root?
   a Files in the document root are, by default, exposed to the public.
   b If there are other hosts being served by Apache, it would cause conflicts.
   c The Nextcloud configuration will only recognize files in /var/www/nextcloud/ directory.
   d Files in the document root can't be given ownership and group attributes that are compatible with Nextcloud.

4 Which of the following will create a symbolic link to the nextcloud.conf file that will be read by Apache?

   a `ln -s /etc/apache2/sites-enabled/nextcloud.conf /etc/apache2/sites-available/nextcloud.conf`

   b `ln -s /etc/apache2/sites-available/nextcloud.conf /etc/apache2/sites-enabled/nextcloud.conf`

   c `ln /etc/apache2/sites-enabled/nextcloud.conf /etc/apache2/sites-available/nextcloud.conf`

   d `ln -h /etc/apache2/sites-enabled/nextcloud.conf /etc/apache2/sites-available/nextcloud.conf`

5 Which of the following commands will unpack the nextcloud-12.0.0.tar.bz2 archive?

   a `tar xcf nextcloud-12.0.0.tar.bz2`

   b `tar xzf nextcloud-12.0.0.tar.bz2`

   c `tar jf nextcloud-12.0.0.tar.bz2`

   d `tar xjf nextcloud-12.0.0.tar.bz2`

Answer key

1. d, 2. a, 3. a, 4. b, 5. d

Securing your web server

This chapter covers

- Securing your infrastructure
- Controlling access to your server using firewalls
- Using encryption to protect your data
- Tightening the authentication process
- Controlling software and processes

The *web* part of *web server* is a bit misleading. After all, most of the security tools I'm going to discuss in this chapter are important no matter what kind of server you're running. In fact, *server* is also kind of redundant, as all computers need securing. Still, because by definition they're exposed to significant external traffic, the security of your web servers should be a particularly high priority. So the best way to test the things you're going to learn about in this chapter is to have an Apache web server running. Consider putting one together right now: `apt install apache2`.

In an IT context, *security* is the protection of hardware, software, data, and digital services from unauthorized access and corruption. Given that networked computer resources are designed to be exposed to client users of one sort or another, ensuring that only the right clients are able to perform only the right operations is a challenge.

You can think of security as the fine art of balancing value against risk. When you consider how many kinds of security threats already exist, and how frequently new ones appear, you'll probably understand that the balance will never be perfect. It will most certainly need to be reassessed often.

There's no single tool or practice that can cover every aspect of security. Although it's not a bad idea to build yourself a checklist of key security to-dos, that's not enough. The most successful administrators I've known were all deeply skilled and knowledgeable, and they also seemed to share a particular attitude: no software, vendor, government agency, co-worker, or even close friend can ever be completely trusted. They may mean you no harm, but it's too easy to make a mistake and leave an important window open to attack. Everything and everyone can use a second pair of eyes and some double checking.

What can you do to secure your servers? It's really about the small things. Lots and lots of small things. So many, in fact, that a couple of them are going to spill over into the next chapter. In this chapter, however, we'll begin with some basics before diving into using firewalls to control network access, protecting website data transfers with SSL/TLS encryption, and limiting what can be done with server resources through the strategic use of tools like Security-Enhanced Linux (SELinux) and system groups.

9.1 The obvious stuff

Let's start by picking some low-hanging fruit. A lot of security is common sense, considering the many security best practices you've seen so far in this book. But, simple as it may be, you can't afford to ignore these basics:

- Back up your data. Today.

  No matter what the bad guys do to your server, if you can rebuild it from a reliable backup, then you're still in the game. Take another look at chapters 4 and 5 and then script yourself a regular, automated, comprehensive, and verifiable backup regimen that covers everything of any value that you've got. Make sure that there's more than one archival version available at all times and that at least one archive is stored off site.

- Apply all software updates to your system. No excuse.

  Oh, there are always excuses: you're afraid that updates might break something your application depends on or it might require a reboot that could end up being disruptive. But do it anyway. Don't get me wrong. I understand that those are real concerns. It's that the alternatives are worse. Here's your friendly reminder for updating your system:

```
# yum update
```

Or (on Ubuntu):

```
# apt update
# apt upgrade
```

NOTE Don't forget that package managers only update packages that were installed through managed repositories. Any applications you added manually will remain *unpatched* (and potentially unsafe) until you either manually apply patches or disable them.

You could avoid most of the risk of disruption by building test (or *staging*) environments (figure 9.1) that run mirror images of your applications that are safely protected from public networks. Applying updates and patches to your staging infrastructure should give you an excellent idea of how it'll work in the real world.

Even better, you could use the infrastructure as the code configuration management software you'll see in chapter 16 to automate your whole deployment process. That way, once you confirm that the staging environment you patched is running properly, it can become your production infrastructure. But that's a discussion we'll leave until later.

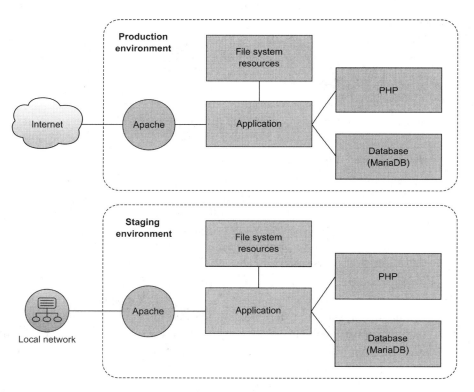

Figure 9.1   You can replicate server infrastructure in a protected staging environment to safely perform maintenance.

9.2 Controlling network access

Think of your server's connection to the network and the big, bad internet beyond as your first line of defense. Networking protocols are designed to be flexible to help you closely control what traffic makes it through. The trick is understanding how the protocols work, and then properly using that knowledge to set things up right.

9.2.1 Configuring a firewall

A *firewall* is a set of rules. When a data packet moves into or out of a protected network space, its contents (in particular, information about its origin, its target, and the protocol it plans to use) are tested against the firewall rules to see if it should be allowed through. Here's a simple example as illustrated in figure 9.2.

Let's say that your company's web server has to be open to incoming web traffic from anywhere on earth using either the insecure HTTP or secure HTTPS protocol. Because your developers and admins will need to get into the backend from time to time to do their work, you'll also want to allow SSH traffic, but only for those people who'll need it. Requests for any other services should be automatically refused. Let's see how that's done.

A Linux machine can be configured to apply firewall rules at the kernel level through a program called *iptables*. Creating iptables rules isn't all that difficult; the syntax can be learned without too much fuss. But, in the interest of simplifying your life, many Linux distributions have added their own higher-level tools for abstracting the job. In this section, you're going to see CentOS's firewalld and Ubuntu's UncomplicatedFirewall (ufw).

Firewall functionality is also available through hardware appliances manufactured by companies like Juniper and Cisco. Those proprietary devices run on their own operating systems with unique syntax and design. For larger enterprise deployments involving hundreds of servers spread across multiple networks, such tools will often

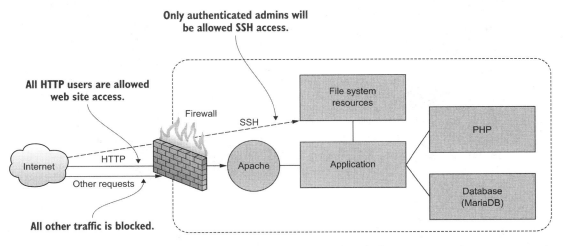

Figure 9.2 A firewall can filter requests based on protocol or target-based rules.

make a lot of sense, but there's a remarkable amount that you can accomplish with any old Linux box for a tiny fraction of the cost. Having said that, this section will introduce you to only a small subset of the full functionality of Linux firewalls. Naturally, if you want to learn more, stick around for a bit more depth in chapter 10 and consult the usual sources of Linux wisdom, like man files and online guides.

FIREWALLD

As you might have guessed from its name, firewalld is part of the systemd family. firewalld can be installed on Debian/Ubuntu machines, but it's there by default on Red Hat and CentOS. If you're just too excited by firewalld to even consider trying anything else, here's how to install it and get it running on Ubuntu:

```
# apt update
# apt install firewalld
```

To confirm that the firewall is working, try browsing to your server's web root. If the site is unreachable, then firewalld is doing its job.

You'll use the `firewall-cmd` tool to manage firewalld settings from the command line. Adding the `--state` argument returns the current firewall status:

```
# firewall-cmd --state
running
```

> ### A few important terms
>
> To be sure no one's left out, let's define a few important terms. The *Hypertext Transfer Protocol* (HTTP) coordinates the exchange of resources between web clients and web servers over a network. A browser might, for instance, request a web page written in the *Hypertext Markup Language* (HTML), to which the server can respond by transferring the page contents. *Metadata* (contextual information attached to a packet) containing information about session status is generated by each data transfer event and consumed later by admins trying to figure out what went wrong. The HTTPS variation of the protocol ensures that data transfers are securely encrypted using the *Transport Layer Security* (TLS) protocol.
>
> A *packet* is a small unit of data that might have been carved out of a larger data file or archive. After transmission, packets can be reassembled into their original form. When the *Transmission Control Protocol* (TCP) is used for a network data transfer, packets being transferred across a network are checked for errors when received and, if necessary, resent. Transfers using the *User Datagram Protocol* (UDP) will complete more quickly than TCP but, because they don't include error correction, they're only appropriate for operations that are highly tolerant of error.

By default, firewalld will be active and will reject all incoming traffic with a couple of exceptions, like SSH. That means your website won't be getting too many visitors, which will certainly save you a lot on data transfer costs. As that's probably not what you had in mind for your web server, you'll want to open the HTTP and HTTPS ports that, by convention, are designated as 80 and 443, respectively. firewalld offers two ways to do that. One is through the `--add-port` argument that references the port number directly along with the network protocol it'll use (TCP in this case). The `--permanent` argument tells firewalld to load this rule each time the server boots:

```
# firewall-cmd --permanent --add-port=80/tcp
# firewall-cmd --permanent --add-port=443/tcp
```

The `--reload` argument will apply those rules to the current session:

```
# firewall-cmd --reload
```

That approach will work for any complicated or customized configuration you can come up with. But if you've got simpler needs, you can use one of firewalld's pre-defined values for many of the more commonly used services. Those values are drawn from the data kept in the /etc/services file.

The `--add-service` argument, when it refers to your HTTP and HTTPS services, would open ports 80 and 443. This may not seem like a big deal in this case, but when push comes to shove and time is short, are you sure you'll remember that the default MySQL port happens to be 3306? Wouldn't it be easier to just type `mysql`?

```
# firewall-cmd --permanent --add-service=http
# firewall-cmd --permanent --add-service=https
```

Curious as to the current settings on your firewall? Run `--list-services`:

```
# firewall-cmd --list-services
dhcpv6-client http https ssh
```

Assuming you've added browser access as described earlier, the HTTP, HTTPS, and SSH ports are all open, along with `dhcpv6-client`, which allows Linux to request an IPv6 IP address from a local DHCP server. You'll learn more about that in chapter 14.

You certainly don't want just anyone getting SSH access to your server, so let's put firewalld to work securing it. You'll restrict SSH access so that only sessions originating from a particular IP address will be allowed. To do that, I'm going to show you how to cut off all SSH access and then open it for only a single IP.

> **NOTE** I should warn you that playing around with firewalls while logged in to an SSH session is a bit dangerous. You could end up locked out of your own server. If this happens, there are some tricks (coming later in this chapter) for getting back in. In any case, if you're using a disposable LXC container or VM, you shouldn't have all that much to worry about one way or the other: if something breaks, destroy it and fire up a clean one.

To shut down the existing SSH access, use `--remove-service` and then reload firewalld (`--remove-port` will work the same way if you're referring to the port number):

```
# firewall-cmd --permanent --remove-service=ssh
success
# firewall-cmd --reload
```

Test your new configuration to make sure it worked. Open a new terminal on any other machine with network access, and try to log in to your server using SSH. Your attempt should fail:

> **Allowing root login via SSH is not a good idea and can be forbidden in the /etc/ssh/sshd.conf file through the PermitRootLogin setting with a value of no.**

```
$ ssh root@192.168.1.22          ⊲
ssh: connect to host 192.168.1.22 port 22: No route to host
```

Now, back on your firewalld machine, add a new rule that will accept TCP traffic on port 22 (the default SSH port), but only from clients using the IP address 192.168.1.5 (or whatever the IP address of your client machine is). The --add-rich-rule argument tells firewall-cmd that this command uses the *Rich Language* set, a high-level syntax designed to simplify the creation of complex firewall rules (see http://mng.bz/872B for more details):

```
# firewall-cmd --add-rich-rule='rule family="ipv4" \
 source address="192.168.1.5" port protocol="tcp" port="22" accept'
success
```

Now try logging in once again from a terminal originating in the specified IP address. It should work. Because you didn't make this rule permanent, everything should go back to normal the next time you boot.

UNCOMPLICATEDFIREWALL (UFW)

Let's see how you can similarly control SSH access on an Ubuntu machine using ufw. The ufw program might not come installed on new Ubuntu installations and, in any case, will be disabled by default, so you'll want to get it running:

```
# apt install ufw
```

Because ufw starts with all ports closed, enabling it prevents you from opening a new SSH session. Any existing sessions shouldn't be affected but, still, it's probably a good idea to add a rule allowing SSH even before enabling ufw:

> **Use the ufw deny ssh command to disable SSH.**

> **Starts the firewall. When necessary, use the ufw disable command to shut down ufw.**

```
# ufw allow ssh          ⊲
Rules updated
# ufw enable          ⊲
Command may disrupt existing ssh connections.
Proceed with operation (y|n)?          ⊲
```

> **A warning that existing or new remote connections might be affected by this action**

If you're running ufw on an LXC container, those commands probably didn't work. Instead, this rather frightening error message was probably displayed:

```
ERROR: initcaps
[Errno 2] modprobe: ERROR: ../libkmod/libkmod.c:586 kmod_search_moddep()
 could not open moddep file '/lib/modules/4.4.0-87-generic/modules.dep.bin'
modprobe: FATAL: Module ip6_tables not found in directory
  /lib/modules/4.4.0-87-generic
ip6tables v1.6.0: can't initialize ip6tables table `filter':
  Table does not exist (do you need to insmod?)
Perhaps ip6tables or your kernel needs to be upgraded.
```

With IPv6 support disabled on the host system, you may encounter this error message.

This is related to the fact that LXC containers might not have IPv6 support enabled by default. Fixing that might be complicated, given that containers lack full access to their host's kernel. If you're not planning to include IPv6 in your network configuration (which, in any case, fits the vast majority of use cases), then it'll be simplest to disable IPv6 support in your /etc/default/ufw configuration file by editing the IPV6=yes line to read IPV6=no.

> **Listing 9.1 Part of the /etc/default/ufw configuration file**

Change the value of IPV6 from yes to no to disable IPv6 support and avoid the ufw error.

```
# /etc/default/ufw
#

# Set to yes to apply rules to support IPv6 (no means only IPv6 on loopback
# accepted). You will need to 'disable' and then 'enable' the firewall for
# the changes to take affect.
IPV6=no

# Set the default input policy to ACCEPT, DROP, or REJECT. Please note that
# if you change this you'll most likely want to adjust your rules.
DEFAULT_INPUT_POLICY="DROP"

# Set the default output policy to ACCEPT, DROP, or REJECT. Please note that
# if you change this you'll most likely want to adjust your rules.
DEFAULT_OUTPUT_POLICY="ACCEPT"
[...]
```

Enabling ufw, adding a rule for SSH, and running `ufw enable` should now work:

```
# ufw enable
Command may disrupt existing ssh connections.
Proceed with operation (y|n)? y
Firewall is active and enabled on system startup
# ufw allow ssh
Rules updated
```

Like firewalld, ufw lets you create rules using either port numbers or service names (like the `ufw allow ssh` you just used). The following two commands will open HTTP and HTTPS access for your web server:

```
# ufw allow 80
# ufw allow 443
```

The `ufw status` command shows you that the service is running and that the three rules you need are now active. Go ahead and test this against your web server:

```
# ufw status
Status: active
To                         Action      From
--                         ------      ----
80                         ALLOW       Anywhere
22                         ALLOW       Anywhere
443                        ALLOW       Anywhere
```

> **NOTE** To properly test web server access through a firewall, don't forget that your browser caches page data. This means that the browser might be able to load a page it's previously visited even though there's now a firewall rule that's supposed to make that impossible. To make sure you're testing the current state of your website, flush the browser cache or refresh your browser page.

One more piece of fine-tuning will limit SSH access to your team members sitting behind a specific IP address. If it's safe (meaning your web server isn't exposed to internet traffic right now), it's a good idea to disable ufw before making these changes. Then remove your allow-SSH rule using `delete 2` (which refers to the rule as the second in the ufw list) and reopen it only for traffic coming from 10.0.3.1. (In my case, because I was logging in to the LXC container from my LXC host, that happens to be the IP I'll use; your mileage may vary.) Finally, restart ufw and check its new state:

```
# ufw disable
Firewall stopped and disabled on system startup
#
# ufw delete 2                          ◁───┐  Deletes the second firewall
Rules updated                               │  rule displayed by ufw status
#
# ufw allow from 10.0.3.1 to any port 22    ◁───┐  Permits SSH traffic
Rules updated                                    │  from only the specified
#                                                │  IP and nowhere else
# ufw enable
Command may disrupt existing ssh connections.
Proceed with operation (y|n)? y
Firewall is active and enabled on system startup
#
# ufw status
Status: active
```

```
To                      Action      From
--                      ------      ----
80                      ALLOW       Anywhere
443                     ALLOW       Anywhere
22                      ALLOW       10.0.3.1     ◁─┐   A new rule permitting SSH traffic
                                                      only from the specified IP
```

You can test your configuration by logging in from both the machine using the permitted IP and from any other machine. The first one should work, but the second one had better not!

With that, you've now seen how to use both firewalld and ufw to securely configure access to a simple web server. Even though firewalls can control traffic using any protocol or port, we've only covered HTTP, HTTPS, and SSH. It's worth also mentioning that, as you'll see a bit later in this chapter, you can use nonstandard network ports for your applications.

RECOVERING A LOCKED VM

If you do manage to lock yourself out of an LXC container, you can use `chroot` (as you did back in chapter 6) to disable or even reconfigure your firewall. First of all, stop the container and then run `chroot` against the rootfs directory that's within the directory hierarchy used by your LXC container (/var/lib/lxc/your-container-name/). The command prompt you'll get lets you execute commands as if the container was actually running. Now disable ufw or, if you prefer, run the necessary commands to fix the problem and then exit the `chroot` shell. When you start the container up again, you should have SSH access:

```
                                                Stops a running
                                                LXC container
# lxc-stop -n your-container-name       ◁─┐
# chroot /var/lib/lxc/your-container-name/rootfs/     ◁─┐   Mounts your container's
# ufw disable                                              file system as chroot
# exit
# lxc-start -d -n your-container-name
```

Closes the chroot shell session

What if it's a VirtualBox VM that's locked you out? That's an easy one: log in through the original terminal that opened when you launched the VM in the first place. That's the equivalent of sitting at a keyboard that's plugged into a physical server and won't require any network connectivity for access.

9.2.2 Using nonstandard ports

One advantage of being able to set network ports by number is that it lets you configure applications to use nonstandard ports. You could, for instance, set port 53987 for SSH rather than 22. The advantage of nonstandard ports it that they let you implement *security through obscurity*.

Let me explain. In and of itself, port 53987 isn't any more secure than port 22: exploiting it is simply a matter of updating the SSH client with the new setting. But it can, nevertheless, add a layer of protection.

Imagine there's a hacker poking away at your infrastructure, trying to find a way in. Perhaps that person has discovered that one of your admins has a bad habit of reusing the same password for multiple accounts—and one of those accounts has already been compromised. The hacker has quite a lot of valuable information from that breach: your server's IP address (it's often the same as the one used by your website) and your admin's user name and password. Assuming you permit password login to your SSH accounts (which, as you know from chapter 3, is not a good idea), there's nothing stopping the hacker from logging in and injecting some mayhem into your life. Except no one told the hacker that port 22 is shut tight and SSH access is only available through some obscure high-range port (like 53987). Because you reset the default port, you've made it a little bit harder to break through your defenses, and that little bit might one day make a big difference.

How does it work? First, you'll need to edit the /etc/ssh/sshd_conf configuration file on your server (the computer that will host your SSH sessions). The file will contain a line that, by default, reads `Port 22`. You'll want to edit that to use whichever port you plan to use.

> **Listing 9.2 Port setting line from the ssh_d.conf file on an SSH host**

```
# What ports, IPs, and protocols we listen for
Port 22                    ◁────┐
                                 │  Change this value to the port
                                 │  number you want to use.
```

When you're done, and you're sure you'll be able to get back into your server should your current SSH session go down, restart the SSH service. If you've got a firewall going, you'll need to tell it to allow access on your new port…that's coming soon:

```
# systemctl restart ssh
```

Now, when you want to log in from a remote machine, add -p followed by the new port number. Your SSH client will then be able to request a session over the new port:

```
$ ssh -p53987 username@remote_IP_or_domain
```

If you're logging in using a different SSH client (like PuTTY), you'll need to similarly tell the client about the nonstandard port number. Let's look at that next.

CONFIGURING A UFW FIREWALL TO ALLOW TRAFFIC THROUGH A NONSTANDARD PORT

Opening up a port by number is fairly straightforward, but you'll need to explicitly specify the protocol you'll be using (TCP or UDP). This example uses the TCP protocol:

```
# ufw allow 53987/tcp
```

You can also open a range of ports with a single command using the colon (:) character. This can be useful for infrastructure planning when, say, you know your developers will be pushing out new applications and will need access to multiple ports. Giving them a range to play with now can save time and frustration later. This particular example opens all the ports between 52900 and 53000:

```
# ufw allow 52900:53000/tcp
```

> **Network ports**
>
> The 65,535 available network ports are divided into three categories:
>
> - Ports between 1 and 1023 are designated as well-known and have been set aside for recognized services like SSH (22) and HTTP (80). You should never use a well-known port number for your own applications, as you're likely to cause a conflict.
> - Ports between 1024 and 49151 are *registered*, meaning companies and organizations have requested that specific ports in this range be set aside for their applications even if they haven't become universally adopted. Examples of this are port 1812, which is used for the RADIUS authentication protocol, and 3306, MySQL's dedicated port.
> - Ports between 49152 and 65535 are *unregistered* and are considered dynamic (or private). These ports are available for any temporary or ad hoc use, particularly on private networks. You can be confident that they won't clash with known applications or services.

CHOOSING A NONSTANDARD PORT NUMBER

What port number should you choose? Well let's first of all get one thing clear: you should never let outsiders (like me) influence such decisions! But, to avoid possible conflicts with active network applications, you'll want to stick to values in the unregistered range between 49152 and 65535. That should give you enough to work with.

Working with nonstandard ports is, of course, not only for SSH. You should consider using this trick for any application that you've either written yourself or can control through configuration files. And remember: like most of the tools in this chapter, this won't be all that effective on its own, but it's a powerful element when used as part of a larger set of security protocols.

9.3 Encrypting data in transit

For two reasons, website encryption is a really big deal:

- Unencrypted sites dangerously expose their data and place their users at significant risk.
- Unencrypted sites generate significantly less business.

The first problem stems from the fact that unencrypted sites display and handle everything in plain text. That means all transfers involving passwords and personal and financial information (like credit cards) are visible to any curious observer with access to the network. This is obviously a horrible idea.

The second problem is the product of a decision made by Google back in January, 2017. Google decided to penalize unencrypted websites by ranking them lower in internet search results. This made it much harder for users to find content that's not secure.

Why should Google (along with other powerful internet companies) care? And why should you care? Because the stability of the internet and everything we all do with it can't survive if we can't trust its content and the way sites handle our private information. Even if your site doesn't process credit card purchases, the fact that it's unencrypted means that it's much more likely to be compromised, with its resources hijacked for use as part of zombie attacks against other sites. Any single weak site makes the whole internet weaker.

If you want to secure your website (which is what this chapter is about, after all), then encryption is a significant part of the process. Mind you, don't think that encryption *guarantees* that your data is safe. It just makes it a great deal more difficult for the wrong people to get at it. To make this work, you'll need a *certificate*, which is a file containing information identifying the domain, owner, key, and a reliable digital signature.

Once you have a certificate, browsers can authenticate the security of your site and exchange only encrypted data throughout a session. All widely used modern browsers come with public root certificates preinstalled, so they can authenticate connections with any site using a private Certificate Authority (CA) certificate. Here's how it works:

1　A client browser requests the server identity so the two can perform a *handshake*.
2　The server responds by sending a copy of the certificate it received from a CA.
3　The browser compares the certificate against its list of root certificates and confirms that your certificate hasn't expired or been revoked.
4　If satisfied, the browser encrypts a symmetric session key using the public key your server sent, and transmits the key to the server.
5　All transmissions will be encrypted using the session key.

The process is illustrated in figure 9.3.

Until 2016, generating and then installing encryption certificates from trusted CAs using the SSL/TLS standard took time and cost money. On Linux, you would use the OpenSSL command-line interface tool to generate a key pair and then put together a specially formatted Certificate Signing Request (CSR) package containing the public half of the pair along with site profile information.

The CSR would then be sent to a CA. If the request was approved, the CA would send a certificate for you to install in your file system. You would also need to update

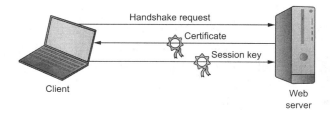

Figure 9.3 The exchange of identifying data, certificates, and session keys for a TLS encrypted browser session

web server configuration files (/etc/apache2/sites-available/default-ssl.conf, in the case of Apache on Ubuntu) so the software would know where in your file system the certificate was kept. That was then.

Since 2016, Let's Encrypt has been issuing certificates as a CA for free. Let's Encrypt (https://letsencrypt.org) is sponsored by the Electronic Frontier Foundation along with a large number of corporate partners including Cisco, Chrome, Shopify, and Digital Ocean. Its mandate is to promote website encryption by making it cheaper and, just as important, simpler.

Forget about configuring files and using OpenSSL to generate CSRs: Let's Encrypt's Certbot ACME client will do pretty much the whole thing for you. Let's Encrypt certificates are valid for 90 days and can be set to automatically renew.

9.3.1 Preparing your website domain

Before you can install a certificate to encrypt your website domain, you'll need to have a domain. That will involve purchasing a name from a domain registrar like GoDaddy or Amazon's Route 53. For more on how that works, you can read chapter 5 in my book *Learn Amazon Web Services in a Month of Lunches* (Manning, 2017).

As you'll want Apache to handle domain-specific requests from external clients, you'll also need to add a section to the /etc/apache2/sites-available/000-default.conf file (on a CentOS machine, it's the settings in the /etc/httpd/conf/httpd.conf file that you'll edit). Here's how it might look on my bootstrap-it.com server. Note how, at this point, it's only configured to accept traffic on the insecure HTTP port 80.

> **Listing 9.3 Possible domain section from an Apache configuration file**

This configuration only listens for traffic on port 80.

```
<VirtualHost *:80>
    ServerName bootstrap-it.com
    DocumentRoot /var/www/html
    ServerAlias www.bootstrap-it.com
</VirtualHost>
```

Your domain name is used as the value for ServerName.

This ServerAlias line adds www as a valid domain prefix.

9.3.2 Generating certificates using Let's Encrypt

From this point, it's quite simple. Browse to the Getting Started page of the Electronic Frontier Foundation Certbot website (https://certbot.eff.org) and, as you can see in figure 9.4, specify the web server software and OS you're using.

From the Certbot home page, you'll be redirected to a page with some brief instructions. For Apache on Ubuntu 16.04, which includes commands to install the software-properties-common repository management tool, add the Certbot repository to your APT list, and then install the Python-based Certbot software for Apache:

```
# apt update
# apt install software-properties-common
# add-apt-repository ppa:certbot/certbot
# apt update
# apt install python-certbot-apache
```

Figure 9.4   Once you select your web server software and OS on the Certbot home page, you'll be shown installation instructions.

Finally, you'll launch the Certbot program as admin (using `--apache` as an argument, in my case). Certbot will read your web server config files to get a feel for the domains you're likely to want to register:

```
# certbot --apache
```

After answering a few questions about contact information and Let's Encrypt's terms of services, you'll be presented with a list of possible domain names that might look like this:

```
Which names would you like to activate HTTPS for?
-------------------------
1: bootstrap-it.com
2: www.bootstrap-it.com
-------------------------
Select the appropriate numbers separated by commas and/or spaces,
  or leave input blank to select all options shown (Enter 'c' to cancel):
```

Once you respond, the bot will try to confirm that your selected domains exist and are registered with a publicly accessible DNS server. The certificate server will finally try to connect to your site. If that's successful, a Let's Encrypt certificate will be automatically installed and any necessary additional sections will be added to your configuration files.

If something goes wrong with the process, Certbot will display useful error messages that you can use to seed your research for a solution. Plus Let's Encrypt hosts an active community help forum where users of all skill levels can safely plead for help: https://community.letsencrypt.org.

Up to now in this busy chapter you've learned how to enhance website security by keeping your applications patched and updated, use firewall rules to control access to your network, add security through obscurity to your mix, and encrypt data as it moves between your website and its visitors. We're not done with security.

Still to come: toughening up your login protocols, using the SELinux kernel module and groups to more closely control the trouble your users can get themselves into, and keeping track of your running processes to make sure there's nothing inappropriate going on in the background when no one's looking.

9.4 Hardening the authentication process

Using secure connectivity solutions, especially SSH, is great. But it's also a good idea to give some attention to the way your team members use SSH. Here are a couple of suggestions for improving your remote-access security. It may not be practical to enforce them in every environment (particularly while you're in the process of setting things up), but they should at least be familiar to you.

Avoid logging in to servers as the root user. It's always better to use `sudo` whenever admin privileges are necessary. In fact, you can prevent incoming root logins using SSH altogether by editing the `PermitRootLogin` line in the /etc/ssh/sshd_conf file:

```
PermitRootLogin no          ◁──┐ The root-login-control
                               │ line in /etc/ssh/sshd_conf
```

You can also encourage your admins to use only passwordless SSH access through key pairs (the way you saw back in chapter 3). This, too, can be enforced from the sshd_conf file, this time on the `PasswordAuthentication` line. With no password authentication, users will be forced to use key pairs:

```
PasswordAuthentication no    ◁──┐ The password-authentication
                                │ control line in /etc/ssh/sshd_conf
```

After each of those edits, make sure you reload SSH; otherwise, the new settings won't take effect until the next boot:

```
# systemctl restart sshd
```

Those are important steps in any environment. But if your deployment needs some industrial-strength isolation, consider enabling SELinux.

9.4.1 Controlling file system objects with SELinux

Remember when we discussed object permissions back in chapter 4? The context was the need to make sure users can access and edit their own files. But the flip side of that coin is ensuring that the wrong users can't get their dirty fingers into other people's files.

You'll recall that a common permissions profile for an object might give the owner full read-write-execute powers, but gives the object's group and others only the permission to read. That would translate as 744 in our numeric notation, or rwx r-- r-- otherwise.

Giving your users full power over their own resources is sometimes described as a *discretionary access control* (DAC) system. A DAC will make a lot of sense if you want your users to be productive, but it comes with a price: having full control carries the risk that they'll apply it without being fully aware of the consequences.

Here's a practical example of what I mean. Suppose a couple of the developers diligently slaving away for your company run into a problem: testing their software locally always fails when trying to write to a data file. Debugging reveals that it's a permissions issue caused by the fact that the application is being run by one user, but the data file belongs to another.

Because this has happened more than once, and to more than one data file (or SSH key file for that matter), the developers take the quick and lazy route: they open up permissions on the data files and on all the files in those directories to 777—fully accessible to the entire world. Now that's a significant security problem. There's also an excellent chance that the application they're working on will eventually be moved out to production with the same system settings. This is the kind of mistake that lies at the root of a lot of the major data breaches you hear about from time to time.

SELinux is another one of those complex topics that, although critically important for many Linux workloads, doesn't have to play a major role in this book's projects. Once again, feel free to skip right past it to our discussion of system groups if you like.

When installed and activated, the SELinux kernel module applies *mandatory access control* (MAC) to file system objects, regardless of a particular object's owner. In effect, as illustrated in figure 9.5, it imposes carefully defined, system-wide limits on what a user can do, making it impossible to set inherently dangerous configurations.

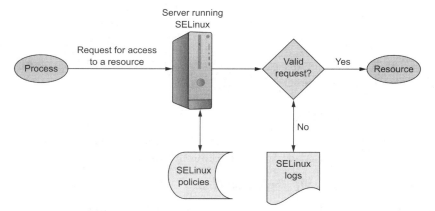

Figure 9.5 The process flow following a request for resource access through the filter of SELinux policies

Had SELinux been active, those two developers could have applied 777 permissions to their data files over and over again until their poor little fingers fell off, but it wouldn't have helped. Instead, they'd have been forced to look for a more appropriate and effective solution. They might, for instance, have considered creating a system group with authority over the data and then adding appropriate user accounts to the group. You'll learn more about that a bit later in this chapter. Sounds great. What's not to love about security?

Well, there's a problem. SELinux has a dark and scary relationship with application compatibility. So dark and so scary that many admins disable it rather than trying to make it work. The problem is that many applications, both off-the-shelf and custom apps you're building locally, need to access and edit system resources. As a result, running such applications within an unmodified SELinux environment will often fail.

I have it on good authority that there are solutions to all those conflicts and that they're not impossible to apply. But just as often, the conflicts can be avoided altogether through a better understanding of file system design and security principles. In particular, you should remember *the principle of least privilege*, which seeks to permit all users and processes only the access they need and nothing more. In any case, you'll need to know your way around SELinux, so the following sections introduce the basics.

9.4.2 *Installing and activating SELinux*

Perhaps because SELinux was developed by and for Red Hat Linux (and CentOS), it comes installed and active by default on those systems. Running it on other distros, including Ubuntu, is definitely possible (although AppArmor is a more common choice for Ubuntu), but I can't guarantee that it will always go smoothly. (Don't even think about trying it on an LXC container; go with VirtualBox for testing, instead.) On Ubuntu, you'll need three packages: selinux, setools, and policycoreutils. Here's how that would look:

```
# apt install setools policycoreutils selinux
```

Once they're nicely tucked in, reboot Ubuntu, and run `sestatus` for a snapshot of the current SELinux status, including important file system locations and policy. With luck, you should see something like this:

```
# sestatus
SELinux status:                 enabled          ◁─┐  The current SELinux
SELinuxfs mount:                /sys/fs/selinux        status is enabled.
SELinux root directory:         /etc/selinux
Loaded policy name:             targeted         ◁─┐  The default policy being
Current mode:                   permissive         │  used is targeted.
Mode from config file:          permissive
Policy MLS status:              enabled
Policy deny_unknown status:     allowed
Max kernel policy version:      30
```

You might sometimes have to run the `selinux-activate` command to incorporate SELinux settings into the boot process:

True to its name, selinux-activate sets SELinux as active following the next boot.

```
# selinux-activate
Activating SE Linux
Generating grub configuration file ...
Warning: Setting GRUB_TIMEOUT to a non-zero value when GRUB_HIDDEN_TIMEOUT
   is set is no longer supported.
Found linux image: /boot/vmlinuz-4.4.0-89-generic
Found initrd image: /boot/initrd.img-4.4.0-89-generic
Found linux image: /boot/vmlinuz-4.4.0-87-generic
Found initrd image: /boot/initrd.img-4.4.0-87-generic
Found linux image: /boot/vmlinuz-4.4.0-83-generic
Found initrd image: /boot/initrd.img-4.4.0-83-generic
Found memtest86+ image: /boot/memtest86+.elf
Found memtest86+ image: /boot/memtest86+.bin
done
SE Linux is activated. You may need to reboot now.
```

SELinux-friendly flags are added to the launch command for each image controlled by GRUB.

Because SELinux relies on kernel-level settings, changes often require a reboot.

Like the man says, you may need to reboot for the changes to take effect.

You can control SELinux behavior through the configuration file in /etc/selinux/. The file contains two settings, SELinux state and SELinux type. Table 9.1 gives a brief overview of the possible values.

Table 9.1   The configuration settings for SELinux in /etc/selinux/config

Category	Value	Description	Use
State	`disabled`	SELinux is off.	
	`enforcing`	Security policy is enforced.	
	`permissive`	Policy breaches trigger only logged warnings.	Useful for testing configurations
Policy type	`targeted`	Enables a domain whose processes are "unconfined" by SELinux restrictions.	Useful for mixed-use systems where not all processes require restrictions
	`minimum`	Only minimal processes are restricted by SELinux.	Can allow finer tuning for experimental systems
	`mls`	Policies are applied based on sensitivity level and capability.	

Besides the config file, you can also set the SELinux state from the command line using `setenforce`, where `setenforce 1` enables the enforcing state, and `setenforce 0` sets SELinux to the permissive state. When in a permissive state, rule violations are permitted but logged. This is a good way to troubleshoot or test a configuration without turning everything upside down in the process:

```
# setenforce 1
```

How about an SELinux example to illustrate how you can control access to an individual file? Consider it done. You should definitely try the example in the next section (or something like it) yourself.

9.4.3 *Applying SELinux policies*

Say that you're the sysadmin responsible for those two developers with the lazy streak you met earlier. Based on past experience, you suspect that they might be tempted to open access to a data file a bit too widely. Here's how you might protect your data no matter what the developers try.

You can use SELinux to control the way any file or process is consumed, but to keep this example simple, let's work with a machine with Apache (or httpd) installed and an index.html file in the document root at /var/www/html/. The file will, by default, be accessible at least to local requests (via wget localhost from the command line of the server). Here's how that will normally look:

```
$ wget locahost
--2017-08-02 10:24:25--  http://localhost/
Resolving localhost (localhost)... ::1, 127.0.0.1
Connecting to localhost (localhost)|::1|:80... connected.
HTTP request sent, awaiting response... 200 OK
Length: 11 [text/html]
Saving to: 'index.html'

100%[======================================>] 11          --.-K/s    in 0s
```

wget successfully saved the index.html file to the local directory.

Now, check out the permissions status of the index.html file using ls -Z (-Z will display the file's security context):

```
# ls -Z /var/www/html/
-rw-r--r--. root root unconfined_u:object_r:httpd_sys_content_t:s0 index.html
```

First, note the regular permissions (-rw-r--r--) that make the file readable (r) by anyone. This is standard for website resources. The SELinux status of the file is displayed as unconfined_u:object_r:httpd_sys_content_t:s0. You can use chcon -t to change the context type of a file. This command replaces the Apache httpd_sys_content_t type with the Samba-related samba_share_t type. I'm not sure you'd ever want to do this in real life, but it should nicely demonstrate one way you can balance the authority you give your users against their potential to mess things up:

```
# chcon -t samba_share_t /var/www/html/index.html
```

A second shot of ls -Z shows that the file is now associated with the samba_share_t type:

```
# ls -Z /var/www/html/
-rw-r--r--. root root unconfined_u:object_r:samba_share_t:s0
 /var/www/html/index.html
```

How will another round of `wget localhost` handle the new SELinux context?

```
$ wget localhost
--2017-08-02 10:27:30--  http://localhost/
Resolving localhost (localhost)... ::1, 127.0.0.1
Connecting to localhost (localhost)|::1|:80... connected.
HTTP request sent, awaiting response... 403 Forbidden
2017-08-02 10:27:30 ERROR 403: Forbidden.
```

Apache responds to the request with a 403: Forbidden fail message.

It's no go. Apache is forced to disappoint you (or, rather, the developers), as Apache itself has no power over the file in its current context. This is true despite the fact that the file attributes include read permissions for all users. No matter how desperately your developers might want to open access to a protected file, they'll be spinning their wheels and getting nowhere.

9.4.4   *System groups and the principle of least privilege*

Those two developers finally got the message. They understand that they've been blocked from opening access too widely. But now they're asking you to help them solve the original problem: how to make files containing sensitive data accessible to multiple accounts without opening those up to everyone.

The short answer is groups. (And the long answer is g—r—o—u—p—s.) A *group* is a system object much the same as a user, except that no one will ever log in to the system as a group. The power of groups is in how they, like users, can be assigned to files or directories, allowing any group members to share the group powers. This is illustrated in figure 9.6.

Try this yourself: use nano to create a new file. Add some Hello World text so you'll be able to easily tell when you can successfully access it. Now edit its permissions using

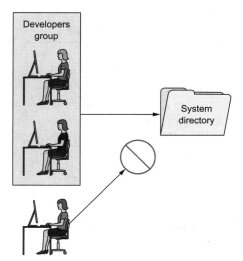

Figure 9.6   Developers who are members of the Developers group can be given access to a particular directory, as opposed to those individuals who aren't part of the group.

chmod 770 so that the file's owner and group have full rights over the file, but others can't read it:

```
$ nano datafile.txt
$ chmod 770 datafile.txt
```

If your system doesn't already have an extra user besides your account, create one using either adduser (the Debian/Ubuntu way) or useradd (if you're on CentOS). Note that useradd will also work on Ubuntu:

```
# useradd otheruser
# passwd otheruser
Enter new UNIX password:
Retype new UNIX password:
passwd: password updated successfully
```

The useradd command (as opposed to the Debian adduser command) requires you to generate a user password separately.

Use su to switch to your new user. Once you enter the user's password, all the commands you execute will be run as that user. You'll be working with only that user's authority: no more and no less. If you try reading the datafile.txt file (using cat), you'll have no luck because, as you remember, others were denied read permission. When you're done, type exit to leave the new user shell and return to your original shell:

```
$ su otheruser
Password:
$ cat /home/ubuntu/datafile.txt
cat: /home/ubuntu/datafile.txt: Permission denied
$ exit
```

All this is expected and easy to understand. And, as you've seen, not being able to read the file belonging to a different reader can sometimes be a problem. Let's see what you can do about that by associating the file with a group and then properly configuring the file's permissions.

Create a new group you can use to manage your application data, and then edit the properties of your data file using chown. The ubuntu:app-data-group argument leaves the file ownership in the hands of the ubuntu user, but changes its group to your new app-data-group:

```
# groupadd app-data-group
# chown ubuntu:app-data-group datafile.txt
```

Run ls with long output (-l) against the file to view its new permissions and status. Note that, as expected, ubuntu is the file's owner and app-data-group is its group:

```
$ ls -l | grep datafile.txt
-rwxrwx--- 1 ubuntu app-data-group       6 Aug  9 22:43 datafile.txt
```

You can use `usermod` to add your user to app-data-group and then, once again, `su` to switch to a shell deploying the other user's account. This time, even though the file's permissions lock others out, and you're definitely acting as an "other" right now, you should be able to read it…thanks to your group membership:

```
# usermod -aG app-data-group otheruser
$ su otheruser                              Use the su command to switch
$ cat datafile.txt                          between user accounts.
Hello World                         This happened to be the
                                    contents of my datafile.txt file.
```

This kind of organization is the correct and effective way to deal with many of the complicated permissions issues that will arise on a multiuser system. In fact, not only is it used to give individual users the access they need, but many system processes couldn't do their jobs without special group memberships. Take a quick look through the /etc/group file and note how many system processes have their own groups:

Listing 9.4   Partial listing of the contents of the /etc/group file

```
$ cat /etc/group
root:x:0:
daemon:x:1:
bin:x:2:
sys:x:3:
adm:x:4:syslog
tty:x:5:
disk:x:6:
lp:x:7:
mail:x:8:
news:x:9:
uucp:x:10:
man:x:12:
proxy:x:13:
[...]
```

I'll close out the chapter with a few quick but vital protocols you can incorporate into your security practices.

9.4.5 *Isolating processes within containers*

Worried that the multiple services you've got running on a single server will, should one service be breached, all be at risk? One way to limit the damage that careless or malicious users can cause is by isolating system resources and processes. That way, even if someone might want to expand their reach beyond a set limit, they won't have physical access.

The old approach to the problem was provisioning a separate physical machine for each service. But virtualization can make it a lot easier, and more affordable, to build a *siloed* infrastructure. This architecture is often referred to as *microservices* and would have you launch multiple containers with one, perhaps, running only a database, another

Apache, and a third containing media files that might be embedded in your web pages. In addition to the many performance and efficiency benefits associated with microservices architectures, this can greatly reduce each individual component's risk exposure.

> **NOTE** By *containers* I don't necessarily mean those of the LXC persuasion. These days, for this kind of deployment, Docker containers are far more popular. If you're interested in learning more, check out Manning's *Microservices in Action* (Morgan Bruce and Paulo A. Pereira, 2018), *Microservice Patterns* (Chris Richardson, 2018), or *Docker in Practice, 2nd ed.* (Ian Miell and Aidan Hobson Sayers, 2018).

9.4.6 Scanning for dangerous user ID values

While any admin user will be able to temporarily assume root authority using `sudo`, only *root* is actually root. As you've seen already, it isn't safe to perform regular functions as root. But it can happen, whether by innocent accident or malicious tampering, and a regular user can effectively get admin rights full-time.

The good news is that it's easy to spot imposters: their user and/or group ID numbers will, like root, be zero (0). Take a look at the passwd file in /etc/. This file contains a record for each regular and system user account that currently exists. The first field contains the account name (root and ubuntu, in this case), and the second field might contain an *x* in place of a password (which, if it exists, will appear encrypted in the /etc/shadow file). But the next two fields contain the user and group IDs. In the case of ubuntu in this example, both IDs are 1000. And, as you can see, root has zeroes:

```
$ cat /etc/passwd
root:x:0:0:root:/root:/bin/bash
[...]
ubuntu:x:1000:1000::/home/ubuntu:/bin/bash
```

If you ever see a regular user with a user or group ID of 0, then you know there's something nasty going on, and you should get to work fixing it. The quick and easy way to spot a problem is to run this `awk` command against the passwd file, which prints any line whose third field contains only a 0. In this case, to my great relief, the only result was root. You can run it a second time substituting $4 for $3 to pick up the group ID field:

```
$ awk -F: '($3 == "0") {print}' /etc/passwd
root:x:0:0:root:/root:/bin/bash
```

⊲ **The awk command is discussed in greater detail in chapter 11.**

9.5 Auditing system resources

The more things you've got running, the greater the odds of something breaking, so it makes sense that you'll want to keep track of what's running. This applies to network ports (if they're open, then by definition, there must be a way in), services (if they're active, then people can run them), and installed software (if it's installed, it can be executed).

For audits to be useful, you'll have to remember to run them once in a while. Because you know you're going to forget, you'll be much better off incorporating your auditing tools into a script that not only executes regularly but, ideally, also parses the results to make them more readable. In this section, I'll focus on introducing you to three key audit tools to help you scan for open ports, active services, and unnecessary software packages. Getting it all implemented will be your job.

9.5.1 Scanning for open ports

A port is considered *open* if there's some process running on the host that's listening on that port for requests. Keeping an eye on your open ports can keep you plugged into what's going on with your server.

You already know that a regular web server is probably going to have HTTP (80) and SSH (22) ports open, so it shouldn't come as a surprise to find those. But you'll want to focus on other, unexpected results. The netstat command displays open ports along with a wealth of information about how those ports are being used.

In this example, run against a fairly typical multipurpose server, -n tells netstat to include the numeric ports and addresses, -l includes only listening sockets, and -p adds the process ID of the listening program. Naturally, if you see something, do something:

```
# netstat -npl                                         The MySQL process is
Active Internet connections (only servers)             running on port 3306.
Proto Local Address        Foreign Address    State       PID/Program name
tcp   127.0.0.1:3306       0.0.0.0:*          LISTEN      403/mysqld       ◁──
tcp   0.0.0.0:139          0.0.0.0:*          LISTEN      270/smbd
tcp   0.0.0.0:22           0.0.0.0:*          LISTEN      333/sshd         ◁──┐
tcp   0.0.0.0:445          0.0.0.0:*          LISTEN      270/smbd
tcp6  :::80                :::*               LISTEN      417/apache2
[...]
                                                       The SSH process has a
                                                       process ID of 333.
```

In recent years, ss has begun to replace netstat for many uses. In case you find yourself at a party one day and someone asks you about ss, this example (which lists all established SSH connections) should give you enough information to save you from truly deep embarrassment:

```
$ ss -o state established                      Displays all TCP sockets
   '( dport = :ssh or sport = :ssh )'   ◁──
Netid  Recv-Q Send-Q    Local Address:Port    Peer Address:Port
tcp    0      0         10.0.3.1:39874         10.0.3.96:ssh
timer:(keepalive,18min,0)
```

9.5.2 Scanning for active services

Getting a quick snapshot of the systemd-managed services currently enabled on your machine can also help you spot activity that doesn't belong. systemctl can list all existing services, which can then be narrowed down to only those results whose descriptions include enabled. This code returns only active services:

```
# systemctl list-unit-files --type=service --state=enabled
autovt@.service                          enabled
bind9.service                            enabled
cron.service                             enabled
dbus-org.freedesktop.thermald.service    enabled
docker.service                           enabled
getty@.service                           enabled
haveged.service                          enabled
mysql.service                            enabled
networking.service                       enabled
resolvconf.service                       enabled
rsyslog.service                          enabled
ssh.service                              enabled
sshd.service                             enabled
syslog.service                           enabled
systemd-timesyncd.service                enabled
thermald.service                         enabled
unattended-upgrades.service              enabled
ureadahead.service                       enabled
```

sshd is the SSH server; ssh is the client software.

If you do find something that shouldn't be there, you can use `systemctl` to both stop the service and make sure it doesn't start up again with the next boot:

```
# systemctl stop haveged
# systemctl disable haveged
```

There's actually nothing dark and sinister about the haveged service I'm stopping in this example. It's a small tool I often install to generate random background system activity when I'm creating encryption keys.

9.5.3 *Searching for installed software*

Could someone or something have installed software on your system without you knowing? Well, how would you know if you don't look? To get the whole briefing, use `yum list installed` or, on Debian/Ubuntu, `dpkg --list`. To delete any packages that don't belong, use `remove <packagename>`:

```
# yum list installed
# yum remove packageName
```

Here's how it goes on Ubuntu:

Outputs a long list of packages that you'll have to visually scan as quickly as you can. I'm not aware of any shortcuts.

```
# dpkg --list
# apt-get remove packageName
```

It's also a good idea to be aware of changes to your system configuration files. That's something you'll learn about in chapter 11.

Summary

- Using firewalls, you control network traffic by protocol, port, and source or destination.
- Configure applications to listen in on nonstandard network ports to add *security through obscurity* to your infrastructure.
- Using certificates received from a CA, client-host browser sessions are encrypted, greatly reducing the chances of the transferred data being compromised.
- Global controls are enforced on a multiuser file system using SELinux.
- Access to resources is closely managed using groups to allow users and processes exactly the access they need.
- Regular (scripted) audits of running processes, installed software, and open ports are critical to ongoing server security.

Key terms

- You can administer firewall rules on Linux using *iptables* or simpler, high-level tools.
- The *Hypertext Transfer Protocol* (HTTP) manages browser-based data transfers over a network.
- The *Transport Layer Security* (TLS) protocol enforces data encryption for host-client network data transfers.
- *Discretionary access control systems* (DACs) allow users control over file system resources.
- Control over resources on *mandatory access control systems* (MACs) is ultimately managed by system-wide policies.
- *Microservices* are individual computer services run from individual containers as part of a larger single application infrastructure spanning multiple containers.

Command-line review

- `firewall-cmd --permanent --add-port=80/tcp` opens port 80 to incoming HTTP traffic and configures it to reload at boot time.
- `firewall-cmd --list-services` lists the currently active rules on a firewalld system.
- `ufw allow ssh` opens port 22 for SSH traffic using UncomplicatedFirewall (ufw) on Ubuntu.
- `ufw delete 2` removes the second ufw rule as listed by the `ufw status` command.
- `ssh -p53987 username@remote_IP_or_domain` logs in to an SSH session using a non-default port.
- `certbot --apache` configures an Apache web server to use Let's Encrypt encryption certificates.

- `selinux-activate` activates SELinux on an Ubuntu machine.
- `setenforce 1` toggles enforcing mode in an SELinux configuration.
- `ls -Z /var/www/html/` displays the security context of the files in a specified directory.
- `usermod -aG app-data-group otheruser` adds the otheruser user to the app-data-group system group.
- `netstat -npl` scans for open (listening) network ports on a server.

Test yourself

1 You're concerned that hackers might have gained access to your server, and you want to make sure they aren't able to escalate their permissions to root powers. Which of the following commands might help?

   a `firewall-cmd --list-services`

   b `netstat -npl`

   c `certbot --apache`

   d `awk -F: '($3 == "0") {print}' /etc/passwd`

2 You noticed that there are network ports open on your server that you can't explain. Which of the following tools can be used to close them?

   a firewalld

   b netstat

   c certbot –apache

   d awk

3 What security advantage can there be in splitting a single application's services among multiple containers?

   a A failure in one won't necessarily affect the performance of the others.

   b A vulnerability in one won't necessarily spread to the others.

   c Such a design pushes authentication further away from the servers.

   d Such a design increases process visibility.

4 Which of the following commands will allow SSH access to a server from only a single IP address?

   a `firewall-cmd allow from 10.0.3.1 to any port 22`

   b `ufw allow from 10.0.3.1 to port 22`

   c `ufw allow from 10.0.3.1 to any port 22`

   d `firewall-cmd --allow from 10.0.3.1 to any port 22`

5 Requesting a TLS certificate from a CA allows you to

   a Prevent unauthorized users from accessing your web server's backend

   b Secure data at rest on a web server

   c Secure data in transit between a web server and clients

   d Permit passwordless SSH access to your web server's backend

6 Which of the following settings in the /etc/ssh/sshd_conf file will force SSH clients to use key pairs?

   a PermitRootLogin no

   b PermitRootLogin yes

   c #PasswordAuthentication no

   d PasswordAuthentication no

7 Which of the following commands will set SELinux to permissive mode?

   a `setenforce 0`

   b `chcon -t samba_share_t /var/www/html/index.html`

   c `setenforce 1`

   d `selinux-activate`

8 Which of the following commands will make the app-data-group the group of the datafile.txt file?

   a `chown app-data-group,ubuntu datafile.txt`

   b `chown app-data-group datafile.txt`

   c `chown app-data-group:ubuntu datafile.txt`

   d `chown ubuntu:app-data-group datafile.txt`

Answer key

1. d, 2. a, 3. b, 4. c, 5. c, 6. d, 7. a, 8. d

10

Securing network connections: Creating a VPN or DMZ

This chapter covers

- Implementing server security configurations
- Deploying an OpenVPN tunnel to secure remote connections
- Using firewalls to control access between segments
- Using iptables and Shorewall to create a DMZ-based network
- Testing network connectivity solutions using virtual environments

They tell us we live in a hyper-mobile world. Not that I'd know: I rarely leave my home office. I get to enjoy the comforts of my home office because all the server resources I could possibly need are available remotely. Apparently I'm not alone.

Almost everyone whose work touches IT will access their professional tools from remote locations from time to time. And given that the public networks through which you access those remote locations are by their very nature insecure, you're going to want to carefully control those connections.

The previous chapter focused on making sure that the data consumed by your remote clients is reliably transferred and invisible to anyone who might be lurking on the connecting network. This chapter, by sharp contrast, will focus on making sure that the data consumed by your remote clients is reliably transferred and invisible to anyone who might be lurking on the connecting network. See the difference? Neither do I.

In fact, there are all kinds of technologies devoted to securing network communication, and the principle of *defense in depth* teaches us never to rely on one. Here's where you'll learn about adding new layers of protection for your remote activities.

In this chapter, you'll revisit a couple of old friends. You'll use VirtualBox VMs and encryption to build a virtual private network (VPN) tunnel to permit secure and invisible remote connections. And, in a separate project, you'll design more sophisticated firewall architectures to strategically divide your network into isolated segments. Finally, you'll build a virtual network environment within VirtualBox so you can test your configurations.

10.1 *Building an OpenVPN tunnel*

I've talked a lot about encryption already in this book. SSH and SCP can protect data transferred through remote connections (chapter 3), file encryption can protect data at rest (chapter 8), and TLS/SSL certificates can protect data in transit between websites and client browsers (chapter 9). But sometimes your requirements demand protection across a broader range of connections because, occasionally, you've got different kinds of work to do. For instance, perhaps some members of your team need to work from the road using public WiFi hotspots. It's definitely not smart to assume that random WiFi access points are secure, but your people do need a way to connect with company resources—VPNs to the rescue.

A properly designed VPN tunnel provides a direct connection between remote clients and a server in a way that hides data as it's transferred across an insecure network. But so what? You've already seen lots of tools that can do that using encryption. The real value of a VPN is that once you've opened a tunnel, it's possible to connect remote networks as though they're all together locally. In a way, you're circumventing that dodgy coffee shop hot spot.

Using such an extended network, admins can get their work done on their servers no matter where they might happen to be. But more importantly, as you can see in figure 10.1, a company with resources spread through multiple branch offices can make them all both visible and accessible to all the teams who need them, wherever they are.

The mere existence of a tunnel alone doesn't guarantee security. But one of a number of encryption standards can be incorporated into the design, making things a great deal better. Tunnels built with the open source OpenVPN package use the same TLS/SSL encryption you've already seen in use elsewhere. OpenVPN is not the only available choice for tunneling, but it's among the best known. And it's widely assumed

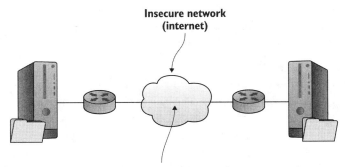

Data moving through a **VPN** tunnel between
company locations over the internet is hidden from
unauthorized users.

Figure 10.1   Tunnel connecting remote private connections through a public network

to be a bit faster and more secure than the alternative Layer 2 Tunnel Protocol using IPsec encryption.

You'll want your team to safely connect with each other from out on the road or between multiple campuses. For that, you'll need to build an OpenVPN server to permit sharing applications and to access the server's local network environment. To make it work, it should be sufficient to fire up two VMs or containers: one to play the role of a server/host and the other of the client. Building a VPN involves quite a few steps, so taking a few moments to think about the big picture of how this is going to work will probably be worthwhile.

10.1.1 Configuring an OpenVPN server

Before getting started, here's a helpful tip. If you're going to follow along with this process on your own, and I strongly recommend that you do, you'll probably find yourself working with multiple terminal windows open on your desktop, each logged in to a different machine. Take it from me, at some point you're going to enter a command into the wrong window and totally mess up your environment. To avoid this, you can use the `hostname` command to change the machine name displayed on the command line to something that will visually remind you where you are. Once that's done, you'll need to exit the server and log back in again for the new setting to take effect. Here's what it looks like:

```
ubuntu@ubuntu:~# hostname OpenVPN-Server
ubuntu@ubuntu:~$ exit                                   Activate your new
<Host Workstation>$ ssh ubuntu@10.0.3.134               hostname by exiting the
ubuntu@OpenVPN-Server:~#                                shell and logging back in.
```

Following that approach to assign appropriate names to each of the machines you're working with should help you keep track of where you are.

NOTE After using `hostname`, you might encounter annoying Unable to Resolve Host OpenVPN-Server messages when running subsequent commands. Updating the /etc/hosts file to match the new hostname should solve that.

PREPARING YOUR SERVER FOR OPENVPN

Installing OpenVPN on your server requires two packages: openvpn and, to manage the encryption key-generation process, easy-rsa. CentOS users should, if necessary, first install the epel-release repository the way you did back in chapter 2. To give you an easy way to test access to a server application, you could also install the Apache web server (apache2 for Ubuntu and httpd on CentOS).

While you're setting up your server, you might as well do it right and activate a firewall that blocks all ports besides 22 (SSH) and 1194 (the default OpenVPN port). This example illustrates the way that will work on Ubuntu's ufw, but I'm sure you still remember CentOS' firewalld from chapter 9:

```
# ufw enable
# ufw allow 22
# ufw allow 1194
```

To permit internal routing between network interfaces on the server, you'll need to uncomment a single line (`net.ipv4.ip_forward=1`) in the /etc/sysctl.conf file. This allows remote clients to be redirected as needed once they're connected. To load the new setting, run `sysctl -p`:

```
# nano /etc/sysctl.conf
# sysctl -p
```

The server environment is now all set up, but there's still a ways to go before you're ready to flip the switch. Here are the steps we'll cover over the next pages of this chapter:

1 Generate a set of public key infrastructure (PKI) encryption keys on the server using scripts that come with the easy-rsa package. Effectively, an OpenVPN server also acts as its own Certificate Authority (CA).
2 Prepare matching keys for the client.
3 Configure a server.conf file for the server.
4 Configure your OpenVPN client.
5 Test your VPN.

GENERATING ENCRYPTION KEYS

For simplicity, you're going to set up your key infrastructure on the same machine that's running the OpenVPN server. Security best practices, however, will usually suggest that a separate CA server be used for production deployments. In any case, figure 10.2 illustrates the process of generating and distributing encryption key resources for use on OpenVPN.

When you installed OpenVPN, a /etc/openvpn/ directory was automatically created, but there isn't a whole lot in it just yet. Both the openvpn and easy-rsa packages

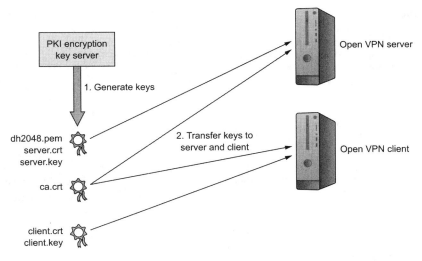

Figure 10.2 **The files that will be created by your PKI server and their distribution targets**

come with sample template files that you can use as a base for you configuration. To jump-start the certification process, copy the easy-rsa template directory from /usr/share/ to /etc/openvpn/ and then change to the easy-rsa/ directory:

```
# cp -r /usr/share/easy-rsa/ /etc/openvpn
$ cd /etc/openvpn/easy-rsa
```

Because the easy-rsa directory will now contain quite a few scripts, table 10.1 gives you a quick preview of the tools you'll be using to bring your keys into existence.

Table 10.1 **Key easy-rsa scripts and their functions**

Script name	Function
clean-all	Removes old key files to prepare for new key generation
pkitool	Frontend for OpenSSL (does most of the key-gen heavy lifting)
build-ca	Uses the pkitool script to generate a root certificate
build-key-server server	Uses the pkitool script to generate a key pair and certificate
build-dh	Sets Diffie-Hellman authentication parameters

NOTE These operations require root authority, so through sudo su, you'll need to become root.

The first file you'll work with is called vars, which contains environment variables that easy-rsa uses when it generates its keys. You'll want to edit the file to substitute your own values for the sample defaults that are already there. Here's what my file would look like.

Listing 10.1   Key excerpts from the /etc/openvpn/easy-rsa/vars file

```
export KEY_COUNTRY="CA"
export KEY_PROVINCE="ON"
export KEY_CITY="Toronto"
export KEY_ORG="Bootstrap IT"
export KEY_EMAIL="info@bootstrap-it.com"
export KEY_OU="IT"
```

Running the vars file will pass its values to the shell environment from where they'll be incorporated into the contents of your new keys. Why would sudo alone not work? Because the first step edits a script called vars and then sources it. *Sourcing* means that the vars file passes its values to the shell environment from where those will be incorporated into the contents of your new keys.

   Make sure to run the file again using a new shell if you need to complete an unfinished process. When that's done, the script will encourage you to run the clean-all script to delete any existing content in the /etc/openvpn/easy-rsa/keys/ directory:

```
$ cd /etc/openvpn/easy-rsa/
# . ./vars                         ⟵── This command requires sudo permissions.
NOTE: If you run ./clean-all,
  I will be doing a rm -rf on /etc/openvpn/easy-rsa/keys
```

Naturally, your next step will be to run that clean-all script followed by build-ca, which uses the pkitool script to create your root certificate. You'll be asked to confirm the identification settings provided by vars:

```
# ./clean-all
# ./build-ca
Generating a 2048 bit RSA private key
```

Next is the build-key-server script. Because it uses the same pkitool script along with the new root certificate, you'll be asked the same confirmation questions to generate a key pair. The keys will be given names based on the arguments you pass, which, unless you're running multiple VPNs on this machine, will normally be server as in this example:

```
# ./build-key-server server
[...]
Certificate is to be certified until Aug 15 23:52:34 2027 GMT (3650 days)
Sign the certificate? [y/n]:y
1 out of 1 certificate requests certified, commit? [y/n]y
Write out database with 1 new entries
Data Base Updated
```

OpenVPN uses parameters generated using the Diffie-Hellman algorithm (by running build-dh) to negotiate authentication for new connections. The file that's created here doesn't need to remain secret, but it must have been generated using the build-dh script against the RSA keys that are currently active. If you create new RSA keys at some time in the future, you'll also need to update the Diffie-Hellman file:

```
# ./build-dh
```

Your server-side keys will now have been written to the /etc/openvpn/easy-rsa/keys/ directory, but OpenVPN doesn't know that. By default, OpenVPN will look for them in /etc/openvpn/, so copy them over:

```
# cp /etc/openvpn/easy-rsa/keys/server* /etc/openvpn
# cp /etc/openvpn/easy-rsa/keys/dh2048.pem /etc/openvpn
# cp /etc/openvpn/easy-rsa/keys/ca.crt /etc/openvpn
```

PREPARING CLIENT ENCRYPTION KEYS

As you've already seen, TLS encryption uses matching key pairs: one installed on the server and the other on a remote client. That means you're going to need client keys. Our old friend pkitool is just the thing to cook some up. This example, run while still in the /etc/openvpn/easy-rsa/ directory, passes `client` as an argument to generate files called client.crt and client.key:

```
# ./pkitool client
```

The two client files, along with the original ca.crt file that's still in the keys/ directory, will now have to be securely transferred to your client. Because of their ownership and permissions, this might be a bit complicated. The simplest approach is to manually copy the contents of the source file (and nothing but those contents) in a terminal running on your PC's desktop (by highlighting the text, right-clicking over it, and selecting Copy from the menu), then pasting it into a new file of the same name you create in a second terminal logged in to your client.

But anyone can cut and paste. Instead, think like an admin, because you won't always have access to a GUI where cutting and pasting is possible. Instead, copy the files to your user's home directory (so a remote scp operation can access them) and then use chown to change the ownership of the files from root to your regular, non-root user so that remote scp action can work. Make sure your files are all settled in and comfy for now. You'll move them over to the client a bit later:

```
# cp /etc/openvpn/easy-rsa/keys/client.key /home/ubuntu/
# cp /etc/openvpn/easy-rsa/keys/ca.crt /home/ubuntu/
# cp /etc/openvpn/easy-rsa/keys/client.crt /home/ubuntu/
# chown ubuntu:ubuntu /home/ubuntu/client.key
# chown ubuntu:ubuntu /home/ubuntu/client.crt
# chown ubuntu:ubuntu /home/ubuntu/ca.crt
```

With a full set of encryption keys ready for action, you'll need to tell your server how you want to build your VPN. That's done using the server.conf file.

Saving keystrokes

Too much typing for your poor, tired fingers? Brace expansion can help reduce those six commands to two. I'm sure you'll be able to study these two examples and figure out what's going on. More importantly, you'll be able to figure out how to apply the principles to operations involving dozens or even hundreds of elements:

```
# cp /etc/openvpn/easy-rsa/keys/{ca.crt,client.{key,crt}} /home/ubuntu/
# chown ubuntu:ubuntu /home/ubuntu/{ca.crt,client.{key,crt}}
```

CONFIGURING THE SERVER.CONF FILE

How are you supposed to know what the server.conf file should look like? Well, remember the easy-rsa directory template you copied from /usr/share/? There are more goodies where that came from. The OpenVPN installation left a compressed template configuration file that you can copy to /etc/openvpn/. I'll use the fact that the template is compressed to introduce you to a useful tool: zcat.

You already know about printing a file's text contents to the screen with cat, but what if the file is compressed using gzip? You could always decompress the file, and cat will then be happy to print it, but that's one or two steps too many. Instead, as you've probably already guessed, you can use zcat to load the decompressed text into memory all in one step. In this case, rather than print it to the screen, you'll redirect the text to a new file called server.conf:

```
# zcat \
 /usr/share/doc/openvpn/examples/sample-config-files/server.conf.gz \
 > /etc/openvpn/server.conf
$ cd /etc/openvpn
```

Leaving out the extensive and helpful documentation that comes with the file, here's how it might look once you're done editing. Note that a semicolon (;) tells OpenVPN not to read and execute the line that follows.

Listing 10.2 The active settings from a /etc/openvpn/server.conf file

```
port 1194
# TCP or UDP server?
proto tcp
;proto udp
;dev tap
dev tun
ca ca.crt
cert server.crt
key server.key  # This file should be kept secret
dh dh2048.pem
server 10.8.0.0 255.255.255.0
ifconfig-pool-persist ipp.txt
push "route 10.0.3.0 255.255.255.0"
keepalive 10 120
```

```
comp-lzo
port-share localhost 80
user nobody
group nogroup
persist-key
persist-tun
status openvpn-status.log
log openvpn.log
;log-append  openvpn.log
verb 3
```

Minimizes privileged system exposure

Writes session logs to /etc/openvpn/openvpn.log

Outputs verbosity, which can go as high as 9

Let's work through some of those settings, one at a time:

- By default, OpenVPN works over port 1194. You can change that, perhaps to further obscure your activities or avoid conflicts with other active tunnels. Because it requires the least coordination between clients, 1194 is normally your best choice.

- OpenVPN uses either the Transmission Control Protocol (TCP) or User Datagram Protocol (UDP) for data transmissions. TCP might be a little bit slower, but it's more reliable and more likely to get along with applications running at either end of the tunnel.

- You can specify dev tun when you want to create a simpler and more efficient IP tunnel that transfers data content and nothing much else. If, on the other hand, you'll need to connect multiple network interfaces (and the networks they represent) by creating an ethernet bridge, then you'll have to select dev tap. If you haven't a clue what all that means, go with tun.

- The next four lines pass OpenVPN the names of the three server authentication files and the dh2048 parameters file you created earlier.

- The server line sets the subnet range and netmask that'll be used for assigning IP addresses to clients when they log in.

- The optional push "route 10.0.3.0 255.255.255.0" setting allows remote clients to access private subnets behind the server. Making this work also requires network configuration on the server itself to ensure that the private subnet is aware of the OpenVPN subnet (10.8.0.0).

- The line port-share localhost 80 allows client traffic coming in on port 1194 to be rerouted to a local web server listening on port 80. (This will be useful in this case because you're going to use a web server to test your VPN.) This only works when proto is set to tcp.

- The user nobody and group nogroup lines should be enabled by removing the semicolons (;). Forcing remote clients to work as nobody and nogroup ensures that their sessions on the server will be unprivileged.

- log sets current log entries to overwrite old entries every time OpenVPN starts, whereas log-append appends new entries to the existing log file. The openvpn.log itself is be written to the /etc/openvpn/ directory.

In addition, it's also common to add `client-to-client` to the config file so multiple clients will be able to see each other in addition to the OpenVPN server. Once you're satisfied with your configuration, you're ready to fire up the OpenVPN server:

```
# systemctl start openvpn
```

> **NOTE** Due to the evolving nature of the relationship between OpenVPN and systemd, starting the service might sometimes require a syntax like this: `systemctl start openvpn@server`.

Running `ip addr` to list your server's network interfaces should now include a reference to a new interface called tun0. This will have been created by OpenVPN for the use of incoming clients:

```
$ ip addr
[...]
4: tun0: <POINTOPOINT,MULTICAST,NOARP,UP,LOWER_UP> mtu 1500 qdisc [...]
    link/none
    inet 10.8.0.1 peer 10.8.0.2/32 scope global tun0
        valid_lft forever preferred_lft forever
```

It's possible that you'll need to reboot the server before everything will fully function. Next stop: the client computer.

10.1.2 *Configuring an OpenVPN client*

Traditionally, tunnels are built with at least two ends (otherwise we'd call them caves). Having OpenVPN properly configured on the server directs traffic into and out of the tunnel at that end. But you'll need some kind of software running on the client side as well.

In this section, I'm going to focus on manually configuring a Linux computer of one sort or another to act as an OpenVPN client. But that's not the only way you might want to consume the service. OpenVPN itself maintains client applications that can be installed and used on Windows or Mac desktop and laptops, or Android and iOS smartphones and tablets. See the https://openvpn.net website for details.

The OpenVPN package will need to be installed on the client machine as it was on the server, although there's no need for easy-rsa over here because the keys you'll use already exist. You'll need to copy the client.conf template file over to the /etc/openvpn/ directory that the installation just created. This time, for some reason, the file won't be compressed, so a regular cp will do the job just fine:

```
# apt install openvpn
# cp /usr/share/doc/openvpn/examples/sample-config-files/client.conf \
 /etc/openvpn/
```

Most of the settings in your client.conf file will be fairly obvious: they'll need to match the values used by the server. As you can see from the next sample file, one setting that's unique is `remote 192.168.1.23 1194`, which points the client to the server's IP address. Again, make sure you use your server's address. You should also force your client to verify the authenticity of the server certificate to prevent a possible man-in-the-middle attack. One way to do this is by adding the `remote-cert-tls server` line.

> **Listing 10.3   The active settings in a VPN client's /etc/openvpn/client.conf file**

```
client                          ←┐  Identifies the computer as a VPN
;dev tap                         │  client whose configuration will be
dev tun                          │  based on a remote server
proto tcp
remote 192.168.1.23 1194        ←┐  The address and network port
resolv-retry infinite            │  used to access the VPN server
nobind
user nobody
group nogroup
persist-key
persist-tun
ca ca.crt
cert client.crt
key client.key
comp-lzo
verb 3                           ┌  Enforces server
remote-cert-tls server          ←┘  certificate verification
```

Now you can move to the /etc/openvpn/ directory and pull those certification keys from the server. Substitute your server's IP address or domain name for the one in the example:

```
$ cd /etc/openvpn
# scp ubuntu@192.168.1.23:/home/ubuntu/ca.crt .        ←┐  The dot (.) at the end tells
# scp ubuntu@192.168.1.23:/home/ubuntu/client.crt .     │  scp to save the file to the
# scp ubuntu@192.168.1.23:/home/ubuntu/client.key .     │  current directory.
```

Nothing exciting is likely to happen until you start OpenVPN on the client. Because you'll need to pass a couple of arguments, you'll pull the trigger from the command line. The argument `--tls-client` tells OpenVPN that you'll be acting as a client and connecting via TLS encryption, and `--config` points to your config file:

```
# openvpn --tls-client --config /etc/openvpn/client.conf
```

Read the command output carefully to make sure you're connected properly. If something does go wrong the first time, it's probably due to a setting mismatch between the server and client configuration files or perhaps a network connectivity/ firewall issue. Here are some troubleshooting steps:

- Carefully read the output from the OpenVPN operation on the client. It will often contain valuable hints to exactly what it couldn't do and why.
- Check for error-related messages in the openvpn.log and openvpn-status.log files in the /etc/openvpn/ directory on the server.

- Check OpenVPN-related and timely messages in the system logs on both the server and client. (`journalctl -ce` will print out a screen full of the most recent entries.)
- Confirm that you've got an active network connection between the server and client (see chapter 14 for details).

10.1.3 Testing your VPN

If everything OpenVPN spat out at you as it loaded on the client looks fine, then you should move on to test your tunnel to confirm that it's working and protecting your connection. Running `curl` from the client against the server address using the OpenVPN port should return the index.html file in your web root directory (/var/www/html/):

```
curl 192.168.1.23:1194
```

Test your setup by removing the port number and the colon preceding it. Assuming your firewall is running with the previous settings, `curl` shouldn't work.

The truth is, that alone is not a useful test. After all, the goal of a VPN is to prevent your session activity from being visible to other people on the network, so being able to load the page proves nothing. Without going into that much detail, the following sections suggest a couple of ways (in no specific order) to confirm that your VPN is working properly.

NETWORK SNIFFING

Set up a regular GUI desktop PC as a client, and use your browser to open a server-based application that will require some kind of data entry. For the application, you could use a simple HTML form like the following.

> **Listing 10.4 A simple HTML page providing a browser data-entry form**

```
<!DOCTYPE html>
<html>
<body>
<form action="/action_page.php">
  First name:<br>
  <input type="text" name="firstname" value="Your">
  <br>
  Last name:<br>
  <input type="text" name="lastname" value="Name">
  <br><br>
  <input type="submit" value="Submit">
</form>
</body>
</html>
```

You could save the file to the server's web document root as, say, form.html. You'll then access the page using the 192.168.1.23/form.html URL (substituting your server's IP address).

To find out if the information you typed into the form would have been visible to unauthorized eyes, you can use network packet-sniffing software like Wireshark to capture and analyze the data. If the tunnel worked to encrypt the session, then the packets containing the names you entered would be unintelligible.

Unfortunately, a useful guide to setting up and using Wireshark for this purpose would require its own complete chapter. As that would be a significant detour away from our beloved Linux, that chapter will have to find a spot within a different book.

NETWORK INFRASTRUCTURE

A second approach to testing your VPN involves setting up resources (servers, routers, and so on) within the server's local network, the one to which you pushed clients from your server.conf file. Building infrastructure of one kind or another to make this work can get quite involved. But if you pull it off, and your client can access those resources, then you'll know things are working. I've added a guide to using VirtualBox to build such an infrastructure at the end of this chapter.

10.2   *Building intrusion-resistant networks*

VPNs, through the magic of encryption, are great for protecting session data. And firewalls can nicely control incoming and outgoing traffic by port, protocol, or routing information. In theory, that should be enough to protect your server networks. After all, if you've locked down all but a couple of approaches into your network and strengthened the locks to the few doors that are still there (using, for instance, passwordless key-pair authentication for SSH), then you should be safe, right? If only it were that simple.

No matter how good you are, there's no such thing as 100% when it comes to IT security. You do your best to keep informed about new kinds of threats, patch your software, audit your processes, and fine-tune your firewall, but someone's always going to find a way through the wall. Besides the risk of human error and buggy or intentionally compromised software, it's only a matter of time before (quantum computing?) machines capable of cracking encryption algorithms become widely available.

Practically, the solution is to over-provision by adding as many layers to your security profile as possible so that even if the bad guys make it past one gate, there should still be two or three others standing between you and the abyss. (Earlier, we called this defense in depth.) After thinking things through, you may decide that one of those layers involves separating your resources into multiple isolated networks in the hope that if one is breached, the others might still be protected.

When everything is said and done, the primary goal is to safely expose all the services that should be exposed and to jealously protect everything else. Let's say you're running a web server hosting a publicly available application. Users' browsers will load their pages from the web server, while user information and application data are handled by a second server running a database. You'll want to give everyone on earth (along with anyone who might be enjoying the view in low earth orbit) access to your web server, but close off all public access to the database server. Let's discuss how that particular magic trick is done.

10.2.1 Demilitarized zones (DMZs)

One popular isolation architecture is known as a *DMZ* (a contraction of the phrase used to describe a geographic buffer between two distrustful nations: demilitarized zone). The idea is to divide your servers, workstations, WiFi routers, and other resources into separate networks. To make it work, each of your devices will need to be physically connected to a separate network interface.

One simple implementation of a DMZ, as illustrated in figure 10.3, is to use a single server as a router to redirect traffic between the internet and two internal networks. One of the networks might contain backend databases or the workstations and laptops used in your office. This network will be heavily protected by tight access rules. The other network will enjoy fairly direct and easy access to the outside world and might include public-facing resources like web servers.

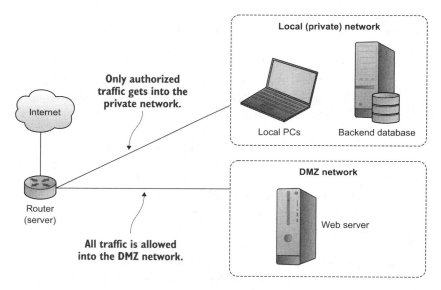

Figure 10.3   A simple three-interface DMZ architecture

Before moving on to building your own DMZ environments, you should at least be aware of a couple alternatives to the DMZ model. I'll mention some in the following sections.

RESISTANT NETWORKS: DESIGN CONSIDERATIONS

In addition to DMZs, which are reliable and flexible enough to be candidates for a wide range of use cases, there are other secure network configuration models that you might consider.

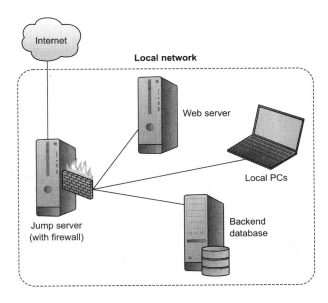

Figure 10.4 A typical jump-server architecture

A *jump server* (sometimes referred to as a jumpbox or, perhaps, a bastion host) is a lightweight server open to the internet that's given only one function: allow remote SSH clients to log in and then "jump" on to other servers running on the jump server's private network. As shown in figure 10.4, the private servers on the network would have some kind of access controls configured to permit access to only remote logins coming from the jump server.

Jump servers (by definition, representing a possible single point of failure and an extra layer of complexity) aren't as popular as they once were. As mentioned in chapter 9, proprietary hardware solutions provided by companies like Juniper and Cisco can be used to manage connectivity and security for larger enterprise deployments. But the costs of such hardware and the significant learning curve you'll need to overcome before you'll be able to competently use it can sometimes outweigh the benefits.

None of those systems will necessarily make all that much sense for hybrid cloud solutions, where company infrastructure is hosted both locally and on remote cloud platforms. But the underlying tools and design concepts are always going to be useful.

WHY USE DMZS?

Next up, I'm going to discuss creating a DMZ using two widely used software firewall packages: iptables and Shorewall. Before I do, though, I should tell you that for all intents and purposes, they're pretty much the same thing. Shorewall is a more user-friendly tool that does nothing more than manipulate iptables rules without you seeing it. Here are two reasons why I'd like you to see both those approaches:

- Usually there are going to be narrow, practical considerations that inform your choice of tools in these things, so having more than one option out of the box gives you a nice head start.

- Even if you do end up using a simpler solution, like Shorewall, it's good to catch at least a quick glimpse of iptables in its natural habitat. That will help deepen your understanding of Linux firewalls in general.

Here we go. Warning: complex and involved topic ahead. Skip to the end of the chapter if you feel like it. Remember to head right back here the next time you're asked to build this kind of infrastructure.

10.2.2 Using iptables

iptables is a tool for managing firewall rules on a Linux machine. iptables? But what about the ufw and firewalld command sets you learned about in the previous chapter? So, you don't like choices? And would it spoil your day if I told you that there was a fourth tool out there called nftables?

OK, I'll admit that the whole thing does smell a bit funny, so let me explain. It all starts with *netfilter*, which controls access to and from the network stack at the Linux kernel module level. For decades, the primary command-line tool for managing net-filter hooks was the iptables rule set.

Because the syntax needed to invoke those rules could come across as a bit arcane, various user-friendly implementations like ufw and firewalld were introduced as higher-level netfilter interpreters. ufw and firewalld are, however, primarily designed to solve the kinds of problems faced by standalone computers. Building full-sized net-work solutions will often require the extra muscle of iptables or, since 2014, its replacement, nftables (through the nft command-line tool).

iptables hasn't gone anywhere and is still widely used. In fact, you should expect to run into iptables-protected networks in your work as an admin for many years to come. But nftables, by adding on to the classic netfilter tool set, has brought some important new functionality. Still, for the sake of simplicity, I'm going to use iptables to quickly show you how to handcraft a DMZ from the command line. When that's done, we'll move on to the somewhat more intuitive Shorewall implementation.

10.2.3 Creating a DMZ using iptables

iptables should be installed by default. To confirm that, you can run `iptables -L` to list all the current rules. If you haven't been playing around with it yet, you should see a completely open (ACCEPT) firewall. Note that the INPUT, FORWARD, and OUTPUT chains are all part of the default Filter table. The NAT table that also exists by default can be used to alter (or translate) a packet's routing information so it can move between networks successfully. We'll revisit NAT a bit later:

```
# iptables -L
Chain INPUT (policy ACCEPT)          <──┐  The output (part of the Filter table
target     prot opt source      destination     in this case) identifies rules by chain:
ACCEPT     tcp  --  anywhere     anywhere     tcp dpt:domain    INPUT in this first example.
ACCEPT     udp  --  anywhere     anywhere     udp dpt:domain
ACCEPT     tcp  --  anywhere     anywhere     tcp dpt:bootps
ACCEPT     udp  --  anywhere     anywhere     udp dpt:bootps
```

```
Chain FORWARD (policy ACCEPT)
target     prot opt source     destination
ACCEPT     all  --  anywhere   anywhere
ACCEPT     all  --  anywhere   anywhere

Chain OUTPUT (policy ACCEPT)
target     prot opt source     destination
```

Once you've got an overall plan, which in this case is separating the kinds of servers you're running using a DMZ setup, you should set a strict default policy.

TIP Firewall admin rule #1: always know how it's supposed to end before you start.

These rules form the baseline of a firewall by blocking (DROP) all incoming and forwarding traffic for all interfaces, but allowing outgoing:

```
# iptables -P INPUT DROP
# iptables -P FORWARD DROP
# iptables -P OUTPUT ACCEPT
```

Because their internet connection comes through the router server (perhaps via a network switch), all of the devices on your networks are automatically bound to these rules. Test it out for yourself. Again, feel free to use the virtual network infrastructure described as follows. We'll assume that the three network interfaces attached to your firewall server are named as described in table 10.2.

Table 10.2 Network interface designations used for the coming examples

Designation	Purpose
eth0	Connected to the internet
eth1	Connected to the DMZ
eth2	Connected to the local private network

Linux naming conventions for network interfaces

Once upon a time, you could have safely assumed that your Linux distro would assign simple and straightforward names for the physical network interfaces attached to your computer. The first ethernet interface recognized would be eth0, the second one, eth1, and so on; wireless interfaces would be wlan0 and wlan1 and so forth. (As you saw in chapter 9, virtual devices like tunnels and bridges can be given names using different conventions.) The point is that even if you didn't happen to know an interface's exact name, you could usually guess it pretty quickly. But run `ip addr` on your modern systemd machine, and you may come face to face with something like enp1s0. Or how about this abomination: wlx9cefd5fe4a18. Just trips off your tongue when you repeat it, no?

> *(continued)*
> Here's what's going on. For many solid reasons, systems using predictable interface names are easier and safer to manage, even if there's a bit of a convenience trade-off. An ethernet interface might be made up of *en* for ethernet, *p1* to indicate bus 1, and *s0* to indicate the first physical slot. And a different device might get *wl* (wireless LAN) and *x9cefd5fe4a18*, where the *x* indicates that the hexadecimal number that follows is the device's MAC address.
>
> As long as you know where a device is plugged in and/or what its MAC address is, you can safely predict its interface name. Nevertheless, for simplicity, I'll use the older conventions for this chapter's examples.

You'll want the devices within your local network to be able to communicate with the public-facing servers, including the router itself, in the DMZ. These two rules added to the FORWARD chain in the Filter table will allow data packets to move (FORWARD) between the networks behind the eth1 and eth2 interfaces. -A indicates that what follows should be added as a new rule. This allows your web server in the DMZ to exchange data with the database server in the private network:

```
iptables -A FORWARD -i eth1 -o eth2 -m state \
 --state NEW,ESTABLISHED,RELATED -j ACCEPT
iptables -A FORWARD -i eth2 -o eth1 -m state \
 --state ESTABLISHED,RELATED -j ACCEPT
```

This next rule will be added to the NAT table (-t nat). It uses the TCP protocol to handle all traffic coming through the eth0 interface that's aimed at your application's (fictional) public IP address (54.4.32.10) and specifies that it wants to use the HTTP port 80. Any traffic meeting all of those conditions will be rerouted to the internet IP address of your web server on the DMZ (192.168.1.20):

```
iptables -t nat -A PREROUTING -p tcp -i eth0 -d 54.4.32.10 \
 --dport 80 -j DNAT --to-destination 192.168.1.20
```

Because you haven't opened any access from the internet through the eth0 interface to either the DMZ or the private network, nothing coming from the outside can reach any local servers.

You may think you're done, only you're not. Wait a half hour or so, and you should start receiving angry emails from the developers on your team wondering why they can't download critical software updates or cute cat videos. Be prepared to customize your firewall settings to accommodate unexpected special needs (like access to and from remote software repositories or cloud resources). Ideally, you should anticipate the things you'll need before building the firewall, but the old "pull the trigger and see what breaks" approach also works.

As I mentioned before, iptables isn't at the vanguard of firewalling technology any more, and this example was very bare-bones basic, but I think it does help illustrate how such things work. If you're curious about how the big boys and girls get this kind of thing done on newer deployments, an official guide to putting together something similar using nftables is available at http://mng.bz/b0DM.

10.2.4 Creating a DMZ using Shorewall

I'm sure you already know the drill: the first step is to get the software. Ubuntu users can use APT to install the shorewall package, although those on CentOS will need to get it through the epel-release repository:

```
# yum install epel-release
# yum install shorewall
```

Unlike the command-line-based iptables, Shorewall is managed through configuration files. There's something about having the solid visual representation of complex settings provided by config files that I personally find reassuring. Once you wrap your mind around the way Shorewall settings are spread across a half dozen or so files, you'll probably find working with Shorewall syntax much less intimidating than iptables.

Shorewall startup options are controlled by the /etc/default/shorewall file, but the firewall configuration itself is normally handled by a number of files in the /etc/shorewall/ directory. /etc/shorewall/shorewall.conf sets the shell environment within which Shorewall will run. It's possible that for simple projects, you won't even need to touch either that file or the params and conntrack files that you'll also find there. You will, however, need to create some other files for which templates exist in /usr/share/doc/shorewall/examples/ (or /usr/share/doc/shorewall-5.0.14.1/Samples on CentOS, where 5.0.x is the version number). If you list the contents of that examples/ directory, you'll see four subdirectories that, in turn, contain sample configuration files covering a number of common scenarios:

```
# ls /usr/share/doc/shorewall/examples/
LICENSE.gz       README.txt        two-interfaces
one-interface    three-interfaces  Universal
```

Even though the three-interfaces option looks like a good match for what we're planning here, we'll put together what we need from scratch so you can see clearly and exactly how the process works. Table 10.3 shows a quick rundown of the /etc/shorewall/ files you might find yourself using.

Table 10.3   Shorewall configuration files kept in /etc/shorewall/

Filename	Purpose	Required
zones	Declares the network zones you want to create	Yes
interfaces	Defines which network interfaces will be used for specified zones	Yes
policy	Defines high-level rules controlling traffic between zones	Yes
rules	Defines exceptions to the rules in the policy file	No
masq	Defines dynamic NAT settings	No
stoppedrules	Defines traffic flow while Shorewall is stopped	No
params	Sets shell variables for Shorewall	No
conntrack	Exempts specified traffic from Netfilter connection tracking	No

There's lots of good documentation available through man by invoking man shore-wall-, along with the name of the particular file you're looking for:

```
$ man shorewall-rules
```

THE ZONES FILE

Let's get started using a text editor to create a zones file. The first line defines the Shore-wall server as type firewall. Each of the three active zones you'll create will use type ipv4 addressing (as opposed to IPv6). The net zone represents the public network (the one all the cool kids call the internet), dmz will be the public-facing zone within your infrastructure, and loc will be the private, local network for your backend servers.

Listing 10.5   /etc/shorewall/zones

```
fw firewall
net ipv4
dmz ipv4
loc ipv4
```

THE INTERFACES FILE

Now you'll need to create a file called interfaces where you'll associate each of your new zones with one of the three network interfaces you've got attached to the Shorewall server. detect tells Shorewall that you want the network settings to be automatically detected; dhcp means that you want IP addresses automatically assigned to your interfaces by DHCP servers. And nosmurfs,routefilter,logmartians on the internet-facing interface will filter suspicious packets and source domains, and log-related events.

Listing 10.6   /etc/shorewall/interfaces

```
net eth0 detect dhcp,nosmurfs,routefilter,logmartians
dmz eth1 detect dhcp
loc eth2 detect dhcp
```

Maps the eth0 interface to the internet (net) zone and establishes behavior protocols

THE POLICY FILE

The policy file establishes the default, baseline behavior you want. The first line in this example will silently delete all traffic coming from the internet (`net`) directed at any destination. Outbound traffic from the private zone (`loc`) to the internet is allowed, enabling local machines to receive software updates. The third line states that traffic originating from the firewall should be accepted everywhere. The final line rejects any packets not covered by other rules.

Listing 10.7 /etc/shorewall/policy

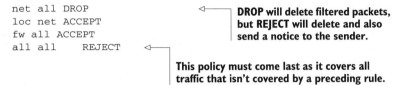

```
net all DROP
loc net ACCEPT
fw all ACCEPT
all all    REJECT
```

DROP will delete filtered packets, but REJECT will delete and also send a notice to the sender.

This policy must come last as it covers all traffic that isn't covered by a preceding rule.

THE RULES FILE

The only other file you'll need to create for this simple configuration is rules. A rules file can, as your needs change, become quite long and complex. For this exercise, however, you'll need only a few lines. The primary goal of the rules file is to fine-tune the broad-strokes exclusions of the policy file.

For instance, because you'll be running a web server in the DMZ zone, you'll want to allow all traffic using the TCP protocol to access via either port 80 (insecure HTTP) or port 443 (secure HTTP). You'll also want to open SSH access from your local servers to machines (including the Shorewall firewall server itself) in the DMZ. Without SSH, how will admin workstations on the local network be able to administer the firewall?

If necessary for remote SSH access, you might also open port 22 from the net network to the firewall. The `Web(DNAT)` rule allows port-forwarding access from the internet to your web server in the DMZ. Although it's not a part of this chapter's example, if you end up running a DNS server on your firewall machine, you'll also open access for port 53 from your local network to the firewall machine.

Listing 10.8 /etc/shorewall/rules

```
ACCEPT all dmz tcp 80,443
ACCEPT net dmz tcp 22
ACCEPT loc dmz tcp 22
ACCEPT loc fw udp 53
Web(DNAT) net dmz:10.0.1.4
```

All that's left is to start up Shorewall on the firewall machine:

```
# systemctl start shorewall
```

NOTE Don't forget to restart Shorewall after making edits to the configuration files. And don't think you won't be making edits to the configuration files as you struggle to get everything working the way it's supposed to.

10.3   *Building a virtual network for infrastructure testing*

You know as well as I do that you have to try a tool out for yourself before you can understand how it works. But trying out the deployments discussed in this chapter will require more than one or two virtual servers to test. To do a proper job here, you'll need to set up multiple networks whose I/O access can be fully controlled.

If you've got a few spare machines, some cabling, and a couple of switches lying around then, great, roll up your sleeves and have at it. I for one really miss playing with server and networking hardware. But what can I do? My world is pretty much all virtual now: I can't even remember the last time I opened up my own workstation.

If, like me, you're stuck with whatever networks you can build for yourself on a command line, here's how it can work. You're going to use VirtualBox to create a couple of virtual NAT networks, provision network interfaces for each of the VMs you'll launch, and manually associate the interfaces with the appropriate networks.

Bear in mind that the number of VirtualBox VMs you'll be able to launch is limited by the amount of free physical memory and CPU power you've got on your VirtualBox host machine. With a Linux host running on 8 GB of RAM, you might be able to squeeze out three concurrent VMs. And don't even think about trying that on a Windows host unless you've got at least 16 GB of RAM. Consider offloading one or two VMs on to a separate PC within your network.

You'll use the vboxmanage command-line tool for the first step (creating the networks for a DMZ configuration). As far as I can see, there's no way to do this from within the VirtualBox GUI. The command `natnetwork add` tells VirtualBox that you want to add a new NAT network. In the first example, the netname will be dmz, and the subnet will be 10.0.1.0/24. The second network will be called loc (for local), and its subnet will be 10.0.2.0/24. When the networks are created, you'll start them using `natnetwork start`:

```
$ vboxmanage natnetwork add --netname dmz \
  --network "10.0.1.0/24" --enable --dhcp on
$ vboxmanage natnetwork add --netname loc \
  --network "10.0.2.0/24" --enable --dhcp on
$ vboxmanage natnetwork start --netname dmz
$ vboxmanage natnetwork start --netname loc
```

Because these are only virtual networks, creating them doesn't require admin permissions.

NOTE Due to a known bug, it might not be possible to create and run NAT networks on VirtualBox versions older than 5.1.

The next step is to create (or, better, clone) the VMs you'll need. (Make sure you've got enough system memory and CPU power on your host machine to handle all the VMs you plan to launch.) Before you start the VMs, click once on the first one's name in the

VirtualBox list, then click the Settings button, and then click the Network item on the left side. If this VM is going to be, say, a Shorewall server, then attach its first network adapter to whichever interface you normally use to give your VMs full internet access.

Now click the Adapter 2 tab and then the Attached To drop-down menu, and select the NAT Network setting. Because you've already created a couple of NAT networks, both should be available as options (figure 10.5). Select one of them for Adapter 2, and then the other for Adapter 3.

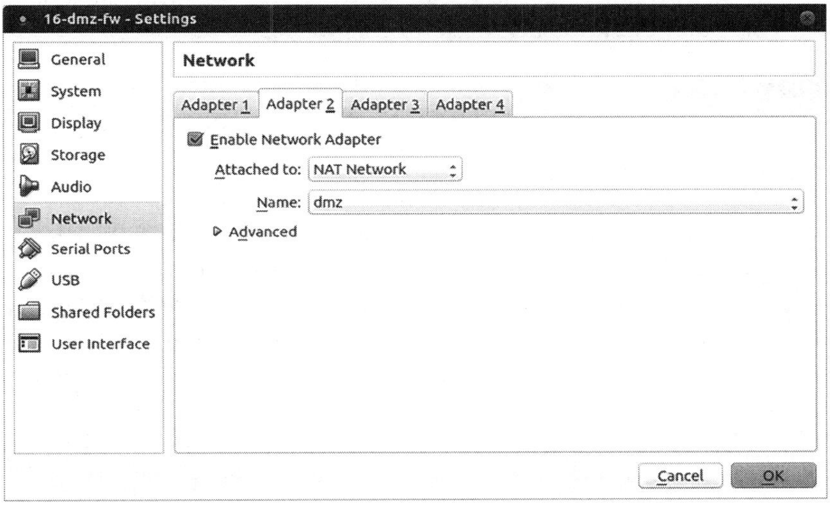

Figure 10.5 Associating a network adapter attached to a NAT network to a VirtualBox VM

To complete a Shorewall test environment, work through the Settings | Network section of your other two VMs and associate one with the dmz NAT network, and the other with loc. Those two VMs will have only one interface each.

With all that done, you can fire up your three VMs and log in. Run `ip addr` on each to confirm that the interfaces have been recognized and are connected to their networks. If you see the right kind of IP address on the inet line (like 10.0.1.5/24), then everything's working:

**This interface is properly connected
to your dmz NAT network.**

```
$ ip addr
2: enp0s3:: <BROADCAST,MULTICAST,UP,LOWER_UP> mtu 1500 qdisc [...]
    inet 10.0.1.5/24 brd 10.0.1.255/ scope global enp0s3          <──
        valid_lft forever preferred_lft forever
```

But if there is no inet address, then you'll need to bring it up manually. Take the interface name (enp0s3, in the example) and use it as an argument for `ifconfig up`. That tells the interface that it had better wake up and get to work. Running `dhclient` will then request an IP address on the dmz network from a DHCP server. (Remember how you set `--dhcp` on when you created the NAT network? That was for a reason.)

```
# ifconfig enp0s3 up
# dhclient enp0s3
```

If this operation fails, there might be something wrong with your network hardware or configuration.

Finally, run `ip addr` once again to make sure everything is as it should be. You've got yourself a test environment. If you're not sure you're quite clear on subnetting and NAT networks, all is not lost: hang on until chapter 14.

Summary

- VPN tunnels can be used to secure remote connections and also to safely expose network infrastructure between remote locations.
- The Easy RSA package contains scripts that can be used to generate a full public key infrastructure (PKI) for TLS encryption applications.
- Firewalls and network architecture can be used together to create protected subnet environments for resources that should not be exposed to public networks.
- The Shorewall firewall tool is configured for varying levels of complexity through plain text files, whereas the iptables firewall implementation is controlled from the command line.
- A DMZ network structure uses firewall configurations to place vulnerable resources in protected, private subnets and public-facing servers in subnets, allowing easier remote access.
- iptables and nftables are deep and flexible command-line implementations of the netfilters Linux kernel firewall tool.

Key terms

- A *virtual private network* (VPN) is a method for connecting remote networks and safely exposing resources between them.
- A *VPN tunnel* describes the way network protocols can be used to obscure VPN traffic as it moves across insecure networks.
- A *VPN client* is a device logging in to or through a VPN server. In the case of OpenVPN, the client could be a smartphone or PC running the OpenVPN GUI client application, or a Linux machine configured using OpenVPN.
- A *packet sniffer* like WireShark can capture and analyze data packets as they move through a network, revealing details about their content, origin, and destination.
- A *NAT network* presents a single external IP address to a public network while managing traffic to and from private devices behind it. This will be discussed in much greater detail in chapter 14.

Command-line review

- `hostname OpenVPN-Server` sets the command prompt description to make it easier to keep track of which server you're logged in to.
- `cp -r /usr/share/easy-rsa/ /etc/openvpn` copies the Easy RSA scripts and environment configuration files to the working OpenVPN directory.
- `./build-key-server server` generates an RSA key pair set with the name server.
- `./pkitool client` generates a client set of keys from an existing RSA key infrastructure.
- `openvpn --tls-client --config /etc/openvpn/client.conf` launches Open-VPN on a Linux client using the settings from the client.conf file.
- `iptables -A FORWARD -i eth1 -o eth2 -m state --state NEW,ESTAB-LISHED,RELATED -j ACCEPT` allows data transfers between the eth1 and eth2 network interfaces.
- `man shorewall-rules` displays documentation on the rules file used by Shorewall.
- `systemctl start shorewall` starts the Shorewall firewall tool.
- `vboxmanage natnetwork add --netname dmz --network "10.0.1.0/24" --enable --dhcp on` uses the VirtualBox CLI to create and configure a virtual NAT network with DHCP for VirtualBox VMs.
- `vboxmanage natnetwork start --netname dmz` starts a virtual NAT network.
- `dhclient enp0s3` requests an IP address for the enp0s3 interface from a DHCP server.

Test yourself

1 A properly configured OpenVPN tunnel can improve security by
   a Applying firewall rules to control access between networks
   b Isolating network-attached devices through subnetting
   c Adding encryption to network connections
   d Obscuring traffic moving through a public network

2 To enable internal routing on a server, you need to uncomment a line in the /etc/sysctl.conf file. Which one?
   a `net.ipv4.ip_forward=1`
   b `net.ipv4.tcp_syncookies=1`
   c `net.ipv6.conf.all.accept_redirects = 0`
   d `net.ipv4.conf.all.accept_source_route = 0`

3 After installing easy-rsa, where will you find the scripts you'll use to generate your keys?
   a /usr/share/easy-rsa/
   b /usr/share/easy-rsa/scripts/

    c /usr/share/easy-rsa/examples/

    d /usr/share/docs/easy-rsa/

  4 Which of the following scripts will do most of the work generating RSA scripts?

    a vars

    b build-key-server

    c build.ca

    d pkitool

  5 After installing OpenVPN, where will you find configuration file templates?

    a /usr/share/doc/openvpn/examples/sample-config-files/server.conf/

    b /usr/share/doc/openvpn/sample-config-files/server.conf.gz

    c /usr/share/doc/openvpn/examples/sample-config-files/server.conf.gz

    d /usr/share/openvpn/examples/sample-config-files/server/

  6 Which of the following values can be added to the /etc/openvpn/server.conf file to port-forward clients to a web server?

    a `port-share localhost 80`

    b `proto tcp`

    c `client-to-client`

    d `push "route 10.0.3.0 255.255.255.0"`

  7 Which of the following iptables commands will silently block all traffic sent to an interface?

    a `iptables -P OUTPUT DROP`

    b `iptables -P INPUT DROP`

    c `iptables -P INPUT REJECT`

    d `iptables -P FORWARD DROP`

  8 Which of the following Shorewall files is used to set a default access profile for your firewall?

    a params

    b interfaces

    c rules

    d policy

Answer key

1. c, 2. a, 3. a, 4. d, 5. c, 6. a, 7. b, 8. d

System monitoring: Working with log files

This chapter covers

- Filtering log entries to maintain system health
- The care and feeding of your Linux logging system
- Filtering text streams using grep, awk, and sed
- Deploying intrusion detection systems

If all you had to work with was just the things you've learned so far in this book, I'd say you're ready to put together a pretty respectable server. It'll be connected, automated, backed up, open for remote clients requesting data and other services, and at least reasonably secure. All the comforts of home.

Time to put your feet up and enjoy the view? Not yet. Your server may be properly configured, but you'll also need to keep an eye on the way it handles the road once it enters its production environment. How does that work? As you'll soon see, most Linux system monitoring consists of reading log files.

A *log entry* is a text-based record of some system event. When a user enters authentication credentials, a remote client requests data from a web server, an application crashes, or a new hardware device is connected, a descriptive note is appended to one or more log files.

229

Even a lightly used system can generate many thousands of lines of log files between the time it's booted up and shut down, and busy applications can easily produce millions of lines a day. Because log files tend to be long and boring, you'll probably want to outsource their reading to software that can intelligently filter only urgent entries, like warnings of imminent failures, and notify you only when absolutely necessary. The better you get at configuring your system's log behavior and managing the ever-growing log files, the better you'll understand your system's strengths and weaknesses—and the more reliable your system will become.

For those who can read them, log files are a treasure chest of valuable insights. They can tell you about weaknesses in your security defenses and past unauthorized intrusions. Log entries can help you anticipate problems with your system security and performance, and diagnose them once everything has already blown up.

You could say that this chapter is about providing you with an inventory of the log resources at your disposal and describing the best-practice approaches to configuring, consuming, and managing your logs. You'll also learn about intrusion detection tools that can be set to regularly scan your server and network environments looking for telltale signs of suspicious activity.

But the chapter is really focused on trouble-proofing your system to protect it from security breaches and performance outages. If you're an admin responsible for a critical public-facing server, then this kind of trouble-proofing is for you.

11.1 *Working with system logs*

For decades, Linux logging has been managed by the *syslogd* daemon. Syslogd would collect the log messages that system processes and applications sent to the /dev/log pseudo device. Then it would direct the messages to appropriate plain text log files in the /var/log/ directory. Syslogd (figure 11.1) would know where to send the messages because each one includes headers containing metadata fields (including a timestamp, and the message origin and priority).

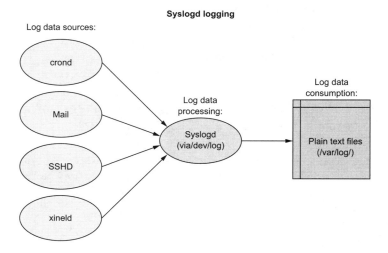

Figure 11.1 The flow of log data from sample sources through the syslogd daemon

In the wake of systemd's relentless, world-conquering juggernaut, Linux logging is now also handled by journald. I say *also* because syslogd hasn't gone anywhere, and you can still find most of its traditional log files in /var/log/. But you need to be aware that there's a new sheriff in town whose (command line) name is *journalctl.*

Like everything else connected to systemd, the move to journald has been contentious. No one will deny the value behind journald's new functionality (illustrated in figure 11.2). You'll soon see for yourself how it introduces some powerful filtering and searches. But the fact that journald stores log data in a binary file rather than plain text is definitely an issue.

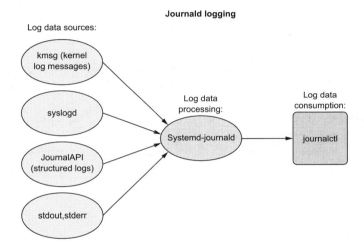

Figure 11.2   The journald logs (including those generated by syslogd) are consumed using the journalctl command-line tool.

Practically, because they're binary, it might sometimes be difficult or even impossible to access your logs. Think about it: when you most need it (while struggling to recover from a system crash, perhaps), journalctl will probably be out of service. Syslogd logs, on the other hand, will always be accessible to you as long as you can mount their drive. This can be immensely helpful when you're trying to figure out what brought down your system and what has to be done to get it back up. The good news is that both systems will continue to coexist for the foreseeable future.

11.1.1   Logging with journald

Here's one that came my way last week. A worried developer brought me his laptop running Ubuntu, complaining that it was dying. The boot had, in fact, stalled, leaving a black screen displaying a single message that read something like this:

```
/dev/sda1: clean, 127663/900212 files, 709879/3619856 blocks
```

The fact that I was getting a reference to /dev/sda1 told me that the hard drive was alive, the boot process had made it past GRUB, and Linux was at least partially loaded. In fact, that particular screen message turned out to be misleading, because it represented the last successful stage the boot process cleared before stalling and had nothing to do with the problem itself.

After a bit of trial and error, including booting the laptop to a live USB drive and mounting the laptop's drive (the way you saw back in chapter 6), it turned out that Linux had fully loaded, but it had failed to launch the GUI desktop. How did I discover that gem? Back in a failed boot (with the /dev/sda1:… showing onscreen), I pressed Alt-F1 and was taken to the login of a virtual console. From there I had full command-line shell access.

> **TIP** It turns out that you can open multiple virtual consoles using Alt-F2, Alt-F3, and so forth. You can also switch back and forth between them through Alt-<the appropriate F-key>. Keep in mind that you can return to the host shell (usually your GUI session) using Alt-F7.

Why was the desktop GUI not loading? And why am I even telling you about this whole business in the first place? The answer to both questions can be found, you guessed it, in the laptop's logs.

To figure it all out, let's take a small detour to learn a bit more about journalctl and then get back to that poor laptop. Typing `journalctl` by itself returns a screen full of the oldest log entries currently on the system. The first line, however, displays the start and end date of the available entries. In the following, there are nearly nine months of log entries, which would require a great many screens to display in order:

```
# journalctl
-- Logs begin at Thu 2016-12-15 08:46:17 EST,
➥ end at Mon 2017-09-04 21:14:54 EDT. --
```

As you're likely to be interested in more recent activity, the -n 20 argument will display only the last 20 entries:

```
# journalctl -n 20
```

It's always a good idea to check your logs every now and then. I ran that command on my own workstation to confirm that it works as expected and discovered an orphaned OpenVPN client. Bless its little heart. Every 5 seconds, the client was faithfully trying to connect with a VPN server that, sadly, no longer existed, and then sending off new entries to tell me about it. To resolve the problem, I used systemctl to first stop and then disable the OpenVPN service.

As I wrote earlier, the more accurately you can narrow down results, the quicker you'll get the information you're after. One useful way to filter logs is to display results by priority. Adding -p emerg, for instance, shows you only those log entries categorized as an emergency. If you know something has broken on your system but can't isolate the problem, emerg would be a good first place to look:

```
# journalctl -p emerg
```

Besides `emerg`, you can also filter for debug, info, notice, warning, err, crit, and alert messages (see syslogd's priority levels in the next section). Adding the `-f` flag (for follow) displays the 10 most recent entries and any subsequent entries as they're created. This allows you to watch events in real time as they occur:

```
# journalctl -f
```

You can also filter logs by date and time. And here's where we arrive back at the GUI-less laptop. If you've got a pretty good idea when the boot process ground to a halt, you can narrow down your search to return only events from that time frame. Fortunately, the `--since` and `--until` arguments take dates and times. If you don't specify a date, you'll get the most recent time meeting those criteria.

In my case, I could specify a 2-minute bracket within which I figured the failure occurred. Two minutes, especially during a system boot, can still produce a lot of log entries—but it will be a whole lot easier to browse than 20 minute's worth:

```
# journalctl --since 15:50:00 --until 15:52:00
```

Had I run that command on the laptop, I might have saved myself some time. As it happened, however, I went with the older syslog log files instead. Let's see how those work.

11.1.2 Logging with syslogd

All the logs generated by events on a syslogd system are added to the /var/log/syslog file. But, depending on their identifying characteristics, they might also be sent to one or more other files in the same directory.

With syslogd, the way messages are distributed is determined by the contents of the 50-default.conf file that lives in the /etc/rsyslog.d/ directory. This example from 50-default.conf shows how log messages marked as cron-related will be written to the cron.log file. In this case, the asterisk (`*`) tells syslogd to send entries with any priority level (as opposed to a single level like `emerg` or `err`):

```
cron.*    /var/log/cron.log
```

Working with syslogd log files doesn't require any special tools like journalctl. But if you want to get good at this, you'll need to know what kind of information is kept in each of the standard log files. Table 11.1 lists the most common syslogd log files and their purposes. (To get you up to speed on the others, check out their man pages. `man lastlog` is one example.)

Table 11.1 Commonly used syslogd facilities

Filename	Purpose
auth.log	System authentication and security events
boot.log	A record of boot-related events

Table 11.1   Commonly used syslogd facilities *(continued)*

Filename	Purpose
dmesg	Kernel-ring buffer events related to device drivers
dpkg.log	Software package-management events
kern.log	Linux kernel events
syslog	A collection of all logs
wtmp	Tracks user sessions (accessed through the who and last commands)

In addition, individual applications will sometimes write to their own log files. You'll often also see entire directories like /var/log/apache2/ or /var/log/mysql/ created to receive application data. Log redirection can also be controlled through any one of eight priority levels, in addition to the * symbol you saw before. Table 11.2 lists syslogd's priority levels.

Table 11.2   Syslogd priority levels

Level	Description
debug	Helpful for debugging
info	Informational
notice	Normal conditions
warn	Conditions requiring warnings
err	Error conditions
crit	Critical conditions
alert	Immediate action required
emerg	System unusable

Now, curious about what I found on that laptop? Well, it's not really relevant to this chapter, but because you've been such a nice reader I'll tell you anyway. This one appeared in the syslog log file itself:

```
xinit: unable to connect to X server: connection refused
```

X server is the Linux system that handles desktop graphical interfaces. If the user was unable to connect, it sounds like one of two things:

- The X server system had become corrupted.
- There was some kind of authentication problem.

It wasn't the former because, by this time, I'd already successfully logged in to a desktop session using a different user account. But it was difficult to see how the laptop's owner would have been able to authenticate in a command-line shell and still be refused access to the desktop. Nevertheless, it seemed worth exploring further, so I opened up the auth.log file, and here's what I saw (with *username* used here in place of the developer's name):

```
lightdm: pam_succeed_if(lightdm:auth): requirement
       "user ingroup nopasswdlogin" not met by user "username"
```

I know that lightdm is the desktop manager used by Ubuntu computers, and pam is a module that handles Linux user authentication. But I'll admit that I didn't understand the full significance of the message until I fed it into my favorite internet search engine.

There I learned that other people facing that message had traced it to incorrect ownership of the .Xauthority file kept in the user's home directory. Apparently X server can only load a GUI session if the .Xauthority file belongs to the user. I checked, and this user's .Xauthority file actually belonged to root. Fixing the problem was as simple as running chown to change the ownership back to username:

```
$ ls -al | grep Xauthority
-rw-------  1 root root  56 Sep  4 08:44 .Xauthority
# chown username:username .Xauthority
```

How did the ownership get mixed up in the first place? Who knows. But it happened. And the smart use of log files helped me fix it.

11.2 *Managing log files*

With hundreds of system processes spitting out thousands of log messages each hour, an unmanaged log system quickly fills all the storage space available to it. At that point logging will break down, along with any other system processes relying on that space. What to do? Continue reading.

11.2.1 *The journald way*

Journald deals with the problem by automatically limiting the maximum disk space the journald system will be allowed to use. Once a limit is reached, older messages are removed and deleted. This setting is controlled by the SystemMaxUse= and RuntimeMaxUse= settings in the /etc/systemd/journal.conf file.

What's the difference between these settings? By default, journald builds and maintains its journal in the /run/log/journal file, which is a volatile file that's destroyed each time the system is shut down. You can, however, direct journald to maintain a persistent journal file at /var/log/journal. You'd use either one or the other of those two journal.conf settings depending on your system setup. Converting to a persistent journal file requires only that you create a /var/log/journal/ directory, and use systemd-tmpfiles to direct log traffic appropriately:

```
# mkdir -p /var/log/journal
# systemd-tmpfiles --create --prefix /var/log/journal
```

11.2.2 *The syslogd way*

By default, syslogd handles log rotation, compression, and deletion behind the scenes without any help from you. But you should know how it's done in case you ever have logs needing special treatment.

What kind of special treatment could a simple log ever require? Well, suppose your company has to be compliant with the transaction reporting rules associated with regulatory or industry standards like Sarbanes-Oxley or PCI-DSS. If your IT infrastructure records must remain accessible for longer periods of time, then you'll definitely want to know how to find your way through the key files.

To see the logrotate system in action, list some of the contents of the /var/log/ directory. The auth.log file, for instance, appears in three different formats:

- *auth.log*—The version that's currently active, with new auth messages being written to it.
- *auth.log.1*—The most recent file to have been rotated out of service. It's maintained in uncompressed format to make it easier to quickly call it back into action should it be necessary.
- *auth.log.2.gz*—An older collection (as you can see from the .gz file extension in the following listing) that, because it's less likely to be needed, has been compressed to save space.

Listing 11.1   Contents of the /var/log/ directory

**The currently active
version of auth.log**

```
$ ls /var/log | grep auth
auth.log
auth.log.1                        The most recently
auth.log.2.gz                     retired version
auth.log.3.gz
auth.log.4.gz          Subsequent versions are
                       compressed using gzip.
```

When, after seven days, the next rotation date arrives, auth.log.2.gz will be renamed auth.log.3.gz, auth.log.1 will be compressed and renamed auth.log.2.gz, auth.log will become auth.log.1, and a new file will be created and given the name auth.log. The default log rotation cycle is controlled in the /etc/logrotate.conf file. The values illustrated in this listing rotate files after a single active week and delete old files after four weeks.

Listing 11.2   Some common settings from the /etc/logrotate.conf file

```
# rotate log files weekly
weekly
# keep 4 weeks worth of backlogs
rotate 4
# create new (empty) log files after rotating old ones
create
# packages drop log rotation information into this directory
include /etc/logrotate.d
```

The /etc/logrotate.d/ directory also contains customized configuration files for managing the log rotation of individual services or applications. Listing the contents of that directory, you see these config files:

```
$ ls /etc/logrotate.d/
apache2  apt  dpkg  mysql-server  rsyslog  samba  unattended-upgrade
```

Here's what the apt config file looks like on my system.

Listing 11.3   Contents of the /etc/logrotate.d/apt log rotate configuration file

```
                /var/log/apt/term.log {
Files will be       rotate 12                    Rotations will take
rotated 12          monthly                      place once a month.
times before        compress
being deleted.      missingok
                    notifempty               Rotated files will be
                }                            immediately compressed.
                /var/log/apt/history.log {
                    rotate 12
                    monthly
                    compress
                    missingok
                    notifempty
                }
```

> **TIP**   Many admins choose to redirect log entries to purpose-built remote log servers where the data can receive all the specialized attention it deserves. This can free up application servers for their immediate tasks and consolidate log data in a single, easily accessible central location.

11.3   Consuming large files

You know you've got better things to do with your time than read through millions of lines of log entries. The following sections describe three text-processing tools that can do it for you—faster and better.

11.3.1   Using grep

Based on my experience, at least, the most versatile and straightforward tool for filtering text is our old friend grep. Here's an obvious example that will search through the auth.log file for evidence of failed login attempts. Searching for the word *failure* will return any line containing the phrase *authentication failure*. Checking this once in a while can help you spot attempts to compromise an account by guessing at the correct password. Anyone can mess up a password once or twice, but too many failed attempts should make you suspicious:

```
$ cat /var/log/auth.log | grep 'Authentication failure'
Sep  6 09:22:21 workstation su[21153]: pam_authenticate: Authentication failure
```

If you're the kind of admin who never makes mistakes, then this search might come up empty. You can guarantee yourself at least one result by manually generating a log entry using a program called logger. Try it out doing something like this:

```
logger "Authentication failure"
```

You could also pre-seed a genuine error by logging in to a user account and entering the wrong password.

As you can tell, grep did the job for you, but all you can see from the results is that there was an authentication failure. Wouldn't it be useful to know whose account was involved? You can expand the results grep returns by telling it to include the lines immediately before and after the match. This example prints the match along with the lines around it. It tells you that someone using the account david (that would be me, I guess) tried unsuccessfully to use su (switch user) to log in to the studio account:

```
$ cat /var/log/auth.log | grep -B 1 -A 1 failure
Sep  6 09:22:19 workstation su[21153]: pam_unix(su:auth): authentication
    failure; logname= uid=1000 euid=0 tty=/dev/pts/4 ruser=david rhost=
    user=studio
Sep  6 09:22:21 workstation su[21153]: pam_authenticate:
    Authentication failure
Sep  6 09:22:21 workstation su[21153]: FAILED su for studio by david
```

By the way, you can also use grep to search within multiple files, which I've personally found useful while writing this book. My problem was that each chapter is saved as a separate file in its own directory, so searching, say, for each reference to the word *daemon* can get tedious. Because copies of the plain text chapter files are also saved to a single manuscript directory, I can move to that directory and search using grep -nr. There it is, in chapter 3:

The n argument tells grep to include line information; the r argument returns recursive results.

```
$ grep -nr daemon
linux-admin-chapter3.adoc:505:
[...]
```

The number 505 in the result tells me that the match appeared on line 505 in the specified file.

11.3.2 *Using awk*

There's a lot that grep can do, but it's not omnipotent. Let's take these entries from the /var/log/mysql/error.log file as an example.

Listing 11.4   A selection of entries from a /var/log/mysql/error.log file

```
2017-09-05T04:42:52.293846Z 0 [Note] Shutting down plugin 'sha256_password'
2017-09-05T04:42:52.293852Z 0 [Note]
➥ Shutting down plugin 'mysql_native_password'
2017-09-05T04:42:52.294032Z 0 [Note] Shutting down plugin 'binlog'
2017-09-05T04:42:52.294647Z 0 [Note] /usr/sbin/mysqld: Shutdown complete
```

```
2017-09-05T12:24:23.819058Z 0 [Warning] Changed limits:
➥ max_open_files: 1024 (requested 5000)
2017-09-05T12:24:23.819193Z 0 [Warning] Changed limits:
➥ table_open_cache: 431 (requested 2000)
```

As you can see, entries are categorized by a priority level enclosed in brackets ([Warning], for example). Suppose you'd like to know how many warning messages there have been since the log was last rotated. Perhaps you regularly compare the numbers with an accepted baseline frequency to know when you might have a problem needing investigation. You can grep for each time [Warning] shows up and then pipe that to wc, which will count the lines, words, and characters in the output:

```
# cat error.log | grep [Warning] | wc
   4219   37292   360409
```

It would seem that [Warning] shows up 4,219 times. Someone is trying to get your attention here. But try the same thing using the awk tool. wc will return only 204 lines! What's going on?

```
# cat error.log | awk '$3 ~/[Warning]/' | wc
    204    3213    27846
```

It seems that grep uses brackets to contain a list of characters and searches the text stream for any one of those. Because there are six unique letters in *Warning*, pretty much every line in the log file was a match. You could always remove the brackets and search for *Warning*, but there might be cases where that returns too many false positives.

As long as the search string is enclosed in forward slashes (/[Warning]/), awk will have no trouble with the brackets. And the sophisticated syntax of awk comes with its own distinct benefits. Take that $3 in the previous example, for instance. By default, awk divides a line of text into individual fields, each separated by one or more spaces. This log entry, for instance, has seven fields:

```
2017-09-05T04:42:52.294032Z 0 [Note] Shutting down plugin binlog
```

grep interprets the final four words (Shutting down plugin binlog) as four distinct data fields, so it would be hard to figure out a way to usefully search those. But the third field represents the entry's priority level, so you can run awk with $3 to return only matching results from that field.

11.3.3 Using sed

In case typing wc to return the number of lines in a stream doesn't appeal to you, you could always do the same thing with sed, in whose universe = will print the current line number (-n tells sed to not print the text itself):

```
# cat error.log | awk '$3 ~/[Warning]/' | sed -n '$='
204
```

OK, but you're not likely to ever need to drag out an industrial-strength stream editor like sed just to do something simple like count lines. I only brought it up as an excuse to introduce you to sed and, in particular, its ability to make complex substitutions on text streams.

Here's a simple example where sed is given the text *hello world* and told to substitute (s) the first instance of the word *world* with the word *fishtank*:

```
$ echo "hello world" | sed "s/world/fishtank/"
hello fishtank
```

Adding a g before the final quotation mark would tell sed to substitute every instance of *world*, assuming there were more than one.

That's nice, but not very useful. Where sed shines is in cleaning up text as part of some larger process. Perhaps the next step of a Bash script you're working on needs to operate on only one part of the input it's receiving. Or maybe you're preparing text so it will be more readable for an end user.

Let's say you've got a file called numbers.txt that contains some code with line numbers. You need to remove the line numbers without messing with the code itself, including the lines that are part of the code. Here's some text you can use (paste it into a file on your own computer to follow along):

Listing 11.5 A sample code snippet with unwanted line numbers

```
4 <menuitem action='Item 1'/>
5 <menuitem action='Item 2'/>
6 <menuitem action='Item 3'/>
7 <menuitem action='Exit'/>
8   <separator/><
```

Now feed the numbers.txt file to sed: use the caret character (^) to point sed to the start of each line. Specify any number, and the instance of any number at that first position will be deleted. Note how the line numbers have disappeared, but the Item numbers are still there:

```
$ sed "s/^ *[0-9]* //g" numbers.txt
<menuitem action='Item 1'/>
<menuitem action='Item 2'/>
<menuitem action='Item 3'/>
<menuitem action='Exit'/>
  <separator/><
```

Alternatively, you could redirect the output to a new file:

```
$ sed "s/^ *[0-9]* //" numbers.txt > new-numbers.txt
```

Finally, sed can selectively print only the subdirectories (and not individual files) from a directory listing. Here's what an unfiltered listing would look like:

```
$ ls -l
total 28
drwxrwxr-x 2 dbclinton dbclinton 4096 Sep  7 14:15 code
-rw-rw-r-- 1 dbclinton dbclinton   55 Sep  6 11:53 file
-rw-rw-r-- 1 dbclinton dbclinton   76 Sep  6 11:54 file2
-rw-rw-r-- 1 dbclinton dbclinton 4163 Sep  6 00:02 mysql.log
-rw-rw-r-- 1 dbclinton dbclinton  137 Sep  7 13:58 numbers
drwxrwxr-x 2 dbclinton dbclinton 4096 Sep  7 14:15 old-files
```

And here's how that would go using sed with ^d to print (p) only those lines starting with a *d* (which, as you know, designates a directory):

```
$ ls -l | sed -n '/^d/ p'
drwxrwxr-x 2 dbclinton dbclinton 4096 Sep  7 14:15 code
drwxrwxr-x 2 dbclinton dbclinton 4096 Sep  7 14:15 old-files
```

11.4 *Monitoring with intrusion detection*

Besides logs, there's another way to monitor your system's health and welfare: intrusion detection. The idea is to create a baseline profile of your system state, the way it's supposed to look, and then scan the system periodically looking for the kinds of changes that suggest there's mischief afoot.

One way to go about this is by implementing a network-based intrusion detection System (NIDS), which relies on software (like Snort, Nmap, and Wireshark) to regularly "sniff" the network neighborhood looking for devices, open ports, and hosts that shouldn't be there. We're not going to spend time on NIDS here (although my "Linux Network Security" course on Pluralsight does).

Closer to home, you can also build a host-based intrusion detection system (HIDS) to keep a steady eye on your server. That's what we're going to learn how to do using an open source package called Tripwire.

Tripwire scans your server and adds key attributes of important system files (like the file size) to its own database. If any one of those files should be edited or deleted, or if new files are added to directories being monitored, those attributes will change. When you later tell Tripwire to check the system, it compares the current values to the ones stored in the database and reports any discrepancies.

> **NOTE** The Tripwire company also provides a commercial version that offers centralized management for multiple installations, policy compliance, support, and compatibility with Windows (not that we'll be needing that one). It's not cheap, but for enterprise-scaled deployments, it can be worth the cost.

To get Tripwire going, you'll first install a plain vanilla mail server to send email reports to any admins you specify. You'll install and configure Tripwire itself, and then edit and encrypt its policy and configuration files (tw.cfg and tw.pol, respectively). Finally, you'll simulate a system change to see how it looks in an emailed report.

11.4.1 *Setting up a mail server*

Creating a basic Linux mail server is a lot easier than you might think. Install the postfix (and, for Ubuntu, mailutils) package. During installation (for Ubuntu, at least), select Internet Site when prompted for a mail configuration type and localhost.local-domain for your system mail name. You'll also want to make sure the inet_interfaces setting in the /etc/postfix/main.cf file is set to localhost. All that's left is to make sure port 25 is open for SMTP on any firewall you've got running and to restart postfix:

```
# systemctl restart postfix
```

That wasn't so bad, was it? You should now have an active mail server that can send emails to remote recipients. It's not ready to handle incoming mail, but you don't need that for this project.

How do you know your mail server is operational?

Send some mail to a local address (named, for example, Steve) using `sendmail steve`. You'll be faced with a blank line on which you're expected to type your message, followed by a hard return, a single dot, and another hard return. Steve can collect his email by typing `mail` on his command line.

11.4.2 Installing Tripwire

Installation is straightforward, although there are some minor variations between Ubuntu and CentOS. I'll cover each in its own section.

UBUNTU

As apt installs the Tripwire package, you'll be prompted to create new passphrases for two sets of signing keys. This process will briefly leave your passphrase unencrypted and exposed to anyone else who happens to be logged in to your system (figure 11.3).

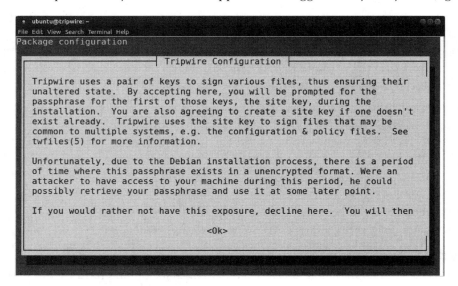

Figure 11.3   Warning screen from the Debian/Ubuntu installation process for Tripwire

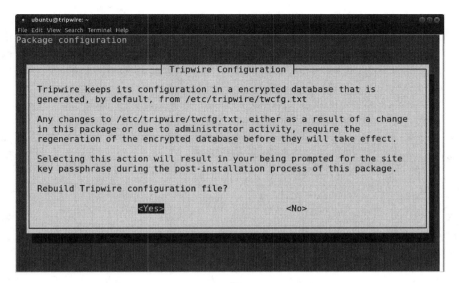

Figure 11.4 Final screen before Tripwire rebuilds the encrypted configuration file

After creating passphrases from both sets of keys, you'll be asked whether you want to rebuild the encrypted Tripwire configuration file (figure 11.4). Rebuilding the configuration and policy files is required after any edits to their source text files. You'll see how to do it manually later, but this first time the Tripwire installation does it for you.

When the installation is complete, you'll be shown a screen (figure 11.5) containing information about the locations of key Tripwire files. Make a note of those, and in particular note the location of the documentation in /usr/share/. As you might expect, there are also configuration files in the /etc/tripwire/ directory.

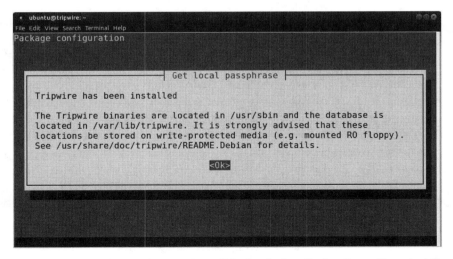

Figure 11.5 When installation completes, Tripwire displays the locations of important files.

CentOS

CentOS installation lacks the fancy, cutting-edge, vintage 1980's graphics accompanying the Ubuntu wizard. In fact, assuming you already have the epel-release repository installed (`install epel-release`), it's a matter of installing the Tripwire package and watching the lines of text fly by.

In CentOS, the signing keys are created by running a program called tripwire-setup-keyfiles after the main installation. There you'll be prompted to create two passphrases. Once the installation is done (for both Ubuntu and CentOS), you'll need to run `tripwire --init` to initialize the database:

```
[...]
Wrote database file: /var/lib/tripwire/tripwire.twd
The database was successfully generated.
```

If you're setting up Tripwire on an LXC container, be aware that you'll likely see a lot of errors like these:

```
The object: "/proc/cpuinfo" is on a different file system...ignoring.
The object: "/proc/diskstats" is on a different file system...ignoring.
The object: "/proc/meminfo" is on a different file system...ignoring.
```

This is happening because some of the system files normally monitored by Tripwire are being shared with the container's host. This means that processes running in the container may not always have full access. Don't worry, though. Other than producing lots of nasty-looking error messages, this won't have any impact on the way Tripwire works.

11.4.3 Configuring Tripwire

You control the way Tripwire behaves through two files kept in the /etc/tripwire/ directory: tw.cfg and tw.pol. The thing is, those files are encrypted and are not only impossible to edit but, unless you've got some special superhero skills, they're unreadable, too. The files are built from the information in two plain text files: twcfg.txt and twpol.txt.

The twcfg.txt file contains some basic environment variables, all of which you can change to fit your needs. Most of them will work perfectly well right out of the box. But changing some of the file locations can add a layer of security through obscurity, especially if you're concerned that the bad guys might be looking to identify and disable the alarm system before getting down to do their work. If you do decide to move things around, twcfg.txt is the file you'll edit.

Listing 11.6   The default contents of the twcfg.txt file

```
ROOT                    =/usr/sbin
POLFILE                 =/etc/tripwire/tw.pol
DBFILE                  =/var/lib/tripwire/$(HOSTNAME).twd
```

Note how the report filename reflects the
server's hostname for easy identification.

```
REPORTFILE              =/var/lib/tripwire/report/$(HOSTNAME)-$(DATE).twr
SITEKEYFILE             =/etc/tripwire/site.key
LOCALKEYFILE            =/etc/tripwire/$(HOSTNAME)-local.key
EDITOR                  =/bin/vi
LATEPROMPTING           =false
LOOSEDIRECTORYCHECKING  =false
MAILNOVIOLATIONS        =true
EMAILREPORTLEVEL        =3
REPORTLEVEL             =3
MAILMETHOD              =SENDMAIL
SYSLOGREPORTING         =false
MAILPROGRAM             =/usr/sbin/sendmail -oi -t
```

You can change the default text editor to
Nano if you're more comfortable with it.

You may find changing the verbosity setting
to 1 will make reports easier to read.

One thing you'll want to add to this file is the email address (or addresses) where you'd like reports to be sent. You do this by adding a GLOBALEMAIL line pointing to your address:

```
GLOBALEMAIL    =info@bootstrap-it.com
```

The twpol.txt file sets the policies Tripwire will use to categorize and scan your file system. The file gives you a working generic policy, but you'll almost certainly need to make at least some customizations to accommodate your particular server setup. You can add those customizations gradually over time, as you get a feel for the kinds of false positives you're seeing in reports, and for the things Tripwire might be missing.

You'll probably get a feel for the kinds of false positives your system will produce pretty quickly. Likely culprits include process ID (PID) files and configuration files for applications you're actively working on. Once you've run Tripwire a couple of times and start to recognize the false positives, look through the twpol.txt file for the line referencing the offending file (the line for the bashrc file, for instance, would look like /etc/bashrc -> $(SEC_CONFIG) ;) and comment it out with the # character (meaning, #/etc/bashrc -> $(SEC_CONFIG) ;).

Browse through the twpol.txt file you've installed on your own server, and note the way policies are defined by rules with names like Invariant Directories. Each rule is assigned a severity level (like SIG_MED, for medium significance, in the following listing). An *Invariant* designation means that you don't expect such objects to change permission or ownership, and that you should therefore be alerted if such events do occur.

Listing 11.7   A sample Tripwire policy rule from the twpol.txt file

```
# Commonly accessed directories that should remain static with  regards
# to owner and group.

(
  rulename = "Invariant Directories",
  severity = $(SIG_MED)
)
```

```
{
  /                                        -> $(SEC_INVARIANT) (recurse = 0) ;
  /home                                    -> $(SEC_INVARIANT) (recurse = 0) ;
  /etc                                     -> $(SEC_INVARIANT) (recurse = 0) ;
}
```

Obviously, you're free to edit the contents and values of any of the dozen or so rules that make up Tripwire policy to suit your needs. The file is well documented, so spending 10 or 15 minutes reading through it should make the kinds of things you can do with it quite clear.

After editing the plain text files, and assuming you're in the same directory, update the encrypted versions using `twadmin --create-cfgfile` and `twadmin --create-polfile`:

```
# twadmin --create-cfgfile --site-keyfile site.key twcfg.txt
Please enter your site passphrase:
Wrote configuration file: /etc/tripwire/tw.cfg
#
# twadmin --create-polfile twpol.txt
Please enter your site passphrase:
Wrote policy file: /etc/tripwire/tw.pol
```

Because the source files are in plain text, you should delete those as soon as their settings have been successfully incorporated into their encrypted cousins:

```
$ cd /etc/tripwire
# rm twcfg.txt
# rm twpol.txt
```

If, sometime in the future, you need to update your configuration, you can recover the original values by running `twadmin --print-cfgfile` or `twadmin --print-polfile`. Those commands give you a file in which you can make any necessary edits:

```
# twadmin --print-cfgfile > twcfg.txt
# twadmin --print-polfile > twpol.txt
```

It's time to take Tripwire out for a test drive. On the command line, `tripwire` takes many arguments with a `-m` prefix, where m stands for module, so `-m c` would load the check module. Running a check prints a report to the screen that will (probably) mostly consist of dozens of file system error messages about files and directories that aren't there:

```
# tripwire -m c
[...]
176. File system error.
     Filename: /proc/pci
     No such file or directory
----------------------------
*** End of report ***
Integrity check complete.
```

Now you can update the Tripwire database based on the results of the previous scan:

```
# tripwire -m u
Please enter your local passphrase:
Wrote database file: /var/lib/tripwire/localhost.localdomain.twd
```

It's possible that Tripwire will complain that it's unable to open the report file. If that happens, run `--update -r` against the most recent file currently in the `/var/lib/tripwire/report/` directory. You'll be shown the report in a text editor. Exit, and the update will continue (`:q!` should do the trick if you find yourself in the vi editor):

```
tripwire -m u -r \ /var/lib/tripwire/report/\
    localhost.localdomain-20170907-102302.twr
```
← **You don't need to include the full filename, including its date/time stamp, as long as you include enough to be unique.**

11.4.4 Generating a test Tripwire report

Let's make some trouble and see whether Tripwire will notice. Adding a new user to the system will leave fingerprints all over the place. At the very least, the passwd, shadow, and group files in /etc/ will be updated. Give your friend Max an account and password:

```
# useradd max
# passwd max
Changing password for user max.
New password:
Retype new password:
passwd: all authentication tokens updated successfully.
```

Now run `tripwire`, specifying that an email report should be sent using level 1 verbosity:

```
tripwire --check --email-report --email-report-level 1
```

If everything works out, you should receive an email that includes text like this:

```
Modified:        "/etc"
Modified:        "/etc/group"
Modified:        "/etc/group-"
Modified:        "/etc/gshadow"
Modified:        "/etc/gshadow-"
Modified:        "/etc/passwd-"
Modified:        "/etc/shadow-"
Modified:        "/etc/subgid"
Modified:        "/etc/subgid-"
Modified:        "/etc/subuid"
Modified:        "/etc/subuid-"
Modified:        "/etc/tripwire"
Modified:        "/etc/tripwire/tw.pol"
Modified:        "/etc/tripwire/tw.cfg"
Modified:        "/etc/passwd"
Modified:        "/etc/shadow"
```

What's left? Once you're done fine-tuning your policies, you can add `tripwire --check` and `tripwire -m u` commands to cron to automate the process. Happy hunting!

Summary

- Journald logging is built around a binary journal file that can be finely parsed using journalctl to target specific matches.
- Log files grow quickly and must be controlled through a rotation regimen that takes business and regulatory needs into account.
- The grep, awk, and sed text-filtering and -formatting tools can be used to manage large volumes of data: grep, by string matches; awk, by breaking strings down into fields; and sed, through string substitution.
- Tripwire can be used for ongoing server monitoring to alert admins should it sense the presence of suspicious behavior.

Key terms

- *Journald* stores its log data in a binary file, which allows for more flexible retrieval but requires a running host system.
- On a *syslogd* system, all log events are written to the /var/log/syslog file.
- *Log rotation* for syslogd log files is controlled through the /etc/logrotate.conf file and through individual files in the /etc/logrotate.d/ directory.
- A *text stream filter* (like grep) searches text for matching strings and, usually, returns the entire line containing the match.
- A *network-based intrusion detection system* (NIDS) monitors a private network for evidence of infiltration.
- A *host-based intrusion detection system* (HIDS) monitors servers for evidence system files have been maliciously altered.
- A *mail server* allows emails to be sent and received by applications or at the command-line level.

Security best practices

- Regularly scan the auth.log file for evidence of repeated failed attempts to access user accounts.
- Configure scanning software like an intrusion detection system to push alerts to admins when potentially compromising events occur.
- The original plain text files used to create encrypted Tripwire configuration and policy files should be deleted immediately after use.

Command-line review

- Alt-F<n> opens a virtual console from a non-GUI shell.
- `journalctl -n 20` displays the 20 most recent log entries in the journal.

- `journalctl --since 15:50:00 --until 15:52:00` displays only events between the *since* and *until* times.
- `systemd-tmpfiles --create --prefix /var/log/journal` instructs systemd to create and maintain a persistent journal rather than a file that's destroyed with every boot.
- `cat /var/log/auth.log | grep -B 1 -A 1 failure` displays matching lines along with the lines immediately before and after.
- `cat /var/log/mysql/error.log | awk '$3 ~/[Warning]/' | wc` searches the MySQL error log for events classified as a warning.
- `sed "s/^ [0-9] //g" numbers.txt` removes numbers at the start of each line of a file.
- `tripwire --init` initializes the database of a Tripwire installation.
- `twadmin --create-cfgfile --site-keyfile site.key twcfg.txt` generates a new encrypted tw.cfg file for Tripwire.

Test yourself

1 The /dev/log pseudo device is used for
   a Storing the journald ephemeral journal file
   b Storing the journald persistent journal file
   c Collecting log event data for syslogd
   d Storing log even data collected by syslogd

2 Which of the following commands will display the five most recent log entries in the journal file?
   a `journalctl -l 5`
   b `journalctl -n 5`
   c `journalctl -f 5`
   d `journalctl --since 5`

3 Which of the following directives would send only kernel-related emergency messages to the existing kern.log file?
   a `kern.emerg -/var/log/kern` in the /etc/rsyslog.d/50-default.conf file
   b `kern.* -/var/lib/kern.log` in the /etc/rsyslog.d/50-default.conf file
   c `*.emerg -/var/log/kern.log` in the /etc/rsyslog.d/30-default.conf file
   d `kern.emerg -/var/log/kern.log` in the /etc/rsyslog.d/50-default.conf file

4 Which configuration file is used to control the log-rotation policies for files in /var/log/?
   a /etc/logrotate.conf
   b /etc/systemd/journal.conf
   c /etc/logrotate.d
   d /etc/rsyslog.conf

5 What arguments will tell grep to include surrounding lines of text along with the matching line it displays?

  a `cat /var/log/auth.log | grep --B 1 --A 1 failure`

  b `cat /var/log/auth.log | grep --since 1 --until 1 failure`

  c `cat /var/log/auth.log | grep -B 1 -A 1 failure`

  d `cat /var/log/auth.log | grep -b 1 -a 1 failure`

6 Which of the following sed commands will remove line numbers from lines of text?

  a `sed "s/^ [0-9] //g"`

  b `sed -n '/^d/ p'`

  c `sed -n '/^d/ [0-9] p'`

  d `sed "s/^ [0-9] //"`

7 Which of the following commands will prepare the Tripwire database for operation?

  a `tripwire-setup-keyfiles`

  b `tripwire --init`

  c `twadmin --create-polfile twpol.txt`

  d `tripwire -m c`

8 Which of these commands contains the appropriate syntax to encrypt and update the Tripwire configuration file?

  a `wadmin --create-polfile --site-keyfile site.key twcfg.txt`

  b `wadmin --create-cfgfile --site-keyfile site.key twcfg.txt`

  c `wadmin --create-cfgfile --local-keyfile local.key twcfg.txt`

  d `wadmin --create-cfgfile --site-keyfile site.key twpol.txt`

Answer key

1. c, 2. b, 3. d, 4. a, 5. c, 6. a, 7. b, 6. b

Sharing data over
a private network

12

This chapter covers

- Sharing documents with Network File System (NFS)
- Fine-tuning restricted access to an NFS share
- Automating remote file shares using /etc/fstab
- Securing and encrypting NFS shares
- Configuring Samba for sharing files with Windows clients
- Organizing your system resources with symbolic and hard links

If you read chapter 8 then you're already up to speed with using Nextcloud to share files between clients over insecure networks like the internet. But for trusted local networks, there are simpler ways to collaborate that are more deeply integrated into the Linux file system itself.

I'm not suggesting that you can only do this locally. It's possible to fully encrypt and secure file system-based sharing tools to safely use them over the internet, but doing it right is not going to be easy. And the particular strengths of these tools are best exploited closer to home.

In this chapter, you're going to learn how to expose carefully defined parts of a server's file system to allow remote trusted clients to collaborate on files and documents. You won't need to create a separate document store the way you did for Nextcloud, as your clients will be able to access the documents where they are in their native locations. This can be useful in a number of common scenarios:

- You want workers to be able to log in to any physical workstation throughout the building and have instant access to the files in their own home directories.
- You want to make specific data collections available to the members of appropriate teams, wherever they might be.
- You want to provide full document read/write access to some remote workers, but read-only access to others.

A bit later we'll look at setting up Samba, which is the tool of choice for sharing Linux-based documents with Windows clients. But most of our attention will be focused on using NFS to permit integrated collaboration among Linux systems.

12.1 Sharing files through Network File System (NFS)

Time to get stuff done. Just how do individuals share full access to documents across a network? As represented in figure 12.1, NFS works by allowing clients to mount specific directories hosted on a remote server as though they were local partitions. Once mounted, the contents of those directories will be visible on the client system both at the command-line level and from the desktop GUI.

Back in chapter 6, you learned how to mount a peripheral media drive to allow access from the file system. Here's a reminder:

```
# mkdir /media/mountdir/
# mount /dev/sdb1 /media/mountdir/
```

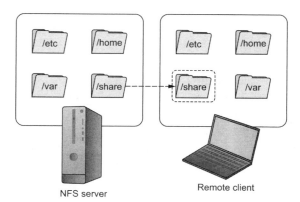

NFS server   Remote client

Figure 12.1   A mounted file share will appear like a local resource on the remote client.

You're going to use the mount command here too, but this time to mount the directories from the remote NFS server as a local partition. We've got some business to take care of before we get there, though. Here, step by step, is how it's going to go:

1 Install NFS on the server.
2 Define client access to server resources through the /etc/exports file.
3 Update NFS on the server.
4 Install NFS on the client.
5 Mount an NFS share.
6 Configure the NFS share to mount at boot time.
7 Open any firewalls you've got running (if necessary).

12.1.1 Setting up the NFS server

Let me show you how to share home directories on your server so that multiple users will be able to access the contents remotely. For a CentOS server, the package you're looking to install is nfs-utils. On Ubuntu, that'll be nfs-kernel-server.

> **NOTE** It may be possible to install NFS server software on an LXC container and trick it into thinking it has sufficient access to the kernel to run properly, but I suspect it won't be worth your time. If you want to virtualize this exercise, stick with VirtualBox.

Either way, the configuration file you're going to work with is called exports, and it lives in the /etc/ directory. On Ubuntu at least, the file comes with a number of useful example directives, each disabled with the # comment character. For our simple example (and assuming the IP address used by your client computer is 192.168.1.11), this is the only active line that file will need:

```
/home 192.168.1.11(rw,sync)
```

Let's break that down:

- /home tells NFS that you want to expose the /home directory on the server along with all its subdirectories. As long as you don't unnecessarily expose sensitive system or personal data, you're free to expose any directories you like.
- 192.168.1.11 is the IP address of the NFS client you want to let in.
- rw assigns that client both read and write permissions on the files in the exposed directories.
- sync maintains a stable environment by writing changes to disk before replying to remote requests.

The default NFS values include ro (read-only, meaning write operations are blocked) and root_squash (remote client users aren't permitted to perform actions on the server as root, no matter what status they have on their own systems). Both settings provide protection for the server and its files. If you're trying to open up some resources to serve as a kind of knowledge library, then the defaults will work best.

If you wanted to override the root_squash default and permit root actions to remote users, you would add the no_root_squash value. Although potentially a serious security vulnerability, no_root_squash can sometimes be necessary when you need your client users to perform administrative work on system files. Here's how that would look:

```
/home 192.168.1.11(rw,sync,no_root_squash)
```

Based on the use-case scenario that provides a single network-based home directory hierarchy for all the users in your company, you'll want to open up access to more than just one client. This next example will permit anyone coming from anywhere on the local network to mount and use the server's /home/ directory. It assumes that there's no one you don't trust with access to the 192.168.1.0 network. If, however, that network is accessible from a WiFi service you provide visitors to your business, then this might not be a good idea:

```
/home  192.168.1.0/255.255.255.0(rw,sync)
```

If you're confused about what that 255.255.255.0 might be doing and how all these network structures work, section 14.1 should set you straight.

> **NOTE** Once again, spelling counts in Linux—and punctuation, too. Be aware that 192.168.1.11 (rw,sync) means that a client from 192.168.1.11 will get read/write permissions. But adding a space so that the directive reads 192.168.1.11 (rw,sync) would give anyone in the world rw rights, and clients logging in from the 192.168.1.11 IP address the default read-only rights!

When you finish editing the exports file, you'll need to run exportfs to force NFS to adopt your new settings. You'll probably see a notice telling you that subtree checking is disabled by default. This is a change to the default behavior because, for most modern use cases, it's generally not worth the trouble:

The r flag tells exportfs to synchronize the file systems, and the flag a applies the action to all directories.

```
# exportfs -ra
exportfs: /etc/exports [2]: Neither 'subtree_check' or 'no_subtree_check'
  specified for export "192.168.1.0/255.255.255.0:/home".
  Assuming default behaviour ('no_subtree_check').
  NOTE: this default has changed since nfs-utils version 1.0.x
```

If you're interested, subtree checking when enabled is used to ensure that file use is consistent with the policies governing both server-based file systems and exported trees.

You can view any NFS file systems currently exposed to clients using `exportfs`:

```
# exportfs
/home      192.168.1.0/255.255.255.0
```

To make it easy to test your share from the client end, create a new file in your home directory on the server, and add some text. If you're running your NFS server on CentOS, don't forget to open the firewall (which comes fully operational by default) and start NFS (which will be stopped by default). And here's how that would look:

```
# firewall-cmd --add-service=nfs
# firewall-cmd --reload
# systemctl start nfs-server
```

You're now ready to set up NFS on a client computer. Learn all about that next.

12.1.2 *Setting up the client*

Things are fast and easy from the client side. Install the same nfs-utils package you used for the server on CentOS, and nfs-common for Ubuntu. Just two more steps from here. First, create a new directory where you'll mount the remote file system. Then mount it using the NFS server's IP address and the file system address you exposed in the server's /etc/export configuration file:

```
# mkdir -p /nfs/home/
# mount 192.168.1.23:/home /nfs/home/
```

◁──────┐ **The -p flag tells Linux to create
any directories in the path that
don't yet exist (like /nfs/).**

At this point, you should be able to open and edit shared files. Navigate to the mount point you created, and you should find at least one subdirectory, the one belonging to your server's main user (ubuntu in my case). Enter the directory, and try opening, editing, and saving the file, then head back to the server to see if you can see the new, updated version:

```
$ cd /nfs/home/
$ ls
ubuntu
```

Success? Congratulations! Although it's kind of creepy that you're having a conversation with yourself. I promise not to tell anyone else.

No success? Here are some troubleshooting tips to consider:

- Make sure your client and the server have basic network connectivity with each other and can actually talk. Ping the IP address of the client from the server and the IP address of the server from the client (for example, `ping 192.168.1.23`) and confirm that you're getting an appropriate response. Remember how you did this back in chapter 3?

- Make sure there isn't a firewall blocking traffic. By default, NFS needs the TCP port 2049 open to do its work. If you're using ufw, you don't need to remember that port number: `ufw allow nfs` will get it done (for a full list of available service aliases, see the /etc/services file).
- Make sure NFS is running properly on the server. Check your configuration with `exportfs` to verify that NFS is using your latest version with `exportfs -a`.
- Make sure the IP address of your server hasn't changed. This can easily happen if the server is getting its IP dynamically from a DHCP server. Ideally, your NFS server should use a static address (see chapter 14 for details). In any case, you can temporarily solve this problem by updating the directive in /etc/fstab (see the next section).

If you want to remove the NFS mount from the client, use `umount`:

```
# umount /nfs/home/
```

12.1.3 *Mounting an NFS share at boot time*

Although you can access those remote files now, I'm afraid your happiness won't persist past the next system shutdown. You could run the `mount` command each time you boot, but that's a habit that probably won't last long. Instead, you can tell Linux to automatically mount the share each time you boot by editing the /etc/fstab file.

Listing 12.1   Contents of a typical /etc/fstab file

```
# /etc/fstab: static file system information.
#
# Use 'blkid' to print a universally unique identifier          <———————┐
# for a device; this may be used with UUID= as a more robust way to name  │
# devices that works even if disks are added and removed. See fstab(5).   │
#                                                                         │
# <file system>      <mount point> <type>  <options>      <dump>  <pass>  │
# / was on /dev/sda2 during installation                                  │
UUID=130fe070-9c44-4236-8227-6b1515baf270 /                               │
    ext4     errors=remount-ro 0        1                                 │
# /boot was on /dev/sda1 during installation          Instructions for finding the
UUID=e06b8003-255f-44b4-ab0f-291367d2928b /boot         UUID identifier for devices
    ext4     defaults      0        2                   that may not yet be listed
# /utility was on /dev/sda5 during installation
UUID=9cae6b93-963d-4995-8d33-5826da106426 /utility
    ext4     defaults      0        2
```

As you can see, an active fstab line will include six fields containing pieces of information about each listed device (see table 12.1).

NOTE Some fstab options include `exec` (or `noexec`) to control whether binaries will be executable from the file system, `ro` to restrict access to read-only, `rw` to permit read and write access, and `defaults` to invoke the default settings (`rw`, `suid`, `dev`, `exec`, `auto`, `nouser`, and `async`).

Table 12.1 Fields in the fstab file

Field	Purpose
File system	Identifies a device either by its boot-time designation (/dev/sda1, which can sometimes change) or, preferably, by its more reliable UUID.
Mount point	Identifies the location on the file system where the device is currently mounted.
Type	The file system type.
Options	Mount options assigned to the device.
Dump	Tells the (outdated) Dump program whether (1) or not (0) to back up the device.
Pass	Tells the fsck program which file system to check first at boot time. The root partition should be first (1).

The fstab file is initially populated with references to attached hardware devices during the OS installation. As admin, you have the right to add your own devices so they too are mounted at boot. Bear in mind the way a device is referenced. Adding a new line (in the client's fstab file) for your NFS share might look like this:

```
192.168.1.23:/home  /nfs/home  nfs
```

Reboot your client. This time, don't manually mount the NFS share, but immediately head over to the directory where it's supposed to be mounted (/nfs/home/) to make sure you can see the server-based files. If it's there, then you know fstab has done its job. Run the mount command by itself; along with a long list of other file systems, you should see your new NFS share with the options that were assigned to it.

Listing 12.2 Partial output of mounted file systems on the client

```
# mount
sysfs on /sys type sysfs (rw,nosuid,nodev,noexec,relatime)
/dev/sda2 on / type
 ext4 (rw,relatime,errors=remount-ro,data=ordered)      ◁── The root partition
/dev/sda1 on /boot type ext4 (rw,relatime,data=ordered)
192.168.1.23:/home on /nfs/home type nfs4
 (rw,relatime,vers=4.0,rsize=262144,wsize=262144,namlen=255,hard,
 proto=tcp,port=0,timeo=600,retrans=2,sec=sys,clientaddr=192.168.1.11,
 local_lock=none,addr=192.168.1.23)
tmpfs on /run/user/1000 type tmpfs (rw,nosuid,nodev,relatime,
 size=204828k,mode=700,uid=1000,gid=1000)
```
The NFS share followed by its boot options

12.1.4 NFS security

Take another quick look at the title of this chapter ("Sharing data over a private network") and note the word *private*. As I mentioned earlier, NFS if left to its own devices won't encrypt the data it hurls back and forth between hosts. You should only use it in private spaces.

But how secure are private spaces? We call a network *private* when it can't be reached from the outside using normal access rules. But if you don't know yet, let me break it to you as gently as possible: hackers aren't shy about using abnormal access rules. Or, more accurately, they're likely to generate and deploy their own homemade rules.

If the security of your NFS server share depends on how well you trust the folks in the office, then it could probably use some improvements. It's not that you should never trust the people you know and work with, it's that you can't always be sure that their workstations and accounts haven't been compromised by outsiders. Nor can you be certain that there's no one from the outside listening in to your network traffic.

Your general approach should be to follow the *principle of least privilege*: never open up a resource any wider than absolutely necessary, and never give users (or clients) any more access than they absolutely need to get their work done. For example, if your clients don't need to edit the files, by all means pass the ro (read-only) option in the /etc/exports file. Or, if your clients need access to only some of the files in a directory hierarchy, block all the others.

FIREWALL RULES

An important line of defense will be your firewall. If there are any individual workstations within your trusted private network that don't need access to your NFS server, lock them out:

```
# ufw deny to 192.168.1.10
```

On CentOS, that would be

```
# firewall-cmd --add-rich-rule="rule family='ipv4'
    source address='192.168.1.10' reject"
# firewall-cmd --reload
```

Speaking of locking them out, following a change of firewall rules on the NFS server, you may need to reboot the client machine before the NFS share is fully blocked.

Sometimes you'll want your server to host more than just NFS files. There might also be unrelated data stores and configuration files needed by developer or admin teams working on their own machines. Here's how you can block a developer, whose laptop has the IP 192.168.1.10, from accessing NFS on the server, while retaining full access to other server resources:

```
# ufw deny from 192.168.1.10 to any port 2049
```

To test this, consider installing the Apache web server in addition to NFS on your NFS server. If your NFS share fails to load on the client, but you can still access the web application on the server, then you'll know you've found your sweet spot:

```
# ls /nfs/home/                              curl retrieves the contents
# curl 192.168.1.3          ◁────┘           of a web page, if accessible.
Welcome to my web server on my NFS machine
```

ENCRYPTION

As always, restricting access to your resources doesn't mean that the data you transfer between servers and clients is safe—at least when that data is not encrypted. If you're only transferring data within your local private network, and you're confident that it truly is local and private, then you can be excused for relying on what you've already got going. But any data that will move across insecure networks requires some extra protection.

Here's a brief list of ways you can deal with the problem (besides squeezing your eyes shut and hoping only good things happen to you, which, strictly speaking, is more of a coping mechanism):

- You can run an NFS share on top of a VPN much the same way you used a VPN to encrypt data movement back in chapter 10.
- The IPSec protocol secures data at the IP network level by preventing IP spoofing and packet tampering. It encrypts all data contained in IP packets through the use of session keys. You can configure IPSec as a tunnel that, in broad terms, would work in a way that's similar to that OpenVPN tunnel.
- NFS can be configured to run over an underlying SSH session, which is another kind of tunnel. It's always good to have multiple options available in case you run into an unusual use case. Note that this is a nonstandard option.
- Assuming you already have a Kerberos authentication server running as part of your infrastructure and you're using at least NFS v.4, adding the `sec=krb5p` line to your NFS configuration will pass managing the problem into the capable hands of Kerberos.
- Finally, an alternative to NFS is SSH Filesystem (SSHFS). SSHFS similarly mounts remote file systems as local volumes, but works through the SFTP protocol using the Filesystem in Userspace (FUSE) software interface.

12.2 *Sharing files with Windows users using Samba*

If your office network includes users who need to access Linux-based files from their Windows PCs, then Samba is a solution that's both simple and devilishly complex. What do I mean? Setting up a basic connection like the one I'm going to demonstrate won't take much work at all. But integrating authentication with a Windows Active Directory domain or struggling with SELinux on the Linux server can give you considerably more trouble. It's no accident that a whole library of Samba configuration books has been published over the years.

For our purposes, you can get away with installing only the samba and smbclient packages on Ubuntu. For CentOS, it's simpler to run `yum` against `samba*` to grab the whole collection of Samba-related tools (remember: the * character is interpreted to return all results containing the preceding text). Here's how the rest of the process will unfold:

1 Create a Samba user account on the Linux server.
2 Designate a share directory.
3 Define the share through the edit smb.conf file.

    4 Test the configuration.

    5 Connect from a Windows client.

You'll need to use a program called smbpasswd to set up a Samba user as an account clients will use to log in to. But because the Samba authority will be added to an existing account, you should first create a new Linux account. I'll call mine sambauser, but you can choose any name you like:

```
# adduser sambauser
# smbpasswd -a sambauser
```

Next, you can create a directory where the share will be based. I'm going to follow the same pattern I used earlier for my NFS share. To make it easier to test things later, I'll create a file within the new directory. Because multiple clients might end up working with files in this directory, you can avoid potential permissions issues by using chmod to open up the directory permissions to 777 (read, write, and execute for all users):

```
# mkdir -p /samba/sharehome
# touch /samba/sharehome/myfile
# chmod 777 /samba/sharehome
```

That's the Samba environment all built up. Now you can add a configuration to the smb.conf file in the /etc/samba/ directory. You should browse through the configuration file to get a feel for how much customization is possible, and how complicated things can get:

```
# nano /etc/samba/smb.conf
```

For your humble aspirations right how, however, you'll only need to add a single section that defines your share. I'll throw all caution to the wind and call the share sharehome. The two entries that you absolutely must include are path, which points to the directory you plan to use for your shared documents, and, assuming you want your clients to be able to create and edit files, writable with a value of yes. With that done, save the file and close your text editor.

Listing 12.3 A file share configuration section from the /etc/samba/smb.conf file

```
[sharehome]
path = /samba/sharehome
writable = yes
```

Now use systemctl to start and enable the Samba daemon. Ubuntu knows Samba as smbd, but on CentOS, it'll be smb (without the *d*):

```
# systemctl start smbd
# systemctl enable smbd
```
◁—— **Note that smbd is the daemon name systemctl recognizes on Ubuntu; on CentOS it will be smb.**

12.2.1 Testing your Samba configuration

It's always a good idea to test your configuration before digging in too deeply, so running `testparm` will show you whether the section you added can be properly read by the Samba service. This output suggests that everything is fine:

```
# testparm
Load smb config files from /etc/samba/smb.conf
rlimit_max: increasing rlimit_max (1024) to minimum Windows limit (16384)
WARNING: The "syslog" option is deprecated
Processing section "[printers]"
Processing section "[print$]"
Processing section "[sharehome]"
Loaded services file OK.
Server role: ROLE_STANDALONE
Press Enter to see a dump of your service definitions
```

testparm tests and displays your Samba configuration.

Confirmation that your sharehome section is recognized

One more test before you invite your Windows friends in: you can use the smbclient program to log in to your Samba share from the local machine. You'll first need to switch the user (`su`) to the sambauser account you associated with Samba earlier. You can then run `smbclient` against the share's host address and name (//localhost/sharehome):

```
$ su sambauser
Password:
# smbclient //localhost/sharehome
Enter sambauser's password:
Domain=[WORKGROUP] OS=[Windows 6.1] Server=[Samba 4.3.11-Ubuntu]
smb: \>
```

Note the special Samba command prompt telling you that you're now in a Samba shell session.

In this case, as you can see from the command-line prompt, you've been dropped into a Samba shell. Run `ls` to display the contents, and you should see the myfile file you created:

```
smb: \> ls
  .            D        0  Thu Sep 14 20:54:32 2017
  ..           D        0  Thu Sep 14 20:36:52 2017
  myfile       N        0  Thu Sep 14 20:54:32 2017

    953363332 blocks of size 1024. 732660884 blocks available
```

By the way, as you already know from chapter 9, poorly trained and/or impatient admins will sometimes be tempted to switch off SELinux at the first sign of conflict. This is a bad thing and certainly nothing highly trained and infinitely patient Linux folk like us would ever consider. Most of the time.

If you're running this demo on CentOS and find yourself unable to access the files in your share, it might be because SELinux is getting in the way:

```
smb: \> ls
NT_STATUS_ACCESS_DENIED listing \*
```

Don't ever do what I'm about to tell you. Not even for a simple demo on a non-production server. Never. But if you did want to disable SELinux for a minute or two to avoid having to read through the smb.conf file documentation to figure out how to fix the problem properly, I'm sure you'll remember that running `setenforce 0` will disable SELinux. But I never told you that. In fact, this whole paragraph never happened.

If you've got a firewall protecting your server, you'll need to open up some ports so Samba can get in and out. But the specific ports you'll need will at least partly depend on what you include in your Samba configuration. Kerberos, LDAP, DNS, and NetBIOS are common services to run in conjunction with Samba.

Using `netstat` on the server to scan for ports being used by Samba (using the `smbd` search term) will give you the key ports on a basic system. This example returns 139 and 445, but there could be many more:

```
# netstat -tulpn | egrep smbd
tcp    0  0 0.0.0.0:139   0.0.0.0:*   LISTEN  2423/smbd
tcp    0  0 0.0.0.0:445   0.0.0.0:*   LISTEN  2423/smbd
tcp6   0  0 :::139        :::*        LISTEN  2423/smbd
tcp6   0  0 :::445        :::*        LISTEN  2423/smbd
```

If you don't have netstat on your machine, install the net-tools package.

12.2.2 *Accessing a Samba server from Windows*

From the Windows client machine, create a desktop shortcut (they've got those things in Windows, too!) and give it a location pointing to the Samba share on your Linux server. Assuming the Linux server's IP address is 192.168.1.23 and the name you gave the Samba share was sharehome, the address you'll enter will look like this:

```
\\192.168.1.23\sharehome
```

To connect, the Windows user must authenticate using the Linux Samba username and password you created earlier, unless you chose to integrate your Samba authentication with a Windows Active Directory domain. That's something that can be both more efficient in the long run and more secure than relying on a simple password. I'd show you how that's done, but first let me grab a quick look at the book cover to confirm my suspicion. Yup. This is a Linux book. Sorry, no Windows configuration guides.

12.3 *Sharing files with yourself using symbolic links*

Granted, the connection to this chapter might seem a bit stretched, but users will sometimes want to share their files with themselves. Creating symbolic links (also known as *symlinks*) can make that happen. Just to be clear, I'm not talking about making your files available to both you and your evil twin, but making them more readily accessible from wherever you might happen to be.

Let me illustrate that. Earlier in the chapter, you used an NFS share to give your users access to a central /home/ directory. The goal was to let any user sit down in front of any workstation in the office and, through the /nfs/home/ directory you created, immediately get to work with their own documents.

But what if not all of your users are so comfortable with the Linux file system hierarchy, not to mention the command line? Perhaps some users don't know where on the file system their files live. Feel free to create a symbolic link to, say, a mounted shared directory that will display on the user's GUI desktop.

> **NOTE** User accounts on GUI Linux systems are given a set of subdirectories (like Documents and Pictures) in their /home/username/ directory where they can conveniently organize their documents. One of those subdirectories is called Desktop, and whatever files are saved to it will appear as icons on the GUI screen users will see first when they log in. Keep in mind that those subdirectories won't be created until the user logs in to the new account for the first time.

You create a symbolic link with the ln command followed by the -s argument, the file system object you want to link, and the location where you'd like the link placed:

```
# ln -s /nfs/home/ /home/username/Desktop/
```

That's all there is to it. In fact, it's so simple that you might wonder why it deserves a section all for itself. It's about the -s argument. The *s* stands for symbolic, which means there must also be a different flavor of link. Indeed, by default, ln will create a hard link.

But what's the difference? A *symbolic link* points to a separate file system object. Reading, executing, or editing the symbolic link will read, execute, or edit the linked object. But if you move or delete the original the symbolic link, being nothing more than a pointer to a separate object, it will break.

A *hard link*, by contrast, is an exact duplicate of its target to the point that the two files will share a single inode. An inode, as you recall from chapter 1, is metadata describing an object's attributes: in particular, its location within the file system.

Let's see all this in action. Create two files, and add a different bit of text to each. Now create a hard link for one of the files and a symbolic link for the other:

```
$ nano file1
$ nano file2
$ ln file1 file1-hard
$ ln -s file2 file2-sym
```

Run ls with the i argument to display inode IDs. Note that the hard-linked files share an identical inode ID number. Note also how the file2-sym file points to file2:

```
$ ls -il
9569544 -rw-rw-r-- 2 ubuntu ubuntu    4 Sep 14 15:40 file1
9569544 -rw-rw-r-- 2 ubuntu ubuntu    4 Sep 14 15:40 file1-hard
9569545 -rw-rw-r-- 1 ubuntu ubuntu    5 Sep 14 15:40 file2
9569543 lrwxrwxrwx 1 ubuntu ubuntu    5 Sep 14 15:40 file2-sym -> file2
```

If you were to delete, rename, or move file2, its symbolic link would break and, depending on your shell's color scheme, be displayed with an angry red background. The hard link, on the other hand, will survive all changes to the original. Try both yourself: rename the file1 and file2 files, and see what happens to their respective links:

```
$ mv file1 newname1
$ mv file2 newname2
```

As you may notice when you run `ls -il` once again, even after using `mv` to rename file1, file1-hard is still there and, more important, still shares the same inode with newname1. Any edits to one file will be reflected in the other. file2-sym, sadly, has been orphaned.

Why bother with all this? Why not just make copies? Think about the case you saw a bit earlier where you created a link to a file system location on a user's desktop. Or what about the connection between the /sbin/init and /lib/systemd/systemd files you saw back in chapter 8, or the contents of /etc/apache2/sites-available/ and /etc/apache2/sites-enabled/ from chapter 3? Those are all examples of links being used to enhance system functionality.

Hard links are much more widely used in Linux, but their purpose is not always so obvious. In one common use case, even though files are kept in disparate locations in the file system, they'll be linked together. This can make it easier to back up important but widely scattered configuration files without having to regularly make new copies. And because hard links don't take up any space, you won't have to worry about extra disk usage.

Summary

- NFS shares expose defined file system resources on remote computers, allowing convenient document access and collaboration among teams.
- File systems and devices can be mounted (and used) either manually from the command line or at boot time through entries in the /etc/fstab file.
- You can secure NFS shares through smart configuration policies, firewall rules, and encryption delivered through third-party solutions like Kerberos and IPSec.
- Windows clients can consume Linux-based files using Samba and Samba-generated account authentication.
- Symbolic links point to file system objects, whereas hard links create objects that are exact copies of the original without taking up storage space.

Key terms

- A *share* is a set of documents or a file system that's shared with a remote client.
- A *Samba server configuration* can be tested using `testparm`.
- *Symbolic and hard links* allow Linux file system objects (files and directories) to be represented in multiple locations.

Security best practices

- NFS shares should be as specific as possible, including only those clients who need access and only the rights needed by each client. This is in keeping with the *principle of least privilege.*
- Where possible, NFS share policies should always include `squash_root` to ensure that remote clients don't get unconstrained root access to the server.
- NFS (and Samba) shares are not encrypted by default. If your clients will be accessing them via an untrusted network, then you should apply encryption.

Command-line review

- `/home 192.168.1.11(rw,sync)` (the entry in the NFS server /etc/exports file) defines a remote client share.
- `firewall-cmd --add-service=nfs` opens a CentOS firewall for client access to your NFS share.
- `192.168.1.23:/home /nfs/home nfs` (a typical entry in the /etc/fstab file of an NFS client) loads an NFS share.
- `smbpasswd -a sambauser` adds Samba functionality (and a unique password) to an existing Linux user account.
- `nano /etc/samba/smb.conf` controls Samba on the server.
- `smbclient //localhost/sharehome` logs in to a local Samba share using the Samba user account.
- `ln -s /nfs/home/ /home/username/Desktop/` creates a symbolic link allowing a user to easily access an NFS share by clicking a desktop icon.

Test yourself

1 Which of the following directives would provide read-only access to an NFS client using the 192.168.1.11 IP address?

   a `/home 192.168.1.11(ro,sync)`

   b `192.168.1.11 /home(ro,sync)`

   c `/home 192.168.1.11(rw,sync)`

   d `192.168.1.11 /home(r,sync)`

2 Which client-side configuration file should be edited to ensure an NFS share is loaded at boot-time?

  a /etc/nfs

  b /etc/exports

  c /etc/nfs/exports

  d /etc/fstab

3 What will the `exportfs -ra` command accomplish?

  a Force NFS to reload the policies from the configuration file

  b List current NFS file systems

  c Test a Samba configuration

  d Reload all attached devices

4 Which of the following will completely block a single remote client machine from server access?

  a `ufw deny ALL 192.168.1.10/UDP`

  b `ufw deny ALL 192.168.1.10`

  c `ufw deny to 192.168.1.10`

  d `ufw deny to 192.168.1.10/255.255.255.0`

5 Which of the following security tools will not help protect data while in transit between server and client machines?

  a Kerberos

  b firewalld

  c SSHFS

  d IPSec

6 Which of the following is the correct name and location of the Samba server configuration file?

  a /etc/samba/smb.conf

  b /etc/smb.cfg

  c /etc/samba/smb.conf

  d /etc/samba.cfg

7 Which of the following commands will start Samba on an Ubuntu server?

  a `systemctl start sambad`

  b `systemctl start smbd`

  c `systemctl start smb`

  d `systemctl start samba`

8 Which of the following commands makes the most sense for creating a link to a configuration file to make regular backups simpler and more reliable?

  a `ln -s /var/backups/important_config_file_backup.cfg /etc/important_config_file.cfg`

  b `ln /var/backups/important_config_file_backup.cfg /etc/important_config_file.cfg`

c `ln  -s  /etc/important_config_file.cfg  /var/backups/important_config_file_backup.cfg`

d `ln /etc/important_config_file.cfg  /var/backups/important_config_file_backup.cfg`

Answer key

1. a, 2. d, 3. a, 4. c, 5. b, 6. c, 7. b, 8. d

Troubleshooting system performance issues

This chapter covers

- Understanding and measuring your system behavior
- Controlling application and client demands on system resources
- Multilevel strategies for addressing resource shortages
- Strategies for effective ongoing monitoring protocols

Do "cascading chaos" and "impending doom" describe your IT operations right now? Are your servers slow and unresponsive? Do your customers complain about poor application performance? Or have you stopped bragging about the unbelievable experience you get from your new-ish workstation?

Even if it's not as bad as all that, life won't always progress smoothly. The fact that, by definition, we're always trying to squeeze the greatest possible value from our IT investments means that sometimes we'll push a bit too far: stressed systems will sometimes break, and complicated software stack elements will sometimes stop working together.

The secret to a long and happy life is to anticipate trouble, quickly identify the symptoms and causes, and apply the right fixes at the right time. And this should help in your work as an IT admin as well.

What do I mean by *system*? It's the hardware and software environment you're using to deliver your service, whether it's an application, database, web server, or the reliable use of a simple standalone workstation. In this chapter, you'll focus on the health and well being of the four core elements of your system: the central processing unit (CPU), memory (RAM, both physical and virtual), storage devices, and network load management. You'll learn about spotting trouble, pinpointing the cause, and then either fixing the underlying problem or, if necessary, throwing more hardware at it.

Of course, you would always prefer to avoid problems altogether. One way to do that is to subject your healthy system to stress testing to see how it stands up. A bit later in the chapter I'll also include a quick look at yes, a great tool for subjecting your infrastructure to cruel and unusual torture.

In any case, I'm going to assume that one of the servers or workstations for which you're responsible has been misbehaving: crashing or slowing down at the worst possible moments. You glare at it with your meanest, nastiest expression for a minute or two, but the machine doesn't seem impressed, nor does it respond. Let's work through this one step at a time.

13.1 CPU load problems

The CPU is your computer's brain. The electronic circuits that make up a CPU, no matter how many cores there might be and how wide the bus they're using, are only expected to do one thing: wait for instructions passed in by software programs, perform calculations, and spit back answers.

By and large, either your CPU will work or it won't. Most CPU-related performance issues (like sluggish response times or unexpected shutdowns) can be traced to pushing them beyond their physical capacity. One of the first things you'll need to do when wondering whether a particular performance issue may be connected to the CPU is find out if you're being too rough on the poor dear.

13.1.1 Measuring CPU load

Two indicators of CPU state include CPU load and CPU utilization:

- *CPU load* is a measure of the amount of work (meaning the number of currently active and queued processes) being performed by the CPU as a percentage of total capacity. Load averages that represent system activity over time, because they present a much more accurate picture of the state of your system, are a better way to represent this metric.

- *CPU utilization* (or usage) is a measure of the time a CPU is not idle (described as a proportion of the total CPU capacity).

A load score of 1 on a single-core machine would represent full capacity. If your system has multiple CPU cores, say four, then full capacity would be represented by the number 4. User experience will probably start to suffer (at least from time to time) once the CPU utilization score rises above 75%, which would be 0.75 for a single core, and 3.0 on a quad-core system.

Getting your CPU load average is easy. Running `uptime` returns the current time, the elapsed time since the more recent system boot, the number of users currently logged in, and, most importantly for us right now, load averages for the last minute, 5 minutes, and 15 minutes:

```
$ uptime
10:08:02 up 82 days, 17:13,  1 user,  load average: 0.12, 0.18, 0.27
```

A load average of 1.27 on a system with one CPU would mean that, on average, the CPU is working to capacity and another 27% of processes are waiting for the their turn with the CPU. By contrast, a load average of 0.27 on a system with one CPU would mean that, on average, the CPU was unused for 73% of the time. On a four-core system, you might see load averages in the range of 2.1, which would be just over 50% of capacity (or unused for around 52% of the time).

To properly understand those numbers, you'll have to know how many cores your system is running. In case that information isn't printed on a chassis sticker and you're not interested in opening up the case and looking for yourself, you can query the pseudo file cpuinfo:

```
$ cat /proc/cpuinfo | grep processor
processor    : 0
processor    : 1
processor    : 2
processor    : 3
```

Looks like there are four cores in that system. Because you're there anyway, take a look through the rest of that file to get a feel for the way Linux describes your CPU. In particular, try to make sense of the flags section, which lists the features supported by your hardware.

13.1.2 *Managing CPU load*

Consistently under capacity (based on the results you get from `uptime`)? You could just enjoy the extra head space. Or you might consider consolidating resources by using the underused computer to deliver additional services (rather than purchasing additional servers) to maximize your return on investment.

Consistently over capacity? You'll either need to switch to a more robust hardware architecture with more CPU cores or, in a virtual environment, provision for more VMs or containers to pick up the extra work. Once in a while, you could also take a closer look at the processes running on your system to see if there isn't something that could be shut down or even something that's been running rogue without your knowledge. Running `top` provides a rich, self-updating display of process information.

Figure 13.1 is a typical screenfull of data from `top`. Notice how the first line provides the same insights you would get from running `uptime`. Because you're trying to resolve performance problems, the columns of data that should interest you the most are %CPU (percentage of CPU capacity currently used by a given process) and especially the processes showing up at the top of the list.

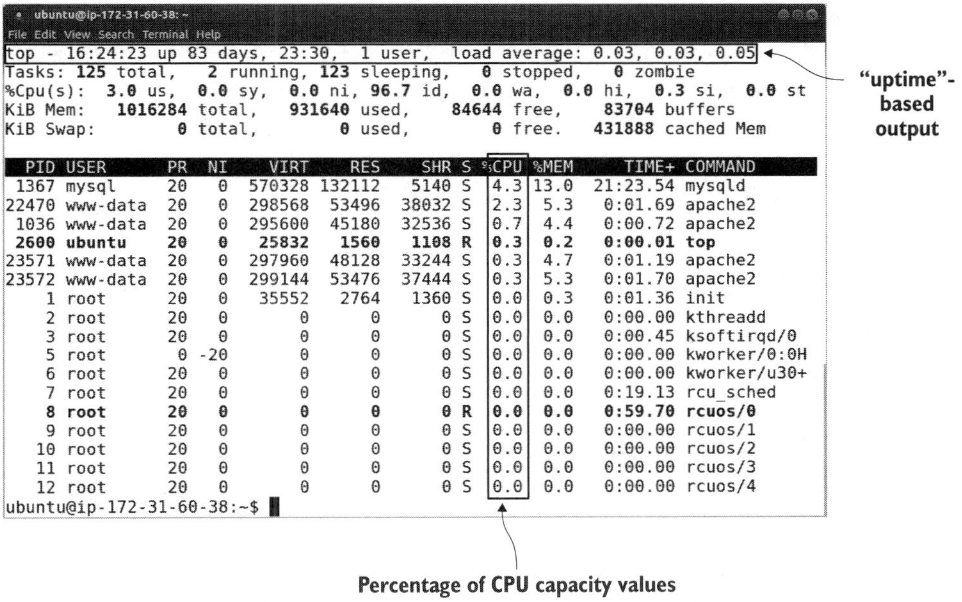

```
● ubuntu@ip-172-31-60-38: ~
File Edit View Search Terminal Help
top - 16:24:23 up 83 days, 23:30,  1 user,  load average: 0.03, 0.03, 0.05    ◀──  "uptime"-
Tasks: 125 total,   2 running, 123 sleeping,   0 stopped,   0 zombie              based
%Cpu(s):  3.0 us,  0.0 sy,  0.0 ni, 96.7 id,  0.0 wa,  0.0 hi,  0.3 si,  0.0 st   output
KiB Mem:   1016284 total,    931640 used,    84644 free,    83704 buffers
KiB Swap:        0 total,         0 used,        0 free.   431888 cached Mem

  PID USER      PR  NI    VIRT    RES    SHR S %CPU %MEM     TIME+ COMMAND
 1367 mysql     20   0  570328 132112   5140 S  4.3 13.0  21:23.54 mysqld
22470 www-data  20   0  298568  53496  38032 S  2.3  5.3   0:01.69 apache2
 1036 www-data  20   0  295600  45180  32536 S  0.7  4.4   0:00.72 apache2
 2600 ubuntu    20   0   25832   1560   1108 R  0.3  0.2   0:00.01 top
23571 www-data  20   0  297960  48128  33244 S  0.3  4.7   0:01.19 apache2
23572 www-data  20   0  299144  53476  37444 S  0.3  5.3   0:01.70 apache2
    1 root      20   0   35552   2764   1360 S  0.0  0.3   0:01.36 init
    2 root      20   0       0      0      0 S  0.0  0.0   0:00.00 kthreadd
    3 root      20   0       0      0      0 S  0.0  0.0   0:00.45 ksoftirqd/0
    5 root       0 -20       0      0      0 S  0.0  0.0   0:00.00 kworker/0:0H
    6 root      20   0       0      0      0 S  0.0  0.0   0:00.00 kworker/u30+
    7 root      20   0       0      0      0 S  0.0  0.0   0:19.13 rcu_sched
    8 root      20   0       0      0      0 R  0.0  0.0   0:59.70 rcuos/0
    9 root      20   0       0      0      0 S  0.0  0.0   0:00.00 rcuos/1
   10 root      20   0       0      0      0 S  0.0  0.0   0:00.00 rcuos/2
   11 root      20   0       0      0      0 S  0.0  0.0   0:00.00 rcuos/3
   12 root      20   0       0      0      0 S  0.0  0.0   0:00.00 rcuos/4
ubuntu@ip-172-31-60-38:~$ █
```

Percentage of CPU capacity values

Figure 13.1   A snapshot of process data displayed by `top`

In this case, you can see that the MySQL daemon is using 4.3% of the server's CPU and, from the next column, 13% of its memory. If you follow that row over to the left, you'll see that the process ID is 1367 and the process is owned by the mysql user. You might conclude that this process was taking more resources than can be justified and will have to be sacrificed (for the greater good, you understand). You can exit `top` by pressing the q key.

That `top` display gave you everything you'll need to kill the process. Because MySQL is a service managed by systemd, your first choice should be to use `systemctl` to bring the process down gently, without putting any application data at risk:

```
# systemctl stop mysqld
```

If it's not managed by systemd, or if something's gone wrong and `systemctl` failed to stop it, then you can use either `kill` or `killall` to eliminate your process (some systems require you install `killall` as part of the psmisc package). You pass the PID to `kill` this way:

```
# kill 1367
```

On the other hand, `killall` uses the process name rather than its ID:

```
# killall mysqld
```

To `kill` or to `killall`, that is the question. Actually, the answer is kind of obvious. `kill` will shut down a single process, based as it is on the PID, whereas `killall` will kill as many instances of a particular program as happen to be running. If there were two or three separate MySQL instances, perhaps belonging to separate users, all would be stopped.

> **NOTE** Before launching `killall`, make sure there aren't any similarly named processes running that could become collateral damage.

You'll also have to use systemctl once again to make sure that the process doesn't restart the next time you boot:

```
# systemctl disable mysqld
```

SETTING PRIORITIES WITH NICE

Sometimes you won't be able to kill a process because it's a necessary part of a mission-critical service. But you can limit the CPU resources it gets using `nice`. By default, a new process is given a `nice` value of 0, but you can change that to any number between -20 and 19. The higher the number, the nicer the process will be when it comes to giving up resources in favor of other processes. And, by contrast, the lower the number, the less nice the process will be as it grabs as many resources as it can get, regardless of the pain and suffering that might cause others.

Let's say that you want to run a script called mybackup.sh that sets a large remote backup operation in motion. The problem is that this is an active server that, from time to time, needs a lot of power to respond to important client requests. If a request comes in while the backup is running at full speed, the performance won't be acceptable. On the other hand, if the backup is throttled back from start to finish, it might never finish.

Here's how `nice` can help you deal with this in a way that leaves everyone relaxed and smiling. Prepend the script (or any other command name) with `nice` and the numeric value you've chosen for it. In this case, the dash (-) followed by 15 tells Linux that the script will run with a very nice attitude. This means that when there's a conflict over resource access, your script will back off, but otherwise it'll take whatever's available:

```
# nice -15 /var/scripts/mybackup.sh
```

If running your script is an urgent priority that has to complete as soon as possible, you could add a second dash to give the process a negative value (-15), as in this example:

```
# nice --15 /var/scripts/mybackup.sh
```

Either way, if you want to see this in action, create a script and, while it's executing, have a second terminal running top. You should see your process running, and its appropriate nice value should appear in the NI column.

For many Linux programs, you can also set default nice values. rsync, on Ubuntu at least, allows you to explicitly define how nice it will be through the RSYNC_NICE setting in /etc/default/rsync.

```
RSYNC_NICE='10'
```

You can also use renice to change the way a process behaves even after it's started. This example will, when necessary, limit the resources available to the process currently assigned PID 2145:

```
renice 15 -p 2145
```

TIPS FOR TOP

In case you ever need them, the third line of the top output you saw a bit earlier gives you time values (as percentages) for a number of other CPU metrics. Table 13.1 offers a quick rundown of the jumble of acronyms you'll see there.

Table 13.1 Symbols for CPU-related metrics displayed by top

Metric	Meaning
us	Time running high-priority (un-niced) processes
sy	Time running kernel processes
ni	Time running low-priority (nice) processes
id	Time spent idling
wa	Time waiting for I/O events to complete
hi	Time spent managing hardware interrupts
si	Time spent managing software interrupts
st	Time stolen from this VM by its hypervisor (host)

Note that the top display can be customized in real time through keyboard input. Type h to learn more.

13.1.3 *Making trouble (simulating CPU load)*

Need to try some of these tricks out but, wouldn't you know it, everything is running smoothly? Why not simulate crisis-level CPU overload for yourself?

Much like children, yes will output (digital) noise continuously until told to stop. On second thought, that's not at all like kids. This command will redirect that noise to the disposable /dev/null file and the ampersand (&) character will push the process into the background, giving control of the command line back to you. To ramp up the pressure, launch the command a few more times:

```
$ yes > /dev/null &
```

That should keep them busy. While all that's running, watch top to see what's happening. You could also try to run other applications to see how much it will take to slow them down. When you're done, run killall to knock off all your yes sessions in one go:

```
$ killall yes
```

13.2 *Memory problems*

For all the great advances in information technology over the years, random access memory (RAM) itself is still used the same way it always was. Computers speed up core compute operations by loading OS kernels and other software code into volatile RAM modules. This permits quick system access to frequently requested software instructions.

The biggest challenge with memory is usually its limits. My first computer had 640 KB of RAM (that's less than 1 MB) and it wasn't enough. I'd leave my computer on overnight just to render a single 640 × 480 GIF image. The workstation sitting under my desk right now has 8 GB and, once I add three VirtualBox VMs to my regular workload it, too, starts to feel the pain.

13.2.1 *Assessing memory status*

Generally, a memory-starved system will fail to complete requested tasks or just slow down. Of course, these problems can describe all kinds of things, so you'll want confirmation before jumping to conclusions. Short of focusing an electron microscope on the memory modules plugged into your motherboard, running free is the most direct way to do that.

free parses the /proc/meminfo file and displays the total physical memory available (described as 7.1 GB in this example) and the way it's currently being used. shared is memory that's used by tmpfs to maintain the various pseudo file systems we've come to know and love, like /dev/ and /sys/. Buffers and cache are associated with memory used by the kernel for block level I/O operations (don't worry too much if you don't understand what that's all about).

Any memory in use by any system process is designated as used. The available value is an estimate of the memory that's currently available for launching new applications, even if it's currently being used by disk caching, without having to dip into swap memory (which you'll meet in much a moment or two). Here's an example:

```
$ free -h
        total    used    free   shared  buff/cache  available
Mem:    7.1G     2.8G    1.3G   372M          3.0G        3.5G
Swap:   7.2G     540K    7.2G
```

You'll notice that I added the -h argument to free, which displays the output in human-readable format, using easier-to-read larger numeric units (GB, MB, and KB) rather than bytes.

This example looks like a healthy system with plenty of room for growth. But if the value of free is consistently a lot closer to 0 and transferring load to swap memory doesn't alleviate the problem, then you may need to add memory. Now, about that swap...

13.2.2 Assessing swap status

Because, byte for byte, RAM modules tend to be more expensive than disk storage, many OS installations designate a file or partition on the storage drive for use as an emergency source of virtual RAM. That way even if, strictly speaking, you don't have quite enough RAM for all of the processes that'll be running, an overloaded system won't fail, although it will run noticeably slower.

You can get a glimpse of the way swap is being used on your system from vmstat. The 30 and 4 arguments added to the command here tell the program to return four readings with 30-second intervals between each reading. In a real-world case, you'd probably want to extend the testing over a longer period, perhaps a couple of hours, to increase the accuracy of your results. The two columns you should watch most closely are si, which measures data transfers from swap into system memory, and so, which reports transfers out of system memory into swap. As promised, here's the command:

```
$ vmstat 30 4
procs ----------memory---------- ---swap-- -----io---- -system-- ------cpu--
 r  b   swpd    free    buff   cache   si  so   bi   bo   in    cs us sy id wa st
 0  0    540 1311400 373100 2779572    0   0   35   41  418   186  4  1 94  1  0
 0  0    540 1311168 373104 2779540    0   0    0    9  671   881  0  0 99  0  0
 0  0    540 1311216 373116 2779508    0   0    0   33  779  1052  1  1 98  0  0
 0  0    540 1310564 373116 2779476    0   0    0    2  592   815  0  0 99  0  0
```

If you're getting consistent movement into and out of swap, you should consider adding physical RAM, unless the slower performance isn't a problem for your workload.

13.3 Storage availability problems

If your application software stack regularly writes new documents, data, or log files to storage drives, then you can't ignore the fact that there are always limits to the space you've got available. Something that can't go on forever will eventually stop. And those data writes will stop when there's no free space left on your drive, taking your system functionality with it.

How can you tell how close you are? Easy. You've already met df. Because devices don't use any actual disk space, you can ignore those listed in the Use% column as using 0% of their maximum space. You already know that they're pseudo file systems. But you should focus on the others, and particularly the root partition (/). In this case, root still has 686 GB (nearly 80%) free, so there's no need to worry right now. But this is obviously something you'll want to check regularly:

```
$ df -h
Filesystem      Size  Used Avail Use% Mounted on
udev            3.5G     0  3.5G   0% /dev
tmpfs           726M  1.5M  724M   1% /run
/dev/sda2       910G  178G  686G  21% /              ◁──┐  The root
tmpfs           3.6G   71M  3.5G   2% /dev/shm              partition entry
tmpfs           5.0M  4.0K  5.0M   1% /run/lock
tmpfs           3.6G     0  3.6G   0% /sys/fs/cgroup  ◁──┐  A pseudo file system;
/dev/sda1       511M  3.4M  508M   1% /boot/efi             note the 0 bytes used.
tmpfs           726M   72K  726M   1% /run/user/1000
```

That's the easy way to track your usage. The hard way happens when you find you're unable to save a file to disk, or you log in to the system and get a message that your session is read-only.

> ### Full or failure?
> To be sure, not every read-only failure is a result of a full storage drive. It could also mean that the physical device is failing. In that case, you'll want to immediately get to work saving any important data on to peripheral drives or online storage accounts before the drive goes down completely. How can you tell the difference? df, if your system is healthy enough to run it, should help, but if in doubt, safe beats sorry every time.

13.3.1 *Inode limits*

Physical space isn't the only constraint on Linux data storage. You'll remember our discussion back in chapter 12 where we noted that all Linux file system objects are identified and managed through metadata contained in unique inodes. It turns out that there's a hard limit to the number of inodes you're permitted on a system, and it's possible to run out of inodes even though there's still plenty of physical space available.

NOTE The number of available inodes is permanently set when the file system is created. Considering that inodes themselves take up space, when creating a file system (using a tool like mkfs.ext4, for instance), the goal is to find a balance that allows for the most potential files while wasting the least disk space.

Here's what it looks like when I run `df` on the same system as before, but this time with the `-i` argument to display inode data:

```
$ df -i
Filesystem        Inodes  IUsed    IFree IUse% Mounted on
udev              914806    546   914260   1% /dev
tmpfs             928143    797   927346   1% /run
/dev/sda2       60547072 701615 59845457   2% /          ◁──┐  This is the root partition,
tmpfs             928143    155   927988   1% /dev/shm          the one whose inode status
tmpfs             928143      5   928138   1% /run/lock         is most important.
tmpfs             928143     16   928127   1% /sys/fs/cgroup
/dev/sda1              0      0        0   -  /boot/efi
tmpfs             928143     31   928112   1% /run/user/1000
```

With so many free inodes, there's no immediate cause for alarm on this system, but you would definitely want to take action if you saw yourself getting within 10% or 20% of your ceiling. One of my servers was once hit with maxed-out inodes, and it took a few minutes before I even understood what had happened. Let me tell you all about it.

The first indication of trouble was when I tried to install some new software using `apt`. The installation failed, displaying an error message that included the words *No Space Left on Device*. Now that was plain crazy talk, as I knew there were still gigabytes free. It took some web searching to prompt me to check my inode levels: sure enough, I was fresh out on that particular partition.

Logically, the next step is to search for directories containing the largest numbers of files. After all, concentrations of inodes will probably be found hanging out in the places frequented by lots of files. Here's how to tune `find` to give you that information:

```
$ cd /
# find . -xdev -type f | cut -d "/" -f 2 | sort | uniq -c | sort -n
```

Table 13.2 explains what it all means.

Table 13.2 `find` command syntax

Syntax	Function
`.`	Start searching within and below the current directory.
`-xdev`	Remain within a single file system.
`-type f`	Search for objects of type `file`.
`cut -d "/"`	Remove text identified by the delimiter (`/` character, in this case).
`-f 2`	Select the second field found.
`sort`	Sort lines of output, and send to standard out (stout).
`uniq -c`	Count the number of lines sent by `sort`.
`sort -n`	Display the output in numeric order.

That's a great command. The trouble was that it failed because find temporarily saves raw data to disk. But because I was out of inodes, saving anything was currently impossible. Terrific. Now what? Free up a little space by finding a couple of unnecessary files and deleting them. With that done, here's what find showed me:

```
# find . -xdev -type f | cut -d "/" -f 2 | sort | uniq -c | sort -n
5 root
48 tmp
127 sbin
128 bin
377 boot
989 etc
2888 home
6578 var
15285 lib
372893 usr
```

The /usr/ directory obviously wins the award for "most files in a single directory tree."

> **WARNING**   Because it might have to search through thousands of files and directories, find can take some time to run.

By far the largest number of files were somewhere beneath the /usr/ directory. But where? No problem, move down a level and run find once again:

```
$ cd usr
# find . -xdev -type f | cut -d "/" -f 2 | sort | uniq -c | sort -n
6 include
160 sbin
617 bin
7211 lib
16518 share
348381 src
```

The directory containing the most files

This time, /usr/src/ is the obvious culprit. Just what goes on in /usr/src/? It turns out that that's where the kernel headers are kept, including those left over from previous kernel versions installed on your machine. If you drill down through the directory tree, you'll see that there are, indeed, a whole lot of files.

13.3.2 *The solution*

To free up space, you may need to manually remove some of the older directories. Then, assuming you're using Ubuntu, let dpkg safely remove whatever else isn't needed through --configure:

```
# dpkg --configure -a
```

To safely remove all the old kernel headers themselves, run autoremove, and everything should go back to optimal working order:

```
# apt-get autoremove
```

On CentOS, install the yum-utils package and then run `package-cleanup`. Adding `--count=2` will remove all but the most recent two kernels:

```
# package-cleanup --oldkernels --count=2
```

> **TIP** It's always a good idea to keep at least one older kernel to fall back on in case something breaks with the latest one.

What can be done to address storage limitations? The most obvious thing is to add more storage. But you can also periodically audit your system to see what can be deleted or transferred to alternate and often cheaper storage solutions. Amazon's Glacier is a great place to keep large data stores that aren't accessed frequently.

You should also work to reduce the sheer volume of data you produce. As you saw in chapter 11, one way to do that is to make sure your logs are regularly rotated and retired.

13.4 *Network load problems*

When the words *network* and *problem* come together in a single sentence, most people probably think first of failed connections. But that's what we're going to talk about in the next chapter. Here, however, is where we discuss how to handle an active and healthy connection that's overloaded.

When should you suspect the load's beyond your capacity? On a regular desktop workstation, you'll probably see downloads that take longer than they should or fail altogether; on a public-facing server, your clients may complain of slow service. Such symptoms could be the result of more than one cause, so you'll want to do some further investigations and then try out possible solutions. That's what you'll learn next.

13.4.1 *Measuring bandwidth*

Literally dozens of Linux tools exist for providing insight into network usage. The two that I'm going to show you are particularly useful for quickly identifying the resources using most of the bandwidth that, in turn, will allow you to intelligently address the underlying issues.

Like top, iftop (acquired by installing the iftop package through the usual channels) displays a self-updating record of the greediest network activity traveling through the network interface: specify `iftop -i eth0`.

As you can see from figure 13.2, iftop lists the network connections between my computer (workstation) and remote hosts, along with the bandwidth consumed in bytes or kilobytes. The connections are listed in inbound/outbound pairs. Obviously, high-consuming connections will have to be examined and, if necessary, removed. The bottom rows of the display track cumulative and peak usage (both inbound and outbound), along with average usage rates.

You should carefully scan and analyze the remote hosts iftop identifies. Regular monitoring could uncover unexpected drains on your network resources and even

```
  dbclinton@workstation: ~/git/linux/manuscript
File  Edit  View  Search  Terminal  Help
                12.5Kb              25.0Kb              37.5Kb              50.0Kb    62.5Kb

workstation                => ec2-107-21-81-34.compute-         0b      278b      216b
                           <=                                   0b    1.40Kb      448b
workstation                => ControlPanel.Home                 0b      230b      173b        An inbound/
                           <=                                   0b      396b      300b        outbound
workstation                => ec2-107-21-1-61.compute-1         0b      147b       37b        connection
                           <=                                   0b      186b       47b        pair
workstation                => ec2-52-90-249-215.compute         0b      134b      227b
                           <=                                   0b       92b      292b
workstation                => ec2-34-204-82-227.compute         0b      134b      180b
                           <=                                   0b       92b      113b
workstation                => jc-in-f189.1e100.net              0b       41b       34b
                           <=                                   0b       49b       39b
workstation                => stackoverflow.com                 0b       42b       10b
                           <=                                   0b       42b       10b
workstation                => 74.125.124.188                    0b       42b       10b
                           <=                                   0b       42b       10b
workstation                => yyz10s06-in-f14.1e100.net         0b       42b       10b
                           <=                                   0b       42b       10b

TX:            cum:   7.65KB   peak:   6.03Kb   rates:    0b   1.06Kb   1.29Kb       Cumulative
RX:                  10.6KB            9.80Kb             0b   2.32Kb   1.79Kb       and peak
TOTAL:               18.2KB           15.8Kb             0b   3.38Kb   3.08Kb        usage data
```

Figure 13.2   A typical iftop display of network connections and their bandwidth usage

previously unidentified malware that iftop catches "calling home." Calls to Amazon or Google might not be noteworthy, but strange and obscure URLs should inspire a second look.

iftop is great for narrowing down network usage from a remote host perspective (something that will be useful for troubleshooting web browser traffic, for instance). But sometimes you'll need to manage local processes through their PIDs; iftop won't help with that. NetHogs (installed through the nethogs repository package), on the other hand, will. Launch NetHogs from the command line by specifying a network interface. Note that this time you don't include a -i flag:

```
# nethogs eth0
```

Figure 13.3 shows a typical NetHogs display on my workstation, including PIDs for both my Linux Slack client (hey, I also need to keep up with my colleagues) and the Chrome browser. If something was misbehaving, I could track it down and control it through its PID.

13.4.2   *Solutions*

Once you've narrowed down a system process that's causing you trouble, you'll have to figure out how to deal with it. If it's not essential or if it's a rogue, malware process, you could shut it down permanently the way you saw earlier using systemctl, kill, or killall. But, more often than not, that won't be possible: most of the processes running on your servers are probably there for a reason.

You could also consider upgrading your network connection. This might involve calling your ISP to discuss increasing the level of service provided. For local on-site

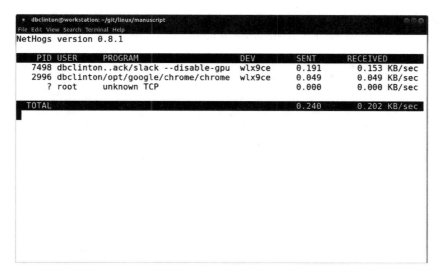

Figure 13.3 A relatively quiet day on my workstation, as seen through NetHogs

networks, you might also think about improving your networking hardware. If your cabling capacity is currently capped at 100 MB/s (CAT 5), you could upgrade to 1000 MB/s (CAT 6). Remember that it's not enough to change the cables. All your routers, switches, and the interfaces attached to your devices must also have that capacity for the benefits to be fully felt. Beyond ethernet cabling, moving to fiber optics can deliver even higher performance but for a much higher price.

13.4.3 Shaping network traffic with tc

A more subtle and sophisticated solution to load problems is *traffic shaping*. Rather than completely shutting down particular services, you can, as an example, place a ceiling on how much bandwidth processes are given. In a way, you want to manage bandwidth the same way that you earlier saw `nice` managing processes. This could make it possible for limited resources to be evenly, or strategically, shared across your system.

For instance, you could limit the bandwidth allowed to web clients to guarantee that other processes (like DNS updates or backups) won't be starved of bandwidth. As a quick and dirty illustration, I'll show you how to impose a basic throttle on an internet-facing network interface using the Traffic Control (`tc`) tool. `tc` is normally installed on Linux by default.

First, ping a remote site and note the response times you get. This example averaged around 37 milliseconds:

```
$ ping duckduckgo.com
PING duckduckgo.com (107.21.1.61) 56(84) bytes of data.
64 bytes from duckduckgo.com (107.21.1.61):
    icmp_seq=1 ttl=43 time=35.6 ms
64 bytes from duckduckgo.com (107.21.1.61): icmp_seq=2 ttl=43 time=37.3 ms
64 bytes from duckduckgo.com (107.21.1.61): icmp_seq=3 ttl=43 time=37.7 ms
```

The time value represents the time needed for a single round-trip operation.

To make sure there aren't any existing rules associated with your network interface (eth0, in this example), list all the current rules:

```
$ tc -s qdisc ls dev eth0
qdisc noqueue 0: root refcnt 2
 Sent 0 bytes 0 pkt (dropped 0, overlimits 0 requeues 0)
 backlog 0b 0p requeues 0
```

> qdisc stands for queueing discipline, a queue through which network-bound data packets must pass.

Now add a rule that delays all traffic by 100 ms. This will add 100 extra milliseconds to each network transfer, allowing other processes a greater share of resources. It'll also slow down your network activity, so you have to be comfortable with the results. Don't worry, I'll show you how to undo all of this in just a moment:

```
# tc qdisc add dev eth0 root netem delay 100ms
```

Once again, list the `tc` rules and note the new rule that delays traffic by 100 ms:

```
$ tc -s qdisc ls dev eth0
qdisc netem 8001:
    root refcnt 2 limit 1000 delay 100.0ms
 Sent 514 bytes 3 pkt (dropped 0, overlimits 0 requeues 0)
 backlog 102b 1p requeues 0
```

> qdisc now has a single rule delaying traffic by 100 ms.

Test your rule. Run `ping` again, and watch the values of `time`. They should now be higher by around 100 milliseconds:

```
$ ping duckduckgo.com
PING duckduckgo.com (107.21.1.61) 56(84) bytes of data.
64 bytes from duckduckgo.com (107.21.1.61): icmp_seq=1 ttl=43 time=153 ms
64 bytes from duckduckgo.com (107.21.1.61): icmp_seq=2 ttl=43 time=141 ms
64 bytes from duckduckgo.com (107.21.1.61): icmp_seq=3 ttl=43 time=137 ms
```

Worked out as you expected? Great. You'll probably want to restore your system to its original state, so run this command to delete the rules, and then test everything again to confirm you're back to normal:

```
# tc qdisc del dev eth0 root
```

`tc` is a complicated piece of software, and a complete guide could probably fill a book of its own. But I think you've seen enough to get a taste of the functionality it offers. As with everything else here, the goal is to put the tools in your hands so you can dig deeper and apply them to your specific problems.

13.5 *Monitoring tools*

As with most administration-related tasks, remembering to get around to running each of the various tools discussed so far in this chapter, well, it just isn't going to happen all that often. Some tasks can be scripted, managed by cron, and programmed to issue alerts when preset thresholds are met. Those are great. But there's also no substitute for having eyes on actual ongoing data at least once in a while. Here are a few ideas to help you set up an effective monitoring system.

13.5.1 Aggregating monitoring data

nmon is a multi-target system monitoring and benchmarking tool. It offers you a customizable single view of limited details into the status of all system components. You get it going by installing the nmon package and then running `nmon` from the command line. The first screen you'll see will look like the one in figure 13.4 and will display the keystrokes used to toggle various views.

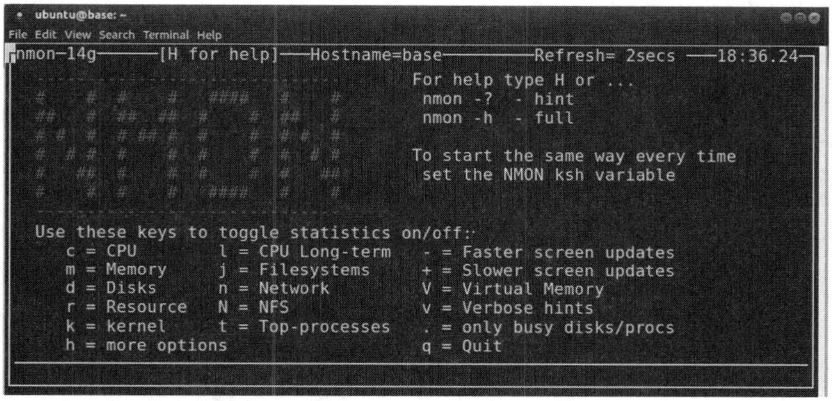

Figure 13.4   The nmon intro screen, including basic usage instructions

The key here is *toggle* because, for instance, pressing c once displays the CPU information view, whereas pressing it again will make CPU go away. This setup makes it possible to add multiple views to the screen. Pressing c, m, and n will enable the CPU, Memory, and Network views all at once, as you can see in figure 13.5. This is a great

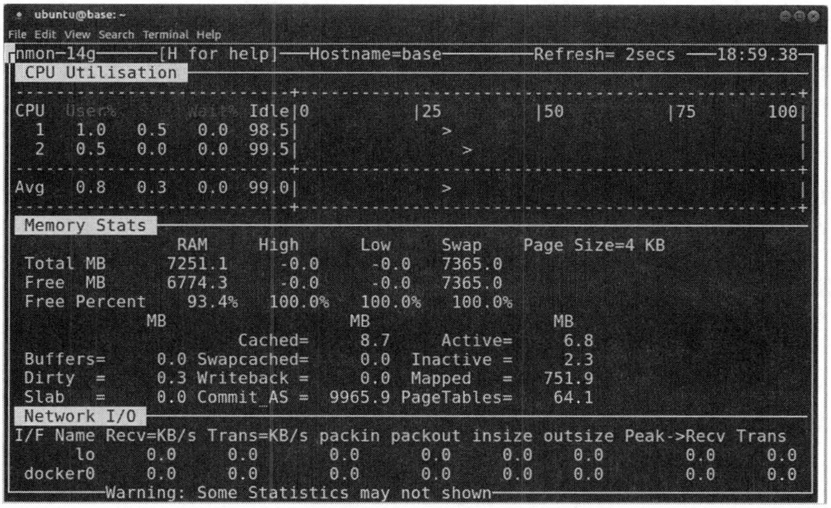

Figure 13.5   Multiple services being monitored in a single nmon screen

way to build a single window view through which you can catch frequently updated overviews of your system. By the way, q will quit the screen.

nmon will only cover you for a single server. If you're responsible for a whole fleet of them, you'll need something a bit more robust like Nagios or collectd for keeping track of the health and activities of multiple servers, and Munin for tracking trends and providing useful analysis.

13.5.2   *Visualizing your data*

Great. But this will still only work when you're actually looking. Head out for an extended coffee break, and you could completely miss a full-scale melt down. Helpfully, nmon lets you record the data it collects over time to a file. This example saves data collected every 30 seconds over a full hour (120 * 30 seconds) to a file in the current working directory:

```
# nmon -f -s 30 -c 120
```

If your system hostname is ubuntu, then the default filename will consist of ubuntu, a date and time stamp, and a .nmon extension:

```
ubuntu_170918_1620.nmon
```

As long as your system has a web server installed, you can use a tool called nmonchart to convert the data files to the much more user-friendly .html format. You'll need to get the tool from the nmon SourceForge site (https://sourceforge.net/projects/nmon/files). The simplest way is to right-click the nmonchartx.tar file (the *x* will be a version number) and copy the URL. From the command line of your server, use wget to download the tar file, and then unpack the archive the usual way:

```
$ wget http://sourceforge.net/projects/nmon/files/nmonchart31.tar
$ tar xvf nmonchart31.tar
```

Here's how you'll invoke nmonchart to convert the .nmon file and save it to your web root directory:

```
# ./nmonchart ubuntu_170918_1620.nmon /var/www/html/datafile.html
```

In case you're faced with an error complaining about the lack of a ksh interpreter, feel free to install the ksh package. A command-line interpreter, ksh is an alternative to Bash:

```
-bash: ./nmonchart: /usr/bin/ksh: bad interpreter: No such file or directory
```

When all that's done, you can point your browser to your server's IP address followed by the filename you specified for nmonchart:

```
10.0.3.57/datafile.html
```

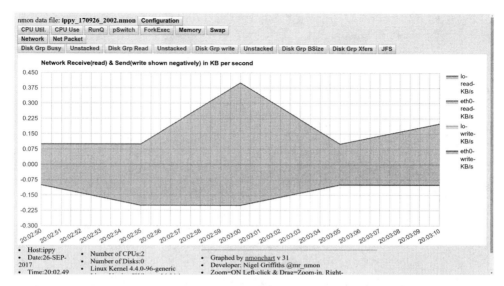

Figure 13.6   An nmap-generated web page with the Network button clicked

That should give you a page looking something like figure 13.6.

You can script all this, including code to generate sequential .html filenames. That makes it convenient to keep up with both new and archived events.

Summary

- The `uptime` tool can provide insight into average CPU loads over time, and unusual results can prompt you to look for and manage high-use processes.
- The `nice` command can closely control the way processes compete with each other for limited system resources.
- Actual and swap memory can be monitored using tools like `free` and `vmstat`.
- Storage limits are defined by both available physical disk space and available inodes.
- iftop and NetHogs are two among dozens of Linux tools for accessing network load data, and tc can be used to control usage.
- Regular monitoring is possible using command-line tools, but scripting them or pushing monitoring data to browser-based visual representations is far more likely to be effective.

Key terms

- *CPU load* is the amount of work being performed by the CPU.
- *CPU utilization* is the proportion of CPU capacity currently being used.
- `nice` lets you control the priority a process has in the face of conflicts for limited resources.

- *RAM memory* holds the OS kernel and other important software to provide fast access to key data.
- *Swap memory* is space on a hard drive designated as virtual RAM, in case you run out of the real thing.
- *Inodes* are metadata containing location and other information and are associated with all Linux file system objects.
- *Network traffic throttling* limits the amount of bandwidth allowed to one process in favor of one or more processes of higher priority.

Security best practices

- Periodically scan your running processes, looking for rogue software that wasn't started by authenticated users or by your base system.
- Running iftop can show you remote network hosts with live connections to your system. If you don't recognize a connection, it might be unauthorized and dangerous.

Command-line review

- `uptime` returns the CPU load averages over the past 1, 5, and 15 minutes.
- `cat /proc/cpuinfo | grep processor` returns the number of system CPU processors.
- `top` displays real-time statistics for running Linux processes.
- `killall yes` shuts down all running instances of the `yes` command.
- `nice --15 /var/scripts/mybackup.sh` raises the priority of the mybackup.sh script for system resources.
- `free -h` displays total and available system RAM.
- `df -i` displays the available and total inodes for each file system.
- `find . -xdev -type f | cut -d "/" -f 2 | sort | uniq -c | sort -n` counts and displays the numbers of files by parent directory.
- `apt-get autoremove` removes old and unused kernel headers.
- `nethogs eth0` displays processes and transfers data related to network connections using the eth0 interface.
- `tc qdisc add dev eth0 root netem delay 100ms` slows down all network transfers through the eth0 interface by 100 milliseconds.
- `nmon -f -s 30 -c 120` records data from a series of nmon scans to a file.

Test yourself

1 Which of the following CPU load scores would likely cause system slowdowns on a two-core system?

   a 1.7
   b 2.1

    c .17

    d 3.0

2 The load scores displayed by `uptime` represent averages over

    a 1, 10, and 25 minutes

    b 1, 5, and 24 hours

    c 1, 5, and 15 minutes

    d 10, 60, and 300 seconds

3 Which of the following files will contain information about the number of processors on your system?

    a /proc/uptime

    b /sys/cpuconf

    c /proc/cpuinfo

    d /etc/proc/envinfo

4 Which of the following commands will shut down a mysqld process with a PID of 4398?

    a `kill mysqld`

    b `killall mysqld`

    c `killall 4398`

    d `kill mysqld:4398`

5 You want to reduce the priority given to your mybackup.sh script. Which of the following will drop its priority the most?

    a `nice -10 /var/scripts/mybackup.sh`

    b `nice -0 /var/scripts/mybackup.sh`

    c `nice --15 /var/scripts/mybackup.sh`

    d `nice -15 /var/scripts/mybackup.sh`

6 Which of the following sets of symptoms most suggests a serious, ongoing memory problem?

    a Slow application performance and high levels of data transfers into and out of swap

    b Slow application performance and low levels of data transfers into and out of swap

    c Slow application performance and high CPU load average scores

    d Slow application performance and high inode availability

7 Which of the following will provide PIDs along with network bandwidth data?

    a `nmon -i eth0`

    b `nethogs eth0`

    c `nethogs -i eth0`

    d `iftop eth0`

8 How should you slow down network traffic through the eth0 interface by 100 milliseconds?

   a   `tc qdisc add dev eth0 root netem delay 1000ms`

   b   `tc qdisc add eth0 root netem delay 100ms`

   c   `tc qdisc add dev eth0 root netem delay 100ms`

   d   `tc qdisc add dev eth0 root netem -h delay 100ms`

Answer key

1. a, 2. c, 3. c, 4. b, 5. d, 6. a, 7. b, 8. c

Troubleshooting network issues

14

This chapter covers

- Using TCP/IP networking to manage network problems
- Troubleshooting networks and network interfaces
- Managing DHCP connectivity
- Configuring DNS for address translation
- Troubleshooting inbound network connectivity

When I was a lad, getting new software for a PC meant either writing it yourself or driving to a store and purchasing a box containing a program stored on one or more 5.25" floppy drives. As often as not, remote collaboration required a dot matrix printer and the post office. Streaming videos? Don't make me laugh. I can't remember if my first PC even had a modem. If it did, I certainly never used it.

These days, network connectivity is as integral to computing as keyboards and strong coffee. And the way things are going with voice interfaces, like Amazon's Alexa, it might not be wise to invest too heavily in keyboard manufacturing. (Coffee prospects still look good, though.) The bottom line is that you and the users you support would be pretty helpless without fast and reliable network access.

To deliver fast and reliable access, you'll need to know how to use network tools and protocols to establish connectivity between your network interfaces and the outside world. And you'll also need to know how to identify and connect network adapters to your computers so the tools and protocols will have something to work with. We'll get to that.

But if you're going to confront the vexing and unpredictable disruptions that can plague your network communication, you'll first need a solid working knowledge of the basics of the *internet protocol suite*, often known as the Transmission Control Protocol (TCP) and the Internet Protocol (IP), or TCP/IP for short. Technically, TCP/IP isn't a Linux topic at all, as the protocols are used universally by all networked devices no matter what OS they're running. Because the work you're going to do in this chapter won't make much sense without taking TCP/IP into account, that's where we'll begin. Feel free to skip this section if you're already comfortable with the material.

14.1   Understanding TCP/IP addressing

A network's most basic unit is the humble Internet Protocol (IP) address, at least one of which must be assigned to every connected device. Each address must be unique throughout the entire network; otherwise message routing would descend into chaos.

For decades, the standard address format followed the IPv4 protocol: each address is made up of four 8-bit octets for a total of 32 bits. (Don't worry if you don't understand how to count in binary.) Each octet must be a number between 0 and 255. Here's a typical (fake) example:

```
154.39.230.205
```

The maximum theoretical number of addresses that can be drawn from the IPv4 pool is over 4 billion (256^4). Once upon a time, that seemed like a lot. But as the internet grew far beyond anyone's expectations, there clearly weren't going to be enough unique addresses in the IPv4 pool for all the countless devices seeking to connect.

Four billion possible addresses sounds like a big number until you consider that there are currently more than 1 billion Android smartphones in use; that's in addition to all the millions of servers, routers, PCs, and laptops, not to mention Apple phones. There's a good chance your car, refrigerator, and home-security cameras also have their own network-accessible addresses, so something obviously had to give.

Two solutions to the impending collapse of the internet addressing system (and the end of life as we know it) were proposed: IPv6 (an entirely new addressing protocol) and Network Address Translation (NAT). IPv6 provides a much larger pool of addresses, but because it's still not all that widely deployed, I'll focus on NAT.

14.1.1   What's NAT addressing?

The organizing principle behind NAT is brilliant: rather than assign a unique, network-readable address to every one of your devices, why not have all of them share the single public address that's used by your router? But how will traffic flow to and from your local devices? Through the use of *private* addresses. And if you want to divide network resources into multiple subgroups, how can everything be effectively managed? Through network segmentation. Clear as mud? Let's look at how NAT addressing works, to gain a little perspective.

14.1.2 Working with NAT addressing

When a browser on one of the laptops connected to your home WiFi visits a site, it does so using the public IP address that's been assigned to the DSL modem/router provided by your internet service provider (ISP). Any other devices connecting through the same WiFi network use that same address for all their browsing activity (see figure 14.1).

In most cases, the router uses the Dynamic Host Configuration Protocol (DHCP) to assign unique private (NAT) addresses to each local device, but they're unique only in the local environment. That way, all local devices can enjoy full, reliable communication with their local peers. This works just as well for large enterprises, many of which use tens of thousands of NAT IP addresses, all behind a single public IP.

The NAT protocol sets aside three IPv4 address ranges that can only be used for private addressing:

- 10.0.0.0 to 10.255.255.255
- 172.16.0.0 to 172.31.255.255
- 192.168.0.0 to 192.168.255.255

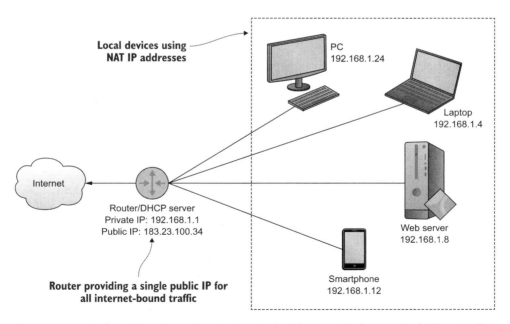

Figure 14.1 A typical NAT configuration, showing how multiple local devices, each with its own private address, can all be represented by a single public IP address

Local network managers are free to use any and all of those addresses (there are more than 17 million of them) any way they like. But addresses are usually organized into smaller network (or *subnet*) blocks whose host network is identified by the octets to the left of the address. This leaves octets to the right of the address available for assigning to individual devices.

For example, you might choose to create a subnet on 192.168.1, which would mean all the addresses in this subnet would start with 192.168.1 (the network portion of the address) and end with a unique, single-octet device address between 2 and 254. One PC or laptop on that subnet might therefore get the address 192.168.1.4, and another could get 192.168.1.48.

> **NOTE** Following networking conventions, DHCP servers generally don't assign the numbers 0, 1, and 255 to network devices.

Continuing with that example, you might subsequently want to add a parallel, but separate, network subnet using 192.168.2. In this case, not only are 192.168.1.4 and 192.168.2.4 two separate addresses, available to be assigned to two distinct devices, but because they're on separate networks, the two might not even have access to each other (see figure 14.2).

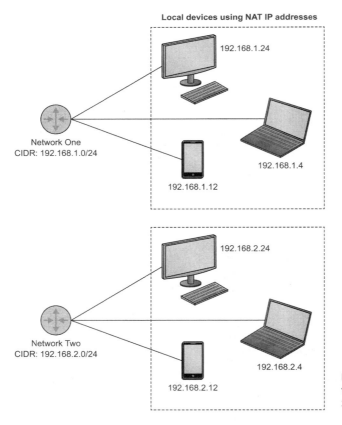

Local devices using NAT IP addresses

192.168.1.24

Network One
CIDR: 192.168.1.0/24

192.168.1.4

192.168.1.12

192.168.2.24

Network Two
CIDR: 192.168.2.0/24

192.168.2.4

192.168.2.12

Figure 14.2 Devices attached to two separate NAT subnets in the 192.168.*x* network range

---

Subnet notation

Because it's critically important to make sure systems know what kind of subnet a network address is on, we need a standard notation that can accurately communicate which octets are part of the network and which are available for devices. There are two commonly used standards: *Classless Inter-Domain Routing (CIDR)* notation and *netmask*. Using CIDR, the first network in the previous example would be represented as 192.168.1.0/24. The /24 tells you that the first three octets (8×3=24) make up the network portion, leaving only the fourth octet for device addresses. The second subnet, in CIDR, would be described as 192.168.2.0/24.

These same two networks could also be described through a netmask of 255.255.255.0. That means all 8 bits of each of the first three octets are used by the network, but none of the fourth.

You don't have to break up the address blocks exactly this way. If you knew you weren't likely to ever require many network subnets in your domain, but you anticipated the need to connect more than 255 devices, you could choose to designate only the first two octets (192.168) as network addresses, leaving everything between 192.168.0.0 and 192.168.255.255 for devices. In CIDR notation, this would be represented as 192.168.0.0/16 and have a netmask of 255.255.0.0.

Nor do your network portions need to use complete (8-bit) octets. Part of the range available in a particular octet can be dedicated to addresses used for entire networks (such as 192.168.14.*x*), with the remainder left for devices (or hosts, as they're more commonly called). This way, you could set aside all the addresses of the subnet's first two octets (192 and 168), plus some of those of the third octet (0), as network addresses. This could be represented as 192.168.0.0/20 or with the netmask 255.255.240.0.

Where did I get these notation numbers? Most experienced admins use their binary counting skills to work it out for themselves. But for a chapter on general network troubleshooting, that's a bit out of scope and unnecessary for the normal work you're likely to encounter. Nevertheless, there are many online subnet calculators that will do the calculation for you.

Why would you want to divide your network into subnets? A common scenario involves groups of company assets that need to be accessible to some teams (developers, perhaps), but not others. Keeping them logically separated into their own subnets can be an efficient way to do that.

14.2 *Establishing network connectivity*

Everyone shows up for work bright and early one Monday morning. They exchange brief but cheerful greetings with each other, sit down at their laptops and workstations all ready for a productive week's work, and discover the internet can't be reached. With the possible exception of the cheerful and productive parts, you should expect that this will happen to you one day soon (if it hasn't already). The source of a network outage could be any of the following:

- A hardware or operating system failure on a local machine
- Disruption to your physical cabling, routing, or wireless connections
- A problem with the local routing software configuration
- A breakdown at the ISP level
- An entire chunk of the internet itself going down

Your first job will be to narrow the focus of your search by ruling out what's not relevant. You do that by following a protocol that starts off closest to home, confirming that the fault doesn't lie within your own local systems, and gradually expanding outward. Figure 14.3 illustrates the process flow.

Let's see how all that might work. You'll begin with fixing problems local computers might have accessing external resources, and then address problems external clients or users might have accessing resources on your servers.

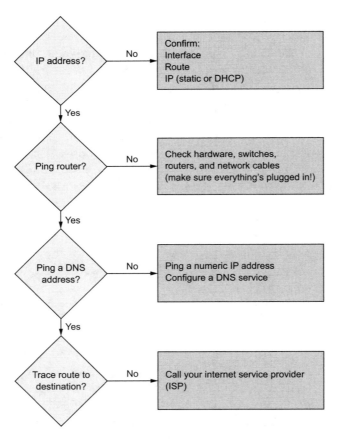

**Figure 14.3   A flow chart illustrating the sequence you might follow
when troubleshooting an outbound connectivity problem**

14.3 Troubleshooting outbound connectivity

It's possible that your computer was never assigned its own IP address, without which it's impossible to exist as a member in good standing of a network. Run `ip` to display your network interface devices, and then confirm you've got an active external-facing device and that there's a valid IP associated with it. In the following, the eth0 interface is using 10.0.3.57:

The loopback (lo) interface through which local (localhost) resources are accessed

The addr argument for ip can also be shortened to a.

Note how the IP used by the loopback device is 127.0.0.1. This follows standard networking conventions.

The interface is listed as UP.

```
$ ip addr
1: lo: <LOOPBACK,UP,LOWER_UP> mtu 65536 qdisc noqueue
        state UNKNOWN group default qlen 1
    link/loopback 00:00:00:00:00:00 brd 00:00:00:00:00:00
    inet 127.0.0.1/8 scope host lo
       valid_lft forever preferred_lft forever
    inet6 ::1/128 scope host
       valid_lft forever preferred_lft forever
7: eth0@if8: <BROADCAST,MULTICAST,UP,LOWER_UP> mtu 1500 qdisc noqueue
        state UP group default qlen 1000
    link/ether 00:16:3e:29:8e:87 brd ff:ff:ff:ff:ff:ff link-netnsid 0
    inet 10.0.3.57/24 brd 10.0.3.255 scope global eth0
       valid_lft forever preferred_lft forever
    inet6 fe80::216:3eff:fe29:8e87/64 scope link
       valid_lft forever preferred_lft forever
```

The computer's current public IP address is displayed as the value of inet.

If there's no IP address listed on the `inet` line, or there's no network interface listed altogether, then that's where you'll focus your attention.

14.3.1 Tracking down the status of your network

First, confirm that you've got a physical *network adapter* (also called a *network interface card*, or NIC) installed on your computer and that Linux sees it. You can list all the PCI-based hardware currently installed using `lspci`. In the following output, `lspci` found a PCI Express Gigabit Ethernet Controller:

```
$ lspci
00:00.0 Host bridge: Advanced Micro Devices, Inc. [AMD]
    Family 15h (Models 10h-1fh) Processor Root Complex
[...]
01:00.0 Ethernet controller:
    Realtek Semiconductor Co., Ltd. RTL8111/8168/8411
    PCI Express Gigabit Ethernet Controller (rev 06)
```

The term ethernet controller refers to a hardware network interface device.

If `lspci` returns no NICs, you should consider the possibility that you've had some kind of hardware failure.

NOTE   The *Peripheral Component Interconnect* (PCI) is a hardware standard used to allow peripheral devices to connect to the microprocessors on computer motherboards through the PCI bus. Various newer standards, like PCI Express (PCIe), also exist, each using its own unique form factor to physically connect to a motherboard.

Besides lspci, you can also use the lshw tool to display the networking hardware your system knows about. By itself, lshw returns a complete hardware profile, but lshw -class network will show you only the subset of that profile that relates to networking. Try it.

A positive result from lspci won't, by itself, get you too far, because it doesn't tell you how the device can be accessed from the command line. But it does give you some important information. Take, say, the word *Ethernet* from the lspci output and use it with grep to search the output of dmesg. As you might remember from chapter 11, dmesg is a record of kernel-related events involving devices. After some trial and error, I discovered that this particular search will work best by including the two dmesg lines immediately following the line containing my search string (using -A 2):

```
$ dmesg | grep -A 2 Ethernet
[    1.095265] r8169 Gigabit Ethernet driver 2.3LK-NAPI loaded
[    1.095840] r8169 0000:01:00.0 eth0<1>: RTL8168evl/8111evl
        at 0xffffc90000cfa000, 74:d4:35:5d:4c:a5, XID 0c900800 IRQ 36
[    1.095842] r8169 0000:01:00.0
        eth0: jumbo features [frames: 9200 bytes, tx checksumming: ko]  ◁
```
Device designation eth0 is shown as associated with the Gigabit Ethernet device.

Success! You can see that the device was given the eth0 designation. Hold on. Not so fast. Even though eth0 was originally given to the device because Linux now uses predictable interface names (refer back to chapter 10), it might not be the designation the interface is actually using. Just to be safe, you'll want to search dmesg once again to see if eth0 shows up anywhere else:

```
$ dmesg | grep eth0
[    1.095840] r8169 0000:01:00.0
        eth0: RTL8168evl/8111evl at 0xffffc90000cfa000, 74:d4:35:5d:4c:a5,
        XID 0c900800 IRQ 36
[    1.095842] r8169 0000:01:00.0
        eth0: jumbo features [frames: 9200 bytes, tx checksumming: ko]
[    1.129735] r8169 0000:01:00.0 enp1s0:
        renamed from eth0                    ◁
```
The eth0 designation was dropped and replaced with enp1s0.

Aha. It seems that at some point in the boot process the device was renamed enp1s0. OK. You've got a properly configured network interface, but still no IP address and still no network connectivity, what's next? dhclient, but first some background.

14.3.2 *Assigning IP addresses*

Network devices can get their IP addresses in these ways:

- Someone manually sets a static address that (hopefully) falls within the address range of the local network.
- A DHCP server automatically gives the device an unused address.

As is usually the case, each approach has its trade-offs. DHCP servers do their work automatically and invisibly, and guarantee that two managed devices are never trying to use the same address. But, on the other hand, those addresses are dynamic, meaning the addresses they're using one day might not be the ones they get the next. With that in mind, if you've been successfully using, say, 192.168.1.34 to SSH into a remote server, be prepared to accommodate for unexpected changes.

Conversely, setting the IPs manually ensures that those addresses are permanently associated with their devices. But there's always the chance that you may cause addressing conflicts—with unpredictable results. As a rule, unless you have a specific need for a static address—perhaps you need to reliably access a resource remotely using its address—I'd go with DHCP.

DEFINING A NETWORK ROUTE

Before looking for an address, you'll need to make sure Linux knows how to find the network in the first place. If Linux can already see its way through to a working network, then `ip route` will show you your computer's routing table, including the local network and the IP address of the device that you'll use as a gateway router:

```
$ ip route
default via 192.168.1.1          <──┐       Address of the gateway router through which the
    dev enp0s3 proto static metric 100       local computer will access the wider network
192.168.1.0/24 dev enp0s3 proto kernel scope           The NAT network (192.168.1.x)
    link src 192.168.1.22 metric 100    <──┐  and netmask (/24) of the local
                                             NAT network
```

If a working route isn't listed, then you'll need to create one, but you'll have to figure out the subnet range of your local network first. If there are other computers using the same network, check out their IP addresses. If, say, one of those computers is using 192.168.1.34, then the odds are that the router's address will be 192.168.1.1. Similarly, if the IP of that connected computer is 10.0.0.45, then the router's address would be 10.0.0.1. You get the picture. Based on that, here's the `ip` command to create a new default route to your gateway:

```
# ip route add default via 192.168.1.1 dev eth0
```

> **NOTE** The `ip` commands discussed in this chapter are relatively new and are meant to replace now-deprecated command sets like `ifconfig`, `route`, and `ifup-down`. You'll still see plenty of how-to guides focusing on those old commands, and, for now at least, they'll still work, but you should get used to using `ip`.

REQUESTING A DYNAMIC ADDRESS

The best way to request a DHCP address is to use dhclient to search for a DHCP server on your network and then request a dynamic address. Here's how that might look, assuming your external network interface is called enp0s3:

```
# dhclient enp0s3
Listening on LPF/enp0s3/08:00:27:9c:1d:67
Sending on   LPF/enp0s3/08:00:27:9c:1d:67
Sending on   Socket/fallback
DHCPDISCOVER on enp0s3 to 255.255.255.255
   port 67 interval 3 (xid=0xf8aa3055)
DHCPREQUEST of 192.168.1.23 on enp0s3 to 255.255.255.255
   port 67 (xid=0x5530aaf8)
DHCPOFFER of 192.168.1.23 from 192.168.1.1
DHCPACK of 192.168.1.23 from 192.168.1.1
RTNETLINK answers: File exists
bound to 192.168.1.23 -- renewal in 34443 seconds.
```

> The address of the DHCP server in this case is 192.168.1.1.

> The new address is successfully leased for a set time; renewal will be automatic.

CONFIGURING A STATIC ADDRESS

You can temporarily give an interface a static IP from the command line using ip, but that will only survive until the next system boot. Bearing that in mind, here's how it's done:

```
# ip addr add 192.168.1.10/24 dev eth0
```

That's great for quick and dirty one-off configurations, perhaps trying to get connectivity on a stricken system while troubleshooting. But the odds are that you'll normally prefer to make your edits permanent. On Ubuntu machines, that'll require some editing of the /etc/network/interfaces file. The file may already contain a section defining your interface as DHCP rather than static.

Listing 14.1   A section in the /etc/network/interfaces file

```
auto enp0s3
iface enp0s3 inet dhcp
```

You'll edit that section, changing dhcp to static, entering the IP address you want it to have, the netmask (in *x.x.x.x* format), and the IP address of the network gateway (router) that the computer will use. Here's an example:

```
auto enp0s3
iface enp0s3 inet static
    address 192.168.1.10
    netmask 255.255.255.0
    gateway 192.168.1.1
```

On CentOS, each interface will have its own configuration file in the /etc/sysconfig/network-scripts/ directory. A typical interface set for DHCP addressing will look as shown in the next listing.

Listing 14.2 Configurations in /etc/sysconfig/network-scripts/ifcfg-enp0s3

```
TYPE="Ethernet"
BOOTPROTO="dhcp"          ◁─────┐  Tells Linux to request a
DEFROUTE="yes"                  │  dynamic IP for the interface
PEERDNS="yes"
PEERROUTES="yes"
IPV4_FAILURE_FATAL="no"
IPV6INIT="yes"
IPV6_AUTOCONF="yes"
IPV6_DEFROUTE="yes"
IPV6_PEERDNS="yes"
IPV6_PEERROUTES="yes"
IPV6_FAILURE_FATAL="no"
NAME="enp0s3"
UUID="007dbb43-7335-4571-b193-b057c980f8d0"
DEVICE="enp0s3"
ONBOOT="yes"
```

The next listing shows how that file might look once you've edited it to allow static addressing.

Listing 14.3 The static version of a CentOS interface configuration file

```
BOOTPROTO=none           ◁─── DHCP addressing won't be used.
NETMASK=255.255.255.0
IPADDR=10.0.2.10         ◁─────┐  Sets the static IP address
USERCTL=no                     │  you want to use
DEFROUTE="yes"
PEERDNS="yes"
PEERROUTES="yes"
IPV4_FAILURE_FATAL="no"
IPV6INIT="yes"
IPV6_AUTOCONF="yes"
IPV6_DEFROUTE="yes"
IPV6_PEERDNS="yes"
IPV6_PEERROUTES="yes"
IPV6_FAILURE_FATAL="no"
NAME="enp0s3"
UUID="007dbb43-7335-4571-b193-b057c980f8d0"
DEVICE="enp0s3"
ONBOOT="yes"
```

If you want your settings to take effect immediately, you'll need to restart networking. Most of the time, networking on modern systems is managed by the systemd service, NetworkManager. Instead, on Ubuntu at least, starting or stopping interfaces that are defined in the /etc/network/interfaces file is handled by the networking service. Therefore, if you want to apply the newly edited settings in the interfaces file, you'll run `systemctl restart networking` rather than `systemctl restart NetworkManager`. Alternatively, you could use `ip` to bring just one interface up (or down):

```
# ip link set dev enp0s3 up
```

It can't hurt to know about some of the places on your system that NetworkManager hides its working files. There's a configuration file called NetworkManager.conf in the /etc/ NetworkManager/ directory, configuration files for each of the network connections your computer has made historically in /etc/NetworkManager/system-connections/, and data detailing your computer's historical DHCP connections in /var/lib/NetworkManager/. Why not take a quick look through each of those resources?

14.3.3 *Configuring DNS service*

If you've got a valid network route and an IP address, but the connectivity problem hasn't gone away, then you'll have to cast your net a bit wider. Think for a moment about exactly what it is that you're not able to do.

Is your web browser unable to load pages? (I don't know, perhaps like bootstrap-it .com, if you're looking for a great example.) It could be that you haven't got connectivity. It could also mean that there isn't any DNS translation happening.

What's DNS?

It may not look it, but the World Wide Web is really all about numbers. There's no place called manning.com or wikipedia.org. Rather, they're 35.166.24.88 and 208.80.154.224, respectively. The software that does all the work connecting us to the websites we know and love recognizes only numeric IP addresses.

The tool that translates back and forth between text-loving humans and our more digitally oriented machines is called the *domain name system* (DNS). *Domain* is a word often used to describe a distinct group of networked resources, in particular, resources identified by a unique human-readable name. As shown in figure 14.4, when you enter a text address in your browser, the services of a DNS server will be sought.

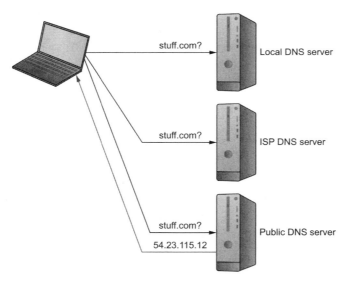

Figure 14.4   DNS address query for stuff.com and the reply containing a (fictional) IP address

HOW DOES DNS WORK?

The first stop is usually a local index of names and their associated IP addresses, stored in a file that's automatically created by the OS on your computer. If that local index has no answer for this particular translation question, it forwards the request to a designated public DNS server that maintains a much more complete index and can connect you to the site you're after. Well-known public DNS servers include those provided by Google, which uses the deliciously simple 8.8.8.8 and 8.8.4.4 addresses, and OpenDNS.

FIXING DNS

Until something breaks, you normally won't spend a lot of time thinking about DNS servers. But I'm afraid something might just have broken. You can confirm the problem using the ping tool. If pinging a normal website URL (like manning.com) doesn't work, but using an IP address does, then you've found your trouble. Here's how that might look:

```
$ ping 8.8.8.8
PING 8.8.8.8 (8.8.8.8) 56(84) bytes of data.
64 bytes from 8.8.8.8: icmp_seq=1 ttl=60 time=10.3 ms
64 bytes from 8.8.8.8: icmp_seq=2 ttl=60 time=10.2 ms
64 bytes from 8.8.8.8: icmp_seq=3 ttl=60 time=9.33 ms
^C
--- 8.8.8.8 ping statistics ---
3 packets transmitted, 3 received, 0% packet loss, time 2002ms
rtt min/avg/max/mdev = 9.339/10.002/10.378/0.470 ms
```

This symbol tells you that the Ctrl-c key combination was used to interrupt the ping operation.

The fix? That depends. A lot of the time, individual computers will inherit the DNS settings from the router through which they connect to the wider network. Which, I guess, means that you'll be spending the next couple of minutes searching through drawers to recover your router's login password (hint: the default password is often printed on the router case itself).

Once you do manage to log in, usually from a connected PC that's running a browser pointed to the router's IP address, work through the GUI menus of the router's OS check to make sure the DNS settings are valid. You can also configure DNS settings on your local computer that will override what's on the router. On a CentOS machine, add references to a couple of public DNS servers to your interface's /etc/sysconfig/network-scripts/ifcfg-enp0s3 file. This example uses the two IPs used by Google's DNS servers:

```
DNS1=8.8.8.8
DNS2=8.8.4.4
```

And on Ubuntu, add `dns-nameserver` values to the appropriate interface in the /etc/network/interfaces files:

```
dns-nameserver 8.8.8.8
dns-nameserver 8.8.4.4
```

14.3.4 *Plumbing*

Yep. It's roll-up-your-sleeves-and-pull-out-the-drain-snake time. If you've got a working interface, a route, an IP address, and DNS service, and you still don't have full connectivity, then there's got to be something out there blocking the flow.

The Linux equivalent of a drain snake, especially the fancy kind that comes with a video camera at the end, is Traceroute—which, as advertised, traces the route a packet takes across the network on its way to its target. If there's anything blocking traffic anywhere down the line, Traceroute will at least show you where the clog is. Even if you're in no position to investigate further, the information could be particularly valuable as your ISP tries to get things going again.

This example shows a successful end-to-end trip between my home workstation and google.com (represented by 172.217.0.238). If anything had gone wrong, the hops displayed would have stopped before reaching the goal. Lines of output containing nothing but asterisks (*) might sometimes represent packets failing to make it back. A complete failure will usually be accompanied by error messages:

**The first hop is my local router; the ~20 ms hop
times displayed are a bit slow, but acceptable.**

```
$ traceroute google.com
traceroute to google.com (172.217.0.238), 30 hops max, 60 byte packets
 1  ControlPanel.Home (192.168.1.1)
      21.173 ms  21.733 ms  23.081 ms
 2  dsl-173-206-64-1.tor.primus.ca (173.206.64.1)          My internet service provider
      25.550 ms  27.360 ms  27.865 ms
 3  10.201.117.22 (10.201.117.22)  31.185 ms  32.027 ms  32.749 ms
 4  74.125.48.46 (74.125.48.46)  26.546 ms  28.613 ms  28.947 ms
 5  108.170.250.241 (108.170.250.241)  29.820 ms  30.235 ms  33.190 ms
 6  108.170.226.217 (108.170.226.217)
      33.905 ms 108.170.226.219 (108.170.226.219)  10.716 ms  11.156 ms
 7  yyz10s03-in-f14.1e100.net (172.217.0.238)  12.364 ms *  6.315 ms
```

Still nothing? Sounds like a good time to put in a phone call to your ISP.

Coming up next: what happens when people within your local network can access everything the big, bad internet has to offer, but your remote workers, clients, and visitors can't get in to consume the services you offer.

14.4   *Troubleshooting inbound connectivity*

Whether it's your company's website, an API supporting your app, or an internal documentation wiki, there are parts of your infrastructure that you'll want to be available 24/7. Those kinds of inbound connectivity can be as important to your business or organization as the outgoing stuff we've just discussed.

If your remote clients can't connect to your services or if their connections are too slow, your business will suffer. Therefore, you'll want to regularly confirm that your application is healthy and listening for incoming requests, that those requests have the access they need, and that there's enough bandwidth to handle all the traffic. `net-stat` and `netcat` can help with that.

14.4.1 *Internal connection scanning: netstat*

Running `netstat` on a server displays a wide range of network and interface statistics. What would interest you most when faced with a screaming horde of angry web clients, however, is a list of the services that are listening for network requests.

`netstat -l` will show you all the sockets that are currently open. If it's a website you're running, then you can narrow down the results by filtering for `http`. In this case, both ports 80 (http) and 443 (https) appear to be active:

```
$ netstat -l | grep http
tcp6 0  0 [::]:http   [::]:*  LISTEN   ◁─── The protocol is shown as tcp6, suggesting
tcp6 0  0 [::]:https  [::]:*  LISTEN        that this is exclusively an IPv6 service. In
                                           fact, it covers both IPv6 and IPv4.
```

> ### What exactly is a network socket?
> To be honest, I'm not 100% sure how to describe it. What it would mean to a C programmer might feel strange to a simple system administrator, like your humble servant. Nevertheless, I'll risk oversimplification and say that a *service endpoint* is defined by the server's IP address and the port (192.168.1.23:80, for instance). That combination identifies the *network socket*. A connection is created during a session involving two endpoints/sockets (a client and a server).

`netstat -i` will list your network interfaces. On the surface, that wouldn't seem like such a big deal; after all, `ip addr` will do that too, right? Ah, yes. But `netstat` will also show you how many data packets have been received (`RX`) and transmitted (`TX`). `OK` indicates error-free transfers; `ERR`, damaged packets; and `DRP`, packets that were dropped. These statistics can be helpful when you're not sure a service is active:

```
$ netstat -i
Kernel Interface table
Iface      MTU Met RX-OK RX-ERR RX-DRP RX-OVR TX-OK TX-ERR Flg
enp1s0     1500 0       0      0    0 0       0      0 BMU
lo        65536 0   16062      0    0 0   16062      0 LRU
wlx9cefd5fe6a19 1500 0 1001876 0    0 0  623247      0 BMRU
```

That example appears to show a healthy and busy wireless interface (with the unfortunate name wlx9cefd5fe6a19), and an interface called enp1s0 that's inactive. What's going on? It's a PC with an unused ethernet port that gets its internet via WiFi. In the code, `lo` is the localhost interface, also known as 127.0.0.1. This is a great way to assess things from within the server, but how do things look from outside?

14.4.2 *External connection scanning: netcat*

You've used `cat` to stream text files and `zcat` to stream the contents of compressed archives. Now it's time to meet another member of the (feline) family: `netcat` (often invoked as `nc`). As you might guess from its name, `netcat` can be used to stream files across networks, or even to serve as a simple two-way chat app.

But right now you're more interested in the status of your server and, in particular, how a client will see it. nc, when run against a remote address, tells you whether it was able to make a connection. -z restricts netcat's output to the results of a scan for listening daemons (rather than trying to make a connection), and -v adds verbosity to the output. You'll need to specify the port or ports you want to scan. Here's an example:

```
$ nc -z -v bootstrap-it.com 443 80
Connection to bootstrap-it.com 443 port [tcp/https] succeeded!
Connection to bootstrap-it.com 80 port [tcp/http] succeeded!
```

If either or both of those services (HTTP and HTTPS) were not available, the scan would fail. That could be because the service isn't running on the server (perhaps your Apache web server has stopped) or there's an overly strict firewall rule blocking access. This is how a failed scan would look:

```
$ nc -z -v bootstrap-it.com 80
nc: connect to bootstrap-it.com port 80 (tcp) failed: Connection timed out
```

This is Linux, however, so you can be sure there's more than one good way to get this job done. Therefore, be aware that nmap can be used to perform a similar scan:

```
$nmap -sT -p80 bootstrap-it.com
Nmap scan report for bootstrap-it.com (52.3.203.146)
Host is up (0.036s latency).
PORT   STATE SERVICE
80/tcp open  http
Nmap done: 1 IP address (1 host up) scanned in 0.37 seconds
```

And this nmap command will scan for any open ports between ports 1 and 1023, an excellent way to quickly audit your system to make sure there's nothing open that shouldn't be:

```
$ nmap -sT -p1-1023 bootstrap-it.com
Nmap scan report for bootstrap-it.com (52.3.203.146)
Host is up (0.038s latency).
Not shown: 1020 filtered ports
PORT    STATE SERVICE
80/tcp  open  http
443/tcp open  https
Nmap done: 1 IP address (1 host up) scanned in 4.69 seconds
```

Which ports "should be" open? That depends on the software you're running on the server. As a rule of thumb, if nmap reports any unfamiliar open ports, search online to find out what software uses those ports, and then ask yourself whether it's reasonable for that software to be running on your server.

Summary

- Practically at least, Linux defines and manages network interfaces and routes within the context of NAT networking protocols.
- Linux needs to recognize attached hardware peripherals like network interfaces, but also designate device labels (like eth0) before they're usable.
- Custom static IP addresses can be assigned to a device both through editing configuration files and from the command line (using ip). Dynamic address can be automatically requested from DHCP servers, but you can't control the addresses you get.
- Confirming that appropriate local services are accessible for remote clients involves scanning for open sockets and ports.

Key terms

- *TCP/IP* is the Transmission Control Protocol and Internet Protocol conventions that define network behavior administration.
- *Public-facing IP addresses* must be globally unique, whereas *NAT addresses* need to be unique only within their local network. The *Dynamic Host Configuration Protocol* (DHCP) is commonly used to manage dynamic (nonpermanent) address assignment.
- A *network route* is the address of a gateway router through which a computer gains network access.
- The *Domain Name System* (DNS) provides translations between numeric IP addresses and human-readable URLs allowing convenient navigation of internet resources.
- A *network socket* is the representation of an IP address and a port through which a network connection can be activated.

Security best practices

It's good to periodically use a tool like nmap to audit your system for inappropriately open ports.

Command-line review

- `ip addr` lists the active interfaces on a Linux system. You can shorten it to `ip a` or lengthened it to `ip address`. It's your choice.
- `lspci` lists the PCI devices currently connected to your computer.
- `dmesg | grep -A 2 Ethernet` searches the `dmesg` logs for references to the string *Ethernet* and displays references along with the subsequent two lines of output.
- `ip route add default via 192.168.1.1 dev eth0` manually sets a new network route for a computer.
- `dhclient enp0s3` requests a dynamic (DHCP) IP address for the enp0s3 interface.

- `ip addr add 192.168.1.10/24 dev eth0` assigns a static IP address to the eth0 interface, which won't persist past the next system restart.
- `ip link set dev enp0s3 up` starts the enp0s3 interface (useful after editing the configuration).
- `netstat -l | grep http` scans a local machine for a web service listening on port 80.
- `nc -z -v bootstrap-it.com 443 80` scans a remote web site for services listening on the ports 443 or 80.

Test yourself

1 Which of the following is a valid NAT IP address?

  a 11.0.0.23

  b 72.10.4.9

  c 192.168.240.98

  d 198.162.240.98

2 How would you describe an IPv4 network subnet using two octets for network addresses, both with CIDR and netmast notation?

  a x.x.x.x/16 or 255.255.0.0

  b x.x.x.x/24 or 255.255.255.0

  c x.x.x.x/16 or 255.0.0.0

  d x.x.x.x/16 or 255.255.240.0

3 Which of the following commands will help you discover the designation given by Linux to a network interface?

  a `dmesg`

  b `lspci`

  c `lshw -class network`

  d `dhclient`

4 You're setting up a PC in your office and want it to have reliable network connectivity. Which of the following profiles will work best?

  a Dynamic IP address connected directly to the internet

  b Static IP address that's part of a NAT network

  c Static IP address connected directly to the internet

  d Dynamic IP address that's part of a NAT network

5 Which of the following commands is used to request a dynamic IP address?

  a `ip route`

  b `dhclient enp0s3`

  c `ip client enp0s3`

  d `ip client localhost`

6 Which file would you edit to configure a network interface named enp0s3 on a CentOS machine?

   a /etc/sysconfig/networking/ipcfg-enp0s3

   b /etc/sysconfig/network-scripts/ipcfg-enp0s3

   c /etc/sysconfig/network-scripts/enp0s3

   d /etc/sysconfig/network-scripts/ifcfg-enp0s3

7 What line would you add to a network interface configuration section of the /etc/network/interfaces file on an Ubuntu machine to force the interface to use a Google DNS name server?

   a DNS1=8.8.8.8

   b dns-nameserver 8.8.8.8

   c nameserver 8.8.8.8

   d dns-nameserver1 8.8.8.8

8 Which of the following will scan the well-known TCP ports on a remote server for accessible, listening services?

   a `nmap -s -p1-1023 bootstrap-it.com`

   b `nmap -sU -p80 bootstrap-it.com`

   c `nmap -sT -p1-1023 bootstrap-it.com`

   d `nc -z -v bootstrap-it.com`

Answer key

1. c, 2. a, 3. a, 4. d, 5. b, 6. d, 7. d, 8. c

15
Troubleshooting
peripheral devices

This chapter covers

- Analyzing system hardware profiles
- Managing kernel modules to administer hardware devices
- Managing kernel settings to solve hardware boot conflicts
- Using CUPS to manage and troubleshoot printers

The connection between clicking a mouse button and seeing something happen on your screen is complicated. In simple terms, you need some kind of software process that'll shuttle data back and forth between the mouse and the computer, between the computer and the software that's running on it, and between the software and the screen.

More than just data transmission, you'll also need a way to translate the data between the mouse that knows only the tabletop on which it sits and software that knows only zeros and ones. Multiply that by thousands of device models and throw in the many connection types (PCI, SATA, USB, serial), and you've got yourself quite a stew cooking away in your PC.

Given the complexity of the whole thing, it's a wonder that it all works as reliably as it does. In this chapter, you're going to learn how to deal with those times that it doesn't...like when the marketing team is waiting for you to activate the webcam so their virtual meeting can begin. Or when their WiFi won't let them connect in the first place. To do all that magic, you'll need to understand how Linux sees your peripheral devices and how you can guide the Linux kernel to take a shy device under its wing and care for it. Because we care about all of our devices.

15.1 *Identifying attached devices*

Webcam plugged in but not broadcasting your smiling face across the internet? Printer not printing? WiFi adapter not adapting (or whatever it is that they do)?

Before you invest too much time and energy working to activate hardware devices, you must first accept the sad truth that an operating system (OS) might sometimes fail to even recognize some of its attached hardware. The first thing you'll do if a newly plugged in device doesn't seem to work is confirm that Linux knows its there. That'll keep you busy for the next couple of pages. If you run the diagnostics I'm about to show you and there's still no sign of life, consider the possibility that

- The device is incompatible with your hardware or with Linux.
- The device is damaged or faulty.
- The hardware interface or cable is damaged or faulty.
- The system needs a reboot.
- You're having a bad day.

Once they're talking to each other, I'll show you how to use kernel modules so Linux and your device can team up to get some work done for you. We'll begin by looking at your hardware through the eyes of Linux. In fact, this whole "find out if Linux recognizes the device you just plugged in" business isn't entirely new. You'll remember how you used `lsblk` back in chapter 6 to discover attached block devices. Well, `lsblk` has some cousins: `lsusb` lists any USB devices Linux is aware of, and, as you saw in the last chapter, `lspci` will do the same for PCI devices. Here's an example:

A Brother laser printer

```
$ lsusb
Bus 005 Device 001: ID 1d6b:0001 Linux Foundation 1.1 root hub
Bus 002 Device 001: ID 1d6b:0002 Linux Foundation 2.0 root hub
Bus 001 Device 008: ID 04f9:0249
     Brother Industries, Ltd                                    A webcam
Bus 001 Device 007: ID 413c:2005 Dell Computer Corp. RT7D50 Keyboard
Bus 001 Device 006: ID 046d:081a Logitech, Inc.
Bus 001 Device 005: ID b58e:9e84 Blue Microphones Yeti Stereo Microphone
Bus 001 Device 004: ID 1a40:0101
     Terminus Technology Inc. Hub          ←── A USB multiport hub
Bus 001 Device 002: ID 148f:5372
     Ralink Technology, Corp. RT5372 Wireless Adapter
Bus 003 Device 002: ID 093a:2510 Pixart Imaging, Inc. Optical Mouse
                                           A USB WiFi adapter
```

Chapter 14 is also where you saw the grand old patriarch of the `ls` family, `lshw`. When run with `root` permissions, `lshw` prints a complete hardware profile of your system. The first thing you'll notice is that `lshw` has an awful lot to say about every piece of your hardware. One way to tame that beast is to convert the output to an easy-to-read .html file that you can view in your web browser. The -html argument does that. Clicking the filename in a GUI file manager like Nautilus should load it into your default browser. Here's how:

```
# lshw -html > lshw-output.html
```

Remember how we used `lshw -class network` in the last chapter to restrict the output to only network-related content? That trick will work for other data subsets, too. For instance, `lshw -c memory` displays detailed information about all types of memory used by your system (including RAM, BIOS firmware, and cache); -c, as you may have guessed, works as a quicker alternative to -class. In addition to those, `lshw -c storage` displays information on SATA and SCSI interfaces, -c multimedia covers audio and video devices, and -c cpu tells you everything you ever wanted to know about the CPU plugged into your motherboard. That's how you can nicely *consume* `lshw` information. But how should you *use* it?

Here's a common scenario. Suppose you're considering adding extra RAM to a system—perhaps the metrics you gathered back in chapter 13 suggest you're running low. You'll need to know how much you've already got and what kind of RAM it is, not to mention what motherboard you're using so you can research how may RAM slots are available and what their maximum capacity is.

OK. So RAM isn't exactly a peripheral device, but it works well as an example of the kind of hardware discovery that's possible. And hardware discovery should always be your first step when troubleshooting problems with your hardware.

By way of illustration, `lshw` shows me that my motherboard has four RAM slots, two of which are currently occupied by 4 GB A-Data DDR3 1600 memory modules. Because you should avoid installing mismatched memory modules on a single system, this tells me exactly what kind of RAM I should purchase to fill those two empty slots and double my capacity.

I should point out that I have no immediate plans to upgrade my workstation. And why should I? The modest hardware profile I've already got allows me to run multiple VMs while editing and/or encoding a small handful of videos (using Kdenlive), and all while keeping at least one web browser busy with more than a dozen open tabs. And the computer I built from the ground up for less than $300 performs significantly better than the $1,000+ rigs used by many of my colleagues. What's the difference? Those poor souls are feeding their resource-hungry Windows and macOS operating systems while I'm using fast and efficient Linux. Take that.

What if your device is recognized by Linux but it still isn't active? Perhaps there's an appropriate kernel module out there waiting to be loaded.

15.2 Managing peripherals with Linux kernel modules

Linux manages hardware peripherals using kernel modules. Here's how that works.

A running Linux kernel is one of those things you don't want to upset. After all, the kernel is the software that drives everything your computer does. Considering how many details have to be simultaneously managed on a live system, it's better to leave the kernel to do its job with as few distractions as possible. But if it's impossible to make even small changes to the compute environment without rebooting the whole system, then plugging in a new webcam or printer could cause a painful disruption to your workflow. Having to reboot each time you add a device to get the system to recognize it is hardly efficient.

To create an effective balance between the opposing virtues of stability and usability, Linux isolates the kernel itself, but lets you add specific functionality on the fly through *loadable kernel modules* (LKMs). Looking at figure 15.1, you can think of a module as a piece of software that tells the kernel where to find a device and what to do with it. In turn, the kernel makes the device available to users and processes and oversees its operation.

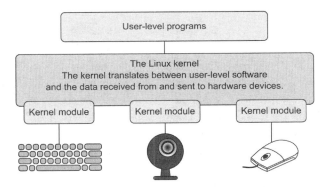

Figure 15.1 Kernel modules act as translators between devices and the Linux kernel.

There's nothing stopping you from writing your own module to support a device exactly the way you'd like it, but why bother? The Linux module library is already so robust that there's usually no need to roll out your own. And the vast majority of the time, Linux will automatically load a new device's module without you even knowing it.

Still, there'll be times when for some reason it doesn't happen by itself. (You don't want to leave that hiring manager impatiently waiting too long for your smiling face to join the video conference job interview.) To help things along, you'll want to understand a bit more about kernel modules and, in particular, how to find the actual module that will run your peripheral, and then how to manually activate it.

15.2.1 Finding kernel modules

By accepted convention, modules are files with a .ko (*kernel object*) extension that live beneath the /lib/modules/ directory. Before you navigate all the way down to those files, however, you'll probably have to make a choice. Because you're given the option at boot time of loading one from a list of releases, the specific software needed to support your choice (including the kernel modules) has to exist somewhere. Well, /lib/modules/ is one of those somewheres. And that's where you'll find directories filled with the modules for each available Linux kernel release, like these:

```
$ ls /lib/modules
4.4.0-101-generic
4.4.0-103-generic
4.4.0-104-generic
```

In my case, the active kernel is the version with the highest release number (4.4.0-104-generic), but there's no guarantee that'll be the same for you (kernels are frequently updated). If you're going to be doing some work with modules that you'd like to use on a live system, you'll need to be sure you've got the right directory tree.

Good news: there's a reliable trick. Rather than identifying the directory by name and hoping you'll get the right one, use the system variable that always points to the name of the active kernel. You can invoke that variable using uname -r (the -r specifies the kernel release number from within the system information that would normally be displayed):

```
$ uname -r
4.4.0-104-generic
```

With that information, you can incorporate uname into your file system references using a process known as *command substitution*. To navigate to the right directory, for instance, you'd add it to /lib/modules. To tell Linux that "uname" itself isn't a file system location, enclose the uname part in back ticks, like this:

```
$ ls /lib/modules/`uname -r`
build    modules.alias        modules.dep      modules.softdep
initrd   modules.alias.bin    modules.dep.bin  modules.symbols
kernel   modules.builtin      modules.devname  modules.symbols.bin
misc     modules.builtin.bin  modules.order    vdso
```

You'll find most of the modules themselves organized within their own subdirectories beneath the kernel/ directory. Take a few minutes now to browse through those directories to get an idea of how things are arranged and what's available. The filenames usually give you a good idea of what you're looking at:

```
$ ls /lib/modules/`uname -r`/kernel
arch  crypto  drivers  fs  kernel  lib  mm
   net  sound  ubuntu  virt  zfs
```

The busiest of the subdirectories listed here is kernel, beneath which you can find modules for hundreds of devices.

That's one way to locate kernel modules, actually the quick and dirty way to go about it. But it's not the only one. If you want to get the complete set, you can list all currently loaded modules along with some basic information using lsmod. The first column is the module name, followed by the file size and number, and then names of other modules on which each is dependent:

```
$ lsmod
[...]
vboxdrv                454656  3 vboxnetadp,vboxnetflt,vboxpci
rt2x00usb               24576  1 rt2800usb
rt2800lib               94208  1 rt2800usb
[...]
```

This small sampling of the results shows modules related to VirtualBox and my USB WiFi adapter.

How many is too many? Well, let's run `lsmod` once again, but this time piping the output to `wc -l` to get a count of the lines:

```
$ lsmod | wc -l
113
```

Those are the loaded modules. How many are available in total? Running `modprobe -c` and counting the lines will give us that number:

```
$ modprobe -c | wc -l
33350
```

33,350 available modules? Looks like someone's been working hard over the years to provide us with the software to run our physical devices.

> **NOTE** On some systems you might encounter customized modules that are referenced either with their own unique entries in the /etc/modules file or as a configuration file saved to /etc/modules-load.d/. The odds are that such modules are the product of local development projects, perhaps involving cutting-edge experiments. Either way, it's good to have some idea of what it is you're looking at.

That's how you find modules. Your next job is to figure out how to manually load an inactive module if, for some reason, it didn't happen on its own.

15.2.2 Manually loading kernel modules

Before you can load a kernel module, logic dictates that you'll have to confirm it exists. And before you can do that, you'll need to know what it's called. Getting that part might sometimes require equal parts magic and luck, and some help from online documentation authors.

I'll illustrate the process by describing a problem I ran into some time back. One fine day, for a reason that still escapes me, the WiFi interface on a laptop stopped working. Just like that. Perhaps a software update knocked it out. Who knows? I ran `lshw -c network` and was treated to this very strange information:

```
network UNCLAIMED
    AR9485 Wireless Network Adapter
```

Linux recognized the interface (the Atheros AR9485) but listed it as unclaimed. Well, as they say, "When the going gets tough, the tough search the internet." I ran a search for "atheros ar9 linux module" and, after sifting through pages and pages of 5 and even 10-year-old results advising me to either write my own module or just give up, I finally discovered that with Ubuntu 16.04, at least, a working module existed. Its name: ath9k.

Yes! The battle's as good as won! Adding a module to the kernel is a lot easier than it sounds. To double check that it's available, you can run find against the modules' directory tree, specify -type f to tell Linux you're looking for a file, and then add the string ath9k along with a glob asterisk to include all filenames that start with your string:

```
$ find /lib/modules/$(uname -r) -type f -name ath9k*
/lib/modules/4.4.0-97-generic/kernel/drivers/net/wireless/ath/
➥ ath9k/ath9k_common.ko
/lib/modules/4.4.0-97-generic/kernel/drivers/net/wireless/ath/ath9k/ath9k.ko
/lib/modules/4.4.0-97-generic/kernel/drivers/net/wireless/ath/ath9k/ath9k_htc.ko
/lib/modules/4.4.0-97-generic/kernel/drivers/net/wireless/ath/ath9k/ath9k_hw.ko
```

Just one more step, loading the module:

```
# modprobe ath9k
```

That's it. No reboots. No fuss.

One more example to show you how to work with active modules that have become corrupted. There was a time when using my Logitech webcam with a particular piece of software would make the camera inaccessible to any other programs until the next system boot. Sometimes I needed to open the camera in a different application and didn't have the time to shut down and start up again. (I run a lot of applications, and getting them all in place after booting takes some time.)

Because this module was presumably active, using lsmod to search for the word *video* gave me a hint about the name of the relevant module. In fact, it was better than a hint—the only module described with the word *video* was uvcvideo, as you can see in the following:

```
$ lsmod | grep video
uvcvideo              90112  0
videobuf2_vmalloc     16384  1 uvcvideo
videobuf2_v4l2        28672  1 uvcvideo
videobuf2_core        36864  2 uvcvideo,videobuf2_v4l2
videodev             176128  4 uvcvideo,v4l2_common,videobuf2_core,
➥ videobuf2_v4l2
media                 24576  2 uvcvideo,videodev
```

There was probably something I could have controlled, for what was causing the crash; and, I guess, I could have dug a bit deeper to see if I couldn't fix things the right way. But you know how it is: sometimes you don't care about the theory and just want your device working. So I used `rmmod` to kill the uvcvideo module and `modprobe` to start it up again all nice and fresh:

```
# rmmod uvcvideo
# modprobe uvcvideo
```

Again: no reboots. No stubborn blood stains.

15.3 *Manually managing kernel parameters at boot time*

Because we're talking about the kernel anyway, now would be a good time to have a serious chat about kernel parameters. You know, the chat we've been putting off for a while because kernel parameters sounds scary. Well, they are scary: getting them wrong can leave your computer at least temporarily unbootable. And spelling counts.

Why make trouble in the first place? Because sometimes your kernel's default boot configuration won't work for what you're doing, and the only way to fix it is to change the way the kernel boots.

There are two ways to pass custom parameters to the kernel at boot time. One involves editing the GRUB menu item during the boot process, and the other, editing the /etc/default/grub configuration file on a running system for the changes to take effect the next time you start up. To illustrate each of those approaches, I'll use two practical use-case scenarios. You'll have to continue reading to find out what those are.

15.3.1 *Passing parameters at boot time*

I'm not sure how common a problem this is, but it'll do nicely as a teaching example. Some unfortunate individuals find it impossible to properly shut down or reboot Linux, experiencing an unwanted system freeze each time. Adding a simple kernel parameter will sometimes solve the issue. Here's how it's done.

With the Linux release you want to boot selected in the GRUB menu (see figure 15.2), press the e key, and you'll be taken to an editing screen. There you'll be able to use the regular cursor and text keys to navigate and then edit the contents.

Scroll down until you reach the Linux entry highlighted in figure 15.3. In this example, after wrapping to the next line, that entry ends with *ro*. (Don't worry if yours is different.) Then add `reboot=bios` to the end of the line and press Ctrl-x to accept the changes and boot. If that doesn't fix the shutdown problem, you can try again using `reboot=pci` instead of `reboot=bios`.

Bear in mind that this edit will not be permanent. After the next boot, the GRUB settings will once again be controlled by configuration files in the file system. To find out how to make changes that will persist through boots, keep reading.

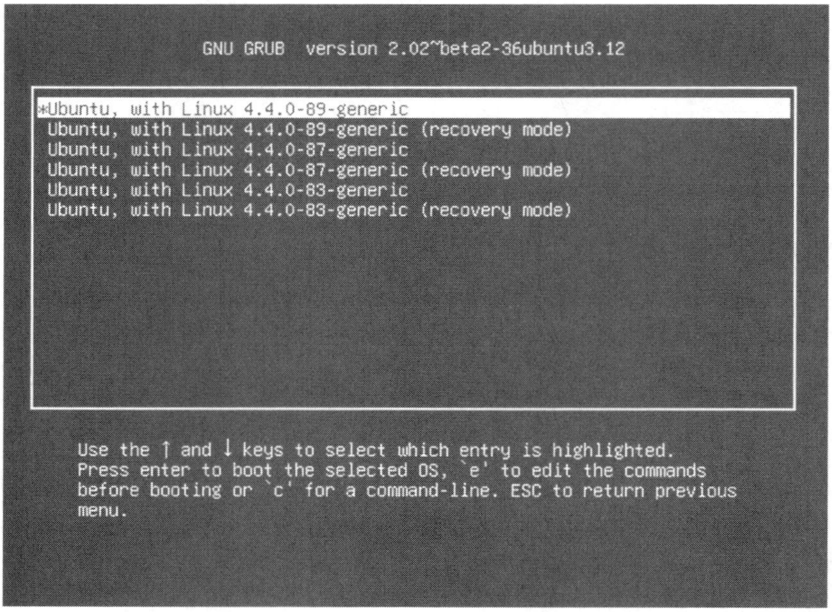

Figure 15.2   The main GRUB menu displaying the multiple Linux kernels available for loading

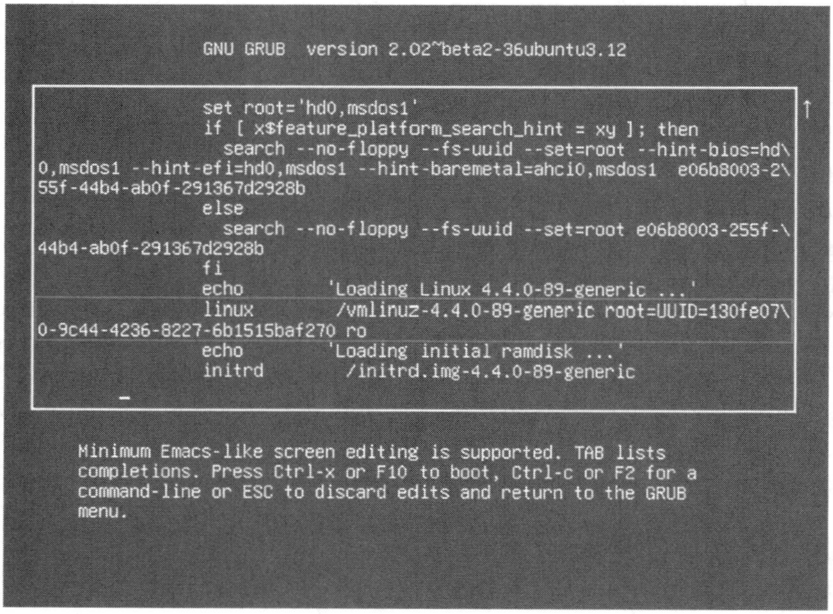

Figure 15.3   The Linux line that shows boot parameters, pointing GRUB to the location of a Linux image

15.3.2 *Passing parameters via the file system*

OK, how about this one? There might be times when you want to boot a desktop machine without its GUI. Perhaps some elements of the GUI itself aren't loading properly, and you need a clean, reliable shell session to troubleshoot. Well waddya know, you can set the default run level to 3 (multiuser, nongraphical mode) through GRUB.

> **NOTE** A *run level* is a setting that defines the Linux system state for a particular session. Choosing between run levels 0–6 determines what services should be available, ranging from a full, graphic, multiuser system to no services at all (meaning, shut down).

Open the /etc/default/grub file, and find the GRUB_CMDLINE_LINUX_DEFAULT line. It often comes with a couple of parameters and looks something like this:

```
GRUB_CMDLINE_LINUX_DEFAULT="quiet splash"
```

Add `systemd.unit=runlevel3.target` to the end of the line so it looks like the following. (`quiet splash` doesn't interest us one way or the other; it controls what you see on your screen as you boot.)

```
GRUB_CMDLINE_LINUX_DEFAULT="quiet splash systemd.unit=runlevel3.target"
```

Run `update-grub` on Ubuntu or `grub2-mkconfig` on CentOS for the changes to take effect. The next time you boot your computer, you'll be dropped into a command-line shell. Once you're done with your troubleshooting, you can remove `systemd .unit=runlevel3.target` from /etc/default/grub, again update GRUB, and reboot.

15.4 *Managing printers*

Ready for a shock? Make sure you're sitting down. I'm going to advise you to pass over a perfectly good command-line tool in favor of its GUI equivalent. The command-line tool? `lp`. Complete with its updated engine under the hood, `lp` is still around, and it can certainly do some interesting things. But trust me, if one of the office printers you support disappears from the network, you're not going to be opening up a command line to troubleshoot. These days it's all Common UNIX Printing System (CUPS), all the time. But before we go there, I'll give you a couple of `lp` commands that might come in handy.

15.4.1 *Basics of lp*

Suppose there's a file on a remote computer that needs printing. You know it's not much fun to launch LibreOffice over a remote X session, right? Wouldn't it be nice to do it through a simple, fast, and reliable SSH shell? Say no more. Use `lpq` to list available printers (along with the current job queue):

```
$ lpq
Brother-DCP-7060D is ready
no entries
```

Then use `lp` to print the file. If there's more than one printer on the system, you'll also need to specify the printer you'd like to use. Here's an example:

```
$ lp -d Brother-DCP-7060D /home/user/myfile.pdf
```

Don't want to print right away? Schedule it for later. The `-H` schedule setting always uses UTC time rather than local:

```
$ lp -H 11:30 -d Brother-DCP-7060D /home/user/myfile.pdf
```

15.4.2 *Managing printers using CUPS*

Once upon a time, before purchasing a printer to use with a Linux system, you'd need careful and time-consuming research to make sure it was compatible. If it was, you'd often need to download and install the appropriate driver and then manually install the printer through the OS. When it worked, it was cause for celebration. Three things have happened over the past years to make Linux printing a lot better:

- The CUPS modular printing system has been adopted by many, if not all, Linux distributions to manage printers and printing. Believe it or not, CUPS is managed on behalf of the community by Apple. As you'll soon see, the CUPS interface greatly simplifies administration and troubleshooting and is quite reliable.

- The major printer manufacturers now generally provide Linux drivers. They're not always perfect, but they're workable. This means that, these days, nearly any modern printer can be deployed with Linux computers. Still, it can't hurt to take a quick look at an online resource like https://help.ubuntu.com/ community/Printers.

- Starting with release 17.04, Ubuntu now offers driverless printing. This means any accessible local or networked printers will automatically be added to CUPS without any setup required.

At any rate, you access the CUPS interface through your browser, pointing it to port 631 on your own machine (localhost:631). The Administration tab (visible in figure 15.4) contains straightforward links to manage finding, securing, scheduling, and tracking all available printers.

You can even manage groups of printers in a class to allow effective use of multiple devices. This can be a great way to organize resources to ensure, for instance, more expensive color printing is only used for high-priority jobs and draft documents are forced to print on cheaper, lower-quality printers.

CUPS handles all the dirty administration details invisibly. Should you need to detach a particular printer from one computer (or network subnet, if it's a network printer) and attach it to another, you'll only need to make the relevant changes within the CUPS interface on the host computer. The appropriate routing information will be automatically updated across the network within a minute or two.

Figure 15.4 The CUPS browser interface that, by default, is available via port 631 on any Linux computer running CUPS

CUPS knows which printers are available because, by default, printers connected to any computer running CUPS will broadcast their existence to all others on the network. This, along with many other configuration settings, can be controlled by the /etc/cups/cupsd.conf file.

Listing 15.1   A section of the /etc/cups/cupsd.conf configuration file

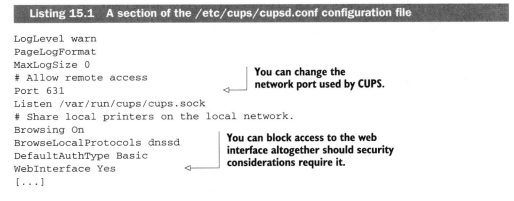

```
LogLevel warn
PageLogFormat
MaxLogSize 0
# Allow remote access
Port 631
Listen /var/run/cups/cups.sock
# Share local printers on the local network.
Browsing On
BrowseLocalProtocols dnssd
DefaultAuthType Basic
WebInterface Yes
[...]
```

You can change the network port used by CUPS.

You can block access to the web interface altogether should security considerations require it.

If CUPS doesn't recognize one of your printers, there are a few things to try even before searching the internet (using the name of your printer and the word *linux*):

- Check for error messages. Running `systemctl status cups` is a good way to view the most recent alerts.
- Run `lsusb` (assuming it's a USB printer) and/or `lpinfo -v` from the command line to confirm that the system sees your printer.

- Make sure there are no duplicate or outdated entries in the /etc/cups/printers .conf file. If there are, shut down CUPS (systemctl stop cups), save a copy of the original file, and then remove any old entries. Start CUPS again, and try adding the printer from the browser interface.
- Make sure that the <Policy default> section of the /etc/cups/cupsd.conf file doesn't have any overly restrictive settings that might be blocking legitimate requests.

Summary

- The visibility and insight into your hardware profile provided by Linux tools like lshw should be used in all hardware upgrades and repair decisions.
- The Linux kernel is isolated from system activity to protect it from destabilizing changes, but kernel modules can safely provide hardware devices with dynamic access to kernel resources.
- The Linux kernel can be modified by adding parameters at boot time, either by editing configuration files or through the GRUB menu.
- CUPS provides an interface to closely administer printers across a network.

Key terms

- A *kernel module* is software that defines the attributes of a hardware device for the benefit of the Linux kernel.
- A *kernel parameter* is an argument that's added to the kernel at runtime to control system behavior.

Security best practices

Use the /etc/cups/cupsd.conf file to control network access to your printers.

Command-line review

- lshw -c memory (or lshw -class memory) displays the memory section of a system's hardware profile.
- ls /lib/modules/`uname -r` lists the contents of the directory under /lib/modules/ containing modules for your current, active kernel.
- lsmod lists all active modules.
- modprobe -c lists all available modules.
- find /lib/modules/$(uname -r) -type f -name ath9k* searches for a file among the available kernel modules with a name starting with *ath9k*.
- modprobe ath9k loads the specified module into the kernel.
- GRUB_CMDLINE_LINUX_DEFAULT="systemd.unit=runlevel3.target" (in the /etc/default/grub file) loads Linux as a multiuser, nongraphic session.
- lp -H 11:30 -d Brother-DCP-7060D /home/user/myfile.pdf schedules a print job to the Brother printer at 11:30 UTC.

Test yourself

1 What's the best way to easily visualize your computer's complete hardware profile?

   a `lsmod`

   b `lshw -class memory`

   c `lshw -html > lshw-output.html`

   d `modprobe -C`

2 What's the best way to reference the file system location containing the active kernel modules?

   a `/lib/kernel/uname -a`

   b `/lib/modules/name -r`

   c `/usr/modules/uname -r`

   d `/lib/modules/uname -r`

3 Which of the following commands will deactivate a kernel module?

   a `delmod uvcvideo`

   b `rmmod uvcvideo`

   c `modprobe -d uvcvideo`

   d `rmmod -r uvcvideo`

4 You need to pass a parameter to the Linux kernel that will be effective immediately and permanently. What are the steps you should take?

   a Edit the linux line in the Edit menu of the GRUB menu at boot time, save the file using Ctrl-x, and boot.

   b Add the parameter to the /etc/default/grub file, update GRUB, and then reboot.

   c Upgrade GRUB from the command line, reboot, add the parameter to the linux line in the Edit menu of the GRUB menu at boot time, save the file using Ctrl-x, and boot.

   d Reboot, upgrade GRUB from the command line, and add the parameter to the /etc/default/grub file.

5 Which of the following commands will schedule a print job for half past ten?

   a `lpd 10:30 -d Brother-DCP-7060D /home/user/myfile.pdf`

   b `lpq -h 10:30 -d Brother-DCP-7060D /home/user/myfile.pdf`

   c `lp -T 10:30 -d Brother-DCP-7060D /home/user/myfile.pdf`

   d `lp -H 10:30 -d Brother-DCP-7060D /home/user/myfile.pdf`

Answer key

1. c, 2. d, 3. b, 4. b, 5. d

16
DevOps tools:
Deploying a scripted server
environment using Ansible

This chapter covers

- Using orchestration tools to automate tiered
  Linux deployments
- Managing Linux servers using Ansible playbooks
- Organizing deployment-related data in a modular
  architecture

You've seen how scripts can automate complicated and boring processes to ensure they're done regularly and done right. You wrote scripts to help with backup jobs back in chapter 5. You also saw how virtual Linux servers can be provisioned and launched in seconds in chapter 2. Is there any reason why you shouldn't be able to put those tools together and automate the creation of entire virtual infrastructure environments? Nope. No reason at all.

Should you want to? Well, if you and your team are involved in an IT project involving multiple developers regularly pushing software versions to multiple

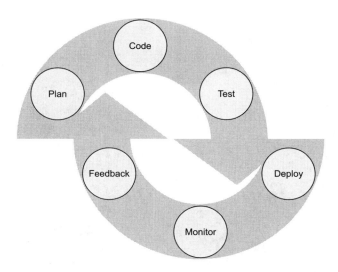

Figure 16.1   A typical DevOps cycle incorporates feedback, testing, and monitoring into the development process.

servers, then you should probably give it some serious consideration, especially if you've got plans to adopt some variation of the DevOps approach to project management illustrated in figure 16.1.

What's DevOps? It's a way to organize the workflow used by technology companies and organizations through close collaboration among a project's development, quality assurance (QA), and system administration teams. The goal is to use templates (*infrastructure as code*) to speed up time-to-deployment and software update cycles, and to allow greater levels of process automation and monitoring.

Many of the automation dividends will come through the smart implementation of orchestration tools like Ansible. Being able to plug new or updated code into a kind of virtual assembly line with all the underlying infrastructure and compatibility details invisibly taken care of can certainly speed things up. But it can also greatly improve quality and reduce errors.

Because most of the DevOps action is built on Linux infrastructure, and because sysadmins are as important to the process as developers, there's a good chance that sooner or later your Linux career will touch DevOps. Before wrapping up this book, it would be a good idea to get a bit of a taste of the world of DevOps and orchestration.

Imagine you're responsible for a complicated platform like the one illustrated in figure 16.2. That includes separate application, database, and authentication servers, all replicated in development, production, and backup environments. The development servers give you a safe place to test your code before pushing it out to production, and the backup servers can be called into service should the production servers crash. Your developers are constantly working to add features and squash bugs. And they're regularly pushing their new code through the production cycle. In addition, the number of servers you run is constantly changing to meet rising and falling user demand.

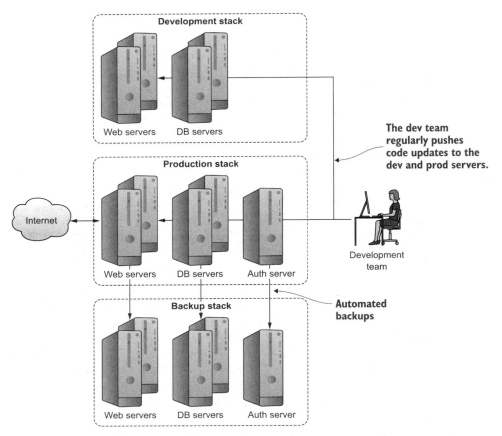

Figure 16.2   A typical application development environment fed by regular software updates from the development team

With so much code flying back and forth in so many directions, you're going to need some help keeping it all straight.

16.1   *What deployment orchestrators can do for you*

Deployment orchestrators will be perfectly happy working their magic on old-fashioned bare-metal servers, but you'll only enjoy their full power when you incorporate them into virtualized deployments. Given how easy it is to script the creation of virtual servers, whether on your own hardware or using the resources of a cloud provider like AWS, being able to automate the creation of software stacks for your VMs will only add speed and efficiency.

The idea is that you compose one or more text files whose contents declare the precise state you want for all the system and application software on a specified machine (usually known as a *host*). When run, the orchestrator will read those files, log on to the appropriate host or hosts, and execute all the commands needed to achieve the desired state. Rather than having to go through the tedious and error-prone process manually on each of the hosts you're launching, you tell the orchestrator to do it all for you. Once your infrastructure grows to dozens or even thousands of hosts, this kind of automation isn't just convenient, it's essential.

But if this is all about automating file system actions, why not use the Bash scripting skills you already have? Well, you probably could, but once you start trying to incorporate things like remote authentication and conflicting software stacks into those scripts, your life will quickly become insanely complicated.

Orchestrators will safely and reliably manage variables and passwords for you, and apply them within the proper context as often and in as many ways as necessary. You don't need to track all the fine details on your own. Because there are all kinds of orchestration tools, the one you choose will largely depend on the specifics of your project, organization, and background. You'll need to ask yourself some basic questions: "Are most of the people involved going to be developers or IT professionals?" "Will you be using a continuous integration methodology?" Table 16.1 provides some quick and dirty profiles of four of the main players.

Table 16.1 Popular deployment orchestrators

Tool	Features
Puppet	Broad community support
	Some coding skills recommended
	Extensible using Ruby
	Requires agents installed on all clients
Chef	Integrated with Git
	Some coding skills recommended
	Extensible using Ruby
	High learning curve
	Broad community support
	Requires chef-client installed on all clients
Ansible	Sysadmin friendly
	Python-based
	No code needed, no host-based agents
	Simple, fast connections work via SSH
	Run via text-based files (called playbooks)
	Minimal learning curve
Salt	Works through agents (called minions)
	Highly scalable
	Sysadmin friendly

As a sysadmin, Ansible sounds like a winner for me, so that's what we'll focus on for the rest of this chapter. But the needs and expectations of your specific project may differ.

16.2 Ansible: Installation and setup

Before starting, you'll need a recent version of Python on your Ansible server and on all the machines you plan to use as hosts. Either `apt install python` or `yum install python` will do that job. Whichever version of Python you use (meaning Python 2 or 3), make sure `python --version` works from the command line.

> **NOTE** As of the time of this writing, Ansible often works better using the older 2.7 version of Python. That, however, will probably not be a long-term condition.

In order to install Ansible on the server (or *control machine*), you'll need to enable the EPEL repository (for CentOS 6), the Extras repository (for CentOS 7), or the ppa:ansible repository for Ubuntu. Before you can enable that repository on Ubuntu using the `add-apt-repository` command, however, you may need to install the software-properties-common package. That'll go like this:

```
# apt install software-properties-common
# add-apt-repository ppa:ansible/ansible
# apt update
# apt install ansible
```

Finally, fire up two or three Python-ready LXC containers to serve as hosts (or *nodes*), the creatures that do all the work. There's no need to install Ansible on any of the hosts, just on the control machine.

16.2.1 Setting up passwordless access to hosts

Let's look at how to set up passwordless access to hosts. Ansible prefers to do its work over SSH connections. Although it's possible to handle authentication from the command line, it's far better to send SSH keys to enable passwordless access with your hosts. You remember how that works from chapter 3, but here it is again:

Run this if you don't already have a key pair on your local system.

The login and IP address of the host machine to which you're copying your server's SSH key

```
$ ssh-keygen                    ◄─┘
$ ssh-copy-id -i .ssh/id_rsa.pub ubuntu@10.0.3.142        ◄──┘
/usr/bin/ssh-copy-id: INFO: attempting to log in with the new key(s),
    to filter out any that are already installed
/usr/bin/ssh-copy-id: INFO: 1 key(s) remain to be installed --
    if you are prompted now it is to install the new keys
ubuntu@10.0.3.142's password:               ◄──┐
```

You'll need to enter a password for the host machine user account to authorize the key transfer.

Now that Ansible is properly installed and connected to your hosts, it's time to configure your environment.

16.2.2 *Organizing Ansible hosts*

Ansible gets its information about which hosts to manage from an inventory file called hosts in the /etc/ansible/ directory. The file can be a simple list of IP addresses or domain names, or a combination thereof.

Listing 16.1   A simple example of a /etc/ansible/hosts file

```
10.0.3.45
192.168.2.78
database.mydomain.com
```

But as the number of hosts you're expecting Ansible to administer grows, along with the complexity of your overall environment, you'll want to organize things a bit better. One way to do that is by dividing your hosts into host groups, which can then be targeted for precise Ansible actions.

Listing 16.2   An example of a /etc/ansible/hosts file organized into host groups

```
[webservers]
10.0.3.45
192.168.2.78

[databases]
database1.mydomain.com
```

Using host groups, Ansible tasks can be configured to run against only a well-defined subset of your hosts, perhaps sending updated public-facing web pages to only the web servers and new configuration files to the databases (illustrated in figure 16.3).

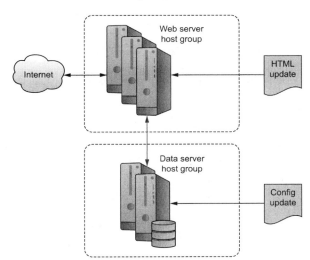

Figure 16.3   Task-specific updates being pushed to servers organized in host groups

There's a lot more control that can be applied to the hosts file. You'll find that the default hosts file created in /etc/ansible/ during installation will already include a nice selection of syntax suggestions, like how you can reference multiple host names in a single line: `www[001:006].example.com`.

> **NOTE** So you'll be able to follow along with the demos in this chapter, add the IP address of your Python-ready LXC (or other) hosts to the hosts file.

16.2.3 *Testing connectivity*

To test that things are set up properly, Ansible can try to contact the hosts listed in the hosts file. This command runs Ansible from the command line in what's known as *ad hoc* mode. The -m tells Ansible to load and run the ping module to send a simple "Are You There?" request to all the hosts listed in the hosts file:

```
$ ansible all -m ping
10.0.3.103 | SUCCESS => {
    "changed": false,
    "ping": "pong"
}
```

The `all` condition in that command means you want this action performed on all the hosts listed in the hosts file. If you only wanted to ping a specific host group, you would use the group name instead of `all`:

```
$ ansible webservers -m ping
```

Now that you're connected, you can run simple commands remotely. This example copies the /etc/group file to the home directory of each of your hosts. Remember, the reason you're able to do this without providing authentication is because you previously used `ssh-keygen` to save your SSH key to the remote host:

```
$ ansible all -a "cp /etc/group /home/ubuntu"
```

You can confirm the operation worked by running `ls` over SSH:

```
$ ssh ubuntu@10.0.3.103 "ls /home/ubuntu"
```

If the username of the account you're logged in to on your Ansible server is not the same as the usernames on your hosts, you'll need to tell Ansible about it. You can do that from the command line using the `--user` argument, which, assuming the host usernames are ubuntu, would look like this: `ansible --user ubuntu all -m ping`.

16.3 *Authentication*

Now suppose you need to execute a command on your remote hosts that requires sudo powers. Imagine you want to push an updated .html file to all of the dozens of web servers toiling away tirelessly behind your load balancer. It sure would make a lot of sense to do it in one go, rather than to repeat the operation individually for each host.

> ### What's a load balancer?
> In case you're curious, a *load balancer* is a server or network router that receives requests for access to a service and redirects those requests to multiple application servers. Load balancers are good at spreading demand among servers to ensure that no one of them is overloaded, and at directing requests away from unhealthy or unavailable servers. Two widely used open source Linux packages for load balancing are HAProxy and, in addition to its web server features, nginx.

Why not try it yourself? See what happens when you try to use the copy module to copy a file in your local home directory (perhaps the group file you copied there earlier) to the /var/www/html/ directory on your remote host. If your host doesn't happen to have a /var/www/html/ directory already, you can produce the same effect by substituting any system directory (like /etc/) that's not owned by your user:

src= points to the location of the source file on the local
machine; dest= points to the target location on the host.

```
$ ansible webservers -m copy -a "src=/home/ubuntu/group \
    dest=/var/www/html/"
10.0.3.103 | FAILED! => {
    "changed": false,
    "checksum": "da39a3ee5e6b4b0d3255bfef95601890afd80709",    A descriptive error
    "failed": true,                                            message explaining
    "msg": "Destination /var/www/html not writable"   ◄──     what went wrong
}
```

Whoops. "Destination /var/www/html not writable" sounds like a permissions issue. Looks like you'll have to find a way to escalate your privileges. The best way to do that is through settings in the /etc/ansible/ansible.cfg file. As you can see from the following example, I edited the `[privilege_escalation]` section of ansible.cfg by uncommenting its four lines.

Listing 16.3 Changed settings in /etc/ansible/ansible.cfg

```
[privilege_escalation]
become=True
become_method=sudo
become_user=root
become_ask_pass=True
```

When you run the copy operation once again, this time adding the --ask-become-pass argument, Ansible reads the updated configuration file and prompts for the remote ubuntu user's sudo password. This time you'll be successful:

```
$ ansible --ask-become-pass webservers -m copy -a "src=/home/ubuntu/group \
    dest=/var/www/html/"
SUDO password:
10.0.3.103 | SUCCESS => {
    "changed": true,
    "checksum": "da39a3ee5e6b4b0d3255bfef95601890afd80709",
    "dest": "/var/www/html/stuff.html",
    "gid": 0,
    "group": "root",
    "md5sum": "d41d8cd98f00b204e9800998ecf8427e",
    "mode": "0644",
    "owner": "root",
    "size": 0,
    "src": "/home/ubuntu/.ansible/tmp/
        ansible-tmp-1509549729.02-40979945256057/source",
    "state": "file",
    "uid": 0
}
```

Log in to your remote server to confirm that the file has been copied. By the way, from a security perspective, it'd be a terrible idea to leave a copy of your group file in the web root. This was just an example. Please don't leave it there.

16.4   *Ansible playbooks*

As you've seen, you can be up and running with some basic Ansible activities in a minute or two. But those basics won't get you far. If you want to exploit the real power of the tool so it can orchestrate the kind of automated multi-tier infrastructure I described in the chapter introduction, you'll need to learn to use playbooks. *Playbooks* are the way you closely define the policies and actions you want Ansible to trigger. They're also an easy way to share working configuration profiles. Here are two ways you can use a playbook:

- As a simple, standalone script
- As a reference that points to resources spread across a specially structured directory tree (for more complicated environments)

16.4.1   *Writing a simple playbook*

Let's learn how to create a simple playbook that can all in one go provision a relatively straightforward web server. To do this, you'll use modules (like the copy module you saw previously), tasks for running Linux system actions, and handlers to dynamically respond to system events. First, make sure your hosts file in /etc/ansible/ is up to date.

> **Listing 16.4   A simple /etc/ansible/hosts file**

```
10.0.3.103
10.0.3.96
```

Next, you'll need to create a YAML-formatted file called site.yml. *YAML* is a text-formatting language related to the more widely used JavaScript Object Notation (JSON). Although you'll need to be careful getting the indentation right, the YAML format does produce configuration profiles that are easy to read, understand, and edit.

After starting with a line containing three dashes (`---`), your file will include three sections: `hosts`, `tasks`, and `handlers`. In this case, the `hosts` section tells Ansible to apply the playbook's actions to all the addresses from the webservers group in the hosts file. The `tasks` section (indented the same number of spaces as hosts) introduces three tasks (or *modules*): apt to install the Apache web server, `copy` to copy a local file to the web document root, and `service`, much like `systemctl` in a systemd environment, to make sure Apache is running.

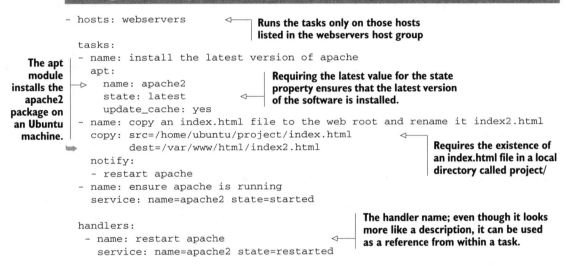

Listing 16.5   A simple Ansible playbook called site.yml

```
- hosts: webservers            ◁──┐  Runs the tasks only on those hosts
                                   │  listed in the webservers host group
  tasks:
  - name: install the latest version of apache
    apt:                            ┌─ Requiring the latest value for the state
      name: apache2                 │  property ensures that the latest version
      state: latest         ◁───────┤  of the software is installed.
      update_cache: yes
  - name: copy an index.html file to the web root and rename it index2.html
    copy: src=/home/ubuntu/project/index.html   ◁─┐
          dest=/var/www/html/index2.html           │  Requires the existence of
    notify:                                         │  an index.html file in a local
    - restart apache                                │  directory called project/
  - name: ensure apache is running
    service: name=apache2 state=started

  handlers:                           ┌─ The handler name; even though it looks
  - name: restart apache       ◁──────┤  more like a description, it can be used
    service: name=apache2 state=restarted  as a reference from within a task.
```

The apt module installs the apache2 package on an Ubuntu machine.

To test this yourself, you could create a simple file called index.html and save it to a directory on your Ansible server. (I used an LXC container for my Ansible lab.) Make sure to properly reference the file location in the playbook (the way it was in the `copy: src=` line from the previous playbook example). The file can, if you like, contain nothing more complicated than the words *Hello World*. It's only there to confirm the playbook worked. Once the playbook has run, a copy of that file should exist in the web document root.

Also, note the `notify:` line within the copy task in the previous example. Once the copy task is complete, `notify` triggers the handler with the name `restart apache` that will, in turn, make sure that Apache is restarted and running properly.

As you build your own playbooks, you'll definitely need more syntax and feature information. Running `ansible-doc` and the name of a particular module will get you going:

```
$ ansible-doc apt
```

RUNNING YOUR PLAYBOOK

Assuming your /etc/ansible/ansible.cfg file is still properly configured to handle host authentication, you're ready to use the `ansible-playbook` command to run your playbook. By default, the command will use the hosts listed in /etc/ansible/hosts, but you can use `-i` to point it to a different file. Here's an example:

```
$ ansible-playbook site.yml
SUDO password:
PLAY ****************************************************
TASK [setup] ********************************************
ok: [10.0.3.96]
TASK [ensure apache is at the latest version] ***
changed: [10.0.3.96]
TASK [copy an index.html file to the root directory] ****
changed: [10.0.3.96]
TASK [ensure apache is running] ************************
ok: [10.0.3.96]
RUNNING HANDLER [restart apache] ***********************
changed: [10.0.3.96]
PLAY RECAP *********************************************
10.0.3.96 : ok=5 changed=3 unreachable=0 failed=0
```

A brief summary of the task's purpose

The ok message tells you that a task has successfully completed.

A summary of the results of running the playbook

Success! With that single command you've built a working web server on all the hosts you listed in your hosts file. Don't believe me? Point your browser to the URL that should be used by the index2.html file you copied (10.0.3.96/index2.html, in my case). You should see your index2.html file displayed.

16.4.2 *Creating multi-tiered, role-powered playbooks*

Once your Ansible-managed infrastructure becomes weighted down with layers of elements, each with its own detailed parameters, keeping them all in a single playbook script is impractical. Try to imagine what it might be like to manage the kind of platform illustrated earlier in figure 16.2.

Breaking out the tasks, handlers, and other data types into separate directories and files will make things much more readable. This kind of modular organization also makes it possible to build new playbooks without having to reinvent any wheels: you'll always have full and easy access to everything you've created.

Ansible organizes its modular elements into roles and even provides its own command-line tool, ansible-galaxy, to manage existing roles and generate the necessary file system framework for starting new roles. Figure 16.4 illustrates the basic Ansible topology.

GENERATING AN ANSIBLE ROLE

Choose a directory to use as your Ansible root. If you're working on a container or VM whose whole purpose is to act as an Ansible server, this might as well be your main user's document root (/home/username/). From the Ansible root, you'll create a directory called roles and then move to the new directory.

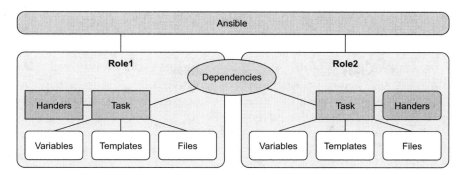

Figure 16.4   Ansible roles shown as self-contained groupings of resources, including access to system dependencies

Once there, initialize the directory using `ansible-galaxy init` followed by the name you want to use for your role:

```
$ mkdir roles
$ cd roles
$ ansible-galaxy init web-app
- web-app was created successfully
```

A new directory called web-app is created. Run `ls -R` to recursively list the new subdirectories and their contents that ansible-galaxy created for you:

```
$ cd web-app
$ ls -R
.:
defaults  files  handlers  meta  README.md  tasks  templates  tests  vars
./defaults:
main.yml
./files:
./handlers:
main.yml
./meta:
main.yml
./tasks:
main.yml
./templates:
./tests:
inventory  test.yml
./vars:
main.yml
```

Each subdirectory within web-app is displayed with a leading ./.

Some directories are already populated with largely empty playbook files of their own.

How does Ansible consume the data contained in those directories? Here's something to chew on: the variable values and parameters set in those files will often control the way Ansible manages the resources launched using that particular role.

Read that one or two more times. Done? OK, there are two things that should stand out: *often control* (but not always?) and *that particular role* (you mean I could have others?).

Right and right. The settings added to files beneath your web-app role directory can be invoked either from a top-level playbook or through an ad hoc command-line action. By way of example, you might have defined a web document root location in the roles/web-app/defaults/main.yml file as `webroot_location: /var/www/myroot/`. Invoking the `webroot_location` variable will always return the value `/var/www/myroot/`.

Except when it doesn't. You see, Ansible was designed for environments encompassing multiple projects. You might have a separate playbook for each of a handful of separate applications and others for internal company services. There's nothing stopping you from managing more than one application from a single Ansible server. This will probably mean that you want a particular variable to mean one thing for application *x* and another for application *y*.

Which brings us to the second notable point: each application or service can be defined by its own Ansible role. But, so that multiple roles can happily coexist on a single system, you'll need a way to prioritize their overlapping variables. The way Ansible does that is quite complicated, but I can summarize it by saying that values found in a role's vars/ directory override those from /defaults, and values explicitly set using `-e` (or `--extra-vars=`) beat everything else.

What might go into each of your roles/web-app/ directories? Here's a short list:

- The vars/ directory is likely to contain information on the file system locations for encryption keys.
- The templates/ directory will hold templates that are meant to be installed as, say, Apache configuration files in Python's .j2 format.
- The files/ directory could contain other files (like that .html file you copied in the previous example) that are used for host-based data.

16.4.3 *Managing passwords in Ansible*

Although you'll probably need to include host passwords in your Ansible infrastructure, you should never store them in plain text documents. Ever. Rather, Ansible provides a tool called Vault that stores sensitive data in encrypted files that can, when necessary, be safely called by a playbook. This snippet opens an editor into which you can enter a new Vault password:

```
$ export EDITOR=nano
$ ansible-vault create mypasswordfile
New Vault password:
Confirm New Vault password:
```

If you don't want Vault to open the password file in Vim, you can export the editor variable as Nano.

You'll be prompted to enter a new Vault password before adding the password you want to use for host access.

Assuming your hosts are all using only a single password, this works by adding the `--ask-vault-pass` argument to the `ansible-playbook` command:

```
$ ansible-playbook site.yml --ask-vault-pass
Vault password:
```

For your information, since Ansible version 2.3, it's also possible to make use of what Ansible calls a *vaulted variable*, which is essentially an encrypted password stored in a plain text YAML file. This makes it possible to manage multiple passwords.

Summary

- Orchestration tools let you automate server infrastructure at scale, whether it's a single host or thousands. The tool you choose will depend on your team's skill set, project needs, and company culture.
- Ansible requires no coding, runs on SSH, and has a light footprint.
- Ansible playbooks, especially playbooks that run resources through roles, are effective and efficient ways to manage security and resources.

Key terms

- *DevOps* is a project organization structure to help development and admin teams speed up and automate product development cycles.
- *Orchestration deployment* tools let you precisely script infrastructure behavior to achieve desired states through automation.
- A *host group* is a way to organize hosts so that Ansible can be directed to manage well-defined subsets of your host fleet.
- In Ansible playbooks, *modules* are predefined command sequences run on a host system, *handlers* are actions triggered by events, and *roles* are bundled resources organized to serve a single project.

Security best practices

- Directing Ansible to access your hosts using passwordless, key-pair-based SSH is preferred to having to enter passwords at the command line for each operation.
- Never include passwords in Ansible playbooks or other plain text scripts. Use Ansible Vault instead.

Command-line review

- `add-apt-repository ppa:ansible/ansible` adds the Debian Ansible software repository to allow apt to install Ansible on an Ubuntu/Debian machine.
- `ansible webservers -m ping` tests all the hosts in the webservers host group for network connectivity.

- `ansible webservers -m copy -a "src=/home/ubuntu/stuff.html dest=/var/www/html/"` copies a local file to the specified file location on all the hosts in the webservers group.
- `ansible-doc apt` displays syntax and usage information on the apt module.
- `ansible-playbook site.yml` launches an operation based on the site.yml playbook.
- `ansible-playbook site.yml --ask-vault-pass` uses a Vault password to authenticate and perform playbook operations.

Test yourself

1 Which of the following orchestration tools would work best for a team of developers with little experience in DevOps who are building a large and complex platform?

   a Ansible

   b Chef

   c Puppet

   d Salt

2 Which of the following packages must be installed on each host for Ansible to work?

   a Ansible

   b Python

   c software-properties-common

   d Ansible and Python

3 Which of the following design considerations is primarily a security concern?

   a Organizing your hosts into host groups

   b Scheduling regular connectivity testing for all hosts

   c Separating environment variables

   d Storing data in Ansible Vault

4 What command tells Ansible to automatically populate the default web document root with a local file on only those hosts running Apache?

   a `ansible all -i copy -a "src=/var/www/html/ dest=/home/ubuntu/stuff.html"`

   b `ansible all webservers -m copy -a "/home/ubuntu/stuff.html /var/www/html/"`

   c `ansible webservers -m copy -a "src=/home/ubuntu/stuff.html dest=/var/www/html/"`

   d `ansible webservers -m copy -a src=/home/ubuntu/stuff.html dest=/var/www/html/`

5 Which of the following commands will create the directories and files you need
   for a new Ansible role?

   a `ansible-root-directory/roles/ansible-galaxy init rolename`

   b `ansible-root-directory/ansible-galaxy rolename`

   c `ansible-root-directory/roles/ansible-init rolename`

   d `ansible-root-directory/roles/ansible init rolename`

Answer key

1. b, 2. b, 3. d, 4. c, 5. a

Conclusion

So that's that. Our journey together is just about done. If I've done my part and you've done yours, then by now you should have picked up some serious Linux skills. In fact, if you've practiced enough, you should feel comfortable taking responsibility for many common server administration tasks, and employers should be comfortable hiring you to perform those tasks on their servers. But before we part, let's spend a couple of minutes covering what you've learned and where it might take you next.

What you've learned

Organizing and absorbing all the many steps you took through *Linux in Action* is going to be a challenge. To make this review more useful, I'll rearrange much of what you read into a half dozen high-level, in-demand themes:

- Virtualization
- Connectivity
- Encryption
- Networking
- Image management
- System monitoring

Virtualization

By working with virtual machines and containers back in chapter 2, you used virtualization to build sandbox computer environments where you can safely experiment with new tools and technologies. In chapters 6 and 9, you launched chroot sessions to recover broken configurations and file systems or to reset an authentication password. And with your understanding of virtualization technologies, along with the introduction to infrastructure orchestration from chapter 16, you're just a step away from diving deeply into the worlds of enterprise cloud and container computing.

Connectivity

Remote connectivity played important roles in nearly every one of the book's projects: from remote server management (chapter 3) to scripted archive backups (chapter 4), from provisioning web servers (chapter 7) and file sharing (chapter 8) to system monitoring (chapter 11). There aren't a lot of critical administrative tasks that would be possible without the existence of safe and reliable connections. You've now got the core Linux tools you'll need to create, manage, and troubleshoot those connections.

Encryption

Business processes that rely heavily on open networks like the internet are going to need ways to secure their data both in transit and at rest. At this point, you're ready to answer that need through the use of encryption tools. You learned about SSH session encryption in chapter 3, encrypted network file sharing in chapter 8, website encryption and TLS certificates in chapter 9, and VPNs in chapter 10.

Networking

In a complex world, your organization will need sophisticated networking solutions to make stuff happen. (I mean good stuff, of course.) Linux certainly pulls its weight on the networking front, and in this book you learned how to use Linux as a platform to build complex connectivity solutions like VPNs and DMZs (chapter 10). You also saw how it's possible to share data over a private network using NFS in chapter 12 and discovered a whole stack of network performance optimization tools in chapter 14.

Image management

You saw how complete images of a file system can be used for data backup and recovery. As you learned from cloning and sharing VirtualBox VMs in chapter 2, images are also important for server orchestration. You'll discover that this will be especially true and useful in the cloud-based infrastructure management world.

System monitoring

In chapter 13, you explored the workings of ongoing system monitoring. You used monitoring tools to keep ahead of problems related to security and system performance, which are connected to the four core computer elements: CPU, memory, storage, and network. Is it all coming back to you now?

What's next

If you came to this book with your own specific goals, then please, don't let me stop you. Get to it. But if you're looking for ideas for some next-level adventures, consider these:

- Number one (two and three): get practical hands-on experience. Hit the command line and don't stop hitting it. Use it to manage anything from simple file transfers to viewing a video on your WiFi-connected laptop from a DVD in a drive on your desktop. As an added bonus, when you run the VLC video application from the command line, you'll be shown all kinds of process output. Reviewing the output can help you figure out why a favorite movie suddenly failed in mid-view.

- Pull out an empty USB drive, and build yourself an emergency toolkit. Load it up with a Linux live-boot image the way you saw back in chapter 6, and add some of your favorite troubleshooting and recovery tools. Test it out at least once before you put it away in a drawer or car storage compartment.

- Dig deeper into Bash scripting. Track down online samples of scripts that use event handling, variables, loops, and inputs. Consider building scripts to automate any administration tasks you commonly perform. Vivek Gite's comprehensive guide to Bash scripting is a good place to start: https://bash.cyberciti.biz/guide/Main_Page.

- Explore the world of encrypted storage drives using tools like eCryptfs and cryptsetup. If you carry sensitive data around with you on your laptop or USB drives, then you'll want to seriously consider what might happen if your devices fall into the wrong hands.

- If you've got coding skills, you might want to open up the Linux kernel and add some customizations of your own. Of course, you'll need to get Linus Torvalds on your side before your changes will be accepted into the official kernel, but you're welcome to deploy your fork for your own use. And the process will teach you a lot about how Linux works under the hood.

- Apply your Linux server skills to the cloud world. You'll be much more effective on AWS or even Azure now that you understand much of what drives cloud infrastructure. Not sure where to start? Manning definitely has you covered. There's my book *Learn Amazon Web Services in a Month of Lunches* (2017), the Wittig brothers' *Amazon Web Services in Action, 2nd ed.* (2018), *Azure in Action* (Chris Hay and Brian H. Prince, 2010), and *Learn Azure in a Month of Lunches* (Iain Foulds, 2018). Your choice.

- Embrace containers through technologies like Docker and Kubernetes. Considering the speed and scalability containers bring to the table, they're the future of enterprise computing. Manning's *Kubernetes in Action* (Marko Lukša, 2017), *Docker in Action* (Jeff Nickoloff, 2016), and *Docker in Practice* (Ian Miell and Aidan Hobson Sayers, 2016) are all great resources.

Resources

What? You want more? All right. But just this once.

You should certainly feel free to visit my own website, https://bootstrap-it.com, where you'll find original content and details of my other books and courses, all certified as Linux- and cloud-friendly. Feel free to follow me on Twitter (@davidbclinton) and be among the first to hear about my next dark plans for world conquest.

Check out the Manning book forum for *Linux in Action* (https://forums.manning
.com/forums/linux-in-action). If you're having trouble with any of the book's projects
or just want to describe your latest successes, share them with the community. I keep a
close watch on that forum, and I should be there when I'm needed.

Go online. Wonderful people have been contributing great documentation and
guides for using Linux for decades now. There are far too many forums, blogs, IRC
channels, Slack groups, and documentation sites to begin listing them here. But
www.tldp.org/FAQ/Linux-FAQ/online-resources.html is a great place to start.

Your favorite internet search engine should be your first choice when looking for
help. And don't forget that (amazingly) man works on the internet pretty much the
same way it does on the command line. The first result you get for a man selinux
search in your browser should be the same man document you'd get in the shell.

I wish you great success in your Linux learning. Be and stay in touch!

DAVID CLINTON

appendix
A chapter-by-chapter, command-line review

Welcome to Linux

- `ls -lh /var/log`—Lists the contents and full, human-friendly details of the /var/log/ directory.
- `cd`—Returns you to your home directory.
- `cp file1 newdir`—Copies a file called file1 to the directory called newdir.
- `mv file? /some/other/directory/`—Moves all files containing the letters *file* and one more character to the target location.
- `rm -r *`—Deletes all files and directories below the current location—use with great care.
- `man sudo`—Opens the man documentation file on using sudo with commands.

Linux virtualization: building a safe and simple Linux working environment

- `apt install virtualbox`—Uses Apt to install a software package from a remote repository.
- `dpkg -i skypeforlinux-64.deb`—Directly installs a downloaded Debian package on a Ubuntu machine.
- `wget https://example.com/document-to-download`—A command-line program, wget downloads files.
- `dnf update`—or yum update or apt update—Synchronizes the local software index with what's available from online repositories.
- `shasum ubuntu-16.04.2-server-amd64.iso`—Calculates the checksum for a downloaded file to confirm that it matches the provided value, meaning that the contents haven't been corrupted in transit.

- `vboxmanage clonevm Kali-Linux-template --name newkali`—Uses the vbox-manage tool to clone an existing VM.
- `lxc-start -d -n mycont`—Starts an existing LXC container.
- `ip addr`—Displays information on each of a system's network interfaces (including their IP addresses).
- `exit`—Leaves a shell session without shutting down the machine.

Remote connectivity: safely access networked machines

- `dpkg -s ssh`—Checks the status of an Apt-based software package.
- `systemctl status ssh`—Checks the status of a system process (systemd).
- `systemctl start ssh`—Starts a system process.
- `ip addr`—Lists all the network interfaces on a computer.
- `ssh-keygen`—Generates a new pair of SSH keys.
- `$ cat .ssh/id_rsa.pub | ssh ubuntu@10.0.3.142 "cat >> .ssh/authorized _keys"`—Copies a local key and pastes it on a remote machine.
- `ssh -i .ssh/mykey.pem ubuntu@10.0.3.142`—Specifies a particular key pair.
- `scp myfile ubuntu@10.0.3.142:/home/ubuntu/myfile`—Safely copies a local file to a remote computer.
- `ssh -X ubuntu@10.0.3.142`—Logs in to a remote host for a graphics-enabled session.
- `ps -ef | grep init`—Displays all currently running system process and filters results by the string `init`.
- `pstree -p`—Displays all currently running system processes in a visual tree format.

Archive management: backup or copy entire file systems

- `df -h`—Displays all currently active partitions with sizes shown in a human readable format.
- `tar czvf archivename.tar.gz /home/myuser/Videos/*.mp4`—Creates a compressed archive from video files in a specified directory tree.
- `split -b 1G archivename.tar.gz archivename.tar.gz.part`—Splits a large file into smaller files of a set maximum size.
- `find /var/www/ -iname "*.mp4" -exec tar -rvf videos.tar {} \;`—Finds files meeting set criteria and streams their names to tar to include in an archive.
- `chmod o-r /bin/zcat`—Removes read permissions for the username others.
- `dd if=/dev/sda2 of=/home/username/partition2.img`—Creates an image of the sda2 partition and saves it to your home directory.
- `dd if=/dev/urandom of=/dev/sda1`—Overwrites a partition with random characters to obscure the old data.

Automated administration: configure automated offsite backups

- `#!/bin/bash`—The so-called "shebang line" tells Linux which shell interpreter you're going to be using for a script.
- `||`—Inserts an "or" into a script, meaning either the command to the left is successful or execute the command to the right.
- `&&`—Inserts an "and" into a script, meaning if the command to the left is successful, execute the command to the right.
- `test -f /etc/filename`—Tests for the existence of the specified file or directory name.
- `chmod +x upgrade.sh`—Makes a script file executable.
- `pip3 install --upgrade --user awscli`—Installs the AWS command-line interface using Python's pip package manager.
- `aws s3 sync /home/username/dir2backup s3://linux-bucket3040`—Synchronizes the contents of a local directory with the specified S3 bucket.
- `21 5 * * 1 root apt update && apt upgrade`—A cron directive, executes two apt commands at 5:21 each morning.
- `NOW=$(date +"%m_%d_%Y")`—Assigns the current date to a script variable.
- `systemctl start site-backup.timer`—Activates a systemd system timer.

Emergency tools—build a system recovery device

- `sha256sum systemrescuecd-x86-5.0.2.iso`—Calculates the SHA256 checksum of a .ISO file.
- `isohybrid systemrescuecd-x86-5.0.2.iso`—Adds a USB-friendly MBR to live-boot image.
- `dd bs=4M if=systemrescuecd-x86-5.0.2.iso of=/dev/sdb && sync`—Writes a live-boot image to an empty drive.
- `mount /dev/sdc1 /run/temp-directory`—Mounts a partition to a directory on the live file system.
- `ddrescue -d /dev/sdc1 /run/usb-mount/sdc1-backup.img /run/usb-mount/sdc1-backup.logfile`—Saves files on a damaged partiton to an image named sdc1-backup.img and writes events to a log file.
- `chroot /run/mountdir/`—Opens a root shell on a file system.

Web servers: build a MediaWiki server

- `apt install lamp-server^`—This single Ubuntu command installs all the elements of a LAMP server.
- `systemctl enable httpd`—Launches Apache on a CentOS machine at every system boot.
- `firewall-cmd --add-service=http --permanent`—Permits HTTP browser traffic into a CentOS system.

- `mysql_secure_installation`—This program resets your root password and tightens database security.
- `mysql -u root -p`—Logs in to MySQL (or MariaDB) as the root user.
- `CREATE DATABASE newdbname;`—Creates a new database in MySQL (or MariaDB).
- `yum search php- | grep mysql`—Searches for available packages related to PHP on a CentOS machine.
- `apt search mbstring`—Searches for available packages related to multibyte string encoding.

Networked file sharing: build an Nextcloud file-sharing server

- `a2enmod rewrite`—Enables the rewrite module so Apache can edit URLs as they move between a client and server.
- `nano /etc/apache2/sites-available/nextcloud.conf`—Creates or edits an Apache host configuration file for Nextcloud.
- `chown -R www-data:www-data /var/www/nextcloud/`—Changes the user and group ownership of all website files to the www-data user.
- `sudo -u www-data php occ list`—Uses the Nextcloud CLI to list available commands.
- `aws s3 ls s3://nextcloud32327`—Lists the contents of an S3 bucket.

Secure your web server

- `firewall-cmd --permanent --add-port=80/tcp`—Opens port 80 to incoming HTTP traffic and configures it to reload at boot time.
- `firewall-cmd --list-services`—Lists the currently active rules on a firewalld system.
- `ufw allow ssh`—Opens port 22 for SSH traffic using UncomplicatedFirewall on Ubuntu.
- `ufw delete 2`—Removes the second ufw rule as listed by the `ufw status` command.
- `ssh -p53987 username@remote_IP_or_domain`—Logs in to an SSH session using a non-default port.
- `certbot --apache`—Configures an Apache web server to use Let's Encrypt encryption certificates.
- `selinux-activate`—Activates SELinux on an Ubuntu machine.
- `setenforce 1`—Toggles enforcing mode in an SELinux configuration.
- `ls -Z /var/www/html/`—Displays the security context of the files in a specified directory.
- `usermod -aG app-data-group otheruser`—Adds the otheruser user to the app-data-group system group.
- `netstat -npl`—Scans for open (listening) network ports on a server.

Secure your network connections: create a VPN or DMZ

- `hostname OpenVPN-Server`—Sets the command prompt description to make it easier to keep track of which server you're logged into.
- `cp -r /usr/share/easy-rsa/ /etc/openvpn`—Copies the Easy RSA scripts and environment configuration files to the working OpenVPN directory.
- `./build-key-server server`—Generates an RSA key pair set with the name server.
- `./pkitool client`—Generates a client set of keys from an existing RSA key infrastructure.
- `openvpn --tls-client --config /etc/openvpn/client.conf`—Launches OpenVPN on a Linux client using the settings from the client.conf file.
- `iptables -A FORWARD -i eth1 -o eth2 -m state --state NEW,ESTAB-LISHED,RELATED -j ACCEPT`—Allows data transfers between the eth1 and eth2 network interfaces.
- `man shorewall-rules`—Displays documentation on the rules file used by Shorewall.
- `systemctl start shorewall`—Starts the Shorewall firewall tool.
- `vboxmanage natnetwork add --netname dmz --network "10.0.1.0/24" --enable --dhcp on`—Uses the VirtualBox CLI to create and configure a virtual NAT network with DHCP for VirtualBox VMs.
- `vboxmanage natnetwork start --netname dmz`—Starts a virtual NAT network.
- `dhclient enp0s3`—Requests an IP address for the enp0s3 interface from a DHCP server.

System monitoring: working with log files

- `ALT+F<n>`—Opens a virtual console from a non-GUI shell.
- `journalctl -n 20`—Displays the 20 most recent log entries in the journal.
- `journalctl --since 15:50:00 --until 15:52:00`—Displays only events between the since and until times.
- `systemd-tmpfiles --create --prefix /var/log/journal` Instructs systemd to create and maintain a persistent journal file rather than one that is destroyed with every boot.
- `cat /var/log/auth.log | grep -B 1 -A 1 failure`—Displays matching lines along with the lines immediately before and after.
- `cat /var/log/mysql/error.log | awk '$3 ~/[Warning]/' | wc`—Searches the MySQL error log for events classified as a Warning.
- `sed "s/^ [0-9] //g" numbers.txt`—Removes numbers at the start of each line of a file.
- `tripwire --init`—Initializes the database of a Tripwire installation.
- `twadmin --create-cfgfile --site-keyfile site.key twcfg.txt`—Generates a new encrypted tw.cfg file for Tripwire.

Sharing data over a private network

- `/home 192.168.1.11(rw,sync)`—An entry in the NFS server /etc/exports file, defines a remote client share.
- `firewall-cmd --add-service=nfs`—Opens a CentOS firewall for client access to your NFS share.
- `192.168.1.23:/home /nfs/home nfs`—A typical entry in the /etc/fstab file of an NFS client, loads an NFS share.
- `smbpasswd -a sambauser`—Adds Samba functionality (and a unique password) to an existing Linux user account.
- `nano /etc/samba/smb.conf`—Samba is controlled by the smb.conf file on the server.
- `smbclient //localhost/sharehome`—Logs in to a local Samba share (using the Samba user account).
- `ln -s /nfs/home/ /home/username/Desktop/`—Creates a symbolic link allowing a user to easily access an NFS share by clicking a desktop icon.

Troubleshooting system performance issues

- `uptime`—Returns the CPU load averages over the past 1, 5, and 15 minutes.
- `cat /proc/cpuinfo | grep processor`—Returns the number of system CPU processors.
- `top`—Displays real-time statistics for running Linux processes.
- `killall yes`—Shuts down all running instances of the yes command.
- `nice --15 /var/scripts/mybackup.sh`—Raises the priority of the mybackup.sh script for system resources.
- `free -h`—Displays total and available system RAM.
- `df -i`—Displays the available and total inodes for each file system.
- `find . -xdev -type f | cut -d "/" -f 2 | sort | uniq -c | sort -n`—Counts and displays numbers of files by parent directory.
- `apt-get autoremove`—Removes old and unused kernel headers.
- `nethogs eth0`—Displays processes and transfers data related to network connections using the eth0 interface.
- `tc qdisc add dev eth0 root netem delay 100ms`—Slows all network transfers through the eth0 interface by 100 milliseconds.
- `nmon -f -s 30 -c 120`—Records data from a series of nmon scans to a file.

Troubleshooting network issues

- `ip addr`—Lists the active interfaces on a Linux system. May be shortened to `ip a` or lengthened to `ip address`; it's your choice.
- `lspci`—Lists the PCI devices currently connected to your computer.

- `dmesg | grep -A 2 Ethernet`—Searches the dmesg logs for references to the string `Ethernet` and displays references along with the subsequent two lines of output.
- `ip route add default via 192.168.1.1 dev eth0`—Manually sets a new network route for a computer.
- `dhclient enp0s3`—Requests a dynamic (DHCP) IP address for the enp0s3 interface.
- `ip addr add 192.168.1.10/24 dev eth0`—Assigns a static IP address to the eth0 interface (doesn't persist past the next system restart).
- `ip link set dev enp0s3 up`—Starts the enp0s3 interface (useful after editing the configuration).
- `netstat -l | grep http`—Scans a local machine for a web service listening on port 80.
- `nc -z -v bootstrap-it.com 443 80`—Scans a remote web site for services listening on the ports 443 or 80.

Troubleshooting peripheral devices

- `lshw -c memory` (or `lshw -class memory`)—Displays the memory section of a system's hardware profile.
- `ls /lib/modules/`uname -r``—Lists the contents of the directory under /lib/ modules/ containing modules for your current, active kernel.
- `lsmod`—Lists all active modules.
- `modprobe -c`—Lists all available modules.
- `find /lib/modules/$(uname -r) -type f -name ath9k*`—Searches for a file among the available kernel modules with a name starting with *ath9k*.
- `modprobe ath9k`—Loads the specified module into the kernel.
- `GRUB_CMDLINE_LINUX_DEFAULT="systemd.unit=runlevel3.target"`—The /etc/ default/grub file loads Linux as multi-user, non-graphic session.
- `lp -H 11:30 -d Brother-DCP-7060D /home/user/myfile.pdf`—Schedules a print job to the Brother printer at 11:30 UTC.

DevOps tools: deploy a scripted server environment

- `add-apt-repository ppa:ansible/ansible`—Adds the Debian Ansible software repository to allow apt to install Ansible on an Ubuntu/Debian machine.
- `ansible webservers -m ping`—Tests all the hosts in the webservers host group for network connectivity.
- `ansible webservers -m copy -a "src=/home/ubuntu/stuff.html dest=/var/ www/html/"`—Copies a local file to the specified file location on all the hosts in the webservers group.
- `ansible-doc apt`—Displays syntax and usage information on the apt module.

- `ansible-playbook site.yml`—Launches an operation based on the site.yml playbook.
- `ansible-playbook site.yml --ask-vault-pass`—Uses a Vault password to authenticate and perform playbook operations.

index

RELATED MANNING TITLES

Amazon Web Services in Action, Second Edition
by Michael Wittig and Andreas Wittig

ISBN: 9781617295119
528 pages, $54.99
August 2018

Learn Amazon Web Services in a Month of Lunches
by David Clinton

ISBN: 9781617294440
328 pages, $39.99
August 2017

Learn Linux in a Month of Lunches
by Steven Ovadia

ISBN: 9781617293283
304 pages, $39.99
November 2016

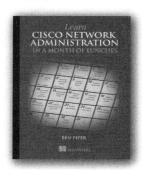

Learn Cisco Network Administration in a Month of Lunches
by Ben Piper

ISBN: 9781617293634
312 pages, $39.99
May 2017

For ordering information go to www.manning.com